EMPIRES AND AUTONOMY

Other volumes planned in the Globalization and Autonomy series:

Global Ordering: Institutions and Autonomy in a Changing World
Edited by Louis W. Pauly and William D. Coleman (2008)

Renegotiating Community: Interdisciplinary Perspectives, Global Contexts
Edited by Diana Brydon and William D. Coleman (2008)

Unsettled Legitimacy: Political Community, Power, and Authority in a Global Era
Edited by Steven F. Bernstein and William D. Coleman (2009)

Property Rights: Struggles over Autonomy in a Global Age
Edited by William D. Coleman and John C. Weaver

Deux Méditerranées: Les voies de la mondialisation et de l'autonomie
Edited by Yassine Essid and William D. Coleman

Indigenous Peoples and Autonomy: Insights for a Global Age
Edited by Mario E. Blaser, Ravi de Costa, Deborah McGregor,
and William D. Coleman

Cultural Autonomy: Frictions and Connections
Edited by Petra Rethmann, Imre Szeman, and William D. Coleman

Globalization and Autonomy: Conversing across Disciplines
Diana Brydon, William D. Coleman, Louis W. Pauly, and John C. Weaver

See also the *Globalization and Autonomy Online Compendium* at
www.globalautonomy.ca.

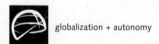 globalization + autonomy

EMPIRES AND

Moments in the History of Globalization

AUTONOMY

Edited by Stephen M. Streeter, John C. Weaver,
and William D. Coleman

UBCPress · Vancouver · Toronto

17 16 15 14 13 12 11 10 09   5 4 3 2 1

Printed in Canada on ancient-forest-free paper (100% post-consumer recycled) that is processed chlorine- and acid-free, with végetable-based inks.

Library and Archives Canada Cataloguing in Publication

Empires and autonomy: moments in the history of globalization / edited by Stephen M. Streeter, John C. Weaver, and William D. Coleman.

(Globalization and autonomy 1913-7494)
Includes bibliographical references and index.
ISBN 978-0-7748-1599-4 (bound); ISBN 978-0-7748-1600-7 (pbk.);
ISBN 978-0-7748-1601-4 (e-book)

1. Globalization–History. 2. Nation-state and globalization–History. 3. Imperialism–History. 4. Autonomy. I. Streeter, Stephen M. II. Weaver, John C. III. Coleman, William D. (William Donald), 1950-   IV. Series: Globalization and autonomy

JZ1318.E46 2009   303.48'209   C2009-901137-9

Canadä

UBC Press gratefully acknowledges the financial support for our publishing program of the Government of Canada through the Book Publishing Industry Development Program (BPIDP), and of the Canada Council for the Arts, and the British Columbia Arts Council.

This book has been published with the help of a grant from the Canadian Federation for the Humanities and Social Sciences, through the Aid to Scholarly Publications Programme, using funds provided by the Social Sciences and Humanities Research Council of Canada. Research for the volume was supported by the Social Sciences and Humanities Research Council of Canada through its Major Collaborative Research Initiatives Program, Grant No. 412-2001-1000.

UBC Press
The University of British Columbia
2029 West Mall
Vancouver, BC V6T 1Z2
604-822-5959 / Fax: 604-822-6083
www.ubcpress.ca

Contents

Preface

The Globalization and Autonomy Series: Dialectical Relationships in the Contemporary World

THE VOLUMES IN THE Globalization and Autonomy series offer the results from an interdisciplinary Major Collaborative Research Initiative (MCRI) funded by the Social Sciences and Humanities Research Council of Canada (SSHRC). SSHRC set up the MCRI program to provide a vehicle to support larger projects with research objectives requiring collaboration among researchers from different universities and across a range of disciplines. The MCRI on Globalization and Autonomy began in April 2002. The research team involved forty co-investigators from twelve universities across Canada and another twenty academic contributors from outside Canada, including scholars from Australia, Brazil, China, Denmark, France, Germany, Slovenia, Taiwan, the United Kingdom, and the United States. Drawing on additional funding from the International Development Research Centre (IDRC), the project became affiliated with a separate interdisciplinary research team of twenty-eight scholars, the Groupe d'Études et de Recherches Interdisciplinaires sur la Méditerranée (GERIM). GERIM is based in Tunisia and includes members from France, Spain, Jordan, and Lebanon as well. Scholars from the following disciplines participated in the project: anthropology, comparative literature, cultural studies, economics, English literature, geography, history, music, philosophy, political science, and sociology.

The project was conceived, designed, and implemented to carry out interdisciplinary research. We endeavoured to put disciplinary-based theories and conceptual frameworks into dialogue with one another, with a view to developing new theories and understandings of human societies. Four conditions needed to be met if research was to be done in this way. First, we brought humanities and social science disciplines into a relationship of mutual influence, where perspectives were integrated without subordinating one to another. To achieve this integration, the team agreed on a set of core research objectives informed by existing writings on globalization and autonomy. Members developed a number of research questions designed to address these objectives and a research plan that would permit them to address these questions in a focused, systematic way. Second, team members individually were encouraged to think inside disciplines other than their own and to respect differences across disciplines in terms of how the object of knowledge is constructed. Third, team members were selected to ensure that the research was carried out using multiple methodologies. Finally, faced with researching the complex relationships involved in globalization, an interdisciplinary approach meant that our work would be necessarily pluri-theoretical. We held to the view that theories would be most effective when, in addition to applying ideas rigorously, their proponents acknowledged the limitations of any particular theoretical perspective and consciously set out to cross boundaries and use other, sometimes seemingly incommensurable, perspectives.

To ensure intellectual integration from the start, team members agreed on this approach at the first full meeting of the project and committed to the following core objective: *to investigate the relationship between globalization and the processes of securing and building autonomy.* To this end, we sought to refine understanding of these concepts and of the historical evolution of the processes inherent in both of them, given the contested character of their content, meaning, and symbolic status.

Given that *globalization* is the term currently employed to describe the contemporary moment, we attempted to:

- determine the opportunities globalization might create and the constraints globalization might place on individuals and communities seeking to secure and build autonomy
- evaluate the extent to which individuals and communities might be able to exploit these opportunities and to overcome these constraints
- assess the opportunities for empowerment that globalization might create for individuals and communities seeking to secure and to build autonomy

- determine how the autonomy available to individuals and communities might permit them to contest, reshape, or engage globalization.

In seeking to address the core objectives for the project, we moved our research in three interrelated directions. First, we accepted that globalization and autonomy have deep historical roots. What is happening today in the world is in many ways continuous with what has taken place in the past. Thus, the burden of a contemporary examination of globalization and autonomy is to assess what is new and what has changed. Second, the dynamics of the relationship between globalization and autonomy are related to a series of important changes in the locations of power and authority. Finally, the globalization-autonomy dynamic plays out in the construction and reconstruction of identities, the nature and value of community, and the articulation of autonomy in and through cultures and discrete institutions. In each of these three areas, the team developed and agreed to answer core questions to provide a clear direction for the research. The full text of the questions is available at http://globalization.mcmaster.ca/ga/ga81.htm.

Over successive annual meetings of the team, our research coalesced around the following themes: institutions and global ordering; democracy and legitimacy; continuity and rupture in the history of globalization and autonomy; history, property rights, and capitalism; community; culture; the situation and struggles of indigenous peoples; and the Mediterranean region as a microcosm of North-South relations. The researchers addressing these themes tended to be drawn from several disciplines, leading to interdisciplinary dialogue within each thematic group. The themes then crystallized into separate research problems, which came to be addressed by the volumes in the series. While these volumes were taking form, the project team also developed an online publication, the *Globalization and Autonomy Online Compendium* (see next page), which makes our findings available to the general public through research summaries; a glossary of key concepts, organizations, people, events, and places; and a comprehensive bibliography. The ultimate objective of all of these publications is to produce an integrated corpus of outstanding research that provides an in-depth study of the varying relationships between globalization and autonomy.

Globalization and Autonomy Online Compendium

Readers of this volume may also be interested in the *Globalization and Autonomy Online Compendium* (available at www.globalautonomy.ca). The *Compendium* is a collective publication by the team of Canadian and international scholars who have been part of the SSHRC Major Collaborative Research Initiative that gave rise to the volumes in the Globalization and Autonomy series. Through the *Compendium*, the team is making the results of their research available to a wide public audience. Team members have prepared a glossary of hundreds of short articles on relevant persons, places, organizations, events, and key concepts and have compiled an extensive searchable bibliographical database. Short summaries of the chapters in other volumes of the Globalization and Autonomy series can also be found in the *Compendium*, along with position papers and peer-reviewed research articles on globalization and autonomy issues.

Acknowledgments

THE EDITORS WOULD LIKE to express their immense gratitude to Nancy Johnson and Sonya Zikic, the project editors for the MCRI on Globalization and Autonomy, for their excellent work, support, and committed professionalism. We are also grateful to Jennifer Clark, Sara Mayo, and Cassandra Pohl for administrative support throughout the project. William Coleman acknowledges that the research for his contributions to the book was undertaken, in part, thanks to funding from the Canada Research Chairs Program. Finally, the editors and volume authors would like to thank the peer reviewers of this book for their helpful and insightful comments and suggestions.

Empires and Autonomy

chapter 1   **Introduction**

William D. Coleman, Stephen M. Streeter, and John C. Weaver

IN *The Communist Manifesto,* published in 1848, Karl Marx and Friedrich Engels described mid-nineteenth-century Europe in a way that seems to foreshadow the modern-day concept of globalization:

> All old-established national industries have been destroyed or are daily being destroyed. They are dislodged by new industries, whose introduction becomes a life and death question for all civilized nations, by industries that no longer work up indigenous raw material, but raw material drawn from the remotest zones; industries whose products are consumed, not only at home, but in every quarter of the globe. In place of the old wants, satisfied by the production of the country, we find new wants, requiring for their satisfaction the products of distant lands and climes. In place of the old local and national seclusion and self-sufficiency, we have intercourse in every direction, universal inter-dependence of nations. And as in material, so also in intellectual production. The intellectual creations of individual nations become common property. National one-sidedness and narrow-mindedness become more and more impossible, and from the numerous national and local literatures, there arises a world literature.[1]

A scarce 150 years later, the late Paul Hirst and his co-author Grahame Thompson looked at their present economic circumstances and then back on the era from 1870 to 1914 and concluded: "The level of integration, interdependence, openness, or however one wishes to describe it, of national economies in the present era is not unprecedented ... This is not to minimize the level of integration now, or to ignore the problems of regulation and management it throws up, but merely to register a certain skepticism about whether we have entered a radically new phase in the internationalization of economic activity."[2]

Two years after Hirst and Thompson published these words, sociologist Anthony Giddens delivered the BBC Reith Lectures, which were broadcast around the world on the BBC World Service. He divided those who debated the novelty of globalization into two camps: the skeptics, such as Hirst and Thompson, and the radicals, those who believed that globalization was not only new but also revolutionary. He supported the radical position but then added that both groups "see the phenomenon almost solely in economic terms. This is a mistake. Globalization is political, technological and cultural, as well as economic. It has been influenced above all by developments in systems of communication, dating back only to the late 1960s."[3] In short, what had been presented as a revolutionary change by Marx and Engels in 1848 had become commonplace in the eyes of globalization skeptics 150 years later; for the radicals, the commonplace was being revolutionized from the inside out in a set of changes as profound as those observed by Marx and Engels in the mid-nineteenth century.

In keeping with the interdisciplinary ambitions of the Globalization and Autonomy project, scholars from many academic disciplines were invited to consider how their research might answer one or more of the historical questions arising out of these debates:

1 What are the historical roots of globalization and autonomy? What are the continuities and differences between past and present?

2 How has capital enlisted political authority (local, national, and global), technologies, and communications media to open new opportunities for expansion and penetration? At what point does capital's enlistment of these factors permit us to speak of a globalization moment?[4]

3 If we find a recent rupture and a decisive globalization moment, what is specific about the current moment? What are the deep foundations for this moment? for globality?

4 How has the practice and concept of autonomy changed over time? How are these changes related to class, citizenship, and identities? How do social and historical memories influence class, identities, citizenship, and autonomy?

5 How and in what ways are globalization and globality engaged and contested across historical moments? How does autonomy at particular historical moments facilitate or hinder the engagement and contestation of globalization and globality? To what extent is the engagement and contestation of globalization and globality a struggle for or against autonomy?

6 How does our research connect globalization and autonomy with the ideas of imperialism and empire? How do these connections and these ideas vary across time and at different moments of globalization?

Continuity, Discontinuity, and Core Concepts

In thinking about how to address these questions, we believe it is important to distinguish between internationalization and globalization. *Internationalization* refers to the growth of transactions and interdependence between countries.[5] The governments of those countries organize the transactions and social relations that result as a unit. The respective "national" communities constitute the governed. In contrast, *globalization* involves "the spread of transplanetary — and in most recent times also more particularly supraterritorial — connections between people."[6] As Jan Aart Scholte emphasizes, *supraterritorial* refers to relations that are somehow "above" territory; that is, they are relatively unconstrained by physical location. For example, Robert Latham and Saskia Sassen have explained how new communication and information technologies augmented the feasibility of supraterritorial connections. Activities by local community organizations, for example, can link horizontally with similar organizations in networks of global scope. In doing so, these organizations can bypass more easily the administrative and institutional components of the nation-state. In this respect, an increasing range of social relations has become "transboundary" — that is, less mediated by territorial-based nation-states.[7] Owing to the development of these new technologies, certain social relations have acquired characteristics

3

of transworld *simultaneity* (they extend anywhere across the planet at the same time) and transworld *instaneity* (they move anywhere on the planet at the same time).[8] In this respect, the supraterritoriality of social relationships alters the nature of some social spaces, which become less defined by their physical location than they might have been in the past.

One of the consequences of the spread of transplanetary connections and supraterritoriality is the growing awareness of the world as an imagined community. In reviewing the conceptual underpinnings of globalization, the sociologist Roland Robertson alludes to "an intensification of consciousness of the world as a whole" over time.[9] When individuals place themselves in a world context, they become more likely to imagine themselves doing things in the world beyond their country or locality.

Analyzing globalization in this manner led us to reject the commonly held notion that internationalization and globalization are always related linearly, with globalization accelerating as internationalization recedes. To the contrary, we show that these processes have often accelerated at the same time, especially over the past two centuries. The relationship between internationalization and globalization can actually be complementary, as nation-states either singly or in combination trigger globalizing processes. Economic historian Samir Saul's study in this volume of global finance over the past 135 years illustrates this positive interdependence. Sociologist Ulrich Beck's analysis of the increased need for states to cooperate on transboundary or transnational issues also demonstrates that internationalization does not necessarily diminish globalization.[10] Of course, it is possible for intensified internationalization to restrict globalization and vice versa. For example, agreements reached by states over the past decade to regulate border crossings illustrate how internationalization has impeded transworld migration. In contrast, emerging digital technologies like the Internet — which reconstitute communication by combining print with oral, visual, and auditory forms — have challenged state boundary controls over the diffusion of culture.

In describing and analyzing such phenomena, the scholars in this book hypothesize that historical ruptures and discontinuities become more likely when particular transworld social relations and spaces become supraterritorial. To date, histories of internationalization stress the importance of the gradual organization and control of the world's territories by nation-states, a process that intensified in the nineteenth century and culminated in the decolonization movements of the mid-twentieth century. As *international* became synonymous with *worldwide* or *global,* primary social spaces became defined as "national" ones, and the mediation of relations in the world took place through national political, economic, cultural, technological, or military institutions. When transworld social spaces became supraterritorial, however, certain social relationships, whether economic, political, or cultural, were also altered. For example, the exchange of visual media like photographs, films, or local video recordings can have more immediate global circulation with unpredictable consequences than in the past. A case in point is the death in 2008 of a disoriented Polish immigrant following the use of a stun gun by the Royal Canadian Mounted Police in the Vancouver International Airport. This local incident was globalized when it was captured on a bystander's digital camera and spread instantly around the world. The video images not only contradicted the police report, leading to an official inquiry and an apology to the man's mother and to Poland, they also helped fuel a growing international debate about the wisdom of using stun guns to apprehend criminal suspects. As this example suggests, in some instances states have increased difficulty defining or containing the spaces in which social relationships emerge and grow.

This volume investigates how the possible historical continuities and discontinuities in globalization might inhibit or promote autonomy. We also are interested in how degrees of autonomy may affect societies' capacity to engage with and shape globalization. We are concerned with both individual and collective forms of autonomy. Scholars Len Doyal and Ian Gough have observed that "our most basic human interest" requires the fulfillment of two basic needs: health or physical capacity and mental capacity or *autonomy.*[11] As Gough has elaborated, "To be autonomous in this minimal sense is to have the ability to make informed choices about what should be done and how to go about doing it."[12] Furthermore, three conditions must be met in order for individuals to enjoy autonomy.[13] First, individuals must have the *cognitive and emotional capacity* to initiate action. Otherwise, a set of disabling symptoms that erode autonomy can be observed, including hopelessness, indecisiveness, a sense of futility, and a lack of energy. Second, individuals must develop *cultural understanding* that permits them to comprehend their own social setting and to know what is expected of them in daily life. Such understanding requires teaching and learning, whether in the family, through community practices and ceremonies, or in schools. Third, individuals must have a *critical capacity,* the ability "to compare cultural rules, to reflect upon the rules of one's own culture, to work with others to change them

5

and, *in extremis,* to move to another culture."[14] To exercise this critical capacity requires some freedom of agency and political freedom.[15] In sum, individual autonomy means being able to formulate aims and beliefs about how to achieve one's choices, seek out ways to participate in social life in pursuit of these choices, and evaluate one's success based on empirical evidence in working towards these aims.

This concept of *individual autonomy* seemingly contrasts with *collective autonomy*, especially the autonomy of states. Collective and individual autonomy may be reconciled, however. Cornelius Castoriadis, a French philosopher of Greek origin, has helped explain the concept of collective autonomy by recalling the Greek roots of the term: to give oneself laws.[16] To be collectively autonomous, a society has to make a place for politics and the exercise of individual autonomy. There must be *public spaces* where citizens are able to freely ask themselves, "Are the rules and the laws under which we exist the right ones?" "Are they just?" "Could they be better?"[17] According to Castoriadis, collective autonomy exists when a society is more reflexive, more able to look at itself critically, and when its members are free, have access to public spaces, and possess the resources, the understanding, and the education needed to interrogate themselves and their laws. Clearly, autonomy in this sense involves an act of the imagination, or what Castoriadis calls the "radical imagination."[18] When individuals and groups are able to imagine different ways of living, they can conceive of an idea, imagine how it might work in practice, and then take action to see if it will work.

In adopting these definitions, the authors in this volume explore how these forms of autonomy are constituted over time for individuals and communities, including nation-states. According to the *Oxford English Dictionary,* the word *autonomy* first appeared in the English language in its collective meaning during the seventeenth century, while the personal meaning of autonomy did not emerge for two more centuries. Both usages became more common as internationalization began to accelerate in the nineteenth and twentieth centuries. Accordingly, the contributors also assess how changes in autonomy over time relate to intensifying globalization and internationalization.

Avenues of Investigation

In seeking to carry out research that would provide some preliminary answers to the historical questions raised in the Globalization and

Autonomy project, we found ourselves focusing repeatedly on several issues. Some of the early celebratory works on globalization cast the present world as the culmination of a long linear process that ended in market economies and democracy. This "end of history" allegedly marked the gradual decline of the most institutionalized form of collective autonomy: the nation-state. Such an argument made implicit assumptions about *time* that we believed deserved to be challenged. That historians had begun to explore the linkages between contemporary globalization and empires as forgers of transplanetary connections also strongly suggested that we had to incorporate the themes of empire and imperialism into our study. Finally, the globalization literature was replete with universal ideas — capitalism, the individual, democracy, free trade, human rights, nature, the environment, and markets. The spread of these ideas and others, and their reconstruction as they became implanted in particular places and varying institutions, was also part of the growth of transplanetary connections that we needed to examine.

Time

Time is a crucial feature in many discussions of globalization. The increase in the speed of communication and of social relations themselves has led to discussions of simultaneity, instaneity, and even "timeless" time by globalization authors.[19] In assessing certain hidden assumptions about time, we discovered many pitfalls. First, there is the hazard of depicting human events as progressing on a smooth plane and arriving at an anticipated endpoint like contemporary globalization. Second, ransacking the past for events to illuminate the present can lead to anachronisms. Third, breaking the past into epochs imposes an implausible uniformity on the defined period.

As the historian Timothy Brook has cautioned, certain intellectual traditions (mostly, but not exclusively, in the West) assume the linearity of time: "An event in the past is not isolated in its unique moment; it is conceived as a point on a line that stretches from the past to the present and beyond the present into the future. Events are thought of as occurring along a timeline that unfolds according to a forward-moving narrative logic."[20] In working uncritically with terms like *continuity* and *discontinuity,* we risk misrepresenting the history of globalization as the rise of the West, the expansion of modernity, or the global penetration of capitalism. To avoid these pitfalls, we seek to distinguish the past from the present while still showing that important interactions in the past "shape future possibilities and closures."[21]

The second hazard, anachronism, arises from attempts to use the past to explain contemporary issues. The danger is that our chosen categories of analysis, formed in the present and addressing current matters, will march into the past to mix with the terms of another time and place. As one historian of colonialism has cautioned, we should not think "as if people acted in search of identity or to build a nation when such ways of thinking might not have been available to them."[22] In other words, historians should not invent a new vocabulary if current terms work well.[23]

The third danger we faced in investigating the history of globalization and autonomy was the temptation to design a teleological project. The historian Anthony Hopkins has divided the history of globalization into a sequence of sweeping epochs: archaic-globalization, proto-globalization, modern-globalization, and postcolonial-globalization.[24] This approach is acceptable so long as we acknowledge that the chief concepts of globalization would have been largely unrecognizable to the people of these eras. Also, it would be a logic-defying leap to speak of global connections in historical epochs when no contacts existed between Eurasia and Africa, or between the Americas and Australasia. In the eighteenth century, several European powers had an extraordinary reach, as did the Ottomans and the Chinese, but large parts of the globe remained unknown to any of these empires. Although some of the essays in this volume do refer to the Hopkins schema, we have been careful to avoid imposing rigid periodization schemes on our contributors that would distort their findings.

Empires, Autonomy, and Globalization

In considering the questions that motivated this volume, it became evident that the concepts of *empires* and *friction* needed elucidation. The concept of friction as an analytical tool in the study of globalization has been described metaphorically by the anthropologist Anna Lowenhaupt Tsing: "A wheel turns because of its encounter with the surface of the road; spinning in the air gets it nowhere. Rubbing two sticks together produces heat and light; one stick alone is just a stick. As a metaphorical image, friction reminds us that heterogeneous and unequal encounters can lead to new arrangements of culture and power."[25] The pursuit of empires played an important role in forging transplanetary connections among particular areas of life and involved, to the advantage of metropolitan centres, some parts of the world more than others.[26] Rarely, if ever, were these connections forged easily or systematically. For these reasons, globalizing processes should not be seen as enveloping the world inexorably or inevitably.

Friction, to varying degrees, accompanied early European expansion into Africa, the Indian Ocean, and America. Where the conquerors found indigenous political authority well established, legitimate, and undivided, they often faced resistance. Where they found small states or tribal divisions with such institutions less developed, they were more likely to establish successful colonies. Historians have long acknowledged that indigenous peoples played a vital role in shaping the pattern of colonization that unfolded during the so-called Age of Discovery. Thus, the Spanish enjoyed momentous successes colonizing the Canary Islands in the fifteenth century, and the Portuguese established enclaves along the west and east coasts of Africa soon thereafter. The historian Alfred Crosby regards the conquest of the Canary Islands as a prototype for later assaults on the personal and collective autonomy of indigenous peoples, and as a stepping stone for the trial-by-error navigators who headed south along the coast of Africa and west to America.[27] Once the Portuguese rounded Africa and entered the Indian Ocean, they found it easy to plant trading forts along the Swahili coast of east Africa and in South Asia because of an abundance of city-states unable to organize a concerted resistance. In their conquest of the New World, the Spanish managed to divide the tribes of Mexico, and they were able to colonize the Philippines for much the same reason.

Europeans took advantage of local disputes and indigenous knowledge wherever they could. The British East India Company extended its rule in India during an age of turmoil for the Mughal Empire. European trading companies could not do the same with a united China or Japan, but they did make commercial inroads in those places because of New World silver, and because of the shipping services that the companies provided. By 1700 Europeans knew how to organize private, large-scale, sustained commercial and manufacturing enterprises, namely, big trading companies and sugar plantations.[28] The management of far-flung commerce and production fostered new skills. Europeans had discovered how to channel wealth into long-term investments that left management in the hands of professional overseers. This approach occurred through the development of the joint-stock company, the forerunner of the modern corporation. It permitted small investors to own part of a venture — say the East India Company or the Hudson's Bay Company — and to be free of the management. Merchants in an empire no longer had to be part of a specific trading community to participate in a major business: individuals in many important cities could invest in a business managed elsewhere, and capital was becoming liquid, not fixed to a place. Networks functioned because of European concepts of joint-stock companies and because of contracts supported by judicial systems that invariably accompanied colonizers and sustained the contracts of trade and the conversion of land into property.[29] In addition to their early establishment of the joint-stock company, the Dutch pioneered the development of stock exchanges, banks, warehouses, and a legal code that serviced commerce. Companies functioned within empires and the legal sanction of a home government; some received government subsidies, but they also admitted non-nationals and outside capital.

Empires tried to put in place law codes and courts based on domestic models that served the institutionalization of law imposed from the outside in dominated lands. Local imperial administrators and jurists had to practise discretion and compromise to achieve order, practices that involved trade-offs between domination and autonomy. In commercial law, empires showed flexibility and adaptation, accepting at first for practical reasons the laws and conventions employed in newly acquired territories and then introducing changes by statutes: informal limits to autonomy thus became more formal. There were adjuncts of empires that retained their own law codes. During the nineteenth century, British financiers, merchant houses, manufacturers, and diplomats exerted so much influence in China, Argentina, and the Ottoman Empire that the populations of these regions found their collective autonomy jeopardized and became incorporated into informal empire. In Nigeria, for example, British colonial authorities of the late nineteenth century relied on indigenous leaders to rule indirectly.

Participation in the empire by local lenders, merchants, and landowners did not mean power sharing. Friction was intrinsic to the imperial form of global integration. Empires may not have always enriched metropolitan powers, but they were organized to benefit Europeans principally, not subject peoples. These organizational steps invariably involved restrictions on collective and individual autonomy. Metropolitan impositions disrupted the structure of local economies and exacerbated local divisions.[30] In India in the nineteenth century, the demise of the Mughal court diminished luxury trades and arts.[31] French incursions in North Africa in the mid-nineteenth century and the Russian occupation of central Asia in the late nineteenth century implanted colonies and assailed customary land and water allocation practices.[32] Empires yielded benefits to specific European families and trading houses, gave employment to Europeans paid out of local revenues, and procured indigenous soldiers for imperial armies.

A thematic description of empires could leave the false impression that European empires operated identically according to a single imperial model. Cultural, social, and legal differences among the imperial powers created distinctive colonies that varied considerably in their autonomy and that left legacies important for understanding forms of autonomy today. Thus, disparate legal traditions, labour availability, the type of commodity produced, and local resistance created different statutes and enforcement practices, even though major colonial law codes in all empires backed labour exploitation. Maps of enclaves, colonies, annexations, and trade can only minimally explain the themes of friction and diversity. Each imperial centre had unique designs, expectations, and capacities. Once the Spanish Crown wrested control of New World colonies from the heirs of the conquistadors, it installed a highly centralized and bureaucratic administration that attempted to control the movements of people and goods. The Royal Council of the Indies, however, proved incapable of preventing smuggling on a widespread scale. As a weak European state, Portugal exerted even less control over its overseas territories and was forced to rely on the British Empire to police its imperial domains. Even the British Empire often proved incapable of regulating land allocation and property rights in its colonies. It is common to remark that globalization has fostered hybrid cultures. In fact, colonialism led to hybridization too.

From 1500 to 1850, European seaborne empires played havoc with local cultures and ecologies, which also led to internal shifts in the distribution of collective autonomy. The slave trade exacerbated intratribal conflicts in western Africa and Angola, and it dramatically altered the cultural landscape of the Americas. Missionary activities in Africa, Latin America, and Asia proved especially disruptive. According to the historian Charles Boxer, the Jesuits developed a worldwide trading entity with activities "far greater in scope than those of either the Dutch or the English East India Companies, which are sometimes termed the first multinationals."[33] Civil authorities did not always welcome missionaries, of course, because of their reputation for interceding on behalf of indigenous people. But whether welcomed, barred, manipulated, or watched with suspicion, Christian churches made irreversible inroads that connected people across oceans.

Empires also appear to have fostered globalization by mixing people, plants, animals, and ideas across oceans. They increased internationalization by aspiring to control their subjects through lines of authority backed by men in national uniforms under national flags. The more zealously intrusive empires practised patriotic indoctrination and precipitated friction with multiple outcomes, including indigenous nationalism. Authorities attempted to maintain more or less uniform law codes within their jurisdictions, but these were often adapted to local circumstances and customs.[34] The attempts of empires to extend metropolitan laws resemble the efforts of transnational bodies in recent decades to initiate judicial bodies; the difference is that transnational bodies attempt to harmonize laws across boundaries, while empires attempted to codify and enforce laws mainly within imperial boundaries. In their chapters, both John Weaver and Adrian Jones consider the reach of imperial law and the later evolution of international criminal law. Apologists for colonialism spoke incessantly of the importance of law but then sanctioned the use of force to trample on the rights of indigenous peoples. Such contradictions in empire provided openings for the contestation of forms of globalization in pursuit of new forms of personal and collective autonomy. Christopher Bayly has proposed that many drivers of change — ideology, economics, and the state — produced chaotic changes in different parts of the world, "which cannot be traced back to any one of these 'drivers' or domains alone."[35]

A new type of imperialism took shape with the economic and military ascendancy of the United States in the first half of the twentieth century. Under the US model, formal collective autonomy might coexist with economic dependency. The first informal colonies in Latin America and the Philippines, for example, were permitted some local political control in exchange for US access to markets and trade. During the remainder of the century, US ambitions for worldwide political and economic supremacy, as well as a strong desire by US allies to avoid another world depression, shaped the formation of international agencies such as the United Nations, the International Monetary Fund, and the World Bank.[36] As is shown in the chapters by Pruessen and Streeter, the compulsion to manage world affairs and to assume international responsibilities that had been shirked in the 1930s led to foreign-aid programs in the postwar period aimed at shaping agrarian and industrial development.

By the 1960s US officials had adopted universal economic development models for the Third World, which were assumed to be free of historical circumstances and constraints. Confronting the US empire was a different imperial system led by the Soviet Union, and later China, with ambitions of implanting Socialist models beyond eastern Europe into the Third World. Both the US empire and the Soviet empire aimed for unprecedented world domination in terms of scale and scope, but they differed in strategy and tactics. The United States eschewed territorial annexation and direct rule, opting instead for informal empire.[37] More than any European empire, the United States unequivocally claimed divine inspiration in carrying out an altruistic mission that would allegedly benefit all of humankind. And, while previous empires had attempted to export languages, religions, and culture, the United States developed new mass communications technologies to promote the American dream on an unprecedented global scale. The Soviets, by contrast, were inspired by leftist secular European heroes, including Marx, Engels, Kautsky, and Lenin, which led to cults of personality around such figures as Joseph Stalin and Mao Zedong. While the Soviets could not match superior American technology, Communism did gain a wide following in certain parts of the Third World for brief periods of the Cold War.[38]

Ideas, Epistemic Communities, and Globalization

When exploring global connections at particular moments, one cannot go very far without running into ideas associated with universal claims. Some of these ideas have particular relevance to collective and individual autonomy: free trade, human rights, property rights and improvement, environmental management, and self-determination, to name but a few. Often, such ideas are nurtured by *epistemic communities,* networks of scholars, savants, and professionals that have recognized expertise and competence in a particular domain and an authoritative claim to knowledge in that domain.[39] Such communities share certain normative beliefs that suggest avenues to action, and they confidently link causal beliefs to everyday problems.

In studying global connections around particular moments, we were drawn to observe how universal ideas travel, how knowledge moves from one locality to another and from one culture to another, and how truces and compromises with the absolute forms of ideas are made. The mission of the universal, Tsing writes, is "to form bridges, roads, and channels of circulation. Knowledge gained from particular experience percolates into these channels, widening rather than interrupting them."[40] As they travel, these ideas become hybridized, reformulated, and recast through dialogue, and sometimes struggle. In these senses, ideas are a source of friction. While free trade can provide a doctrine for the expansion of pharmaceutical transnational corporations' intellectual property rights and control over the sale and distribution of medicines, it also is invoked by developing countries seeking access to wealthier countries' markets for agricultural commodities and foods. References to law can back impositions of order by force but also bolster appeals for justice and restitution.[41] Economic development schemes can and have served the Leviathan, but some societies have embraced them to good effect to house and feed their hundreds of millions. Human rights can cut in more than one direction; political rights follow a convoluted history of struggles.[42] Strands of ideas in Enlightenment thought may have been egregiously misrepresented in some accounts so that their pertinence to "still debated principles, intellectual tendencies, and institutions" is neglected. Leading Enlightenment figures argued from universalistic positions that imperialism was manifestly unjust.[43] As Tsing observes, "Universals beckon to elite and excluded alike."[44] In exploring such dualities implied by the metaphor of friction, we are able to better understand the relationships between globalization and autonomy.

Moments and Friction: Our Approach

Any study attempting to connect empire with globalization and autonomy will likely invite the criticism that empires have rarely adhered to a grand design. As many studies have shown, empires administered dependencies haphazardly, lacked cultural coherence, and met resistance nearly everywhere.[45] Globalization as a conceptual framework needs similar qualification. How can scholars convey globalization's incompleteness, offer a sense of the muddled encounters of states and globalization, and capture globalization's many contradictory consequences for people's lives, particularly as they bear upon autonomy? Instead of trying to construct grand-scale narratives, we directed our contributors to begin their essays with a select moment in history that covered an incident, an innovation, a movement, or a round of negotiations related to their research. We hoped that these moments would demonstrate that global encounters that involved the securing or denial of autonomy in specific places inevitably involved friction. We believed that focusing on moments of friction would offer a useful way to explore the dialectic between globalization and autonomy. As Tsing puts it: "Friction makes global connection powerful and effective. Meanwhile, without even trying, friction gets in the way of the smooth operation of global power. Difference can disrupt, causing everyday malfunctions as well as unexpected cataclysms. Friction refuses the lie that global power operates as a well-oiled machine. Furthermore, difference sometimes inspires insurrection. Friction can be the fly in the elephant's nose."[46]

Whether globalization stole or burst upon the world, whether globalization transpired in an evolutionary fashion or by convergences resulting in sudden ruptures, we recognized the need to measure certain qualities of global connections over time. These include the actual geographic scope of the connections; the depth of their penetration, both spatially and socially; the speed of transfers of people, articles, and information; and the thickness or tenuousness of the connections. Similar to other globalization scholars, the Portuguese historian Cátia Antunes has identified the key variables as extensity, velocity, and intensity.[47] To this list should be added the global consciousness of agents and degrees of individual and collective autonomy. Using such indices, most of the contributors to this volume would probably agree that appreciable globalization had transpired by the late nineteenth century and decisive globalization had arrived by the end of the Second World War, or the height of the Cold War. After lengthy discussions about periodization, however, we realized that fixing a precise date for the origins of globalization was less important than agreeing to investigate globalization and autonomy using the concepts of historical moments and friction.

This Volume's Contributions

Using the device of historical moments, this book provides a series of windows at different times and places to view the dynamic relationships between two sets of processes: globalization and the loss or gain of autonomy. Such a historical analysis is important if we are to have a deep understanding of these relationships. We also recognize that personal and collective forms of autonomy are themselves dynamically linked. Our research suggests several tentative conclusions.

First, over the past three centuries, globalization, understood as expanding transplanetary connections, has brought higher levels of interdependence to more places in the world and involved more persons than at any time in the past. Moreover, this interdependence has featured, in one way or another, in the daily lives of more societies and more persons in the world than at any previous time. Finally, over the past half-century, these changes in the levels of interdependence have occurred more rapidly and through more channels than at earlier times. They are generally less constrained by politically defined territorial boundaries than in the past and are characterized by increased openness across the world.

Second, the expansion in the global coverage of interdependence, its importance in the daily lives of people, and the rapidity of the social changes involved are more pronounced in the wealthy countries as a group than between the wealthy countries and those with lesser wealth. As Samir Saul demonstrates in his chapter, what changes over time is not the degree of interdependence between the wealthier societies and the poorer ones, but the ability of some to leave the club of the poor to join the club of the wealthy. Moreover, certain sectors of poorer societies might be incorporated into these relations of interdependence, thereby intensifying the differences between these parts and the given society as a whole. In these respects, globalizing processes can be supraterritorial in the sense that they create new geographies, or what Appadurai calls "process geographies," which undermine or come to exist alongside territorial or "trait geographies."[48] In each of these respects, then, globalization processes contribute to deepening fissures between those societies participating in globalization and those sidelined by it. Again, Saul's analysis of financial globalization at the end of the twentieth century demonstrates this point. Looking at these processes from the point of view of the Maghreb countries, the scholar Yassine Essid's chapter captures the despair and difficulties originating from this widening gap, particularly when contrasted, for example, with the hope that existed at the time of decolonization and independence.

In researching how autonomy relates to globalization, we concluded that, rather than trying to measure the gain or loss of autonomy in the world, it is more useful to think about changes in the ideas and forms of autonomy. John Weaver's chapter, which explores the life of a slave woman in South Africa at the beginning of the nineteenth century, reveals how the European idea of personal autonomy was strongly opposed by commercial and patriarchal interests when it came to the institution of slavery. Still, he shows how the idea that slaves deserved some personal autonomy became planted in people's minds and worked its way, bit by bit, into law, eventually leading to emancipation. Jeremy Stolow's chapter illustrates how imaginaries fuelled by emerging technologies like the telegraph created new spaces in society for women to be autonomous in a personal sense, even if that autonomy turned liberal notions of autonomy on their head. Ironically, autonomy is enhanced for some women when they become the medium for the words of a spirit from the past.

Ideas of autonomy also have staying power. The philosopher Charles Taylor maintains that a modern moral order based on natural rights and a presumption of equality has "undergone a double expansion: in extension (more people live by it; it has become dominant) and in intensity (the demands it makes are heavier and more ramified)."[49] Weaver's findings suggest that such expansion does not take place smoothly but inevitably involves friction. Attempts to implement the Enlightenment notions of individual rights, which circulated in South Africa at the beginning of the nineteenth century, bogged down in the transition between empires. In the end, these emancipatory ideas offered little solace to a female slave cut off from her community. Two centuries later some of these same ideas of personal autonomy anchored the founding of an International Criminal Court. In his analysis of the Nuremberg trials, which articulated the notion of individual autonomy as a global concept, Adrian Jones suggests that the paradigm of thinking enunciated at the trials was finally institutionalized globally with the creation of the court and its early operations in 2002. When applied more broadly, the paradigm on individual responsibility invoked at the trials opened up avenues for individuals to claim rights to social justice irrespective of sex, property relations, and even citizenship in a particular state. So one particular notion of individual autonomy, a thoroughly modern one, has become the focus of a global institution many centuries after the idea was conceived.

In short, the past three centuries of globalization have seen the emergence of an idea of personal autonomy — the self-reliant individual who is a bearer of rights. The groups entitled to this form of autonomy have expanded from propertied males to include former slaves, peasants, women, and minorities — in short, the subaltern groups that have gradually won more rights over time. This expansion is not linear, nor does it take the same form everywhere. Other chapters underline variations in these processes, whether they involve indigenous peoples (Ravi de Costa), the transition of the Ottoman Empire from imperial power to semi-colonized client (Virginia Aksan), the subjugation of Tibet (Timothy Brook), or the control of workers in export-oriented production (Neil White). The legacies of imperialism and colonization shape how personal autonomy comes to be understood in different parts of the world.

Autonomy in the collective sense of self-government has existed in a variety of forms for centuries, if not millennia. Here, too, our book indicates that, when placed in conjunction with globalization, the forms and ideas of autonomy have changed over the past three centuries. In particular, as Anthony Giddens has observed, this period has seen the globalization of the nation-state form of political organization of territory.[50] Gradually, the nation-state has supplanted earlier forms of organization like city-states and, more recently, the territorial subjugation of empires. The American sociologist Saskia Sassen refers to this development as the hierarchy of scales, which ascends from the local, subnational (province, state, canton, etc.), and national to an international system of states.[51] Collective autonomy becomes understood and defined within this hierarchy of scales. This containment of collective autonomy within states, themselves shaped by patterns of imperial organization of territory, is often a violent process when experienced by indigenous peoples, the colonized, and the subjugated.

Several chapters address these issues. De Costa's assessment of indigenous peoples in Australia shows how practices of collective autonomy based on a long-standing cosmology are undermined and often destroyed by discourses of racial inferiority and backwardness. From the point of view of indigenous peoples, and in some other cases that involve cultural or religious minorities, the nation-state itself is a colonizing force. Aksan and Brook show that the matter of autonomy is particularly acute in land-based empires. To control territory, imperial forces need to use force and occupy land in ways rarely needed by maritime-based empires. As the ability to mobilize these forces declined in the Ottoman Empire because of rising nationalism and increasing competition from the Russian, British, and French empires, the empire as a whole entered into a long crisis that culminated in its dissolution. The modern secular state of Turkey was built on its ashes. Tibet's struggle with China,

Brook explains, also demonstrates how empires impose domination and deprive regions of collective autonomy. By contrast, the sea-based British Empire learned to allow some self-rule in its domains, provided that commerce was protected and that certain British institutions remained intact. Finally, White demonstrates how community and individual autonomy, particularly for the working class, changed as globalization intensified. He contrasts the situation of workers in company towns over the course of the twentieth century with the increasing number of workers employed in export-processing zones in the late part of the century. Social welfare policies that initially governed these towns stand in sharp contrast to these zones, which are commonly devoid of any social safety net. White's findings reflect the process, described by the cultural anthropologist Aihwa Ong, whereby states restrict the personal autonomy of citizens and migrants in slices of territories specifically designated to produce commodities for global markets.[52] White's study emphasizes that these limits on autonomy often include the denial of social rights available to citizens inside the same state but outside the export-processing zones.

In short, the depth and form of collective autonomies in a world moving towards the globalization of the nation-state system are by no means uniform from one part of the world, and from one community in the world, to another. The historian Arif Dirlik has explained global modernity as a world in which the institutions of modernity — the nation-state, the market economy, industrialism, and militarism — take root throughout the world.[53] How these institutions take root, however, depends upon the histories of cultural practices in given places, their relations with imperialism and other forms of domination, and the ways in which they engage with global capitalism. The hierarchy of scale — local, subnational, national, international — that is globalized with the nation-state system is explicitly a political one that does not necessarily correspond to patterns of economic relationships. Over the past two centuries, few states have succeeded for very long in sustaining economic autarky. Nor has this hierarchy of scale corresponded very neatly to patterns of cultural relationships, including religious ones. As we know, the boundaries of many nation-states were constructed by imperial powers that often ignored cultural or economic boundaries in the interest of maximizing their own economic plundering.

Contributors that look at the contemporary period argue that the lack of correspondence among political, cultural, and economic geographies has become more pronounced than ever. Saul's analysis of the possible shift from financial internationalization to financial globalization demonstrates this point well. He argues that over the last hundred years foreign direct investment has come to replace portfolio investment as the spearhead of internationalization. The relative greater importance of foreign direct investment, the transnationalization of firms, and international production has created an economic environment in which nation-state boundaries, particularly in the Global North, are commonly surmounted by economic transactions, as is evident by the use of such phrases as "supraterritorial relationships" or "capital flows." But this phenomenon, he emphasizes, is largely confined to the North. Reversing nineteenth-century patterns, capital now flows mostly to capital-rich countries, as the North-South component of such capital flows is proportionately less than in the past. Admittedly, there are new entrants to the ranks of capital-rich countries such as Japan, South Korea, Turkey, and the Czech Republic, not to mention others on the horizon such as China, India, and Brazil. Nonetheless, the developing world remains marginalized, but in new ways. Capital flows are now mostly a North-North or rich-rich affair, in which developed countries serve more than ever as one another's main creditors and debtors. This economic marginalization of the less wealthy states contrasts sharply with previous phases of international economic relations, most notably the period between 1870 and 1914.

Saul's analysis provides an essential background — autonomy relationships after the First World War — for the more explicitly political focus of other chapters that wrestle with the role of the United States in shaping globalization. Each of these chapters in its own way offers the argument that contemporary globalization in its initial stages was led by the United States to defend its economic interests, which required a more institutionalized and stabilized global economy. Gorman's chapter on the regulation of the radio frequency spectrum presages some of the key battles between the United Kingdom and the United States over institutional arrangements that shaped global economic systems following the Second World War. He shows that the International Radio Conference of 1927 marked a "change from international coexistence to international cooperation and interdependence," wherein nation-states, almost exclusively from the developed countries, came to share collective autonomy. In doing so, they were able to achieve the regulation of what is essentially a "global" commodity, namely, radio spectrum frequencies. The United States gave precedence to private rights and the interests of private radio broadcasting firms, while the United Kingdom and other European powers viewed the radio spectrum as a public good in which public rights ought to predominate. How the United States won the radio battle foreshadowed how economic globalization would unfold under the influence of us hegemony after 1945.

In this regard, Ronald Pruessen probes the thinking of President Franklin D. Roosevelt in the early 1940s as he looked ahead to a postwar world that would prosper under us-led development. An Open Door approach to the world economy demanded, Roosevelt argued, the end of colonialism and the global spread of the liberal democratic nation-state form. In reviewing Roosevelt's ruminations, however, Pruessen detects a strong sense of paternalism and noblesse oblige in the president's views on colonial peoples' right to development opportunities and how much autonomy they might be able to handle.

As globalizing processes are supported, if not enforced, by neo-imperial powers, they call into being new ideas and practices of autonomy in several ways. First, the denial, removal, or repression of collective autonomy in societies through us-led globalization can bring the values, advantages, and need for collective autonomy into the social consciousness of subjugated groups. Acting on this kind of social consciousness will vary in form over time as globalization itself becomes more extensive, intensive, and rapid. As Stephen Streeter observes in his chapter, liberal developmentalism, or the idea that other nations could and should replicate the us developmental experience, was forced on much of the Third World by the us-led globalization project during the 1960s. The battle for "hearts and minds" waged by the United States in Guatemala and Vietnam, for example, can be seen as attempts to steer formerly colonized peoples away from alternative forms of globalization. He notes that during the Cold War, us government officials and academics frequently described Third World peoples as "primitive" or "childlike" and in need of uplift by the "advanced" cultures of the West, sentiments that echoed Franklin Roosevelt's paternalism as described by Pruessen. Vietnamese revolutionaries became famous, if not models, throughout the Third World for how to achieve autonomy, especially in places where similar liberation struggles against us hegemony were unfolding.

Yassine Essid also examines the influence of us economic doctrine, but from the perspective of the Maghreb countries in North Africa. He describes how the promise of Third World development made by

President John F. Kennedy in his 1961 speech to the UN General Assembly was never fulfilled. In this respect, US-led globalization demonstrates disturbing similarities with previous imperial experiences, which have / shattered alternative forms of globalization that might have preserved collective autonomy. In short, globalization and imperialism seem to be part of the same long, bad dream from the perspective of many so-called developing countries. The political shell of collective autonomy that remains in many of these states becomes controlled by autocratic and corrupt leaders who repress their citizens, sometimes violently, all the while attempting to shape their economies to fit with constantly changing development models.

Fortunately, some globalization processes, when abetted by digital technologies and mass media, can impel, if not compel, the work of the imagination and, through it, novel notions of autonomy and agency.[54] An increasing number of persons in the world are able to challenge the assumptions in official thinking, regardless of whether they are extreme forms of enterpreneurial development or oppressive forms of collectivism. Part of the critical imagination is focused on the realization of collective and personal autonomies in situations where these are denied. Streeter sees national liberation movements as examples of these struggles. Essid observes the growing force of Islamic fundamentalism, a movement that makes effective use of digital technologies and mass media, and sees it as constructing a new global Islam that offers (false) hope to the millions being marginalized by US-led globalization.

Ulf Hedetoft's concluding chapter begins with the meeting of Ronald Reagan and Mikhail Gorbachev in Iceland in 1986, an event that signalled the beginning of the end of the Soviet empire. His essay connects to the earlier chapters through his argument that the United States placed severe limits on the autonomy of the developing countries by military means and by its design and direction of global financial institutions such as the International Monetary Fund and the World Bank. In the post-Soviet era, he uses the term *neo-imperialism* to describe the ability of the United States to project its power beyond its formal sphere of sovereign authority to curb the collective autonomy of other states, which are induced or coerced into pursuing choices that are consonant with Washington's prerogatives.

By looking through the keyhole of a moment in history, the essays in this book underline the need for histories of globalization processes and of ideas and forms of autonomy. Autonomy has existed in particular forms for a very long time. Consciousness of autonomy and reflection upon it in a directed way have shorter histories and appear to have arisen with the onset of modernity, which can be identified with the advent of the nation-state or doctrines of development — free market and collectivist. The state and the ideologically opposed doctrines of development have had a deep impact on individuals and communities, so it is no wonder that consciousness of autonomy has emerged most fully with modernity. Consciousness of connections with far away places and the interdependence that arises from such consciousness are phenomena that reach back millennia. Awareness of connections that are planetary and of connections that are specifically transworld is more recent. Historians argue that such consciousness predates modernity, but it is not clear by how long. There is much work to be done to uncover how and when consciousness of globalization and autonomy came into being.

For scholars who are interested in studying the origins of globalization and the implications of globalization for individual and collective autonomy, looking at the past will benefit our thinking about the future. Not only do we benefit from understanding the historical roots of globalization and autonomy, the past is ripe with incidents of friction that, when examined closely, can help us find better solutions to current and imminent global predicaments.

chapter 2   **Tibet and the Chinese World-Empire**

Timothy Brook

THE HISTORY OF GLOBALIZATION since the seventeenth century is usually narrated from the water, not from the land. We regard land as discour-
aging the propensity to travel and reducing the face-to-face interactions
that are essential for maintaining active networks of communication and
exchange. Water, on the other hand, enables networks of information to
proliferate over distances that once seemed endless and commodities to
be shipped in quantities and at speeds that carts and pack animals cannot
equal.

This differentiation between land and water is enshrined in the early
stories Europeans used to tell about the global spread of capitalism, with
Vasco da Gama sailing around Africa and Christopher Columbus crossing the Atlantic. If Europe can be said to have "risen," it did so on water.
Land returns to the story of global capitalism in the nineteenth century
with the building of railways and in the twentieth century with the un-
spooling of highways, both of which supplemented mobility by water.
The opening of the new rail line from Beijing to Lhasa in 2006, to noisy
official fanfare inside China and protest from Tibetans outside China,
shows that these land-based modes of transportation continue to have
a place in how contemporary states make the globe accessible. But globalization in the postwar years has been foremost about container ships;
trains have dwindled to a supporting role.

This contrast is too stark to reveal all facets of globalization. China
was certainly not the landlocked realm hostile to maritime connection

that older histories suggest. Some zealous authors have enjoyed pillorying this stereotype by making Columbus-like claims about the imperial eunuch Zheng He and the fleets he commanded in the Indian Ocean during the fifteenth century. But that is not the only story, nor even the main story, when we look at China through the imperial era, particularly under the Qing dynasty of the Manchus in the eighteenth century. The Qing inhabited a world of military alliances, negotiated sovereignties, and trade networks that extended primarily across land, not water. The Manchus calculated their imperial reach in terms of continents, not oceans, and their projection of power followed land routes rather than water passages.

This continental versus maritime difference underlies the profound divergence in the state systems that have come into being in Europe and China. I will seek to capture this divergence by contrasting the concepts of world-system and world-empire. In a world-system, expansive states interact within a field of competing sovereignties; in a world-empire, one expansive state strives to monopolize all sovereignty. Since the seventeenth century, European nations have constituted a world-system on the basis of technologies of trade and political communication facilitating maritime expansion. Qing China, pursuing a different model of political authority and economic enlargement, constituted a world-empire. This contrast, like that between land and water, is too stark to express the full complexity of the historical reality of globalization. Nonetheless, I shall invoke these concepts later in this chapter to make better sense of the policies that the Chinese state, then and now, has pursued with regard to Tibet.

Tibet in the World

Tibet today is the great paradox of the contemporary global condition. It is a polity without national status in the global nation-state system, an economy with few external ties in an era of global economic integration, and a restricted zone in an age of unprecedented international travel. It is a community whose members live all over the world, a culture whose religious and moral practices have found new soil in other cultural traditions, a place that exceeds its boundaries. The region called Tibet is relatively inaccessible, yet knowledge of Tibet's saga is nearly universal. In geographical reality, it is cut off from the world; in virtual reality, it is thoroughly global.

Inside the Tibetan Autonomous Region (the official designation of the portion of Tibet that the Chinese government allows to retain that name), the same sense of paradox prevails. The region is distant from everywhere and environmentally foreign to the Chinese heartland to the east, yet it is rife with signs of foreign influences. Lhasa, the city that spreads out around the foot of the Potala, the Dalai Lama's now empty residence, exists in an economic and political regime much like what prevailed in the China of three or four decades ago, when a closely watched and desperately underfunded society wilted under the military surveillance of the Communist state. Only the diversity of the clothes that some Tibetans wear on the streets of the old city recalls Lhasa's former status as an Inner Asian hub, rather than as it is today, an outpost of Chinese colonialism. In towns outside Lhasa, the presence of commercial China is also ubiquitous, from the casino-style leisure facilities of Shigatse, home of the Panchen Lama (the lama who is second in authority to the Dalai Lama), to the knock-off merchandise shops in Gyantse, to the starkly divided city of Tsetang, where Stalinist wedding-cake architecture and a busy network of undercover police impose a mode of state colonization indifferent to the squalor of the Tibetan neighbourhoods. At first glance, Tibet might look like a place that globalization has not touched, a place whose isolation makes it attractive to tourists and seems to justify China's intervention. Yet that judgment ignores Tibet's historical openness to outside forces. It also neglects the fact that China would not be remaking Tibet according to Chinese needs and policies were that country not pursuing the opportunities offered to it in the current phase of globalization.

China has used Tibet's comparative continental isolation to justify its own presence as a liberating force. According to the liberationist discourse underlying this justification, Tibet has been a closed and backward place in which the majority suffered under "feudal" oppression until the Chinese arrived to modernize Tibet and bring it into the present. Closure versus opening is the polarity structuring this logic, but that polarity assumes that continentality equals isolation. Although Tibet has not been easily accessible to the outside world, Lhasa has for centuries been a significant nexus of trade in the connections that stretch across Inner Asia. The first Portuguese Jesuits who gazed at the Himalayas in the 1620s were aware of the networks that ran from India up through Lhasa and on into northern and eastern Asia. They knew Tibet not as an impasse but as "the door that opens onto all of Tartary [Mongolia],

China, and many other pagan monarchies."[1] It would be almost a century before the first Jesuit set up a mission in Lhasa. When he got there, Ippolito Desideri reported that the city in the late 1710s was "densely populated, not only by natives, but by a large number of foreigners of divers nations, such as Tartars [Mongols], Chinese, Muscovites [Russians], Armenians, and people from Cascimir [Kashmir], Hindustan, and Nepal, all established there as merchants, and who have made large fortunes."[2] Tibet was not a mountain retreat lacking contact with the outside world but a realm through which economic and political integration linked trade and people in South Asia with Inner and East Asia.

Connections made over land tend to be more vulnerable to control than those over water, especially where topographical conditions are harsh. It is perhaps surprising, then, to discover that the continental space of Inner Asia has, historically, exhibited a peculiarly fluid quality. It has been invaded, armed, and claimed, often simultaneously by several parties seeking, alternately, war or truce as conditions of change. The historian Peter Perdue describes this "unboundedness" of Inner Asia as "the great indeterminacy of the cultural characteristics and territorial borders of this zone, which resulted in constant competition by empires, religions, and cultural groups to define and control it."[3] Less so than the trading networks that laced the world's oceans, continental trading networks were vulnerable to political and military control and more likely to be interrupted and broken as the balance of power among continental peoples shifted. What Perdue calls "the great plasticity of the landscape" defied fixity and territorialization until the eighteenth century, when Russia and China brought to bear resources that no competitor could match and incorporated Inner Asia into their two political empires. This gradual fixation of territories and borders would impede Tibet from becoming a distinct political entity in the modern era.

Tibet and China

The formation of a political unity among the scattered ethnic groups inhabiting the Tibetan massif in the sixth century marked the emergence of Tibet as one of the six great empires — alongside the Chinese to the east, the Turks to the west, and the Arabs, Greeks, and Franks further west — of the late medieval world. The Tibetan empire fractured into independent principalities in the ninth century, though not before its cultural transformation by Buddhism, which crossed the Himalayas from

India in the seventh century.[4] Tibet thereafter would not regain the political stature or military capacity of its early empire, but the religious authority of Tibetan Buddhism grew to become its major strategic resource. The religious authority of key Tibetan leaders gave them power to shape outcomes at many key points in Tibetan history: in the mid-thirteenth century, when one Buddhist monk (Phagspa) became Khubilai Khan's advisor in Mongol-ruled China; at the turn of the fifteenth century, when another (Tsongkhapa) rebuilt Tibetan monasticism; and in the mid-seventeenth century, when yet another (the Fifth Dalai Lama) managed to play off the many polities that recognized him as the highest earthly manifestation of Amitabha Buddha to manoeuvre Tibet into political equality with Manchu-ruled China. Religious authority was the only resource Tibetans could use to assert their autonomy vis-à-vis their neighbours, as is still the case today. This religious dimension explains why the globalization of Tibetan Buddhism since the 1970s had political consequences for Tibet that no one could have foreseen when the Fourteenth Dalai Lama fled to India in 1959.

Religious authority, like any source of power, works to the benefit of the political leadership that invokes it to assert autonomy, but it can also expose its holder to challenges from the political ambitions of states that covet that authority and the territory it controls. Tibet found itself in this position early in the eighteenth century when, through a complex sequence of political and military events involving many state entities, it came under East Asian political suzerainty, a condition that continues to define its relationship to the world. The chief winners in this sequence of events were the Manchus, a Tungusic people from southern Siberia who consolidated their conquest of north China in 1644 by installing their great khan as the emperor of all China, thereby initiating the Qing dynasty. The main losers were the Zunghars, a powerful confederacy of Mongols that controlled Turkestan (now Xinjiang) to the far northwest of Tibet. It was not a loss they were content to bear, and their challenge early in the eighteenth century would lead to the event at the heart of this chapter, the Manchu invasion of Tibet in 1720.

Between the Manchu winners and Zunghar losers were four other groups. On the Manchu side were the Khoshots, a western Mongol confederacy based in Kokonor, northeast of Tibet, who asserted great influence in Tibet throughout the seventeenth century before being forced to throw their lot in with the Manchus. Squeezing the Zunghars from the other side were the Cossacks, whose movement into Siberia brought the Russian and Qing empires into contact and led in 1689 to the signing of the Treaty of Nerchinsk (using Jesuit negotiators, who finalized the treaty document in Latin), which divided up Inner Asia.[5] Then there were the Tibetans. They found themselves constantly having to negotiate with external powers that were eager to patronize their religious leaders, who had undisputed spiritual authority throughout most of Inner Asia. Finally, there were the Chinese, who come into this story principally as the foot soldiers who were recruited or pressed to serve the Manchus campaign into Tibet in 1720. "China" would only come into the equation after 1911, when the Republic of China that replaced the Qing dynasty declared its authority over all the Manchu empire, the consequences of which are still shaping Tibet's history.

The Manchu invasion of Tibet in 1720 was one of a series of interventions imposed on Tibet by external patrons through the seventeenth and eighteenth centuries. Many Tibetans actually welcomed this intervention because it ended a seventeen-year period of occupation (most recently by the Zunghars [for three years] and before them by the Khoshot Mongols) and brought twelve-year-old Gesang Gyatso, the Seventh Dalai Lama, to Lhasa. The politics of religious succession and Mongol suzerainty conspired to place Gesang Gyatso in Lhasa, where, ironically, he would not have gone had the Manchus not transported him there.

The Manchu occupation began well enough. Galbi, the Manchu commander of one of the two invading armies, records the army arriving with the Dalai Lama on 16 October 1720: "The Dalai Lama, proceeding westward, arrived at his residence in Tibet. Both lamas and laity showed their support and bent to his authority. Jubilant shouting shook the heavens and Sanskrit chants echoed over the land as people prayed for the [Manchu] emperor's limitless longevity and celebrated the consolidation of our realm."[6] Even the Italian Jesuit Desideri, who was no friend of the previous occupiers of Lhasa and had good reason to oppose a change in secular leadership, had to admit, in his characteristically backhanded way, that the new Dalai Lama was given a "rapturous reception by these superstitious people."[7]

Rapture over the Dalai Lama's restoration arose from two sources. One was delight that this boy, the highest manifestation of the Buddha on earth, had returned to the place where he should reside; the other was satisfaction that the Zunghar occupiers were forced out. Yet Tibetans were understandably cautious as to whether the Manchus would simply replace the Zunghars as military conquerors, just as the Zunghars had replaced the Khoshots, thereby continuing the shadow of protection/occupation under which Tibetans had lived since the sixteenth century. Their fears were soon justified. Eight years later, when the Dalai Lama began to demand political autonomy for Tibet, his Manchu patrons forced him into exile. Only in 1735 did the Manchus permit his return, though with a much reduced political status. The current half-century exile of the Fourteenth Dalai Lama is but the latest in a series of ruptures between successive Dalai Lamas and patrons in Beijing stretching back to the 1720s. Each rupture has resulted from the irreducible conflict between the Beijing-centred state, striving to assert exclusive territorial control of a grandiose national geo-body, and the aspirations of local authorities in Lhasa, striving for autonomy from external patrons.[8]

Religion and Diplomacy

The origins of the Manchu occupation of Tibet go back to the relationship that Mongol rulers established with high Tibetan lamas since at least the time of Genghis Khan in the twelfth century. Tibetan lamaism is a unique form of shamanistic Buddhist practice that helped to consolidate Tibetan culture after its political empire crumbled in the eighth century. A lama or "superior master" was one who had achieved the wisdom of the Buddha but deferred his own entry into nirvana so that he could assist others in attaining the same salvation. After the twelfth century, when Tibet fell under the sway of Genghis Khan's Mongols, the high lamas enjoyed unrivalled spiritual authority throughout Inner Asia. Even after the empire of Genghis' descendants crumbled in the mid-fourteenth century, lamaism continued to exert huge religious authority throughout Inner Asia until Islam partially eclipsed Buddhism in the nineteenth century.

The spiritual perfection of a lama posed a theological problem for Buddhists: what happened to him after he died? Did he end his mundane existence by entering nirvana, thereby relinquishing his vow to aid all who continue to suffer in ignorance? Or did he return to continue his work? The solution for some high lamas, developed in the fifteenth century, was self-willed reincarnation. According to this doctrine, the lama could continue to re-enter the cycle of rebirth until the task of enlightening the entire world was completed. Institutionally, this solution entailed a shift in how the highest lamas of Tibetan Buddhism, including both the Dalai Lama and Panchen Lama, were selected. No longer did monasteries fill vacancies at the upper level of the religious hierarchy by electing a mature monk from a group of able candidates. Instead, the deceased's reincarnation became the successor. That reincarnation had to be discovered among children (usually but not exclusively boys) born within a year or two of the lama's death. The search was often controversial, with competing clerical and aristocratic factions promoting different candidates. Once the church hierarchy agreed on a particular incarnate, it set to work instructing him in the teachings of Buddhism and fashioning him into the religious leader he had to become. Succession by reincarnation kept the upper echelons of Tibetan society from becoming entirely closed, but it also made Tibet vulnerable to manipulation from outside political forces.

The Dalai Lama lineage was established in the sixteenth century under Mongol patronage. The greatest of this lineage was the fifth incarnation. The Great Fifth (1617-82), as he is affectionately known, was a deft diplomat who used the patronage of Gushri Khan, the leader of the Khoshot Mongols, to defeat his religious and secular rivals linked to the Panchen Lama (both his teacher and rival) and consolidate his position as Tibet's supreme religious authority. When Gushri Khan retired to his homeland in Kokonor on the border with northwest China in 1642, he granted the sovereignty of Tibet to the Great Fifth. The rise of the Manchus to imperial authority in Beijing two years later suddenly posed a new challenge to the Great Fifth. The Manchus recognized his spiritual authority, yet the Fifth managed to evade any posture of submission. In a delicately orchestrated diplomatic visit to Beijing in 1653, the Dalai Lama recognized the reigning Manchu emperor as an incarnation of the Buddhist deity Manjusri. In return, the emperor appointed the Dalai Lama the Buddhist ruler of the empire. This exchange of titles represented more than appeasement: it was a political exchange in which each leader acknowledged and agreed to respect the authority of the other. The Great Fifth saw the relationship as a way of asserting Tibet's desire for autonomy against Mongol encroachments, while the emperor used the Dalai Lama to block the aspirations of Mongol leaders who might seek to draw Tibet into an alliance against the Manchus.

The arrangement outlasted both men, but it disintegrated in the next generation. The agent of its undoing was Gushri Khan's grandson, Lhazang Khan. Lhazang seized the Khoshot succession in 1700, claimed for himself the coveted title of Genghis Khan, and then asserted his right to reassume his grandfather's patronage of the Dalai Lama, now the Sixth.

Finding the Sixth Dalai Lama not to his liking, he deposed him and immediately produced a replacement Sixth in 1707. His choice was unpopular, rumour having it that the new Dalai Lama was actually Lhazang's son. When the first Sixth perished on his way into exile in Kokonor, the plot unravelled, for if the first Sixth was indeed the real Sixth, then the Seventh was on his way.

Lhazang Khan took these actions in oblique defiance of the Manchus. When the Qing emperor, Kangxi (1662-1722), heard about this new Sixth, he remarked at court that Lhazang Khan was not to be trusted. Still, he had no strong reason to challenge him so long as the Khoshot leader showed appropriate deference. Besides, the cost of intervening in so distant a region was prohibitive, especially because the Manchus' main concern at the time was the growing power of another Mongol confederacy, the Zunghars, further west. Emperor Kangxi sent a Manchu official to Lhasa in 1709 to investigate the succession and size up the political situation.[9] The emperor decided not to regard the replacement of the Sixth as a threat to Manchu dominance and duly acceded to the installation of the second Sixth in 1710. Three years later, however, he extended special honours to the Second Panchen Lama (1663-1737), hoping that he might serve as a counterweight to the Dalai Lama (a policy of divide and rule that Chinese governments have used down to the present).

Lhazang Khan's gamble did not pay off. The popularity of the deposed Sixth produced the expected result: his rebirth as the Seventh. Less than two years after the first Sixth's death, Gesang Gyatso was discovered in Kokonor, the region where the Sixth had died, and was recognized as the next reincarnation. The first Sixth was having posthumous revenge on Lhazang Khan by coming back as the Seventh. This birth opened an opportunity for Lhazang's rivals among the Khoshot Mongols to challenge Lhazang's power in Tibet. Competing Dalai Lamas put the Manchus in an awkward position: should they support the status quo in Tibet, or should they strengthen their own hand by backing the challenger? Like many imperial powers, they carefully prevaricated. Rather than burden themselves with a candidate whom they might later have to renounce, they continued to acknowledge the second Sixth in Lhasa while extending patronage to the new Seventh in Kokonor. What was at stake, after all, was not the correct theocratic candidate, but the authority of the patron.

The Zunghar Threat to the Manchu Empire

The instability of lama succession attracted the attention of another confederacy of western Mongols, the Zunghars. Their power, like that of the Khoshots, was eclipsed in the seventeenth century by the rise of the Manchus.[10] By 1715 a new Zunghar leader, Tsewang Rapten (1697-1727), was able to rebuild the Zunghar empire and become a contender for supremacy in Inner Asia. To legitimize his claim, Tsewang turned, as so many other contenders had, to the religious authority of Tibet. The confusion over the status of the Sixth Dalai Lama was an ideal pretext to intervene. Tsewang sent agents to Lhasa to convince Tibetan elites that he would get rid of Lhazang Khan and the Khoshots for them. To throw Lhazang off his guard, Tsewang gave Lhazang his sister in marriage and invited Lhazang's eldest son to marry his adopted daughter. Emperor Kangxi was rightly suspicious. When he heard about the son's marriage, he cynically observed that Tsewang Rapten was "using his love for his son-in-law as a pretext to keep hold of him." "Is it possible," the emperor wondered aloud, "that things can stay as they are without anything happening?"[11]

Three years later Tsewang Rapten dispatched six thousand soldiers into Tibet under his cousin, Tsering Dhondup (d. 1743). The main army moved south through mountainous terrain to avoid detection, but a mobile unit of three hundred men was sent to Kokonor to kidnap the Seventh Dalai Lama. The plan was to use him to break the Khoshot hold over Tibet. The bid to capture the Seventh failed, which meant not only that the Zunghars had no political capital to bring with them to Lhasa but also that they were directly threatening Manchu authority. Tsering Dhondup pushed on to Lhasa, killing Lhazang Khan and driving out the Khoshots. His soldiers then pillaged Lhasa and despoiled the surrounding region, nullifying any possibility of Tibetan support.[12] Deposing the Khoshot's second Sixth Dalai Lama was a pointless gesture when the Zunghars had no Seventh to replace him. So the Khoshot occupation simply became a Zunghar occupation. Nothing changed except the disruption of the careful balance that the Manchus thought they had achieved among the Mongol confederacies. By directly thumbing their noses at the Manchus, the Zunghars were about to draw the Manchus into Tibet for the first time.

The Manchu Occupation of Tibet

The Manchu invasion of eastern Tibet the following year, 1718, became a fiasco. Misjudging Zunghar tactics, underestimating their military power, and failing to mobilize Tibetan support, the Manchu army
was almost entirely annihilated. The second invasion two years later
would not repeat these mistakes. The linchpin for gaining Tibetan support would be the adoption of the Zunghars' original strategy: bring the
Seventh Dalai Lama to Lhasa and install him on his rightful throne in
the Potala. This move seemed to require accepting that the child Seventh was indeed a true incarnation, though the Manchus remained carefully uncommitted as long as possible. Yinti (1688-1755), widely regarded
as Kangxi's heir apparent and acting as his father's representative in
Kokonor, told the boy as late as April 1719, "I don't know whether you
are the real Dalai Lama or not, but since everyone regards you as such, I
am willing to pay homage as though you were the real Dalai Lama." The
boy was alert to the delicacy of this prevarication. "You need not trouble
yourself," he replied. "I cannot receive your obeisance anyway, because
your father is an incarnation of the bodhisattva Manjusri, which makes
you a bodhisattva as well. How could a bodhisattva bow to the Dalai
Lama?"[13] The young Seventh could play the politics of imperial prevarication just as well as Yinti.[14]

The second invasion succeeded. The Zunghars readied themselves
against the combined Manchu-Mongol force bringing the Dalai Lama
from Kokonor to the northeast, but they were unprepared to fight a second army, led by General Galbi, coming from the southeast. Galbi's army
crushed its opponents and took Lhasa before the first army arrived. "The
fleeing mob of bandits scudded like clouds from morning to night without finding any place from which to escape, and so we gained complete
victory with nary an arrow lost," declared one Manchu commander.
"On the day the soldiers entered Tibet, Tibetans young and old lined
both sides of the route, bowing and bearing food and drink to welcome
the kingly army. Drawing up his reins, the General [Galbi] declared his
Majesty's benevolent pacification. The tribesmen danced and the roar of
their joyful shouts shook heaven and earth."[15] The Zunghars attempted
a bold countermove by trying to grab the Dalai Lama from the Manchus before they reached Lhasa, but Tsering Dhondup's remaining force
of four thousand soldiers did not have the strength to fight its way to the
Dalai Lama. According to Desideri, "after heavy fighting, the Zunghars

were defeated and that insolent usurper general, Tsering Dhondup, fled with a handful of followers toward the great western desert."[16] Galbi describes his defeat by noting that "Tsering Dhondup, depleted in food and arms and at the extremity of exhaustion, slunk away like a rat."[17]

The installation of the Seventh Dalai Lama in Lhasa ended the Zunghar occupation of Tibet and effectively sidelined any future Mongol claim to exclusive patronage of the Dalai Lama. Manchus supremacy in Mongolia, not Tibet itself, was the Manchus' main concern because an unsecured Tibet was simply an invitation for Mongolian adventurism and empire building. The Dalai Lama's installation did not yet entail the absorption of Tibet into the Qing empire. The emperor and the Dalai Lama still related to each other as patron to holy man, not sovereign to vassal, although the Dalai Lama's power was much diminished in reality. Only in the nineteenth century, however, would Tibet be fully incorporated into the political structure of the Qing empire. But the Jesuit Desideri saw the future. "After nigh twenty years of tumult and disaster," he noted at the end of his account of his mission, Tibet "was thus subjugated by the emperor of China in October, 1720, and here his descendants will probably continue to reign for many centuries."[18]

Tibetan elites imagined their relationship with the Manchus differently. They accepted Manchu patronage as a condition of being free of Zunghar patronage, but they hoped the change in patrons would enhance their autonomy. When the Manchus reduced their military presence in 1722 by cutting the garrison to 1,900 soldiers for economic reasons, Tibetans interpreted this as a normalizing move that would eventually release them from Manchu control. The Manchus, however, had no intention of allowing Tibet to slip into other hands. A Khoshot attempt to stage a comeback in Tibet in 1723, allegedly with the Dalai Lama's blessing, provoked a brutal response from the Manchus. "The war was one of the bloodiest," notes a modern scholar. "All who made a stand were killed. All the provisions and property of the people had disappeared. All the lamaseries were destroyed or burned down. The depredation of the country was wicked and ruthless, the destitution of the people tragic."[19] When a powerful pro-Manchu aristocrat from the Panchen Lama's region was assassinated five years later, a second invasion was launched and the Dalai Lama was forced into exile for several years.[20] It is a pattern that would be repeated many times down to the most recent Chinese military invasion in 1959.

World-Systems and World-Empires

The history of Tibet since the 1720s has been a struggle for autonomy, sometimes overt, but usually submerged, first against the Manchus and then later against Chinese claims to superior authority in secular and religious affairs. Attempts to form alliances with other powers to counter the Manchu/Chinese claim, including with the British in India in 1910, have consistently failed to solve Tibet's geopolitical conundrum: how to assert autonomy against a state that, since the eighteenth century, has regarded all such claims as a direct challenge to its authority, not just in Tibet but throughout Inner Asia and East Asia.

The Chinese Republic emerged when Chinese revolutionaries overthrew the Manchus in 1911. As heir to the Manchu empire, the Chinese state, then as well as today, conceives of its territorial sovereignty as a world-empire. This conception is fundamentally at odds with the conventions of Westphalian statehood. It is also indifferent to claims for regional autonomy by non-Han-Chinese peoples living within the old Manchu imperial borders. Tibetans in 1911 understood that Manchu suzerainty had collapsed, which allowed them to reclaim their autonomy, but this was not an expectation that the new Chinese Republic was willing to tolerate. From the Chinese perspective, any devolution of power along ethnic lines had to be stoutly resisted for the same reason that the Manchus invaded Tibet: a challenge to the authority of the imperial centre in any one region can only be interpreted as implying a challenge to authority throughout the realm. Such a challenge must be countered; even mild federalism is inconceivable.

To grasp the particularity of the Chinese state's concern with its authority over Tibet, consider two alternative models for understanding the configuration of economic and state power within a large system: a world-system of multiple states or a world-empire. A world-system of multiple states is a system of production and exchange within which states and firms compete for power. Immanuel Wallerstein, who pioneered world-systems analysis, maintained that the capitalist world-system formed in the sixteenth century through a process of European expansion across the oceans.[21] Despite the recurring urge to control zones of supply and demand by annexation and colonization, states in this system have more often accumulated wealth through networks of exchange (however coercively enforced) than through direct control by colonization or military occupation.

A world-empire rests on a different logic of accumulation. In such a structure, there is a single political authority. The competition for resources and power within the system is carried out between the single state and its own agents or subunits, not with other states. Within a world-empire, high military expenditure tends to produce constant revenue hunger. The state and the imperial household try to accumulate wealth outward by extending the borders of the empire and inward by devolving revenue collection through tax farming, which invariably drives the imperial state to the lowest level of accumulation. The best way for a world-empire to achieve a higher efficiency of accumulation is to exploit a more efficient fiscal administration in its territories, as the Manchus did after they conquered China in 1644.

How the multiple-state world-system and world-empire, respectively, perceive threats constitutes one of their key differences. An adept hegemon in a multiple-state world-system can potentially tolerate the loss of a node in its network of accumulation by reconfiguring the network away from that node (at least in theory; most hegemons are inept when dealing with challenges to their power). A world-empire is much less flexible because its regime of control depends on dominating the full range of its territory. A threat to that territory becomes a threat to the entire system because its own sovereignty is not only absolute but also unbounded. A world-empire is a single realm — "all under heaven," in the Chinese usage — rather than an entity within a multiple-state system. As such, it acknowledges only its own sovereignty, which it regards as legitimately extensible to any contiguous territory, as security or its need for access to resources dictate. The capitalist world-system, shaped as it is by European historical experience, accepts that a world-system legitimately consists of many states, not one state. Hence the attention given in the Westphalian model to state-to-state power relations, which in the contemporary world-system is enshrined as the principle of inviolable state sovereignty.

The concept of inviolable sovereignty belongs to our modern image of the world. The historical reality of multiple-state systems has been different, with states coming into being, shifting boundaries, and disappearing through their interactions with other states. The institutionalization of state sovereignty and the claim of autonomy attached to it were not fully instituted until the nineteenth century, which is somewhat late in the history of the capitalist world-system. The concept remains an important fiction of the international order today.

China is a fierce defender of the inviolability of state sovereignty on the international stage, but only for existing states. China's defence of its foreign policy arises from a different historical experience, not that of a state within a multiple-state world-system but of a world-empire that has had to reconfigure itself in a multiple-state system without relinquishing either its imperial possessions or its imperial presumptions with regard to conquered territories. China is not the only imperial successor state to deny the right of territories — acquired earlier through military force or colonial subjugation — to negotiate other terms of association. This denial underpins China's refusal to negotiate Tibetan autonomy and China's insistence that it has the right to develop Tibet in accordance with China's national strategic and economic goals.

Tibet in the Global Present

The invasion of Tibet by the People's Liberation Army in 1950 enacted the claim of the People's Republic of China that it had the right to inherit the Manchu imperial realm. The Fourteenth Dalai Lama had no choice but to accept a Seventeen Point Agreement that surrendered Tibet's independence in return for a guarantee of limited autonomy. Unable to bear the limitations of autonomy that Chinese encroachments brought on them, Tibetans rose in 1959 with disastrous results, and the Dalai Lama fled to India. Despite succession crises and policy changes in China, the Chinese government has been unwilling to negotiate with the Dalai Lama to deal with the problem of failed autonomy. An energetic global campaign to bring Tibet's plight to world attention has made Tibet the world's best-known stateless nation and the Dalai Lama the most respected religious leader in the contemporary world. The Nobel Peace Prize in 1989 confirmed his symbolic stature in the global community, to the considerable annoyance of the Chinese government. Despite this widespread publicity, however, the Tibetan Government-in-Exile has still not been recognized as the legitimate government of a sovereign Tibet. Foreign state leaders are willing to meet the Dalai Lama, but none is willing to bring the case of Tibet before any international body. Tibetans in the twenty-first century face the sentence of being a "national minority" within China and a virtual nation outside it.

Tibet's dual status expresses a paradox of globalization: the global integration of economic and cultural networks has created and destroyed nations without actually abandoning the principle of state sovereignty. The global economy today is largely indifferent to matters of sovereignty, which neoliberals accept only to the extent that it does not unduly restrict capital accumulation. In this context, Tibet's inability to achieve autonomy cannot be blamed solely on China; the entire global system is complicit in the persistence of China's world-empire. Water may have been the capitalist world-system's preferred medium of expansion, but land continues to define China's relationship to its own empire. And so the impairment of Tibetan autonomy continues as Chinese state enterprises pursue development schemes geared to national growth and international trade that grind away at customs inside the region traditionally inhabited by Tibetans. At the same time, outside Tibet, globalization is undercutting the capacity of Tibetans to sustain a Tibet-based cultural identity in the diaspora and threatens to consign them to the museum of extinct world cultures.

The "foreign occupation" of Tibet, as the Fourteenth Dalai Lama calls it, shows no sign of ending.[22] The only certainty is that there will be a search for the incarnation of the Fifteenth Dalai Lama after the Fourteenth dies. This search will pit Tibetans seeking greater autonomy against Chinese leaders anxious to hold onto their world-empire. Both sides will fight over how the incarnation is to be recognized. Already the Chinese government has declared that unauthorized reincarnations of the Buddha are not permitted, an ironic trace of Manchu religious practice and utterly meaningless to Tibetans. The struggle to prevent Tibetan autonomy has thus obliged the government to insist that it alone has the authority to announce to the world the next reincarnation of the Buddha, which at least some Communists must find odd.

The struggle over reincarnation will sit at the core of the coming political struggle within the Chinese world-empire. However strange it may seem to those who are used to other ideologies of empire and resistance, the reincarnation issue at least alerts us to a key observation: the rules governing the accumulation of power and the assertion of authority in this part of Eurasia are not reducible to those that govern change elsewhere in the capitalist world-system, though the outcome will be a matter of little consequence to that system. For Tibet does not exist apart from that process any more than it exists apart from Chinese aspirations to continental power. At the same time, however, without the current phase of globalization, the Dalai Lama would not enjoy his immense reputation as the most respected voice of wisdom and non-violence among world leaders. Tibetans abroad would be just one more ethnic diaspora facing annihilation — though the executor of that fate may not be China as much as globalization itself.

chapter 3

Litigating for Freedom in the British Empire, 1815-22: The Universal and Local in Tension

John C. Weaver

FROM 1815 TO 1822, a handful of activists in Cape Town worked to free a slave known only as Steyntje. Eventually, the British Empire's most renowned legal authorities battled over the fate of the slave and her children. The Cape Town episode pertains to a conflict between local, oppressive practices and universalistic, liberal ideals. Accounts of comparable efforts in other Atlantic-world locales form a genre of writing in which white protagonists who battle over the fate of a slave symbolize dyads of good and evil, justice and injustice, morality and immorality. Yet, simultaneously, these narratives expose spheres of domination in which such clashes are performed.[1] The present episode follows these tales but describes antecedents of globalization in the shape of capital mobilization, imperial legal institutions, and the movement and influence of ideas. To follow pleadings through the Cape Town courts and to the Privy Council in London is to travel in the era of European seaborne empires, to encounter ingenuity in early market economies within empires, to wonder at the migration of Enlightenment ideals, to catch sight of the virtues as well as the limitations of a rights revolution that emphasized individual freedom. The anxieties provoked by claims to rights, the modern rise of litigation, and an empire-wide debate over emancipation depict a shrinking world. In themselves these topics are neither unusual nor challenging to recount. A more distinctive and complicated line of historical writing is suggested by political scientist James Rosenau who has written that to study contemporary world affairs requires looking at how "the forces pressing for greater globalization and those inducing greater localization interactively play themselves out. To do otherwise, to focus only on globalizing dynamics, or only on localizing dynamics, is to risk overlooking what makes events unfold as they do."[2] That simple prescription, although a demanding one, should nevertheless influence how historians press beyond recounting the antecedents of globalization. They can do this by locating the friction that makes events unfold as they do. The challenges include identifying sites of conflict between global and local, assessing the outcomes, commenting on the latter's implications for more recent encounters of the global and the local, and uniting these goals by a documented narrative thread. To prepare for such an experiment in historical writing, three brief preliminary discussions are offered concerning the utility of an intimate scale of historical writing, a conceptualization of globalization, and the idea of autonomy, which is a less bounded concept than localization and one that can apply to individuals.

Historical inquiry into globalization, building on the world history movement of the last four decades, has adopted the preference of these pioneers for long chronological periods and synthesis from secondary studies.[3] The events covered in this chapter could thus be described as occurring within what Anthony Hopkins labelled an age of "proto-globalization," when there was a knowledge revolution, a strengthening of states, growth of state finance, and an expansion of the circuits of seaborne trade.[4] A complementary but different scale and technique is feasible. An incident can supplement — not displace — the world history method of understanding globalization. We can treat unheralded events unearthed in archives as probes to test generalizations and to coax out contradictions, anomalies, and inconvenient problems. We can deploy these pointillist episodes to express a human scale that is needed, because grand organizing schemes leave little space for passion, confusion, the intimacy of seeing the consequences of major events on common lives, or accounts of how things worked. Contributors to this volume have used a historical moment as either a discursive device or as a turning point. In common with chapters by Tim Brook, Virginia Aksan, and Ulf Hedetoft, in this chapter an episode becomes an opening into large topics.

Globalization amounts to an erosion of national boundaries through the recognition, across political jurisdictions and by many agencies, movements, and individuals, that local problems and opportunities must be understood globally. As compared with internationalism, globalization involves the expansion of transplanetary and supraterritorial links that operate at great speed. Questions of scope of global coverage, depth of penetration, and thickness of connecting layers complicate this conception and point towards the idea that globalization is uneven, and has certainly been very uneven in antecedent stages.[5] Autonomy can apply to the autonomy of individuals, family groups, work groups, regions, cities, or states. At one level, the campaign to free a slave engaged individual rights in pursuit of individual autonomy; however, at the collective level it was about women, racism, the marginalized, and the exploited.

Both globalization and autonomy raise normative concerns. Globalization has often been equated narrowly with an ideology or agenda of Westernization. Early declarations of rights were deemed universal by their champions, and these prescriptions inspired mid-twentieth-century human rights declarations and provoked late twentieth-century critical assessments. Advocacy of individual rights by intellectuals and politicians from western Europe and North America has engendered skepticism. Critics can point to historical contradictions or hypocrisies like American slavery, the race and class barriers that pervaded the British Empire, or the persistence of racism and poverty in countries vigorously espousing human rights. Rights, in the instance we are about to describe, elicited circumventions. Critics allege there were acts of imperialism evident in the foisting of values formulated in one part of the world onto others. Or they detect a pernicious ranking of cultures when certain types of rights mark the scale on the yardstick of progress. Or they detect in individual rights the roots of a rampant individualism they dislike. Universal rights insofar as they applied to anyone, moreover, long applied principally to men. In the Cape Town case, women are glimpsed fleetingly and almost always passing through the hands of males. Nevertheless, there was a migration of ideas about individual freedom that travelled far and inspired people to act. Europeans in the instance under review did not thrust their vision of rights on another people; they used the conception of rights inspired by some Europeans to act against other Europeans in a long global struggle against slavery.

This incident involved assertions of universal rights that had surfaced in the American and French revolutions, but it also exposed the argumentation of strict legality and the appeals to order and prosperity summoned to counter appeals to freedom. The words *liberty, equality,* and *freedom* triggered anxieties among men of property and rank. Rights language motivated a few men to challenge bondage, and when they did they shook some local foundations of wealth. In response, spokesmen for slaveholders appealed to prosperity, property, social order, and respect for the law. The case shows, too, how a court-based struggle for rights, a struggle for rights within a system of authority, engendered potentially costly and protracted judicial battles. Today, the settlement of disputes by state-based courts and transnational courts and tribunals shows the same problems of access and duration.

Along with demonstrating the portability and inspiration of ideas about individual rights, the incident exposes hostile reactions and containment strategies. In the shrinking world of the early nineteenth century, freedom, order, and property figured in assorted legislative and administrative acts in many jurisdictions. The case describes these matters and also indirectly captures a connected world or, rather, distant parts of the world connected by the slow movement of documents, people, and ideas. The European seaborne empire's reliance on wind power meant a relatively plodding global flow of goods, people, and writings. That had consequences for the way empires were governed. Decision making had to be decentralized; administrative and judicial discourse was punctuated by weeks of waiting. Electronic communications have had revolutionary implications for government, enterprise, and social interaction, but wind and ink sustained the early beachheads of globalization.

Empires, Markets, and Slave Codes

On 18 June 1815, at Waterloo, more than a half-century of intermittent, worldwide conflict between France and the United Kingdom ended. Parliamentarians overseeing a triumphant British Empire had abundant, world-spanning postwar business. Two matters proved fateful for the people of southern Africa. The easiest to resolve was what to do with the former Dutch colony, the Cape of Good Hope. The weak, cosmopolitan, and far-flung Dutch empire came under French control in 1795; British forces seized Cape Town in 1796, returned it to the Dutch in 1803, took it again in 1806, and then retained the colony for the strategic purpose of better connecting India to the United Kingdom. A second issue also involved empire-wide concerns. In 1807 the British outlawed the slave trade, but slavery remained. Encountering parliamentary opposition financed by wealthy planters, emancipationists had to ensure social order in post-emancipation societies and find a way to compensate owners. The Empire's colonies were now unavoidably and haphazardly integrated through hugely significant debates; colonies and the imperial centre were not only linked by government authority and trade, but by debates around slavery, freedom, law, and order. Acquisition of the Cape Colony added another slave-holding colony in which, as always in a conquered European colony, the British retained existing civil laws, because sudden revisions to contracts and business habits could not be achieved without disturbing commerce. The British discovered that the slavery laws in the Dutch East Indies differed from those in their other colonies, and Cape Town practices deviated from Dutch East Indies law.

The Dutch East India Company (Verenigde Oostindische Compagnie, or VOC), which governed the Cape from 1652 to 1796, was arguably the world's first transnational corporation. In the seventeenth century, the Dutch Republic had fostered the first modern economy.[6] Few citizens of the republic relished living in distant and, for Europeans who lacked resistance to tropical diseases, unhealthy places. Thus, the VOC hired sailors and soldiers from across Europe, notably the German states, Bohemia, and Hungary. These men took the risks for the Dutch in Africa and Asia. In addition to Cape Town, the VOC in 1660 had enclaves in India, Ceylon, the East Indies, Taiwan, and Japan.[7] The VOC mixed people; transportation by sail power, adequate for the movement of goods and people, proved awkward for imperial control. Within a sprawling empire, communication was slow and intermittent; consequently, compliance with company orders was indifferent. By the late eighteenth century, multiple centres of authority managed the VOC. In the Dutch Republic, the Heren XVII determined policy and sent orders to the East Indies; the Governor-General and Council at Batavia (Java) issued decrees as the Government of India. A Court of Policy for the Cape of Good Hope prepared local laws.[8]

On 10 April 1770, the Government of India at Batavia drafted an ordinance governing manumission. Article 8 stipulated that children begotten by female slaves and their masters were never to be sold, even if an estate was insolvent. This condition made them poor security for loans.[9] Article 9 specified that slaves, if baptized and if their owner died or left the colonies, were to be freed, unless they had been donated or willed to the owner's relations, in which case they remained servants for life but could not be sold.[10] Dutch law also permitted the freedom of slaves to be purchased, although manumission required government consent, payments to a church to assure that manumitted individuals would be a

45

part of a community responsible for their welfare, and a bond for good conduct. Slavery did not necessarily impose barriers to capitalism, but religious injunctions and security concerns complicated the legal nexus between slavery and capitalism. In order to make slavery compatible with advances in the financial circuit of proto-globalization, ways were found to permit liquidity. Finance capital has always sought to destroy or circumvent inefficiencies.

For slaves in VOC territories, several narrow doors opened to freedom, but the 1770 ordinance complicated the administration of estates that under Roman-Dutch law often required liquidations to accomplish partitions among heirs and creditors. It also inconvenienced the mortgaging of slaves to raise capital. Liquidation practices had evolved in the Dutch mercantile community, where assets included shares in vessels and warehouse receipts. Both the mortgaging of slaves and Dutch estate law imposed stand-by liquidity demands on slaves.[11] Dreading measures that locked capital into non-transferable servants or, worse, required manumission, slave owners ignored articles 8 and 9 of the 1770 law.[12] Heirs also ignored wills in which testators freed slaves.[13] Mild humanitarianism and religious imperatives collided with capital needs and sophisticated Dutch mercantile liquidity practices; defeats for the former was the result, until a new array of values arrived in the colony. Thus, the dynamics mentioned by Rosenau are apparent in two stages — the effects of finance and the subsequent effects of the rights revolution. Let us first see how finance cleared the obstacle of religion that was evident in the 1770 ordinance and created a hybrid arrangement; then we can look at how the rights revolution destabilized the hybrid arrangement and precipitated a host of new measures and strains.

Tension between liquidity preferences in Dutch law and constraints imposed by the ordinance — between Christianity and a local mode of slave-centred capitalism — was palpable when the Reverend Mr. Vos — "one of the most pious and enlightened of the Dutch clergymen" — complained to Governor Sir John Cradock in 1812 that article 9 obstructed conversion. "It was not to be supposed that the Dutch inhabitants or others would encourage any exertion on this subject [conversion], whereby they were to suffer in their property."[14] Cradock repealed article 9. Article 8 went unheeded. British administrators did not pay attention to Dutch slave laws until Cradock, stirred by Vos, asked a Dutch advisor to report on slave laws in late 1812 or early 1813.[15] The findings shocked him. In 1814 he reported to Lord Bathurst that "there are many persons in this colony, in a state of slavery, who are not under any just, or legal claims in that unfortunate situation." Traders "brought with them persons in their service from India, Java, Ceylon, and many other places — upon whose original lot, time, distance, deception, and avarice have thrown impenetrable mystery. Every reasoning and supposition may be in their favour, that they were not slaves, but it seems impossible at this hour to overcome the obstructions, even in the Court of Justice."[16] As a bulwark of Cape Dutch influence during British occupation, as an agency of local autonomy, the Court of Justice sustained evasion. The British government's supervision of slavery intensified with the arrival of Cradock's successor, General Lord Charles Somerset, whose mother, the Duchess of Beaufort, was a champion of anti-slavery and a friend of emancipationist William Wilberforce.[17] Incrementally, the colony was becoming connected with a metropolis in which there was controversy over slavery.

A Female Slave and an Enlightened Cabal

Steyntje was born at George Stadler's house in the early 1780s.[18] When Steyntje was fifteen years old, Stadler, an elderly widower, "frequently and repeatedly endeavoured to prevail upon her to have carnal conversation with him, which, however, was refused by her." Her master flogged her until she submitted. Stadler coerced Steyntje and her sister Pamela to have intercourse with him regularly.[19] Coercion for sex accompanied slavery throughout the Atlantic; it extended to contemporaneous relations between white men — traders and whalers — and indigenous people in the Pacific. The globalization of a sex trade and pornography in the late twentieth century had precursors in slavery and empire.[20] Steyntje delivered a son, Jacob, on 10 September 1799, and, according to the ordinance of 1770, he should not have been treated as moveable property. Mother and child went to live at Stadler's Zwartland estate. Shortly afterwards, Stadler died in 1800 without a will.[21] One of the colony's most important financial institutions, the Orphan Chamber, entered the picture.

To manage the estates of colonists who died far from relatives, the Dutch East India Company in 1683 created a trust, the Orphan Chamber. Profits from the chamber's management of estates went to support and educate orphans, including mulatto children whose fathers did not acknowledge them. Adept at creating instruments and bodies that mobilized capital — shares, insurance, banks, and stock exchanges — the Dutch advanced capitalism; even at the Cape, their robust ideas about keeping capital working were evident. Leading Cape families managed the fund, which lent to the VOC.[22] Stadler's estate came to the chamber, which auctioned his assets, including his slaves. The chamber was then administering roughly two hundred estates. Six clerks maintained journal entries on nine thousand people.[23] The chamber's auction of people whose legal status as slaves was obscure or dubious explains the alarmist claim that *Steyntje v. Anderson* could shake "the security of perhaps one-third of the whole property of the Colony."[24] Capitalism, which the Dutch had done so much to advance, was capable of accommodating slavery and illegal slavery.

The Orphan Chamber listed Steyntje and Jacob for sale. Hendrik Weeber purchased Steyntje "as his bed companion."[25] Quite likely, the Orphan Chamber did not sell her as a slave, but it did let Weeber pay for her manumission. Weeber then secured Steyntje's fidelity through the debt she incurred. Weeber, however, had failed to complete the formal manumission process, which required government consent, a payment to the reformed church, and a bond for good behaviour. Steyntje and Weeber had a daughter, Christina. They "lived as man and wife." They dined, slept, and walked together. "She was burgherly dressed." He recognized the child as theirs. Weeber became insolvent. When the Insolvent Estates Board — another Dutch innovation to mobilize capital — took over his estate, he beseeched the board's secretary to exclude Steyntje and her children from the inventory. Scrounging to liquidate a debtor's property on behalf of creditors, the board insisted on selling her with her children. Merchant Carl Willem Dieleman, who acquired Steyntje and her children on 11 January 1804, died in 1813. George Anderson, a rich wine exporter and major Cape Town real-estate owner, married Dieleman's widow.[26] The concurrent presence of international trade, the operation of institutions that cleverly mobilized capital, the presence of urban rentier capitalism, the endurance of slavery, the importance of dress as a feature of class, and the persistence of religious conversion as a serious matter suggest a society in which globalizing forces and local traditions mixed. They also clashed.

European men exploited Steyntje; now other European men entered her life and treated her as a cause. Outspoken professionals who shared liberal ideals plotted to disrupt slavery in Cape Town by using its court. The central conspirator was Jan Bernhard Hoffman, a translator and former secretary of the city's government, the Burgher Senate. Hoff-man's grandfather had arrived at the Cape in 1744 aboard the *Vryheyt* (Freedom); he named his Stellenbosch estate Libertas.[27] Jan Bernhard Hoffman was a habitual troublemaker implicated in attempts to free il-legally held slaves.[28] Anderson claimed that Hoffman collected witnesses on Steyntje's behalf and that "many other persons of rank have assisted him."[29] One was Roedolph Cloete.[30] Son of Hendrik Cloete, owner of Groot Constantia vineyards, Roedolph arranged for a deposition by one of Steyntje's witnesses in November 1815. Roedolph's nephew, also named Hendrik Cloete, was a conspirator.[31] In 1803 Hendrik had gone to Europe for studies, earning a Doctor of Laws and Philology from the University of Leiden in 1811. He was tested on theses about liberty, ra-tionality, the just society, honour, virtue, the glory of Rome, and the value of the liberal arts; his thesis questions quoted Blaise Pascal, Jean-Jacques Rousseau, Montaigne, and Alexander Pope.[32] He left the Con-tinent for London, and, after briefly studying common law at Lincoln's Inn, returned to Cape Town in 1813.

Cloete was not a participant in the Steyntje case; however, in Janu-ary 1824, only months after that case's conclusion, Hoffman and Hendrik Cloete were associated in a libel action. Hoffman and friends accused the collector of customs of facilitating illegal enslavement. Cloete defended them against a charge of libel by arguing that, under English law, one had a right to expose abuses of power. The Cape fiscal (attorney gen-eral) accused the defendants of fomenting disorder.[33] In a remote cor-ner of an empire, a few men grounded in European learning appealed to freedom and freedom of speech. Other Europeans worked to silence them. In Europe the Enlightenment was often beleaguered, because "it implied no one view of race or difference."[34] Its enemies at home could not abide subversion of faith, blood, and tradition, and its enemies in colonies could not accept the importation of universalistic ideas that would not spare them from criticism simply because they constituted a distinct polity. Conspirators included notary Rynier Beck.[35] When oth-ers found witnesses helpful to Steyntje, Beck notarized their statements. Beck collected evidence to embarrass slaveholders in other cases.[36] Dutch litigation involved pleadings by notarized documents. People marshalled depositions before they struck. Attorney Michiel Adriaan Smuts joined the cabal. Smuts had gone to the Netherlands for studies in 1800 and, in 1807, earned a doctorate in Roman law at Leiden. He made his way home in 1814.[37] When Roedolph Cloete died in 1816, Smuts took over as attorney. The Court of Justice confirmed Smuts as Steyntje's Curator *ad Lites* — guardian of a person without competence.[38] A slave woman could not act on her own behalf.

Anderson's attorney derided the cabal as "false advocates of humanity, who, either through affection, or too much sensibility, launch out onto high sounding phrases, and who continually call in favor to be shewn to the cause of liberty, contrary to the most approved principles of law and justice."[39] The Age of Revolutions thrust ideas of liberty into public forums, where slavery's defenders posed as champions of law. Pleadings in *Steyntje v. Anderson* were not held until 8 September 1818. The British governor had already moved against abuses in slavery. Almost a year after the conspirators started to assemble their case, Somerset issued a proclamation requiring owners to register slaves, transfers, births, deaths, and manumissions. In this proclamation of 26 April 1816, Somerset sounded an alarm about free persons or their offspring "merging into a state of slavery, or being confounded with the domestic or other slaves."[40] Unregistered slaves would be considered manumitted.[41]

Smuts presented depositions to the Court of Justice alleging that Steyntje's two eldest children were born to white burgers and should be freed on that basis.[42] The court knew what this case meant for many mulatto slaves. Freedom for Steyntje's other children depended on Weeber's presumed act of manumission.[43] Council for Anderson, J.A. Joubert, attacked the credibility of all depositions, pointing out that Letje, who gave a notarized statement about Jacob's parentage, later professed that Steyntje met her on the street, plied her with wine, and told her to agree with whatever Beck asked.[44] The Court of Justice concluded that Steyntje could not prove that she had been emancipated by Weeber and there was no proof on the matter of who fathered her children.[45] The court added a "Condemnation of the Plaintiff [Smuts] in his capacity in the costs incurred in this suit at the taxation and moderation of this court."[46] Joubert fulminated that there was a "set of men, who either from interest, malice, or some secret design, have used every art to kindle the desire and foster the hope of emancipation among the slaves of this Colony."[47]

The Court of Justice was a court of first instance. On 30 May 1807, the British established a Court of Appeals. Smuts approached it on 14 September 1818. With much at stake, this case would be fought in every accessible court. The Court of Appeals had one judge, the colony's governor, Somerset, who granted an appeal. Respondents argued that the depositions were untrustworthy and that if the slaves were emancipated, it should happen through a positive law that granted compensation. The sanctity of private property was one of two issues in discussions of abolition in the Atlantic world.[48] The second was social order. Hard-working people might be worthy of emancipation, argued respondents, but freedom should "not be the crown of the profligate and vicious."[49] Steyntje was vicious, because she made allegations about dead men — Stadler and Weeber — who could not answer.[50] If she won, people lacking deference would upend social order. If she and her children were freed, slavery would be thrown into confusion. "Where the chances are unknown, the hope is equal to all." Hope could "kindle a spirit of revolt."[51]

Smuts introduced more depositions and a note by Weeber written on 11 August 1802, some months after Weeber acquired Steyntje, that suggested that Weeber believed he had purchased her freedom.[52] Somerset overturned the Court of Justice's ruling. His decision of 5 June 1819 outraged the city's slaveholders. They condemned his lack of respect for local autonomy. Empires precipitated innumerable struggles between universalities and parochialisms, and in that sense empires were antecedents of globalization. In Cape Town universalisms included Enlightenment ideals and due process. The parochialism or localism was a deviant branch of Dutch colonial law managed by local elites and a hybrid form of capitalism that accommodated slavery, Christian-inspired restraints on slavery, and liquidity demands. Anderson petitioned to appeal Somerset's decision to "the Lords Commissioners appointed for hearing and determining Appeals from the Colonies and Plantations." Somerset consented. The Empire could not be supervised closely from the centre, but there were abundant slow-moving connections that checked fragmentation: initial instructions to new governors, further instructions, and Privy Council rulings. A local dispute migrated to London. Anderson forwarded papers on the case to his agent who sought the opinion of England's foremost civil law authority, Stephen Lushington. Lushington brought Henry Peter Brougham into the case. Lushington and Brougham, parliamentary opponents of slavery, would argue, paradoxically, against Steyntje's freedom before the Privy Council.[53] As prominent Whigs, they seized this opportunity to censure Somerset's one-man government. The fate of a slave entered partisan sparring at the imperial centre.

An Embryonic World Court?

When appearing for Anderson before a committee of the Privy Council in May 1822, Lushington and Brougham insisted on their emancipation credentials. "Let it never be understood," said Lushington, "that I should be anxious to press, or be justified in pressing these points [the pleadings] so strongly against a claim to freedom; but your Lordships know that as long as a state of slavery subsists in the Cape of Good Hope, sanctioned by the existing laws, the right of property in slavery must be regulated by the same evidence, and brought to the same tests of truth as any other matters whatever."[54] Brougham felt obliged to explain himself too. When attacking Weeber's alleged act of manumission, he said, "There are certain dues to be paid, according to what I consider a great injustice and impolity of that law, which I am not here to defend, which imposes a restraint on emancipation."[55] In an ideologically charged era, freedom was admired and feared. In *Steyntje v. Anderson,* all men claimed to love freedom. Anderson's Cape Town advocate, Joubert, allegedly sympathized with the abolition of slavery, if accomplished gradually.[56] Anderson himself claimed to love freedom, but he insisted that "the first and surest step toward a rational freedom, in every country, is a strict maintenance of the existing laws until it is found expedient to alter or abolish them."[57] The early rights revolution had enough currency to make educated men seek to retain cultural capital by bowing to freedom rhetorically and, if they disliked its implications, containing it by appeals to rationality and the law.

Lushington and Brougham faced familiar protagonists: Nicolas Tindal and Attorney General James Scarlett. Brougham had been Tindal's student. In the recent Queen Caroline affair, in which the King refused to acknowledge his wife as the Queen, Lushington, Brougham, and Tindal represented Caroline and Scarlett represented the King.[58] The Empire's leading jurists, intimates to royal scandal, now argued the fate of a Cape Town slave and her children at Whitehall. On the surface, lawyer-fashioned remedies were available to all classes — to queens and to slaves. Pleadings occurred in May 1822. Lushington attacked Steyntje's character to show her as unworthy of trust or respect. "This lady, who amongst her virtues, does not seem to have numbered chastity as one of her principle ones, has two children more, so that here are four children; one by Stadler, one by Weber [sic], and two by God knows whom, and why your Lordships should suppose that these two first children, upon such evidence as this, were the children of Stadler, or Weber, I cannot conceive." He continued, "It would have puzzled the lady extremely to have fixed, with any degree of certainty, the father of any one of the children."[59] A dedicated Anglican, Lushington juxtaposed freedom and wantonness. Brougham tried to undermine the Court of Appeal's credibility, proposing that the Court of Justice was closest to the customs of the colony. "The Dutch lawyers have decided in my favor, the English General has decided against."[60] The attorney general replied that the Court of Appeals had considered more evidence, namely Weeber's note and additional depositions. Tindal made the case that in claims of illegal slavery Roman law favoured giving benefit of doubt to the slave.[61] The Privy Council agreed.[62]

A handful of Cape Town conspirators thought of a common humanity, but their ideals would have been without any effect had there not been governors committed to restricted slavery and eventual abolition and reasonably fair judicial bodies beyond the compromised local court. The case the conspirators made reached a judicial body that had jurisdiction in many places in the world. Important and difficult cases were forwarded there from colonies; that fact indicates both a stage in global integration and a difference between that stage and true globalization. The British government was no world government; the Privy Council was no world court. Moreover, the judgment was no unmitigated triumph of individual rights, no achievement of individual autonomy. The Privy Council was moved by Weeber's refusal to turn Steyntje over to the insolvency board but concluded she owed service to Weeber for freeing her, and that service — an estate asset — came into the possession of Dieleman and Anderson. No one maintained that Steyntje should be free of duties to a succession of men.[63] Steyntje faced dependency of one kind or another. From the day of Somerset's decision until word of the Privy Council's ruling reached the Cape, Steyntje and her children were subject to three conditions. They had to pay church dues, which theoretically placed them in a community responsible for their welfare. They were to report to Somerset's office on the first day of every month. If they obtained leave to quit Cape Town, they had to deposit security to compensate Anderson if the Privy Council reversed the appeal court's decision. On 2 September 1823, Somerset informed Joachim Wilhelm Stoll, landdrost of the Cape District, that the Privy Council upheld the court's 1819 decision. He then directed the landdrost to implement orders relating to the placement of the liberated appellants, because Steyntje now was reported as a dissipated prostitute.

The secretary of the Court of Appeals reported to Somerset that only Christina had paid church dues. Steyntje had not, though she often had been called upon to do so. She "is a woman of indifferent character, and at present living in open prostitution and as such unfit to have the guardianship of her said children."[64] The court ordered the landdrost "to have the said Steyntje and her minor children put under the superintendence of the Magistrate [landdrost] of the District and by him placed under careful and humane masters or mistresses of good religious and moral conduct until the said Steyntje shall have paid her proportion of the Church dues and until the minors shall have attained their full age, at such wages and upon such terms as can be procured for the benefit of the such persons."[65] Masters or mistresses were to advance church dues for the minors and deduct these sums from their wages. Freedom came with restrictions; Steyntje and her children had to be bound to a community. The assignment of the children as indentured servants would be a cheap source of household labour and a supposed moral uplift tactic for indigenous or non–white children in many colonized places. In these instances, colonizing powers curtailed individual autonomy and put people in communities not of their own choosing; the colonized were treated as subjects not citizens.

The governor's instructions to the landdrost on the disposition of Steyntje and her family foreshadowed slavery's replacement by social control measures. These included policing, master and servant contracts, and segregation. Social order figured in Somerset's thinking on slavery. On 23 March 1823, he wrote Earl Bathurst proposing to end slavery at the Cape by purchasing newborn children at government expense. "To emancipate the adult slaves would be almost as cruel to them as it would be dangerous to the state."[66] There was perverse sense in the forecast, but only because no slave-holding part of the Empire prepared for a post-emancipation society. Nor would other slave-holding empires and states. The American and French revolutions, with their assertions of individual freedom, were preconditions for emancipation, and for the laissez-faire disarray in post-emancipation societies. Anxieties about social order effloresced into policing and laws that granted employers authority to use corporal punishment against indentured labourers.[67] The rights revolution accented individual rights and individual autonomy, and, if Steyntje's plight is metaphor, then that revolution provided gains for the oppressed. But these rights were also vulnerable, and across the Cape Colony various non-white communities were denied the autonomy of their communities, denied that collective autonomy that may help ensure individual autonomy. However, the elevation of collective autonomy as an unqualified good has problems and risks. Collectives can abuse others, and being readily identified as an outsider can single one out for abuse.

Slavery, its forced intercontinental movements of people, emancipation debates, the exploitation of labour and women, and problems in post-emancipation societies depict an integrating world. Global issues — today's environmental concerns, fears of pandemics, human rights, weapons control, peacekeeping, and the gap between rich and poor — are not a new class of concerns. The long nineteenth-century debate over slavery was almost a global issue and, at least, a prominent issue in the English-speaking and French-speaking world. However, slavery was not hotly debated in all slave-holding parts of the world, and not in every European empire with slave-holding territories. To explain why slavery persisted in the Dutch empire until 1863, Seymour Drescher criticized theories of economic determinism and proposed that the Dutch empire lacked intense intellectual ties between a progressive metropolis and slave-holding colonies.[68] European empires had different transmission belts.[69] Had Cape Town remained a Dutch colony, emancipation would have been delayed; *Steyntje v. Anderson* would not have moved beyond the local Court of Justice, because the Dutch empire lacked the British administrative and legal apparatus that linked metropolis and colonies and formed a political world that included affiliated religious and intellectual movements. Just as we should judge empires as distinct entities, we should be discriminating in our assessments of the many aspects of globalization. Some of these aspects may offer prospects for individual and collective autonomy, just as the rights revolution had done in its time. By the same token, unreflective preference for collective autonomy in opposition to globalization should be treated warily.

Beyond Cape Town

Empires advanced global integration, but their coalescence was, at best, confined to their scattered global holdings or to as far as their power could reach. Within an empire, the depth of imperial influence proved suspect. Colonists hijacked colonies; indigenous peoples worked out their arrangements with the Empire's agents and rogue colonists alike. Behind the Empire's port cities there was pandemonium. For the British

Empire, the question of impact has been explored in many ways, such as looking at disruptions to agriculture caused by the impingements of a market economy, assessing the influence of utilitarian reformers on distant places with established institutions, considering the consequences of favour shown to a social or religious group in a subject territory, or studying the imposition and modification of metropolitan law codes. In the current instance, the European impact upon a faraway place is traced through mainly legal discourses. We know something about several people who went to Europe and studied Enlightenment classics and law. All this we know because they were from affluent Cape families that preserved genealogies and documents. The transmission of universalistic ideas proceeded through an educated urban elite. Transmission was also socially circumscribed and limited by rudimentary communication. It is possible to read in a few days all of Somerset's dispatches to London, including his report on *Steyntje v. Anderson*. No copious real-time dialogue transpired between periphery and core. Real-time contact or even telegraphic-relay contacts are altogether different modes of communication from dispatches sent with sailing ships. The global integration that empires achieved before the mid-nineteenth century was shallow and intermittent.

Sequels to the end of slavery in the colony demonstrate the fragility of imperial power beyond the city. Appeals to respect local autonomy clashed repeatedly with imperial designs in colonies. London instructed governors to change local practices. Somerset and his successors had to enforce more humane practices. Parliament abolished slavery in 1833-34. Slave-holding, rural Dutch families harboured grievances about the amount of compensation and the difficulties of securing payment. They also resented British land reforms. When coerced to change, people flee or rebel, if they can. The Great Trek of thousands of Afrikaners across the Orange River, which began in 1836, originated in complaints about British control, and in opportunities for seizing land. The extension of European laws upset collective autonomy and alienated some Afrikaners to the point of provoking a defiant flight into new territory. This exodus had unanticipated consequences, including a war between the semi-autonomous southern African states and the British Empire from 1899 to 1902. That attempt to curb autonomy, during which the British countered guerrilla warfare with concentration camps, intensified Afrikaner identity. Nearly a century after the decision to hold onto the Cape Colony, the British government, with aid from its other settlement colonies, could barely enforce its will on southern African states, and after the Second World War Afrikaner nationalists asserted effective autonomy. The largely Afrikaner National Party would implement apartheid.[70]

Philip Curtin observed that "human cultures have been converging since the invention of agriculture ... What if anything should or could be done about it?"[71] A short answer is that convergences should leave no party worse off than before, but that has been uncommon. Individual rights and legal systems can help address this problem, but on this score history suggests that they are not sufficient and there have to be means of sustaining vigilance, skepticism, criticism, and challenges. These desiderata require open political systems and access to information. Rights and law in this incident had limited purchase and reach due to racial prejudice, hypocritical moral stigmatization, and exceedingly confined political rights. Slavery was readily replaced by another means of subordination, the master-servant laws. Another focal point of discourse in this case, namely, the rule of law, has an ambiguous standing. Law facilitated trade, finance, elite fraternization, cultural chauvinism, slavery, slavery's demise, liberty, and checks on liberty. In the estimation of the rulers of the British Empire, English common law epitomized their civilization's best. Continental law, or Roman law, had sponsors; even the Privy Council accepted it. Global integration today includes efforts to reconcile law codes and establish jurisdictions that transcend or influence national governments. Most importantly, *Steyntje v. Anderson* depicts the law as passive and available to parties with knowledge and resources. Access to the legal and technical knowledge required for effective disputation will be a significant determinant of the courses taken by global integration and their legitimacy. Steyntje and her children had the benefit of idealistic volunteers, but that is not a robust solution for assuring justice in the world of burgeoning legal protocols that is described in other volumes in this series on globalization and autonomy.

Steyntje's plight teases out complex issues of individual and collective autonomy that promote reflection about globalization and the potential for individual and collective autonomy historically and more generally. With respect to personal autonomy, at no point in her life, either as slave or manumitted slave, was she autonomous; at no point was she free from legally enforceable obligations in male-controlled households, although households have been sites of autonomy for women in the past and today.[72] There are glimpses of her meetings with enslaved or newly emancipated women, of her living with Weeber in a burgherly fashion. Her life story, however, depicts a male-centred world. To be a slave and a woman was to be absent as a person but present as a cause. The status of women has changed and continues to do so in many places on account of campaigns for rights, campaigns that had scarcely begun in 1815. It is difficult to imagine the defence of rights without the Enlightenment that animated the Cape Town cabal, but it is also difficult to leave the case without wondering if, in the end, the cabal put Steyntje out of sight during the litigation and regarded her as a cause only.[73] Her champions were certainly not of the same ilk as those who exploited her, but she was not one of their people and they had no interest in alleviating subsequent curtailments of her individual autonomy. Individual autonomy is best cultivated and defended by communities that have an interest in their own people. Steynje's case may therefore stand as a metaphor for the powerlessness of the world's many poor when their lives are affected by laws and other modes of technical knowledge that advance without their participation. In terms of collective autonomy, the incident may be instructive from another critical angle. Global integration today, particularly identification of the term with corporate capitalism, draws seekers of social justice to respect "place-based movements." Certainly, as Neil White points out in his chapter on the export production zones, there is a great need for such action to improve conditions in places made by footloose capital movements that are often identified as synonymous with globalization. "Place-based consciousness" also appeals as "an antidote to many of the supraplace essentializations of identity around race, religion, etc."[74] However, events at Cape Town recommend a critical pause in this privileging of place qua place, a pause before endorsing local or collective autonomy, a pause to assess by questioning. Who can speak for culture in a grounded place, or what constitutes traditional, local, or indigenous culture?[75]

European empires make these questions difficult to answer because they occasionally made the colonial local. On the peninsula of the Cape of Good Hope, the indigenes were the Khoikhoi. The destruction of their society by the early eighteenth century happened because their livestock and labour were dragged into the Cape economy, their lands were encroached upon and seized by individual colonists, and they suffered in the 1713 smallpox epidemic.[76] This cataclysm caused by colonization indicts the imperial mode of global integration. However, by the time of Steyntje's case, slaves from many lands, as well as the Cape

Dutch colonists, had claims to culture in a grounded place. Local autonomy pursued by some Cape Dutch meant an insistence on slavery. Those with weaker claims to place — the British imperial authorities and Cape Dutch liberals educated abroad — were cosmopolitan agents. Place-based consciousness may be less ambiguously praise-worthy in recent times, more connected with the struggles of the oppressed than in the episode at hand; however, sorting out the circumstances that privilege place at various times is different from an unqualified preference for place or collective autonomy.

Enduring Dilemmas

Lessons can be drawn from this incident's clash between the rights revolution and oppression during what Hopkins called the age of proto-globalization. First, the antecedents of globalization included colonization and slavery, which were hugely significant, oppressive, and reprehensible assaults on individual and collective autonomy. Second, the antecedents of globalization also included the rights revolution and the spread of the idea of the rule of law; these are imbedded today in a number of global institutions and declarations. With his chapter on the International Criminal Court, Adrian Jones reminds us that rights and the rule of law persist and grow as powerful ideas. Third, not all empires were alike, coherent, or effectual from within; if globalization has been built on the back of empires, then globalization's unevenness and points of friction are explicable, in part, as legacies of empire. Fourth, in the age of proto-globalization, individual autonomy was almost unheard of, and although the rights revolution started to change that, the swift introduction of containment measures indicated that a struggle was in play and remains so. Globalization is neither oppressor nor liberator; it is an environment for struggle. Fifth, the formation and persistence of groups with political rights, often called collective autonomy in this chapter and book, is one means to advance and protect individual autonomy. Whether all collectives have completely praiseworthy objectives harnessed to their autonomy is another matter. Sixth, a few legal remedies are better than none and superior to violence, but generally those who have the resources to secure technical expertise and the capacity to endure long proceedings have the advantage. Structural inequality must be taken into account. Seventh, the foregoing dilemmas, imperfections, and unrealized potentials require not blanket condemnation of globalization or unrestrained enthusiasm for collective autonomy but thinking creatively about both in specific encounters. And eighth, thinking creatively includes framing ethics for globalization that, building upon the rights revolution, attempt to balance individual and collective autonomy.

chapter 4

Ottoman Military and Social Transformations, 1826-28: Engagement and Resistance in a Moment of Global Imperialism

Virginia H. Aksan

ON THE MORNING OF 12 June 1826, a handful of Ottoman troops, dressed in the smart blue European-style pants and tunic of the reformed army of Sultan Mahmud II (1809-39), demonstrated their new regimental drills before a select assembly of Ottoman officers and members of the religious class in Istanbul. Within two days, this deliberate demonstration orchestrated by the Sultan provoked a massive rebellion of the traditional army, the Janissaries, who assembled to protest the imposition of the new discipline and uniforms. By the afternoon of 15 June, the rebellion was over. Well prepared beforehand, disgusted city residents and loyal combat-ready artillery troops combined to trap the remnants of the once proud organization in their barracks and mow them down. The event was publicized thereafter as the "Blessed Affair" or the "Auspicious Occasion." Incredibly, by 1828, Sultan Mahmud II had eliminated the last of the Janissaries and mustered thirty to forty thousand young conscripts, marching them to battle Tsar Nicholas I at the mouth of the Danube. While European observers remarked on their youth, they were even more impressed with the new disciplinary environment. These new and raw recruits defended the mountain passes to Istanbul.[1]

This crisis of 1826-28 will serve here as a global moment to illustrate the friction, both external and internal and centre and periphery, in the Ottoman encounters with modernity and other empires. In the process, the Ottoman Empire moves from imperial power to semi-colonized client state. During this moment of severe crisis, the Ottoman dynasty hovered on complete collapse, eliminated an obsolete army, fought a civil war on the streets of Istanbul, and confronted the reality of enemies within who were stimulated by the revolutionary nationalism of Greece and Serbia. Reorganizing defensive frontiers and diplomatic practice, increasing the visibility of the Sultan, reordering provincial government, and clarifying loyalty to the empire along ethno-religious lines were all new tactics for an Ottoman sovereign under siege. Such initiatives altered the dynasty's premise of rule, and it reconfigured the social and spatial map of empire in ways that presaged or facilitated the emergence of republican Turkey after the First World War.

Inserting the Ottomans into this larger global narrative of modernity and change has proven to be an elusive task, for, as Tim Brook discusses in this volume, in the Hegelian temporal worldview that informs the writing of history, there is no room for spatial, or "timeless," empires such as those of China, India, or the Middle East. Meaningful history, for Hegel, was that which moved towards "empires in which people could genuinely engage in the secular political life that produces real change in consciousness."[2] Hegel did not envisage a space for Asian societies, because historical authority belonged with Europe. Hence, the Ottoman Empire has remained largely undifferentiated in imperial stories, except to the extent that it is seen to have been transformed by the friction arising from encounters with European military and political ascendancy.

Many scholars, consciously or unconsciously, reformulate the progressive (liberal) nationalist narrative even as they try to interrogate it. In the Ottoman case, this might be called the "empire to nation-state" or "Ottoman to Turk" story, which each generation has massaged and formulated around the question of the liberalization and secularization of individual rights while ignoring the frictional encounters that arose in the spread of modernity.[3] Ottoman sovereignty after 1800 was clearly challenged not only by continuing external threats to state security but also by internal constitutional impulses that challenged the Sultan's right to rule. That trajectory of events has been much belaboured; but missing from the story is a better definition of the indigenous voices of discontent and their expressions of alternative paths to the modern state.

The focus here is on the ideologies of modern state organization — that is, new systems of order and discipline introduced by Mahmud II. For the sake of argument, order and discipline may be assumed to be two obligations primary to the sustainability (and survival) of empires and nation-states alike.[4] Mahmud II reorganized the geography of his empire literally and figuratively through new defensive strategies on the northern tier; he restored order after confronting, in Istanbul from 1808 to 1809, the most significant rebellion of the entire span of empire; and, after the destruction of the traditional army, he disciplined not only his new troops but also society at large. Along the way, new spaces for expressions of collective autonomy emerged along with new sources of friction, which were much contested. Ulf Hedetoft's observation in this volume that "ideational hegemony cannot be politically ordered, imposed, or manipulated at will" because "it challenges deeply held beliefs in the benefits of ethnic, national, and local cultural autonomy" applies especially to the Ottoman population, which is deeply divided along cultural and religious lines yet remains loosely gathered under the imperial umbrella and pervasive culture of Mediterranean Islam.

The Sultan's initiatives described here represented radical departures from the normal behaviour of the dynasty and resulted in a new understanding of Ottoman imperial space in a globalizing world. Interventions into individual lives, such as conscription, registration systems, property laws, and municipal government, are all components of Mahmud II's transformation, which was continued by his successors. No sphere remained untouched. Examining this particular set of initiatives allows the interrogation of several autonomies: state sovereignty primarily, but also local ethno-religious communities and individuals compelled to serve in the new military. What was different about this Ottoman moment? Can that difference elucidate the dynamic of imperial autonomy in the face of the overwhelming frictions that arose from inclusion in a global economy and reconstruction of an imperial worldview?[5]

A Brief Rehearsal

The period from 1760 to 1841 was one of immense crisis and upheaval within the Ottoman territories. These years bracket the era when Britain cast its imperial net worldwide, though haphazardly, and begin and end with the defeat of its rival, France, the loss of the American colonies, but not the Caribbean, and the extension of control over India. The new British order, built out of a unique blend of military and industrial capitalist adventures, was underwritten by an extraordinary confidence in the legal and moral imagination of a virtuous society on a mission to improve the world. This was also the same period of the great revolutions that changed the social and political discourse of the world. All had an impact on the impetus for reform that became an imperative for Ottoman survival.

French and British rivalries moved into the Middle East after 1750. Between 1798, when Napoleon Bonaparte invaded Alexandria, Egypt, and 1841, when the Treaty of London was signed, the French lost out to the British in the contest for control of Middle Eastern markets. After 1841 British consuls dominated their French counterparts in all the ports of the Arab world, which was drawn into the British trading system of the Indian Ocean. The wildcard of the period was Russia, whose expansionism shocked western European thinking about the future of the Ottoman Empire. The Ottomans fought four separate wars with the Russians in 1768-74, 1787-92, 1806-12, and 1828-29. By 1829 Russia was nominally in charge of the northern banks of the Danube, had annexed the Crimea and the northern Black Sea coast, and occupied and annexed large parts of the Caucasus. Russia had thus absorbed large and disparate communities of Christians and Muslims and achieved what it took to be protectorate status over the remaining Orthodox Christians of the empire. In the same period, Greece and Serbia gained independence, and three successive sultans were challenged by rebellious warlords in Janina (Greece), Vidin (Bulgaria), Acre (Syria), Sinop (Eastern Turkey/Caucasus), and, most significantly, Egypt, which was under Mehmed Ali from 1805 to 1848. In 1826 the Ottoman Sultan Mahmud II eliminated his traditional army; in 1827 his allies, Britain and France, "accidentally" sank his (and Mehmed Ali's) entire fleet at Navarino; in 1828 the Sultan declared a jihad and went to war against Russia with forty thousand hastily assembled new-style conscripts; and, by 1833, Russian ships and troops were in Istanbul to protect Mahmud II against his own subject, Mehmed Ali, whose son Ibrahim invaded Anatolia in 1831 and challenged Istanbul itself from 1833 to 1841. British warships, supporting the Ottomans, fired on Beirut in 1841 to bring an end to the challenge of Mehmed Ali.

The Ottomans before 1826

The evolution from a highly centralized to a federative military environment, the economic and military collapse that resulted, and the rebirth of the centralized army after 1826 characterize the period under discussion. Prior to 1800 Ottoman society was organized as a series of discrete orders, or loosely defined classes, such as the army, the *ulema* (scholars), and the peasantry. At the apex of the society stood the highly privileged, centralized Janissary army, originally formed of Christian children from conquered territories, who were brought to Istanbul, raised Muslim, and became the nucleus of the ruling elite and formed the ranks of the Ottoman infantry. They were never the only Ottoman army, however. The *sipahis,* largely cavalrymen who were provincially based, received land in return for military service. They added roughly eighty thousand men for large campaigns. Provincial governors were appointed from the ruling elite in Istanbul; provincial judges *(kadis)* guaranteed that the system operated according to Muslim law, as ameliorated by sultanic prerogative, or *kanun.* The Sultan and his deputy, the grand vizier, stood at the apex of the system, with the Sultan, God's representative on Earth, representing justice at the Gate of Felicity, as his court was called in the capital, Istanbul. The right of appeal by the lowliest subject was repeatedly demonstrated during the Sultan's weekly Friday procession to prayers, when he accepted petitions from one and all.

The Ottoman worldview generally divided subjects into two categories: rulers, who were untaxed *(askeri,* also meaning "soldier," presumably Muslim), and ruled, who were taxed *(reaya,* often translated as "peasant" or "flock," both Muslim and non-Muslim, but by the nineteenth century quite often referring to just non-Muslims). Tax differentiations of the ruled were determined by religion: non-Muslims paid an additional poll tax but, it should be emphasized, were exempt from military service; if they served, it was as auxiliaries with tax exemptions.

By 1800 the traditional Ottoman military organization, especially the highly privileged and caste-like Janissary army, had run its effective course. Related developments contributed to the conditions: large and costly campaigns in the seventeenth and eighteenth centuries tended to mobilize large parts of the population of warrior communities; these communities, in turn, were not adequately reintroduced into the countryside economy. These trends led increasingly to uncontrolled, semi-nomadized fringe populations on the peripheries of empire. For self-protection, cities and outlying suburbs hired private armies. Janissaries dispatched to the provinces to restore order often merged into the countryside and competed for land and tax rights with native families. The Sultan and his bureaucrats lost control over tax revenues and developed ruinous means of financing the dynastic continuance by devaluing currency, confiscating estates of "disloyal" statesmen, and selling offices. Janissary demands in the capital were exorbitant, especially in the change of sultan, when they requested an accession price for loyalty. The palace was increasingly isolated and insulated from both its own public and the larger, non-Muslim world. The Sultan himself, having abandoned campaigning altogether by this period, was invisible to anyone outside Istanbul. Campaigns were led by the grand vizier.

By 1800 the central government had lost control over the muster rolls of its standing army, and it had no idea as to the size of an effective force. Janissary entitlements (pay/ration certificates) were sold publicly and traded on the open market, much like the stock exchange, to whomever had the wherewithal to invest. By one estimate, some 400,000 entitlements were in circulation, but barely one in ten men could be mustered.[6] The concentration of resources and manpower on the northern frontier to confront the Russians loosened the imperial bonds even further with the southern Arab tier of the empire. This reorientation had an impact on sources of manpower and on revenue generation. It also allowed the Arab and Kurdish dominated provinces of the empire to develop considerable autonomy, and it permitted the growth of a particular kind of centrifugal governance that would challenge the capital of the empire itself under Mehmed Ali and his son Ibrahim.

The armies fielded by the Ottomans had become largely nomadic, multi-religious and multi-ethnic warrior bands, a confederative military symbiosis that arose out of the disintegration of the janissary and *sipahi* organizations across the empire. The challenge to the dynasty lay in reorganizing such a federative force and sharing power, while replacing a paper army with actual troops to confront the Russians. On the northern frontier itself, the Ottoman sultans had to rely on regional armies, which were enlarged and consolidated precisely because of their usefulness against the Russians. They were organized by a series of provincial governors, essentially independent warlords, who often had forced the Sultan to appoint them into their positions.

The radical transformation enacted by Mahmud II included deploying new defensive and diplomatic techniques, going "public," radically and violently realigning politics in both the core and periphery, and "turning Turk." He began a process that responded to western European and Russian pressures on his military and ideological autonomy but led, as a consequence, to a radical reconfiguration of the relationship between sultan and subject.

Defending the Borders and Rallying Ottoman Subjects

Imagine the Danube as defining a northern boundary arc, stretching from Belgrade to Kars in the Caucasus (besieged first in 1828, and contested thereafter until the end of the empire). After 1768 this line became the killing grounds for the Russians and Ottomans alike. The formidable Ottoman Danube fortress line fell bit by bit. Ochakov and Ismail garrisons were slaughtered by Russian troops in 1788 and 1791, respectively, while Ruschuk town and fortress were completely demolished in 1810. By 1828 Russian troops had been present (and often in occupation) in most of Moldavia and good parts of Wallachia for close to forty years.

Protracted negotiations between Ottomans and Russians from 1774 to 1829 indicate an obsession with the persistent Russian incursions into the Caucasus. Mahmud II proved particularly obdurate about surrendering further autonomy to Moldavia and Wallachia (present-day Moldova and Romania), and about the concession of any of the eastern Black Sea ports. In spite of the humiliating state of the Ottoman army, Mahmud II adamantly refused to cede those territories. He was particularly sensitive about the eastern Black Sea littoral on the Asian frontier. The two years of war, 1828 and 1829, and the Russian invasion and occupation of Kars (and Adrianople, present-day Edirne) finally forced Mahmud II to give up his ferocious diplomatic defence of the northern and eastern frontiers.

After 1828 the four fortresses of the mouth of the Danube — Varna, Ruschuk, Silistre, and Shumla — became the focus of the Sultan's defensive strategy. Less than two years before Mahmud II's death in 1837, he and the young Prussian officer Helmuth von Moltke toured the mouth of the Danube, starting out by steamship and continuing overland on a tour of the towns mentioned above. The purpose of the journey appears to have been largely to survey fortifications under reconstruction, but on several occasions Mahmud II also made public appearances. The Sultan reviewed the new provincial militias and addressed all the religious communities as one — as his subjects. He gave presents to the assembled schoolchildren of all the Muslim and non-Muslim schools. This public performance of sovereignty, combined with a military surveillance tour, was completely novel. He made five different trips after the 1829 treaty. Previous tours included surveys of the fortresses of the Dardanelles and all of the Gallipoli Peninsula.[7]

These trips represented an effort to reincorporate territories that had just suffered extensive warfare and continued to be in danger of being lost to the empire. It was the first time a sultan had left the capital in over a hundred years, and it was unprecedented in terms of public assemblies outside Istanbul. Mahmud II provided his subjects with new public spaces, and along the way he redrew what would become the final frontier of the Ottoman Europe. He embarked on extensive rebuilding on a very large scale for a nearly bankrupt empire, legitimated the work with his presence, and, by doing so, reconceptualized Ottoman public discourse and territorial boundaries. Except for speculations that his model may have been Europe, very little is known about the reasons for the initiatives or what influenced Mahmud II's thinking in this regard.

Centre-Periphery Frictions

Public initiatives like Mahmud II's were, however, part of a larger effort to bring disparate and highly autonomous provinces back into the imperial fold. *Fitne* (rebellion, disorder, or sedition), while deplored by the Ottoman dynasty (and by all Muslims who follow Qur'anic teaching), figured as an endemic aspect of its history. Hence *nizam* (order) was considered an obligation of sultanic rule. Many contemporary histories exhort the sultans to restore *nizam,* expressed as a return to an older, idyllic, orderly age. Sultan Selim III (1789-1807) introduced Nizâm-ı Cedid, or New Order, which tapped into that discourse. Janissaries, loyal servants of the Sultan, served as arbiters of his justice and, hence, of sultanic legitimacy. By the 1790s the army and police (i.e., the Janissaries) had become the locus of *fitne*. Their demands usually centred on questions of salary payment, currency debasement, and entitlement. Latterly, they protested marching to war at all, especially in the Caucasus and Iran. Their revolts in Istanbul became a regime-weakening method of restoring the balance of the traditional order, an essential check that the Janissaries made to sultanic rapacity.

The rebellions against the regimes of Selim III and Mahmud II, by contrast, resemble a civil war for the soul of the empire, fomented by the military and economic transformations underway. After the revolt, which ended in the removal of Sultan Selim III, the Danube fortress of Ruschuk became the centre of refugees from Istanbul reform circles. The refugees managed to persuade Ruschuk Governor Alemdar Mustafa of the advantage of reinstalling Selim III, by force if necessary. Alemdar

Mustafa joined Grand Vizier Çelebi Mustafa in Adrianople, and in mid-July 1808 he and the grand vizier marched on Istanbul with fifteen thousand troops, restored order to the city, and eliminated much of the opposition. This event was completely novel in Ottoman annals. Revolts were endemic to the city, but relief by a combined imperial and provincial army was previously unknown. Selim III died in the events, but Alemdar Mustafa enthroned Mahmud II and made himself grand vizier.[8]

What is striking in this unprecedented coalition is the evident independence of the provincial warlords, made wealthy and powerful precisely because of the centre's lack of control over the military system. Such local autonomy was traditionally unacceptable to the Ottoman dynastic view and especially odious to Mahmud II. The chiefs of many of the great houses of Anatolia and some from the Balkans, accompanied by perhaps as many as seventy thousand of their own troops, convened in Istanbul in order to convince the new sultan to take the steps they considered necessary to reform the empire at large. In effect, the notables who gathered in 1808 represented the major regional forces whose territories would make up the empire by the end of the nineteenth century: that is, the parts of Europe described above and Anatolia, heartland of republican Turkey. Twenty-five of them signed a Deed of Agreement (Sened-i İttifak), outlining the relationship and obligations between the Sultan and his notables. Article 2 committed the signatories to cooperate in the provision of state troops *(devlet askeri)* for the benefit of the survival of the empire and to assist the Sultan against foreign and domestic enemies when required. Article 5 regulated the relationships among the warlords, the Sultan, and the central bureaucracy on the basis of mutual guarantees. In return, the warlords were confirmed in the possession of their lands and the rights of their heirs.[9]

Never truly enacted, the Sened is still an extraordinary document, sometimes called the Ottoman Magna Carta and elsewhere described as the origin of public law in modern Turkey. It was innovative in striking a balance between the Sultan and his notable, provincial subjects. Real opposition to the document came from the Sultan himself, who found his power proscribed by an agreement negotiated between the grand vizier and the warlords.[10]

In early November Istanbul erupted in resistance to the new military organization established by Alemdar Mustafa. The grand vizier had envisioned a new army of 100 regiments of 1,600 men each, or 160,000 men, organized in units called *sekbans*. In the end, he likely had only twenty-five thousand men to resist the revolt instigated by Janissaries who refused to enrol in the new disciplined forces, were struck off the rolls, and denied their livelihood and privilege.[11] The initial rebellion turned into a general riot, which left six hundred sekbans, and perhaps as many as five thousand rebels, dead. Continued disorder forced the Sultan to reach an accommodation with the Janissary commanders, who were ready to pledge obedience if the sekban corps was dissolved and reformers who had escaped were punished. At least one contemporary account, probably an exaggeration, estimated as many as fifty thousand deaths from the events of November 1808.[12] Nominally, it appears the Janissaries restored order, as they understood it. The ancient order, as it turned out, had been broken forever. The new element in 1808 was the coalition of provincial forces that offered the Sultan the opportunity to recover and reorganize his empire. It is possible, in drawing a line from the agreement of 1808 to significant new regulations for the Ottoman reformed army of 1828, to see a number of crucial changes as the empire sought to engage with modernity on its own terms: an empire-wide construction of a new military force based on universal conscription, the establishment of a national militia in 1834, and military reorganizations that required the cooperation of the provincial power brokers and re-empowered notable local families. The descendants of these families were to serve Turkey and the successors Arab states in the early years after the Ottoman collapse in 1918.

Disciplining Subjects: The New Ottoman Army

After 1812 Mahmud II tamed provincial warlords who threatened his power by having his chief henchmen and advisor, Halet Efendi, appoint individuals who would be loyal to him and amenable to the new disciplinary universe. This development, too, looks much like what Europe was undergoing as standing armies and police forces emerged, only the results were less satisfying in Ottoman territories, where that kind of pressure from Istanbul often had adverse effects. For example, the suppression of the famous "Lion of Janina," Ali Pasha, in 1821, which is credited with precipitating the Greek revolt and bringing down Halet Efendi himself, must be counted a setback for Ottoman state building. Mahmud II earned the sobriquet "infidel sultan" because his armies proved to be more effective at putting down Muslim rebellions than protecting the borders of empire.

Military discipline had long since been abandoned by the Janissaries. Traditional punishments for infractions involved the bastinado (*falaka*, a stick or cudgel), which was used to inflict blows on the soles of the feet. Investigation and punishment were controlled internally, not by sultanic law but by two supreme military judges *(kazıaskers)*, and administered by the hierarchy of Janissary commanders.[13] In the guild-like corporatism of the latter-day Janissaries, ordinary discipline and punishment proved unenforceable. Such a lapse of disciplinary controls occurred in an age when systematic mobilization and severe discipline were being applied in other parts of the globe: the punishing drill, the nation under arms, or the citizen's army of France, and the notorious use of the gauntlet for the smallest infractions. It was precisely that kind of systemic discipline that Mahmud II wished to instill into his unruly army.

The Ottoman military reforms of 1827 introduced radical forms of discipline, punishment, and categories of crimes for both officers and enlisted men, with repeated exhortations that the hierarchies of command be maintained, punishment equitable, and the laws enforced by a new military bureaucracy controlled by the palace, not the Janissaries themselves. Absence at roll call, drills, and firearm practice were all punishable infractions, as was misbehaviour both in and outside the barracks.[14] The new troops on the Danube in 1828 impressed von Moltke and others with their docility and enthusiasm for drilling and artillery.[15] New forms of discipline were needed if other global empires, themselves newly disciplined, were to be engaged.

These regulations have not been systematically compared to any European counterpart, but the innovations are consistent with historical accounts of European armies, especially those of Napoleon. In the post-Napoleonic era, demobilized officers of all European armies became officers-for-hire, but Mahmud II was notoriously stingy with foreign advisors (unlike his Egyptian rival, Mehmed Ali). He declined the services of most, except for the young Prussian von Moltke, who, it must be noted, never asked for or was offered officer rank in the new army. Mehmed Ali astutely refused to obey Mahmud II's command to send him his experienced French officers. British military missions to Istanbul always foundered on the question of command. The few foreigners of any note were junior officers with little impact on the reform climate. The first few commanders-in-chief of the new army, came, not from abroad or the provinces, but from within the Sultan's court. Paranoia, insularity, and lack of funds crippled the development of a proper officer corps for another two decades.[16] In that context, the transformation of the enlisted man seems all the more remarkable.

The army that Mahmud II sent from Istanbul to the Danube in 1828 was also repeatedly identified as Turkic and Muslim, partly because of the lack of time for systematic recruitment, partly because of geopolitics (Muslims were loyal, and Turks were nearby), and partly because of the poor census information that was available to army recruiters. Internal and external pressures on the capital and the Sultan, however, also drove Mahmud II to restrict enrolment in his new army to born Muslims and "loyal Turkish lads." He rejected all non-Muslims *and* converts and, specifically, Greeks and Albanians, who were considered both treasonous and unruly.

After 1800 Ottoman legitimacy was challenged from many directions. By 1821 the empire was embroiled in both Greek and Serbian revolts. In the decade or so between 1826, when Mahmud II eliminated the Janissary corps, and 1839, when he died, Mahmud II was challenged by a plethora of Muslim voices resisting his reforms. Russian expansionism and emerging nationalisms combined to force Muslim populations to relocate into the heart of empire. Strident views, which included accusations that the Ottomans were no longer legitimate Muslim rulers, forced Mahmud II to address not just the Janissary problem but also the ideological direction of the empire.

After successfully eliminating the last Janissary revolt, Mahmud II assembled a great council to formally abolish the traditional corps and replace it with the Muallem Asakir-i Mansure-yi Muhammadiye (Trained, Victorious Soldiers of Muhammad). An edict was read in public by Esad Efendi, Ottoman historian and ideologue of the new order.[17] He reported that he "kissed the precious banner of the Prophet with trembling lips, retired respectfully a few steps down the pulpit staircase, faced the immense crowd of Muslims and read aloud the order ordaining the destruction of the Janissary corps ... whose existence had desecrated the temple of Islam for too long a period." The edict continued,

Today, they are nothing more than a useless and insubordinate body which has become the asylum of the spirit of unrest and seditions in which the number of evil men have outgrown the number of good ones ... Among those who have just been executed were found some Janissaries who bore tattooed on their arm ... the cross of the infidels. This simply proves that traitors, parading in the disguise of Muslims, have for a long time been using the Janissary corps to further their own nefarious ends by spreading false rumors. Hence, let all the congregation of Muslim people, and the small and great officials of Islam and the *ulema,* and members of other military formations, and all the common folk be of one body. Let them look upon each other as brethren in faith.[18]

This edict is a clear reassertion of an Ottoman-Muslim universalism, however fictitious, and quite emblematic of the ideologies expressed as part of military reform throughout the Middle East of the period.[19] The edict clarifies a line, a point of friction, between loyal, disciplined (and thus modern) subjects and disloyal subjects. By 1826 the Janissary corps had come to include Muslim, non-Muslim, and foreigners of all stripes, such as Baron François de Tott and other foreign adventurers.[20] The army had become notionally Muslim, so the edict abolishing the corps should be read as a re-imposition of the "Muslimness" of the Ottoman military as asserted in its very name — Trained, Victorious Soldiers of Muhammad. But Mahmud II went one step further by declaring a jihad and issuing a general call to arms against the Russians in 1828, partially to reassure his subjects but also in the hope of expanding the volunteer base. The initial fervour wore off rather quickly, and the thirty to forty thousand youngsters of the 1828-29 campaigns were all the volunteers that could be secured. Mahmud II then had to turn to a conscription system as his enthusiastic pool of volunteers dried up. In order to beef up the forces for impending confrontations, orders were once again sent to Anatolia and the Balkans to enrol available manpower. Much of the assembled force came from the handpicked "conscripts" of the provincial governors, while the rank and file were drawn from the Anatolian, Turkish peasantry.

Turning Turk

Nationalist revolts led the Sultan to harden the line on ethnic categories, which, prior to the period under discussion, had served little purpose in court circles other than as epithets, as in "unruly Albanians," "loyal Turks," or, increasingly in this era, "traitorous Rum" (Orthodox Greeks). The point here is that ethnography, or ethnic profiling, as a tool in the imperial kit, originated in this period of transition, when Europeans pressed for recognition of the rights of their preferred religio-ethnic group.[21] Armenians, Greeks, and Jews, to mention the most prominent, lived side by side with Muslims in both urban and rural settings. In many instances, non-Muslims of all ethnic persuasions outnumbered Muslims. After 1841, in particular, missionaries poured into the empire, intensifying religious strife and forcing the crisis over religious ownership of Jerusalem, which would be one cause of the Crimean War (1853-56). Confessionalism became political licence, precisely as the dynasty had begun the transformation to a constitutional regime that guaranteed equality of citizenship. Such engagements with modern concepts gave rise to external and internal sources of friction that, in turn, forced the Sultan to turn to the Turk.

One of the constant themes of the Ottoman Empire throughout its history was the loyalty and steadfastness of the soldier "Turk." Beyond the military sphere, however, it never meant more than "rube" or "hick." Even as late as the end of the nineteenth century, to ask a resident of Ottoman territories if he or she was a Turk was to offend, and, like as not, Muslims, non-Muslims, or Turks would answer that they were Ottoman.[22] In the challenges to sovereignty here described, the term *Turk* began to acquire an ideological content for the Ottomans. Mahmud II's recruiters found it practically impossible to enrol Bosnians, loyal (Muslim) warriors, or Arabs (Muslims or otherwise) into the new army unless they were under the aegis of one of their local lords and guaranteed their ancient privileges.[23] So, time after time, Mahmud II found himself turning to the "Turkic" populations of Anatolia and the Balkans, who were situated close to Istanbul and the Caucasus frontiers; these populations had experienced the era of reforms most intensely and had proved amenable to the new disciplinary regime. After a decade of less than successful voluntary, and sometimes brutally enforced, recruitment tactics, Mahmud and his commanders understood that they were exhausting the region by continuing to recruit Muslims, a minority in many of the territories of the late empire until after 1850. From that date to 1918, some 5 to 7 million Muslims are estimated to have immigrated into remaining Ottoman lands from lost territories.[24] Universal conscription failed, as non-Muslims (and probably just as many Muslims) found ways to buy their way out legally or otherwise avoid army service. Further regulations about military mobilization followed in 1843 and again in 1848, when a true conscription system based on a census of eligible young men was enacted. It proved unworkable. In 1870, when the Prussian military model was introduced, the conscription system was completely overhauled. The Committee of Union and Progress (known as the Young Turks) seized power and decreed universal conscription in 1909, the only time it was actually enforced across the Muslim and non-Muslim divide of the empire.[25]

Contested Ottomanism

The tragedy of ethnic and religious nationalism as it unfolded in the last century of the Ottoman Empire has a complicated script. Within a decade after the elimination of the Janissaries, Mahmud II's speeches on his public tours began to articulate a more inclusive definition of Ottoman subjecthood: "It is our wish to ensure the peace and security of all inhabitants of our God-protected great states, both Muslim and raya," he reportedly said to mixed Muslim and non-Muslim audiences in the Balkans.[26] On another occasion, he was heard to refer to his subjects as his children, whom he treated equally, "the only difference perceived among them being of a purely religious nature."[27] At Shumla he declared: "Your faith is different, but all of you equally guard the law and my Emperor's will. Pay the taxes I charge you with; they are employed to ensure your safety and welfare."[28] Such language anticipated the promulgation of equality of citizenship following Mahmud II's death in July 1839.

Mahmud II's sixteen-year-old son and successor, Sultan Abdülmecid I (1839-61), asked his advisors what to focus on as he ascended the throne. The response of his ministers was that he should enumerate "full guarantees for soul and property and for the preservation of the honour and dignity — to extend to all the Sultan's subjects, Muslim as well as non-Muslim." They advised that taxes should be fixed according to the wealth and means of each subject, and that there should be an "even distribution of the burden of military service according to the size of the population in each province." The last is a tacit acknowledgment of the necessity of conscripting soldiers from the entire population, not just from the Muslim, the loyal, and the reliable. The official text included a paragraph in which the Sultan "pledged to take an oath in the hall of the sacred relics, not to act contrary to its stipulations, and that the senior ulema and state functionaries take a similar oath, an action no Ottoman sultan before Abdülmecid had ever undertaken."[29]

The substance of the Gülhane decree of November 1839 referred to equality of citizenship and the equation of the burden of taxation and military conscription as described above. European observers (and most historians since) have hailed the edict as inaugurating the new (secularized) Ottoman order, but the text seems just as likely to have reflected an adjustment of sovereignty to the realities of a war-torn, ideologically fractured society that was still bound by shari'a law.[30] What the Gülhane decree delineated was a hybrid "Ottomanism," which became the central source of friction of Ottoman rule during the Tanzimat period from 1839 to 1876. Major legislation altered property laws, attempted land reform, introduced municipal councils, privileged both Muslim and non-Muslim religious organizations and leaders, created mixed Muslim-non-Muslim tribunals, and repeatedly introduced conscription as described above, but it did not address the inconsistencies in shari'a law and modern constitutionalism. The historian Carter Findley once described the ideological mix expressed in such documents as so "mutually incompatible ... that one gropes for ballistic metaphors to give an idea of their explosive potentials."[31] The new Ottoman citizens in Istanbul and the empire's major cities were divided by conflicting loyalties: an elite, increasingly impoverished Muslim class, which ran the government as officers, administrators, and provincial officials; and a wealthy commercial class made up of Greeks, Armenians, and Jews, who often acquired extraterritorial privileges from the major powers and maintained separate schools and religious organizations.[32] The attempt at universality unintentionally bifurcated a society already rocked by national separatist movements.

Sultan Abdül Mecid's new Ottoman-Muslim absolutism promoted imperial civilization, equality of citizenship, and the rule of law. It took most of the rest of the nineteenth century for Ottoman intellectuals to make sense of the merging of Ottoman-Islamic political traditions and European thought. Ottoman Tanzimat statesmen had access to Vienna, London, Paris, and Berlin, where a similar and vigorous debate over alternative systems of law was underway. The international scope of the debates was reflected in the discussion that began among Ottoman intellectuals of the 1840s. They sought to situate the Ottoman Empire among civilizations and assert its civilizing mission over rebellious nomads and tribes: Druze, Arab Bedouin, Kurd, Albanian mountaineers, and, latterly, Yemenites. In particular, the conquest of Yemen was explicitly argued for on the model of British India. In effect, the Ottomans had joined the putative pantheon of European empires.[33]

The Ottomans in the Face of Friction: Success or Failure?

In 1800 the territories of the Ottoman Empire still included most of what we today call the Middle East, with the addition of the Balkans, the northern shores of the Black Sea, and large parts of the Caucasus. By 1841, Greece, Serbia, Moldavia, and Wallachia had broken free; Egypt, Syria, Crete, and Arabia were up in arms. The Russians had acquired Crimea, Bessarabia, and large parts of the Caucasus. Bosnia, Albania, and Tripoli obeyed Istanbul in name only, and the Russians passed the Balkan range to threaten Istanbul itself. The Treaty of London in 1841, signed by the great powers and the Ottomans, confirmed a regime of international free trade and free passage of the Dardanelles and Bosphorous into the Black Sea, which essentially drew the Ottomans into the emerging global trading system. The British established a semi-colonial regime in most of the Arab provinces, secured the routes to India, and occupied Egypt by 1882. The Ottoman Empire was reduced to Anatolia (present-day Turkey), Bulgaria, Thrace, and the Arab provinces of the Levant and Iraq. British consuls were found in every major port city of the Arab southern tier of the empire, where they had not been before. Foreign powers, in effect, established an informal colonial rule over a large part of the Ottoman territories and found themselves contesting the territory with a rival, but fragile, colonial power, the Ottomans themselves.[34]

Mahmud II laid the groundwork for an army that made a good showing in later conflicts, such as in the Balkans in 1853-54 and even in the Russo-Turkish War of 1877-78. He secured a circumscribed autonomy for the Ottomans while he sketched a social space, at least its putative boundaries, for them, and he identified a preferred (Turkic) ethnicity for the future Turkish (Muslim) Republic. He guaranteed its economic collapse by signing the Anglo-Ottoman Convention. The Ottomans began to look decidedly European, but such a reorientation ultimately destroyed them, as was ruefully acknowledged by reform-minded minister Fuad Pasha, who told a European visitor: "Our state is the strongest state, for you are trying to cause its collapse from without, and we from within, but still it does not collapse."[35] It took decades of internal strife, external provocation, and enormous human costs to finally tear it apart. Some of the continuities from the nineteenth to the twentieth century may be obvious. With his definition of the final frontier of the Danubian-Caucasus arc, his public journeys around the Balkans, his increasing reliance on his loyal "Turkic" citizens, Mahmud II defended and re-imagined the very territories and the nationality that was to emerge. This re-imagination culminated in Mustafa Kemal Ataturk establishing the republic in the National Pact of 1920, when he drew the borders of present-day Turkey and proclaimed that everyone inside the borders was a "Turk."

What was different about the Ottoman modern turn in the global crisis, and in the frictions of 1826-28 prompted by this engagement, may well be the particular way in which the external and internal pressures restricted the full development of constitutionalism and economic autonomy. The costs of the top-down, radical modernization, or defensive developmentalism, by Mahmud II and his successors were considerable. The failure of the constitutional experiment and the inability to extend the rule of law across the empire led to the re-emergence of sultanic absolutism in 1876 under Abdülhamid II (1876-1909). Official bankruptcy followed in 1881, when the Public Debt Administration was created by France and Britain. The final collapse came during the First World War.[36]

The crisis at the imperial hub in 1826-28 offers us a glimpse into a society in extremis, where a web of contradictions, contestations for autonomy, and competing world forces effected a transformation that has universal implications. Although the resulting loss of autonomy and its reconstitution in the nation-state form took its own path, other empires in Britain, France, and China also emerged transformed in their own engagements with the universals of modernity.

chapter 5

Wired Religion: Spiritualism and Telegraphic Globalization in the Nineteenth Century

Jeremy Stolow

FOR SEVERAL WEEKS DURING the spring of 1848, the modest home of the Fox family, outside Rochester, New York, served as a stage for a nightly performance of inexplicable and unrelenting rapping sounds. Over time the young Fox daughters, Kate and Margaretta, began to recognize patterns in the noises and eventually established a rapport with their preternatural visitor — as it turned out, the spirit of a peddler who had been murdered by a former occupant of the house. Their communications were based on a system of rappings not unlike the code Samuel Morse had devised for his electrical telegraph, an instrument that had been introduced to the American public only four years earlier and which was already beginning to turn the town of Rochester into a crucial hub in the expanding communications network of the American interior. The telegraph had also begun to service a rapidly growing and increasingly integrated newspaper industry, which played its own part in helping to spread rapidly the news of the Fox sisters' discovery across the United States, and thence to Canada, Britain, France, Germany, and points beyond. Thus the young Fox sisters were propelled onto the path of media stardom, and, in lockstep with their ascent to the world stage, an eruption of public discussions, spectacles, scientific studies, and transnational exchanges was consolidated around the movement commonly known as modern Spiritualism.

Of course, creation myths do not do much justice to the complexities of historical origins, lines of influence, regional variations, or inconveniently contradicting details. But the Rochester Rappings, as they came to be known, do provide a wonderful illustration of just what made Spiritualism such a potent cultural force in the latter half of the nineteenth century. Here was a fertile intersection of popular religiosity — in this case, a predominantly feminine religiosity — and a transnational public sphere consolidated in new ways through advancing communications media. Emerging technologies such as the telegraph empowered a new class of spirit mediums to exchange knowledge and renegotiate existing lines of cultural, scientific, ecclesiastical, and political authority, which became linked on a worldwide scale. And telegraphy, as it so happens, was particularly well suited to such efforts, since it provided both a practical analogue and a material infrastructure for sustaining contact with various "worlds beyond" the local everyday life situations of relatively powerless people. As this chapter aims to show, the story of Spiritualism was inextricably bound up with the story of the telegraph. By examining their conjoined history, one gains fresh insight into the reshaping of the Atlantic world in the nineteenth century, and perhaps also a new purchase on the very ideas of globalization and autonomy.

Spiritualism is the name for a family of movements centred on the practice of communication with and on behalf of the dead, with various benefits accrued from such activities, including personal solace, health, prestige, and a type of political authority that came with public speaking. This family includes American, British, and Canadian variants of self-defined Spiritualists, adherents to Christian Science and Theosophy, as well as French, Brazilian, and Caribbean followers of Spiritism. All of these emerged during the latter half of the nineteenth century, spread around the Atlantic, and eventually penetrated nearly every region in the world, from Russia to the Philippines, India, and Australia. As a globally resonant movement, Spiritualism drew literally millions of people into its penumbra, including working-class women and men as well as social elites — doctors, artists, scientists, politicians, and engineers — who often lent an aura of respectability and authority to the cause.[1] Such appeal was grounded in part by Spiritualism's unique capacity to draw upon a multiplicity of overlapping philosophical legacies, with varying degrees of accommodation to established Christian doctrines and in dialogue with mystical traditions both from within and outside Europe and the North Atlantic world. Spiritualism was also distinguished by its intense engagement with various Western sciences and para-sciences, from physics to phrenology, as well as with the theoretical and practical frameworks of emerging professions, such as electrical engineering and psychology. For these reasons, the movement cannot readily be contained within the simple binaries of religious-secular, Western–non-Western, modern-primitive, erudite-popular, or scientific-magical, since it so readily moved across and between such social and conceptual spaces. Spiritualism's omnivorous character and its global reach in fact make it a particularly instructive case study from which to survey the dramatic cultural changes that accompanied broader processes of technological modernization, colonial encounter, and the formation of new national and international public spheres over the latter half of the nineteenth century. Indeed, a growing scholarly literature has established this movement's remarkable influence on such disparate phenomena as the birth of psychoanalysis, the rise of first-wave feminism, and the entrenchment of various forms of popular and high culture, from poetry to stage hypnosis and cinema going.[2]

Like many forms of popular religious activity that enjoyed a considerable transnational reach, such as Catholic movements organized around sightings of the Virgin Mary, Spiritualism was predominantly a women's movement. In fact, spirit mediums — the indispensable technicians in the control of access to the supernatural world — were overwhelmingly women, and mediumship in general was culturally coded as a "female gift." Spiritualism offered women of virtually any background opportunities for social advancement through participation in seance practice and, more broadly, the social networks that such associations opened up for them. They could enjoy a high-profile career, lay claim to otherworldly insight, entertain friends, confound skeptics, console the bereaved, and earn considerable money, all the while conforming to nineteenth-century ideals of feminine passivity. Making artful use of the feminine tropes of moral purity, and assumptions about the sensitive nature of "the weaker sex," Spiritualist women were able to speak out while avoiding the responsibilities of authorship by proclaiming that they merely conveyed the judgments of the world of the spirit upon the world of the living. This placed the authority of dead voices in alliance with Spiritualist women's desire to make themselves seen and heard and thereby to transgress prescribed conventions of polite society that depended on the feminine virtues of silence and bodily restraint. In some cases, spirit mediumship served as a gateway to public speech and activism in arenas outside the seance chamber, as is evident in the involvement of notable Spiritualist women in political movements that advocated abolitionism, temperance, anti-vivisectionism, dress reform, and women's suffrage, among other globally resonant liberal causes of the nineteenth century.[3] Most Spiritualists, however, were not much interested in reformist politics, let alone mounting overt challenges to the normative representations of femininity that dominated the nineteenth-century Atlantic world. They were more squarely concerned with the intensely personal goals of assuaging grief, securing health, and satisfying their own curiosity about the fortunes that awaited them in the afterlife.

Nevertheless, unlike many other popular religions, Spiritualism was distinct for having exhibited a striking proclivity for new organizational forms and techniques within the religious field. Its expansion did not depend on the existence of a circle of virtuosi (such as priests) who monopolized religious knowledge, guarded the portals of access to ritual practice, or derived their authority from routine exchanges of money, gifts, and services with ordinary folk. Rather, Spiritualism was very much a do-it-yourself movement: a network of like-minded actors who established their own local circles, largely on the basis of information acquired from the popular press. The movement was also distinguished by its uniquely intense engagement with the world-transforming technologies of Western modernity: not only telegraphy but also photography, telephony, and radio, among others. Spiritualists in fact developed a rich vocabulary for making sense of these ascendant technologies and a repertoire of ritual activities designed specifically to accommodate the performative demands they elicited in various contexts of private and public life. The history of what here will be called the Spiritual Telegraph is, therefore, an instructive tale concerning the cultural reception and social consequences of an emerging technology: how it was inculcated into daily habits and how its powers and its disciplining effects were related to the production of new forms of sociability and subjectivity. This history also has much to offer to current thinking about the triangulation of religion, technology, and individual autonomy, inviting us to revisit some of the reigning assumptions about how these terms relate to one another and also how they relate to larger social transformations gathered under the sign of globalization.

Circum-Atlantic Spirit

One of the difficulties in tracing the legacy of the Spiritual Telegraph is that histories of Spiritualism have tended to be written within the parochial framework of discrete nation-states, as one finds in many accounts of the movement in England, the United States, or France. Such narratives understate the extent to which Spiritualism functioned as a sort of travelling theory, propelled along and productively transformed through a series of transnational trajectories and routes, such as those linking France and England; England, Canada, and the United States; England, the United States, and the Caribbean; France and Brazil; and so on. An examination of Spiritualism's rapid spread along these routes establishes that the proper scale of analysis is not national but transnational, if not global. For this reason, it is most productive to locate this movement within the shifting social spaces, contact zones, and fractal patterns of economic exchange and cultural hybridization that make up what historians have recently characterized as the circum-Atlantic world of the nineteenth century.[4]

The Atlantic world has long been understood as a site of cultural, economic, and political transactions crucial to the formation of the modern world: the fateful encounters between European explorers and "New World" empires (such as the Aztec or the Inca), the slave trade and the establishment of plantation economies, the staging of colonial rebellions that ushered in the age of modern nationalisms, and the migration of millions of European peasants and members of the working class in search of a New Jerusalem, to say nothing of the transatlantic connections among political reformers, social engineers, abolitionists, suffragists, Socialists, Romantics, scientists, evangelicals, artists, and entertainers.[5] The Atlantic world has also served as a privileged site for tracking the confluence of economic, political, and cultural forces normally identified with the formation of the modern world-system, and thus it constitutes the key prototype of our contemporary age of economic and communicational globalization. Indeed, by the middle of the nineteenth century, technologies of steam, rail, and electrical telegraphy together formed an architecture unprecedented in its capacity to contract space and time, transplant populations, extract resources, and supply markets; it transformed the Atlantic basin into the undisputed central arena of global economic exchange and the core of an industrial system dominated by the British Empire.[6]

Placing the history of Spiritualism within this circum-Atlantic framework throws into sharper relief how this movement reflected broader processes of globalization in the nineteenth century. It also demonstrates how Spiritualism worked to translate the forces of technological, economic, and cultural modernization into locally meaningful discourses and performative repertoires of conduct in public and private life. Only a transnational perspective can show us how, and with what effects, the news of Spiritualist activity circulated around the Atlantic. This transnational framework is also needed in order to explain how images of the Atlantic world and, more broadly still, the image of global space itself figured within the Spiritualist imagination.

Nowhere is Spiritualism's global consciousness more colourfully illustrated than in the many cases of seance practitioners who, from their location in bourgeois living rooms of Western metropolises, summoned spirits that represented a diversity of "other worlds" and then subjected themselves to their authority. A survey of articles, notices, and letters published in *La Revue Spirite* (the leading French Spiritualist journal of the nineteenth century, which enjoyed a wide international readership) gives one a sense of how frequently nineteenth-century mediums received visitations, not only from the spirits of great figures from the pantheon of Western history (such as Socrates, Julius Caesar, Mozart, Goethe, Charlemagne, Rousseau, Benjamin Franklin, Thomas Paine, Abraham Lincoln, and Jeanne D'Arc) but also from exotic personalities such as "Hitoti, a savage chief from Tahiti," "Manouza, a woman from Baghdad," "a young peasant girl from Algeria," "a black slave from Louisiana," "a doctor from Russia," "a Queen from Delhi," "a pasha from Egypt," and "a widow from Malabar," among many others.[7] The seance chamber, it seems, was not only a place of congregation but also a site for opening avenues of dialogue and symbolic exchange across and beyond what Peter van der Veer has termed "the colonial divide."[8] Spiritualism thus became deeply implicated in a new mode of imagining community commensurate with the expanding telecommunications networks of the nineteenth-century Atlantic world. Its representations of world community — both living and dead — reflected larger processes of development of mass markets for print, an expanding franchise of readers, the contraction of space and time through improvements in transportation systems, and the growing penetration of new media into every imaginable arena of social life.

Consider the case of Spiritism, the variant of Spiritualism that first blossomed in France in the late 1850s and was eventually transplanted to various New World locations, most notably Brazil, Cuba, and Puerto Rico during the late nineteenth century. Its founder, Allan Kardec (1804-69), helped legitimize Spiritualist knowledge as it spread across western Europe and around the Atlantic by providing a patina of scientific respectability to popular ideas about the afterlife and practices of somnambulism and clairvoyance. Kardec's theories resonated with various social groups, including successive generations of artists, intellectuals, and what the historian Benedict Anderson would refer to as "pilgrim bureaucrats" who had come to Paris to study administration or civil engineering.[9] Through such carriers, Kardec's doctrine of Spiritism was brought back to the New World, where it was fruitfully combined with rituals of possession and other religious practices originating in West Africa and the Americas, giving birth to entirely new, syncretic religions, such as Umbanda in Brazil and Santería in Cuba and Puerto Rico.[10]

Much of the literature on Kardecian Spiritualism fits well within these historical narratives concerning the creolization of European religious and scientific texts, African performative traditions, and Native American cosmologies within New World localities. In this sense, Kardec's influence can be traced back to patterns of exchange that first emerged in the eighteenth century, if not earlier. Such a genealogy, however, offers little insight into the material, institutional, and communicational infrastructures that actually enabled Kardec's ideas to take root in diverse locales of the Atlantic world. In other words, Kardec should not be regarded simply as a philosophical exponent of Spiritualism or solely as a collector and interpreter of knowledge about the spirit world culled from a variety of "primitive" sources. And Kardec's ideas, for that matter, should not simply be regarded as raw material that was "transplanted" from the Old to the New World. We are better served by treating Kardec in terms of his position as the manager of a major cultural enterprise, an epistolary correspondent with Spiritualist organizations around the world, and as a metropolitan (Parisian) intellectual located at the intersection of a rapidly thickening network of communicative lines that extended around the circumference of the Atlantic. In this regard, it is no accident that the most influential vehicle through which Kardec propagated his theories took the form of a periodical publication, the aforementioned *La Revue Spirite,* which he founded in 1858. In fact, Kardec's project to collect, document, and classify stories about spirit communication cannot be disentangled from the conditions that allowed for the rapid expansion of serial publications in the mid- to late nineteenth century. These conditions included the development of steam presses, industrial papermaking techniques, advances in rail and shipping, and the use of electrical telegraphy for reporting news rapidly across vast distances. These same infrastructures help to explain how New World locales provided such fertile soil for the spread of Kardecian Spiritualism, as in the case of Brazil, an early recipient of electrically mediated technologies in the nineteenth century. Cities such as Rio de Janeiro in fact experienced rapid technological modernization in close step with their European and North Atlantic counterparts, laying the groundwork for Brazil to emerge in the twentieth century as the world centre and leading exporter of Spiritualist practices, texts, and organizational forms.[11]

Kardecian Spiritualism thus crystallized the ways that new communication technologies such as the telegraph helped to reorder the circum-Atlantic world of the nineteenth century. This story highlights the ways that telegraphy contributed to transformations, not only in the more commonly noted realms of journalism, finance, trade, and diplomacy but also in the shifting public presence of religious actors. This technology's epoch-making character was further dramatized by the successful laying of submarine cables that connected England, Ireland, Canada, and the United States in 1866, the Caribbean and Latin America in the 1870s, and much of the West African coast in the 1880s and 1890s. In the words of one (perhaps overly excited) contemporary observer, thanks to submarine telegraphy, "the breadth of the Atlantic, with all its waves, is as nothing."[12] This nothingness lies at the heart of the conjoined histories of Spiritualism and telegraphy.

Wired World

According to James Carey, the telegraph merits a privileged place among the new media technologies of the nineteenth century, because communication was for the first time "freed from the constraints of geography."[13] Thanks to telegraphy, information transmission could now proceed much faster than physical transportation and on this basis could redefine longstanding spatio-temporal relations of centre and periphery, the global and the local, or the proximate and the distant. Of course, no technology is created *ex nihilo,* and in this respect it is important to recall that electrical telegraphy was preceded by a variety of techniques and instruments for what we might here call "deterritorialized" communication, such as semaphores, optical telegraph systems, and even the ancient

practices of sending signals by smoke and mirrors.[14] But the electric telegraph involved a far more radical separation between signifying systems
and the physical movement of objects, engendering entirely new possibilities for social relations based on the "economy of the signal."[15] These
were relations predicated on (relative) simultaneity, impersonal contact,
and increasingly centralized administrative control, as was quickly made
evident in a variety of economic, technical, and social arenas: the coordination of capital investments and strategic transactions in international
commodity markets; the standardization of news reporting; shifting protocols for international diplomacy; and even new possibilities for ro-
mance, fantasy, and criminal enterprise.[16]

   As the first successful application of electrical energy outside the realms
of scientific experiment and medical therapy, telegraphy constituted
what some have designated the world's first truly globalizing telecommunications infrastructure, not least because of the systemic nature of its
technical application. Telegraphic communication was characterized by
its capacity for rapid, unidirectional, and asynchronous transmissions of
information across potentially limitless distances, thanks to its innovative use of integrated electrical circuitry and its ability to compress complex language through the use of a binary system of signs (Morse code).
The electric telegraph was also distinguished by the restrictive interface
between the medium and its end-users, which was materialized in the
institutional space of the telegraph office, its bureaucratized labour force,
and its hierarchical ordering of communication processes according to
criteria of efficient time management and priorities of commercial and
governmental interest.[17] In all these respects, the telegraph represented
a significant harbinger of our contemporary global communications environment, with its proliferation of computer and satellite networks,
and the institutional architecture governing transnational flows of digital information.[18] Indeed, through the networking of regional, national,
and international telegraph systems, the design of the human-machine
interface, and the organization of institutional environments for these
communicative practices, telegraphy stood at the forefront of a radical
revolution in mediated communication that had global consequences.
The administration of telegraphic communications not only demanded
new forms of cooperation among states (epitomized by the founding of
the International Telegraph Union in 1865; see also Gorman's chapter
in this volume), it also contributed to a dramatic transformation in the
exercise of political power within and across state structures, in part by

drawing peripheral regions of the world into evermore intimate contact with the great metropoles of Europe and the United States.

By the dawn of the twentieth century, telegraph cables had reached even the most remote hinterlands of the world. This relentless expansion was dominated by British-owned cabling companies, such as the Electric Telegraph Company, the Submarine Telegraph Company, and the Eastern Telegraph Company, that benefited from British hegemony in related fields, including marine traffic and control of the trade in copper and gutta percha (rubber).[19] By drawing all regions into the orbit of this new, global communications system, telegraphy contributed to the formation of a supraterritorial social space that existed everywhere and nowhere. This geography was defined by the logic of the grid — a single, temporally homogeneous map of world space, as reflected, for instance, in the division of the planet's surface into standardized time zones. Admittedly, throughout the nineteenth century, the telegraph's potential remained only partially realized, as it was forever plagued by financial and technical impediments, regional and local resistances to standardization, and dramatically uneven levels of access and control. All the same, for contemporary observers, telegraphy seemed to herald a new alignment of knowledge, representation, and communicative practice that encompassed the entire planet, from the most temporally remote locales of human habitation to the darkest corners of the natural order.[20]

This emergent globality was the great product of electrical engineering in the nineteenth century, and with it came the technological capacity for not just rapid but, more specifically, disembodied communication and contact. The building of the infrastructure to sustain telegraphic modernization accelerated and expanded communication on a global scale and radically expanded its possibilities. With telegraphy came new opportunities, and new expectations, for sustaining one's presence in an autonomous, ethereal world of electrical currents and flows. This universe was one into which human bodies — covered in flesh, impaired by weak sensory organs, prone to fatigue, and slow to move — could never really enter. To the extent that electrical media were capable of duplicating and distributing human presences in this ethereal world of information exchange, the very terms of human communication had been forever changed. To interact with others now meant to read the traces of their virtual presence.[21]

Spiritual Telegraphy and the Inversion of the Autonomous Self

The telegraph proved itself a productive thing to think with, not only for the technological literati, whose experience with electrical instruments afforded them symbolic power as experts, but also for those engaged in the business of occultism. In the context of an expanding reading public conversant in scientific discovery and the marvels of modern engineering, Spiritualists seized upon the example of telegraphy in order to elaborate a grand theory of supernatural presence grounded in the power of electromagnetism. The invisibility and intangibility of electric current, and its capacity to collapse time and space into a single, continuous plane of reference, provided the perfect analogy for the existence of the human soul beyond the body. After all, if telegraphic technologies could harness electromagnetic forces in order to communicate intentional messages, why should it not be possible to develop comparable techniques in order to communicate with the dead? From this perspective, Spiritualists proposed merely to enlarge the range of possible interlocutors within the new social environment created by the telegraph. By presenting a technically plausible explanation for occult knowledge, aligned with the authority of nineteenth-century science and engineering, they offered tantalizing promises of an emerging world order mediated by electrical energy.

This analogy between spirit mediumship and telegraphy worked because it referenced a deeper set of claims about the enigma of electrical energy, popularly conceived as a "universal fluid" that permeated all forms of animate and inanimate beings and facilitated communication between the two. As a master trope, electricity facilitated the articulation of new modes of industrial and political power with new scenes of scientific inquiry and new regimes of cultural production. On its terms, new homologies were forged between the representation of social life, and even of the human body itself, and the geography of industrial modernity. Thus, the electrical flow of a telegraph network could be likened to the arterial architecture of the human nervous system.[22] And, much like a cable transmitting an electric charge, spirit mediumship was frequently described as a means of receiving fluid energies emanating from somewhere beyond. In each case, reception and transmission required the proper attunement of the host. For the spirit medium, this attunement meant being endowed with the correct "electro-medianimic machinery," as Kardec called it.[23] Claims about the receptivity of spirit communication were thereby tied to claims about the body of the spirit medium itself, understood here to comprise a complex of nervous pathways and "cerebral batteries" that connected the material and the immaterial.[24] More than simply a metaphor, the Spiritual Telegraph thus provided a model for the working of the body, and also for the practice of communication itself, worked out through the electrical principles of current and charge, capacity and resistance, circuit and field. ·

In short, telegraphy pointed towards a new type of human agent enveloped by the technological promise of bringing together the visible and the invisible, the public and the private, and the global and the local. This new agent was located in a cosmos defined by the performative goals of erasing distance, freezing time, and circumventing what seemed otherwise to be the inevitable decay of bodies and things. On these terms, the act of being possessed by a spirit was phenomenologically comparable to the autotelic labour of electrical devices, such as occurs when a message is communicated through a telegraph circuit. In both cases, what was brought into existence was a system for the circulation of discourse freed from the "normal" conditions of individual human subjectivity, where one is supposed to enjoy mastery over one's conscious intentions and one's own body. Indeed, from the Spiritualist perspective, passivity was not a sign of the inadequacy of "feminine frailty" in social life; rather, it was understood as a special "gift" and a crucial condition for the receptivity of otherworldly inspiration. Here appears a curious inversion of the liberal ideal of individual autonomy in the sense discussed elsewhere in this book — as the capacity for actors to formulate, assess, and execute choices regarding their paths in social life. Insofar as spirit mediums aimed precisely to relinquish control of their own bodies and — like a telegraphic cable — to serve as "channels" for the messages of others, they dramatized some of the most striking contradictions that shaped gendered conventions of liberal autonomy in the nineteenth-century Atlantic world. On the one hand Spiritualists readily embraced stereotypes of feminine powerlessness, while on the other hand they often flagrantly transgressed the ordained strictures of feminine sociability. Such transgressions could be witnessed in the "scandalous" spectacles of possessed women divulging intimate details about the lives of their clients or discussing at length complex topics about which they had no apparent prior knowledge.

In light of these contradictory pressures of presence and absence, knowledge and ignorance, conformity and transgression, and acquiescence and resistance, spirit mediumship has sometimes been interpreted as a weapon of the weak, as a ritualized (as opposed to a real or enduring) violation of cultural norms, and as a staging of the inconsistencies and conflicts that shaped the psychic lives of seance participants, including the countless "frail" women who were drawn to seance rituals in search of solace. [25] In this reading, Spiritualist seance practice was, for the most part, an expression of a traumatic reaction to the rapid and wrenching transformations associated with the rise of transatlantic modernity, which increasingly confined women to the domestic sphere and pathologized their minds and bodies. This line of interpretation risks obfuscating the important role of emerging technologies within the Spiritualist imagination, and within seance practice in particular. What, indeed, is one to make of the many cases in which Spiritualists incorporated into their seance practices the latest available apparatuses, such as magnets, metal cables, clocks, scales, pressure gauges, and other instruments culled from the emerging electrical industries?[26] From a Spiritualist point of view, the use of such devices revealed something about the nature of the cosmos in general, namely, the susceptibility of all things, spirits included, to the laws of electromagnetism. At the same time, through these technological engagements, Spiritualists sought to demonstrate to their competitors and critics their deep commitment to the language of investigation, exhibition, exposure, and evidence. Such commitments allowed the seance chamber to function as a sort of laboratory: a stage for investigating the spirit world, for obtaining its secrets, and for surveilling the body of the spirit medium through what could be presented as scientifically accredited methods of precise manipulation and controlled observation.[27] In all these ways, the practice of spirit communication was rendered an empirically confirmable condition of the body, the performative gestures of which enacted forms of automatism and mechanization that mimicked the work of modern electrical machinery.

Far from simply reacting to the rapidly transforming culture of nineteenth-century metropolitan life, Spiritualists openly embraced this strange new world that was increasingly governed by invisible electrical flows. In so doing, they also explored and enacted new modes of action and new conceptions of human agency, and they did so in ways that generated considerable friction with the liberal image of the rights-bearing, self-reliant, and self-controlled individual. The global reach of this movement, moreover, raises some troubling questions about the putative universality of the enlightened goals of personal autonomy.

In sum, spiritualism's techno-culture also offers an instructive point of entry into larger discussions about the place of modern technologies within the social order. The readiness with which Spiritualists around and beyond the Atlantic appropriated the telegraph — as a metaphor, as a telecommunications infrastructure, and as the raw material for establishing new forms of otherworldly contact — poses a serious challenge to the unfortunately tenacious assumption that religious modes of discourse and practice are somehow incompatible with the habits and ways of seeing the world that are said to accompany technological modernization. On the contrary, to the extent that the Spiritual Telegraph evinces the inseparability of religion and technology as two dimensions of a shared realm of discourse and practice, we require a new language for defining the search for collective and individual forms of autonomy — and also for defining the impediments to such goals in the technologically infused landscape of the global present.

chapter 6   The Internationalization of
Capital: The Late Nineteenth
and Twentieth Centuries

Samir Saul

Two historical events can be taken as defining moments in the
long-term process of financial globalization: a French law restricting the
export of capital in 1918 and Great Britain's decision, following the collapse of the Bretton Woods system, to abolish exchange controls in 1979.
On 3 April 1918, France's Chamber of Deputies passed an awkwardly
worded law banning the import "of all shares and bonds and in general
of all securities representing, directly or indirectly, a share in property
or in debt."[1] Although the deputies had prohibited the export of French
capital abroad, the law per se was a minor event. Wartime conditions had
forced the imposition of exchange controls and the prohibition of gold
exports, and they had progressively tightened restrictions on the outward movement of capital from the belligerent countries. After the war
France's rentiers, having borne heavy losses from the failure of Russia
and other nations to honour their debts, were less than keen to send their
savings abroad. Worldwide monetary instability and failure to achieve
adjustment hampered the movement of capital, as available funds found
use at home in the reconstruction of a war-ravaged country.[2]

However obscure, this 1918 French law can be considered a defining global moment in the continuum of the history of international capital flows for several reasons. The law represented an epitaph to more
than half a century of considerable and largely unfettered exports of capital, and it presaged the next half-century of more modest levels of exports and impediments to the cross-border mobility of capital. After all,

prohibition of capital flows clashed with the established liberal doctrine that had enabled France to become the world's second largest exporter of capital until 1914.[3] Restrictions over international capital transfers lasted well into the 1970s. From the standpoint of financial regulation, the post-1945 era was not fundamentally new. International capital flows were not encouraged, in part because they were associated with the easy money of the late 1920s and the subsequent crash of 1929. Controls became so much a part of the international financial landscape that lifting them could only be done piecemeal.

During the 1960s and 1970s, Eurocurrency creation and flows developed rapidly, in a sort of offshore environment, outside mainstream financial channels. With exchange controls still limiting the access of foreign borrowers to European securities markets, Eurodollar operations (conducted in dollars but outside the United States) became an attractive alternative because they were exempt from tight regulations and expenses for transactions on national capital markets. By the end of the 1960s, flotations of Euro-issues (i.e., securities denominated in currencies other than those of the markets where they are floated — largely Eurodollars) had become the most important transactions in European markets for long-term foreign issues.[4] Consequently, these capital flows eventually tore at the seams the Bretton Woods system of fixed exchange rates.[5] When the flows slowed in the early 1970s, exchange markets internationalized quickly with the support of government policies. In 1974 the United States removed a tax that had been imposed in 1963 to stem the outflow of capital. The decisive step in the dismantlement of exchange controls, however, occurred on 23 October 1979, when Great Britain abolished all restrictions on outward capital movements.[6] Within a decade most industrialized countries had adopted similar measures. This deregulation represented a defining moment on the way to financial globalization because it facilitated liberalization of capital movements. In the 1980s bond markets internationalized; equity markets followed suit in the 1990s. Capital flows gathered momentum, and their volume soared.

These two defining moments concern attempts to regulate the mobility of capital. Whether regulation took the form of prohibition, as in 1918, or the form of permission, as in 1979, these financial laws reflected current realities more than they represented active agents. Taken together, these moments indicate the direction that capital was taking, and they portray the era in a way that anonymous statistics by themselves do not. From 1928 to 1979, events seemed to have come full circle. The tide of untrammelled movement and increasing amounts of capital flows prior to the First World War ebbed with the onset of restrictions over the next six decades. At the end of the twentieth century, a loosening of constraints accompanied and smoothed the resumption of capital movements.

This chapter compares four successive eras of international capital flows, each defined by the prevailing regime of capital movement: (1) *open*, from 1870 to 1914, (2) *controlled*, from 1918 to 1940, (3) *managed*, from 1945 to the early 1970s, and (4) *deregulated*, from the 1970s to the present. The contemporary era, beginning around 1975 and marked by soaring capital flows, is counterpoised by the open, pre-contemporary era. Following standard economic analysis, capital transfers can be divided into two streams: portfolio flows (equity and debt securities bearing fixed interest, such as bonds and certificates of deposit, acquired with a view to earning income rather than obtaining control) and foreign direct investment (FDI) (stock purchased in order to participate in management and gain control of a company). This investigation seeks to determine what, if anything, is different about capital movements in the present as compared to the past. The guiding thread is the classic dialectic between continuity and change in relation to the extent of globalization. After quantifying capital flows and capital stocks accumulated abroad, I analyze their geographic distribution and sector composition over time. Finally, I outline the stages of international production, using a methodology based primarily on an empirical investigation of the statistical data. The latter suggest that there is more continuity than change, although the foundations of important changes are being laid. It also appears that financial globalization characterizes relations among the wealthier countries of the North. Although changed in form and reduced in overall importance, contemporary economic relations between the North and the poorer Southern countries are similar to those at the end of the nineteenth century. Nevertheless, the forms of autonomy changed in the intervening decades. Although the Global South now enjoys formal political autonomy, its lack of economic autonomy suggests continuity with the colonial era, with the important qualification that the rise of global corporations has added a new layer of complication to the traditional picture of economic dominance by the imperial powers.

Upsurge, Downturn, and Reorganization: 1870s to 1960s

In order to better appreciate the historical importance of the two global financial moments, a background account of capital movements across international borders is required. The history of international finance can be divided into three relatively distinct periods. Between 1870 and 1914, the fixed exchange rate system, an absence of regulatory restrictions, an abundance of capital in industrialized western Europe, and strong demand for capital outside western Europe greatly accelerated the internationalization of capital. From 1914 to 1945, internationalization receded. The First World War led to a breakdown of international economic relations, which came to be characterized by inflation, floating exchange rates, devaluations, and deficits in public finances. The Great Depression provoked autarkic reactions, placing great strain on international financial relations and reducing capital flows sharply, even before the Second World War undid what remained of the international economy. The third period, which commenced after the war, saw the reconstruction of national economies and the framework for international economic relations (see Pruessen and Hedetoft, this volume). Growth, restoration of international commercial relations, and stable currency arrangements by means of fixed exchange rates were the order of the day under the aegis of the International Monetary Fund (IMF). The Bretton Woods system, which lasted only a quarter century, disintegrated in the late 1960s under the pressure of productivity slowdowns, mounting deficits, runaway inflation, and increasingly unrealistic fixed exchange rates.

The international economy was Europe-centred during the period from 1870 to 1914, as most investment flows were unidirectional, emanating from western Europe and radiating outwards. Except for the United States, a sharp divide separated creditor and debtor nations as well as investors and recipients of foreign investments. The bulk of investments tended to move from capital-rich, slowly growing areas to capital-poor, rapidly growing areas, usually on a rate-of-return basis (higher marginal profit or interest-rate differentials). Because the capital was mostly of private origin, it was invested in infrastructure (often export-related, such as railroads and ports), social overhead expenditures (transportation, public utilities, public works, real estate, and urban development), and natural resource extraction, or it served to finance government expenditures. Loans to foreign governments were prominent, but holdings in debentures (fixed-interest bonds backed by the general credit of the issuer rather than specified assets) and the equity of firms increased.

The exact mix between portfolio and FDI remains open to debate. Much of the investment that was originally considered to be portfolio now appears to have been under the control of non-residents. According to one study, the amount of direct investment as a proportion of total private foreign investment was much higher than was originally believed in what would later be called the Third World or developing countries, where two-fifths of accumulated foreign private investment was located in 1914.[7] Foreign direct investment probably represented about 35 percent of total long-term international assets in 1914, a ratio that is higher in relation to the national income of the capital-exporting countries than at any time before or since.[8]

Britain served as the hub of the international economy during the period from 1870 to 1914. Wealth generated by industrialization, revenue from sales of manufactured goods abroad, and profits derived from empire accumulated into a mass of capital available for export to other countries. Annual outflows from Britain in current value swelled from £40 million (US$195 million) in the 1860s to £175 million ($US852 million) in 1910-14.[9] At its peak, net capital outflow from Great Britain represented 9 percent of GNP.[10] From 1865 to 1914, £4,082 million (US$19.9 billion) was raised in London through the issue of foreign securities.[11] Estimates of the stock of outstanding long-term publicly issued foreign investment accumulated by the British in 1913 ranged between £3,714 million (US$18.1 billion) and £3,990 million (US$19.4 billion).[12] Overseas assets in 1913 were equivalent to 1.5 times GDP.[13] They amounted to 30 percent of national wealth and produced 9 percent of national income.[14]

Approximately 60 percent of British capital went to independent countries; self-governing colonies received most of the remaining 40 percent, which went to the Empire.[15] Less than 10 percent went to the dependent Empire.[16] British overseas investment was employed for social overhead purposes, taking the form of loans to governments and municipalities (30 percent) and holdings in railway securities (40 percent). Resource extraction, mainly mining (10 percent), public utilities (5 percent), and manufacturing (4 percent), were the other leading sectors.[17]

The world's second largest capital exporter before 1914 was France. Although capital outflows were slow in the 1870s, they gradually accelerated in the 1890s, reaching a peak on the eve of the war. Stocks of foreign securities rose steadily to around 45 billion francs (US$8.6 billion) in 1914, or one-sixth of national wealth. Government bonds made up half of foreign securities negotiated on the Paris stock exchange; the balance was split evenly between equity and debentures issued by companies.[18] In 1914 over 60 percent of French long-term investments were in European countries; Russia alone accounted for 25 percent.[19] Sector breakdown resembled that of Great Britain.

Germany arrived late to foreign investment. Less than one-tenth of its savings went abroad from 1900 to 1914.[20] Throughout the nineteenth century, the United States was a borrower, mainly in Britain. In 1914 British investors held five-eighths of foreign-owned stocks and bonds in the United States.[21] At the end of the nineteenth century, the United States became an international lender, even while it remained a net debtor owing US$3.7 billion. American investment was especially concentrated in FDI, most likely for the sake of proximity to foreign markets after it introduced mass-produced consumer items. Mass production and transnationalization went hand in hand, so that, by 1914, three-quarters of US accumulated assets overseas were concentrated in FDI.[22]

At the outset of the First World War, Britain held 44 percent of the world's stock of long-term foreign investments, while France held 20 percent, Germany 13 percent, and the United States 8 percent. War conditions radically transformed the international financial environment: belligerents had to liquidate assets overseas in order to finance the war, while debt repudiation meant outright losses. Britain sold securities worth about US$4 billion and lost another US$600 million to depreciation. The aggregate amount and the proportion of loss were higher for France due mainly to its decision to write off the Russian portfolio. Total French losses ranged between 28 billion and 33 billion francs (US$5.3 and US$6.3 billion), or 62 to 73 percent of its foreign assets.[23] Whereas continental Europe became a net debtor, the United States became a creditor country and the prime source of capital flows in the world. In 1919, US assets abroad amounted to US$6.5 billion, nearly double the 1914 level, excluding the US$10 billion it had granted as official loans to its wartime allies.[24]

The interwar period contrasted with the so-called golden age of the previous forty years. Alongside reconstruction, stabilization plans and debt relief were the order of the day. Inflation, budget shortfalls, external balance of payments deficits, unstable exchange rates, exchange controls, transfer difficulties, and defaults exemplified the financial disequilibrium

Table 1: Nominal value of capital invested abroad in 1914 (millions of current US$)

	Europe	European-peopled countries	Latin America	Asia	Africa	Total
United Kingdom	1,129	8,254	3,682	2,873	2,373	18,311
France	5,250	386	1,158	830	1,023	8,647
Germany	2,979	1,000	905	238	476	5,598
Other countries	3,377	632	996	1,913	779	7,697
United States	709	900	1,649	246	13	3,517
Total	13,444	11,172	8,390	6,100	4,664	43,770

Source: Angus Maddison, *The World Economy*, 106.

that made long-term investments risky. Short-term capital flows increased and became more volatile in response to currency fluctuations. International financial relations were in a state of turmoil, but they did not grind to a halt. Despite the reflux in long-term capital flows, it would be an exaggeration to describe this era as one of complete financial disintegration.[25] International flows resumed slowly in the interwar period, reaching a plateau at the end of the 1920s before falling off sharply. Outflows reached their highest level in 1928.

Table 2: Foreign issues (annual averages in millions of current US$)

	1919-23	1924-28	1929-31	1932-38
United States	531	1,142	595	28
United Kingdom	416	587	399	143

Source: United Nations, *Les mouvements*, 28.

The United States had over US$3 billion of FDI in Latin America and US$2 billion in Canada. In the case of investments made by the United Kingdom, the British Empire's share was US$3 billion, while Latin America took US$2.7 billion. One-fifth of US and less than one-tenth of UK FDI went to manufacturing, mainly in developed or partly developed countries.[26] Company financing tended to take the form of FDI. Meanwhile, both the United States and the United Kingdom became sources of government funds as nearly three-quarters of American and British portfolio investment went to governments and public agencies.[27] Foreign direct investment was probably stimulated by a dominant feature of the 1920s — exchange uncertainties. In the following decade, import restrictions, tariff barriers, quotas, and prohibitions threatened access to foreign customers, forcing exporters to open subsidiaries within the newly protected markets.

The Wall Street crash of 1929 and the ensuing economic depression led to wholesale defaults and sell-offs of depreciating assets. Exchange controls replaced free convertibility, leading to wildly erratic capital movements. Large amounts of floating capital travelled nervously to and fro in reaction to economic, monetary, or political anxiety. The flight of capital was followed by repatriation, then its return to the same foreign haven or a new one. The United States, for example, experienced waves of refugee capital seeking security. The interwar period did not lead to an increase in the stock of assets amassed abroad, so the historical trend of rising levels of long-term lending and investments was finally broken.

Table 3: Nominal value of capital invested abroad in 1938 (millions of current US$)

	Europe	European-peopled countries	Latin America	Asia	Africa	Total
United Kingdom	1,139	6,562	3,888	3,169	1,848	16,606
France	1,035	582	292	906	1,044	3,859
Germany	274	130	132	140	—	676
Netherlands	1,643	1,016	145	1,998	16	4,818
Other countries	1,803	1,143	820	101	646	4,513
United States	2,386	4,454	3,496	997	158	11,491
Japan	53	48	1	1,128	—	1,230
Total	8,333	13,935	8,774	8,439	3,712	43,193

Source: Angus Maddison, *The World Economy*, 106.

Following the Second World War, many governments gave priority to reconstituting the fabric of international economic relations. The Bretton Woods system was primarily a means of establishing a stable currency framework in order to promote trade. Its architects did not favour the international mobility of capital or the integration of financial markets; the crash of 1929 had left a legacy of mistrust of financial markets.[28] Key objectives of the system were regulation and safeguarding national economies from instability that originated abroad. Fixed exchange pegs were an incentive to maintain or reinforce statutory barriers to the cross-border movement of capital.

The resumption of the process of internationalization of capital was gradual. It took place as the long search for autonomy by formerly colonized peoples was culminating in political independence (decolonization) and a yearning for economic development. The global financial system after 1945 was as American-centred as the pre-1914 period had been European-centred. The United States became the primary source of capital once its banks had gained experience in the international transfer of funds. With limited convertibility of currencies, controls on exchange, and restrictions on capital issues in force practically everywhere, most capital transfers were at first officially arranged. Net private flows from the capital-exporting countries intensified in the 1950s.

Postwar private investment displayed several distinctive features, including the predominance of FDI over portfolio investments, the greater proportion of reinvested profits of branches and subsidiaries relative to injections of fresh imported capital, and flows towards industrial rather

Table 4: Net long-term private flows

	Annual average (millions of current US$)		Share (%)	
	1946-50	1951-59	1946-50	1951-59
United States	1,085	2,011	59	70
United Kingdom	600	530	33	18
Switzerland	77	197	4	7
Belgium-Luxembourg	67	89	4	3
Federal Republic of Germany	—	49	—	2
Sweden	—	2	—	—
Total	1,829	2,878	100	100

Source: United Nations, *Le courant international des capitaux à long terme et les donations publiques, 1959-1961* (1963), 42.

than developing countries. Foreign direct investment accounted for three-quarters of private outflows from the United States and the United Kingdom, with the two leading exporters representing 90 percent of the total.[29]

Private US capital yielded to official transfers in the developing world and went mainly to industrial countries. From 1951 to 1959, private long-term capital outflows from the United States amounted to US$18 billion, while official grants amounted to US$17 billion and official and private loans amounted to US$4 billion, for a total of US$39 billion, or 72 percent of net international flows.[30] American FDI went mainly to Canada until 1958, when the establishment of the Common Market began to divert capital to western Europe. British overseas investments continued to head mainly for sterling zone countries, with Australia taking precedence. Whereas FDI in developed countries went into manufacturing, most FDI in the developing world flowed to resource extraction, mainly oil. The importance of the periphery continued to be viewed in terms of natural resources.

Table 5: Accumulated stock of FDI by country of origin (billions of current US$ and percentage)

	1914		1938		1960		1971		1978	
	$	%	$	%	$	%	$	%	$	%
United States	2.7	18.5	7.3	27.7	32.8	49.2	82.8	48.1	162.7	41.4
Canada	0.2	1.0	0.7	2.7	2.5	3.8	6.5	3.8	13.6	3.5
United Kingdom	6.5	45.5	10.5	39.8	10.8	16.2	23.7	13.8	50.7	12.9
Germany	1.5	10.5	0.4	1.3	0.8	1.2	7.3	4.2	28.6	7.3
France	1.8	12.2	2.5	9.5	4.1	6.1	7.3	4.2	14.9	3.8
Belgium	–	–	–	–	1.3	1.9	2.4	1.4	5.4	1.4
Netherlands	–	–	–	–	7.0	10.5	13.8	8.0	28.4	7.2
Switzerland	–	–	–	–	2.0	3.0	9.5	5.5	27.8	7.1
Japan	–	–	0.8	2.8	0.5	0.7	4.4	2.6	26.8	6.8
All countries	14.3		26.4		66.7		172.1		392.8	

Source: John Dunning, "Changes in the Level and Structure of International Production," 87.

Surge in the Internationalization of Capital since 1975

In developed Western countries, the exhaustion of the postwar economic boom became manifest by the end of the 1960s. For three decades high levels of investment, aimed at mass production and encouraged by the prospects of continuing growth and profits, had met high levels of demand sustained by near-full employment, rising real income, state-run distributive mechanisms, and demand by the public sector. Then falling productivity, slower market growth, and stagnant profits upset the Fordist-Keynesian nexus. The stage was set for employers and state authorities to dismantle the macro-economic foundations of the postwar era and challenge the social "contract." Heightened competition for diminishing opportunities led to the reconfiguration of internal productive and distributive arrangements, resulting in greater regulation by market forces, stagnation of real wages for some, unemployment for others, more reliance on cost-cutting, profit-enhancing technology, and a greater urge to expand abroad as a way to offset sluggish internal growth. An outburst of cross-border capital movements ensued. The pace of externalization accelerated in both investor and recipient economies.

To cover US civilian and military spending, especially for the war in

Indochina, the US Treasury expanded the money supply by issuing great quantities of dollars during the 1950s and 1960s. Outside the United States there were more dollars (so-called Eurodollars) than gold in the United States to back them. In 1971, when the value of the dollar could

Table 6: Global capital flows (current US$ billions and percentage)

	1971-75	1976-80	1981-85	1986-90	1991-95	1995-2000
FDI	67 (19.7)	168 (11.1)	282 (14.9)	770 (17.8)	1,105 (19.9)	4,623 (28.0)
Portfolio investment liabilities	69 (20.5)	186 (12.3)	393 (20.7)	1,274 (29.5)	2,633 (47.5)	6,680 (40.5)
Other investment liabilities	203 (59.9)	1,159 (76.6)	1,219 (64.4)	2,273 (52.7)	1,803 (32.5)	5,199 (31.5)
Total inflows	339	1,513	1,895	4,316	5,541	16,503

Source: Yu Ching Wong and Charles Adams, "Trends in Global and Regional Foreign Direct Investment Flows," 19.

no longer be sustained, the US balance of trade became negative for the first time since 1893. As currencies were left to float against each other, the Bretton Woods system of fixed exchange rates unravelled between 1971 and 1973. The collapse of Bretton Woods marked a prelude to a gradual return to the unfettered movement of capital characteristic of the pre-1914 era.

Table 7: Composition of private long-term flows (percentage)

	1975-79	1980-84	1985-89	1990-94	1995-98
FDI	18	19	49	48	55
Portfolio	5	4	11	38	29
Loans	63	62	17	7	15
Other	14	15	23	7	–

Source: Ashoka Mody and Antu Panini Murshid, "Growing Up with Capital Flows," 5.

During the 1980s, many countries relaxed restrictions on cross-border capital flows. After Britain lifted exchange controls in 1979, other countries followed suit and reduced regulatory burdens and fees. Financial markets were increasingly liberalized, deregulated, and integrated into a worldwide network. As authorities permitted financial institutions to expand their range of activities, distinctions between banks and non-banks faded. The multiplication of financial instruments provided new opportunities for conducting transactions and moving capital.

As ways and means of transferring money multiplied, total volume of capital inflows and outflows rose sharply, both in absolute terms and relative to basic economic indices. Gross flows from the main industrial countries in the form of bonds and equities went from about US$100 billion in the first half of the 1980s to about US$850 billion in 1993.[31] Relative to their GDP, the stock of external assets and liabilities of the fourteen leading industrial countries nearly tripled between 1983 and 2001; equity, plus FDI assets and liabilities, taken alone, quadrupled.[32]

Major providers of capital changed little. Members of the "Triad" (North America, the European Union, and Japan) remained simultaneously the main investors in the world and the main recipients of one another's capital. Three-quarters to four-fifths of total flows occurred between developed countries. In the northern hemisphere, capital moved from east to west and from west to east. Only a trickle of capital flowed from north to south, mostly towards a few selected spots. Salient features of the period were the increasing role of European countries and Japan in the import and export (only export for Japan) of capital relative to the United States, the transformation of the United States into a net importer of capital, the concentration of inward flows in a handful of countries in eastern and southeastern Asia, as well as Latin America, and the relative abandonment by capital of the great majority of developing countries. The two main forms of capital movement after 1975 can be divided into portfolio flows and bank loans, and FDI.

Portfolio Flows and Bank Loans since the 1970s

The volume of portfolio investment (equities and bonds) rose from one-fifth of total outflows in the late 1970s to nearly one-half in the 1980s. In current values, the amount of cross-border equity transactions exceeded US$1,500 billion in 1989, compared to US$73 billion a decade earlier.[33] By the early 1990s, it had overtaken FDI and syndicated commercial bank lending, which had been prevalent in the 1970s. Institutional investors entrusted with colossal assets "went global" in their desire to buoy up investment returns.

The US market became highly attractive during the 1980s and 1990s as military spending swelled the public debt, control of inflation protected

Table 8: Equities investment flows (billions of current US$, annual averages)

	1975-79	1980-84	1985-89
Aggregate inflows (14 industrial countries)	3.6	10.8	23.1
United States	1.5	3.4	8.6
Japan	0.6	3.5	-9.1
9 major European countries	1.5	2.0	18.8
Aggregate outflows (14 industrial countries)	1.2	8.7	36.6
United States	0.2	1.7	4.1
Japan	0.1	0.2	9.2
9 major European countries	0.8	5.9	19.9

Source: Philip Turner, "Capital Flows in the 1980s: A Survey of Major Trends," 56.

Table 9: Bond investment flows (billions of current US$, annual averages)

	1975-79	1980-84	1985-89
Aggregate inflows (14 industrial countries)	8.8	17.1	102.4
United States	0.6	4.1	30.3
Japan	2.3	4.2	37.2
9 major European countries	3.9	5.9	29.3
Aggregate outflows (14 industrial countries)	16.7	40.1	147.3
United States	5.6	4.0	5.3
Japan	2.5	13.7	80.8
9 major European countries	8.6	21.7	59.6

Source: Philip Turner, "Capital Flows in the 1980s: A Survey of Major Trends," 58.

the value of investments, and stagnation of real wages shored up profits. A massive influx of Japanese funds went into US bonds, while equities drew investors from the United Kingdom and Japan. In 1984 the net international position (assets minus liabilities) of the United States became negative. Once again, the world's leading debtor lived beyond its means and faced a mounting trade imbalance. Foreign governments, especially in Asia, bought US bonds to uphold the dollar and sustain their export markets. Huge and recurring US government deficits drained world savings. At the end of 2002, foreigners owned more than $9 trillion of US assets, while US assets abroad fell just short of $6.5 trillion, leaving a negative net international investment position equivalent to a quarter of GDP.[34]

Because portfolio investment is based on the decisions of numerous agents and is, in principle, not aimed at control, it normally attracts less attention than unit lumpy (large amounts of capital per transaction) and sometimes spectacular (involving major or symbolic companies) FDI.

Portfolio visibility increases markedly when turbulence, instability, or crises occur. As this form of capital is relatively liquid and subject to the bandwagon effect, it is more rate-of-return sensitive than FDI, which normally has a longer time horizon. Stocks, bonds, and debentures can be acquired or unloaded more quickly than production facilities.

Since the 1970s liberalization and the greater interconnectedness of capital markets have intensified and perpetuated local crises. Herd behaviour by inadequately informed, risk-averse portfolio investors tended to become contagious. So-called shocks were followed by panic selling of securities of countries rightly or wrongly perceived to have the same creditworthiness as the source of the scare (known as the "spillover" or "neighbourhood effect"). Overnight, capital flows were reversed and economies whose fundamentals appeared sound suddenly suffered inflation and plunged into recession. Outflows deepened current account deficits, which led to monetary crises. Holders, fearful of devaluation, dumped the local currency, while runs on banks dried up deposits. Economies became highly vulnerable to externally triggered crises.

Until the late 1960s, international private capital tended to shun developing countries. Capital received by the Third World consisted largely of concessional lending, development assistance, and other official bilateral and multilateral aid. Private financial flows in the form of bank loans, which began in earnest in 1969, were fuelled by US money creation and the booming Eurodollar market. As domestic inflation and international commodity prices skyrocketed, developing countries became interested potential borrowers. After 1974 bank loans received a new impetus from deposits made by oil-exporting countries. These deposits were recycled into syndicated commercial bank loans, mostly to official borrowers such as governments and public-sector companies.

As bank credits replaced bond finance, governments of the South turned to foreign loans to finance their development programs. After several decades of circulating primarily in the developed world, private capital was returning to the Third World, where it had gone in appreciable amounts until commodity prices plummeted as a result of the Great Depression. Such flows were in keeping with established patterns of internationalization. Aggregate (official and private) net long-term resource flows to developing countries, in current values, rose from US$16 billion in 1970 to about US$75 billion in the 1980s, then they rose steeply to US$237 billion in 1995.[35]

When the United States raised interest rates to control inflation, the

Table 10: Gross amount of stock of foreign capital in developing countries (billions of US$ and percentage)

	1870	1914	1950	1973	1998
Total in current prices	4.1	19.2	11.9	172.0	3,590.2
Total in 1990 prices	40.1	235.4	63.2	495.2	3,030.7
% Stock/GDP of developing countries	8.6	32.4	4.4	10.9	21.7

Source: Angus Maddison, The World Economy, 136.

cost of servicing external debt became prohibitive for developing countries. As the dollar's exchange rate rose and the industrialized world experienced the worst recession in fifty years, export markets weakened and commodity prices fell. Caught in the cyclical downswing, developing countries saw export earnings plummet. In August 1982, Mexico, one of the largest borrowers, suspended payments on its debt, sending shock waves through the banking world. Major institutions in the developed countries had lent to Mexico and were highly exposed. By the end of 1983, over thirty countries were in arrears. Commercial bank credits dried up and private capital flows to developing countries ebbed. The few credits that were extended went to rescheduling or refunding previous loans. External liabilities of less developed countries measured in current values soared from US$751 billion in 1981 to US$1,351 trillion in 1991.[36] Private international financing of developing countries resumed in 1987 and increased by more than 150 percent between 1990 and 1996.[37] Developing countries' share of global FDI flows rose from 12 percent in 1990 to 38 percent in 1995.[38]

The structure of international flows towards the South had changed in at least seven ways. First, the private share of total aggregate flows, which had fallen from nearly one-half in 1970 to one-third in 1987, rose to four-fifths by 1994.[39] Second, the share of bank lending fell considerably, while FDI and portfolio (equity and bonds) flows made up nine-tenths of the intake of foreign private capital.[40] Third, portfolio flows, barely noticeable until 1987, grew in real terms to US$82 billion in 1996 and more than sevenfold from 1989 to 1993.[41] Accounting for more than one-third of total inflows, they nearly overtook FDI. Fourth, in the portfolio portion of total private flows, equity was more important than bonds.[42] Fifth, equity (FDI and portfolio) weighed more than debt (bank and portfolio). Sixth, the public sector gave way to the private sector as the main recipient of foreign capital. Seventh, flows increasingly took place through capital market channels. As for autonomy, it remained largely out of reach as the recently decolonized South remained enmeshed in the hegemonic workings of international finance.

The restoration of investment flows to developing countries came at a high price. Banks, the IMF, and the World Bank rescued several debtor countries, but they also pressed them to restructure their economies, espouse liberalization, and adopt market-based policies. With the return to full-scale borrowing from banks no longer a possibility, attracting investment in the private sector appeared to be the only way out of deepening impoverishment. Portfolio investment in Mexico exploded from US$500 million in 1989 to US$17 billion in 1993.[43] A high proportion of capital inflows was made up either of "hot money" in search of interest rate differentials or foreign exchange market inefficiencies, both of which were prone to quick reversals. When the influx upset the Mexican balance of payments, the exchange rate of the national currency came under downward pressure. The devaluation of the peso in December 1994 spread panic and caused the stock market to plunge. A massive sell-off forced the central bank to float the peso, which lost 40 percent of its dollar value.

The Mexican fiasco was the harbinger of crises to come in the era of globalizing finance before a period of recovery then set the stage for the surge of FDI in the late 1990s. Asia, once held up by pundits in the early 1990s as a model of open, foreign capital-driven, export-oriented growth, would become a financial storm centre by the end of the 1990s. Capital poured into Thailand during the 1990s, predominantly because of borrowing by banks and financial institutions. Bank credit soared and capital inflows pushed up the real effective exchange rate of the baht by more than 25 percent. Over the same period, Indonesia's rupiah also appreciated by 25 percent, while the Korean won gained 12 percent.[44] Asian currencies, pegged to the US dollar, were overvalued, reducing to a standstill the exports on which the economy had come to depend. Excess capacity plagued the export industries. Slower growth burst a real estate bubble that resulted from intensive office-building construction. Declining property values weakened banks and finance companies holding non-performing loans.

The dream of the so-called Asian miracle soon became a nightmare. The baht came under speculative attack in 1997. Official devaluation spun out of control and the exchange rate fell precipitously as panic selling continued. Since credits to financial institutions were denominated in foreign currencies, currency depreciation turned into a banking crisis as foreign investors withdrew in panic. The Thai shock spread to neighbouring countries. Anticipating turmoil, foreign capital poured out of the region in June 1997. Speculation hit the Philippine peso, the Korean won, the Malaysian ringgit, and the Indonesian rupiah, causing a free fall of these currencies. The IMF had to devise the largest bailout scheme in its history, and capital flight led to mass layoffs, skyrocketing prices, a drop in the standard of living, and political instability.

In 1998 the epicentre of the international financial crisis shifted from Asia to Russia and Brazil, both of which suffered from overvalued currencies and budget deficits. Foreign capital made a mass exit from both countries before the value of the currency collapsed and official devaluation occurred. Ecuador's turn came in 2000, Turkey's and Argentina's came in 2001, and Uruguay's came in 2002. Developing countries suddenly began experiencing their worst financial crises since the nineteenth century. Investment booms went bust as colossal amounts of foreign capital rushed in and out of receiving economies, jeopardizing what little autonomy developing countries had managed to achieve during the era of decolonization.

Foreign Direct Investment

Foreign direct investment deserves special attention because it lies at the heart of the internationalization of production, often considered the embodiment of globalization. While portfolio investment, which is controlled by transnational corporations (TNCs), has increased at the same rate as FDI, the potential of FDI to foster the integration of the world economy suggests the need to pay close attention to its soaring volume and widening geographic scope as old and new forms of capital flows expand simultaneously. This section examines the overall growth of FDI, the distribution of flows and stocks by geographic region, and the origin of TNCs.

Since the 1990s, expectations of economic growth in different parts of the world spurred the movement of FDI outwards in search of positional advantage. Technological advances, a key feature of globalization, helped accelerate this trend. The combination of information processing and communications technologies, for example, reduced or abolished the barriers of distance and time, allowing more direct management of far-off businesses and a greater presence in far-away markets. The enhancement of the technological component as a competitive asset meant

Table 11: Annual growth rates (percentage)

	1986-90	1991-95	1996-2000	2001	2002
GDP of foreign affiliates	17.3	6.7	7.9	14.7	6.7
Global GDP	10.8	5.6	1.3	-0.5	3.4
GFCF	13.4	4.2	1.0	-3.9	1.3

Source: UNCTAD, World Investment Report 2003, 3.

escalating research and development costs, shorter product lifespans, and a consequent need for wider markets to ensure adequate turnover. Favourable institutional arrangements, specifically market-oriented policies, also contributed to the flows of FDI.

Some 63,000 parent TNCS — a sixfold increase over thirty years — and their 690,000 foreign affiliates managed one-quarter of the world's GDP of about US$32 trillion in 1997. The GDP of foreign affiliates alone, that part of output that can be associated with international production, tripled between 1982 and 1994. By 2001, TNCS controlled 11 percent of global GDP, which was up from 5 percent in 1982 and significantly higher than the growth of world GDP and gross fixed capital formation.[45]

Since 1987 global sales by foreign affiliates grew relative to the exports of goods and services by a factor of 1.2 to 1.3, thus outweighing exports as the dominant mode of servicing foreign markets. From sales of US$3 trillion in 1980, they climbed to US$14 trillion in 1999, which was almost two times that of global exports of goods and services.[46] The tendency to view FDI as synonymous with TNCS and international production, however, may be misleading. Foreign affiliates of TNCS often raise funds locally, a practice that lowers the proportion of FDI in their equity and makes the value of their assets greater than FDI. An investment recorded as FDI may be, at most, marginally foreign. Affiliates also seek equity or loans on international markets. Investment in foreign affiliates, which amounted to US$1.4 trillion in 1996, was four times the value of FDI inflows. Assets of foreign affiliates worldwide are estimated to be three to four times the amount of FDI stock.[47]

Foreign direct investment is a cyclical phenomenon: it accelerates in periods of rapid growth in developed countries, and it slows down when their growth is sluggish. Generally, upward movement of rates of change in FDI inflows occurred in 1970-74, 1977-81, 1984-90, and 1993-2000. Sharp downturns were felt in 1975-76, 1982-83, 1991, and after 2001. Whatever the extent of the bulges and troughs, levels of FDI maintained a consistently upward direction. Cyclical booms and busts occurred, but levels of FDI flows were higher than in the previous period of growth or recession. This point is illustrated by the fact that the nominal value (at current prices) of inward and outward flows of FDI worldwide tripled during the 1980s, doubled between 1993 and 1997, and more than doubled between 1997 and 2000. By 2001 inflows were ten times the yearly average of the 1980s.[48] Lest sight be lost of relative volumes, it must be remembered that inflows represented no more than 0.4 percent of world GDP in 1980 and 1985 and 4.4 percent in 2000. Moreover, portfolio flows were greater than FDI flows even during the peak years of FDI flows at the end of the 1990s.[49]

A yardstick of transnationalization is provided by the ratio of flows of FDI relative to gross fixed capital formation (GFCF) or productive capacity. The role of these flows rose significantly in the 1980s and 1990s, even if a reversal set in with the 2001 recession.[50] Foreign direct investment stocks can be a measure of the investment that underpins international production. Assets accumulated under the governance of TNCs tripled during the 1980s and tripled again in the 1990s.[51] Relative to global GDP, the importance of FDI stocks grew by a factor of 1.6 in the fifteen years from 1980 to 1995 and by a factor of 2.2 in the subsequent seven years.[52]

Notwithstanding the apparently triumphal march to international production, caution is in order. Transnationalization is an index of ownership; it implies greater integration but not necessarily increased production. Cross-border mergers and acquisitions (CBMAs) became the preferred means of carrying out FDI. The flurry of CBMAs in the late 1980s turned into a flood in the late 1990s. The aggregate value of CBMAs never represented more than 3.5 percent (in 2000) of GDP, but it constituted about 60 percent of FDI inflows from 1987 to 1990 and 40 percent of FDI inflows from 1991 to 1995.[53] While CBMAs meant further concentration of ownership and management, their contribution to expanded production, greater productivity, and better performance is not established. In fact, they could have been counterproductive if the deals were fire sales or if they crowded out local capital.[54] Takeovers may even have led to a scaling down or a dismantling of existing facilities.

Although the discussion of FDI has so far highlighted significant changes, the full story is not without contradictions and uncertainties. Examination of flows reveals more stability than movement in the proportional distribution of FDI around the world.[55] Some change is occurring, but it does not foretell a major redistribution or reorientation of

FDI, and it does not seem irreversible. Despite fluctuations, developed countries dominated in all respects. Three-quarters of FDI flowed into developed countries (mainly the Triad), and nine-tenths of exiting FDI originated from these countries. Among the developing countries, the forty-nine least developed received minuscule inflows. A distinguishing feature of FDI was its geographic concentration. The top thirty host countries accounted for 93 percent of inflows and 90 percent of inward stocks; the top thirty home countries accounted for 99 percent of outflows and 99 percent of outward stocks.[56]

In the 1970s western Europe supplanted the United States as the home of the largest flows of outgoing FDI. Inflows to the United States rose in the 1970s, when the lower exchange rate of the dollar made US assets attractive. Western Europe became a more important venue for foreign capital than the United States at the end of the 1980s, even when the United States was generally the principal recipient and home country. There were exceptions. In the 1980s the United Kingdom was the largest outward investor; its participation in CBMAs in the United States contributed to making the United States the largest recipient country.

Rapidly rising amounts of FDI, as well as foreign portfolio investment, flowed into developing countries in the 1990s, mostly in a few countries located in Latin America and East and Southeast Asia. The five largest host countries — Mexico, Brazil, China, Malaysia, and Argentina — received more than three-fifths of FDI inflows; the ten largest host countries received more than three-quarters of FDI inflows. Less than 1 percent went to the hundred smallest recipients. Africa usually took a distant third place behind Asia and Latin America.

The Latin American and the Caribbean share of inflows and outflows in 2002 did not change radically from twenty years earlier. The low intake of the 1980s, stemming from the debt crisis, was more than made up for in the 1990s. Foreign direct investment amounted to three-fifths of total foreign capital inflows of US$107 billion in 1997.[57] South and Southeast Asia's involvement in FDI increased notably. The half dozen "tigers" garnered the bulk of Asia's FDI. China, the largest host country in the developing world, received the lion's share of inward FDI — almost half of South and Southeast Asia's total from the late 1990s — and Hong Kong was the main source of outward FDI. The growing number of countries in the region involved in international capital flows was noteworthy.

In the early 1990s, nearly seven-tenths of the FDI flows out of East and Southeast Asia were intraregional. The pattern was similar in other developing countries: the main recipients of outflows were other developing countries. Insufficient experience of internationalization and lack of means to confront stiff competition from the firms of developed economies gave precedence to more familiar markets where transaction costs (knowledge of local conditions, internal transportation and communications costs, regulations and standards, etc.) were lower.

The predominance of developed countries in FDI stocks was just as pronounced as it was for flows.[58] In fact, the relative size of the portfolio of FDI assets located in the developed world grew during the past two decades. About three-fifths of inward FDI stock was in the developed countries and nearly nine-tenths of outward stock worldwide was owned by companies based in those countries. Western Europe increased its share of outward stock from two-fifths to over one-half of the world's total, while the American portion shrank from two-fifths to one-fifth. The United States retained the largest foreign portfolio held by a single country and improved its position as the most important single venue for assets owned by foreign companies.

The rest of the portrait is mixed. While foreign investment by developing countries remained at around one-tenth of the world's total outward stock, relatively less inward stock was located in those countries. The picture is one of unevenness and sharp contrasts, from overwhelming concentration in developed countries to the increasing predominance of China and the marginalization of the least developed countries. No less salient was the geographic concentration of TNCs in one part of the world. More than 90 percent of parent firms and 60 percent of affiliates were based in developed countries.[59] The composition of the hundred largest TNCs remained stable.[60] Between 95 and 100 were headquartered in developed countries, and there was little change in the national distribution or the identity of firms. The foreign assets of the top fifty developing country TNCs represented 2.5 percent of the foreign assets of the fifty top TNCs in the world in 1994 and 8.2 percent in 2001.[61] Major non-Triad companies were transnationalizing, but the preponderance of developed country TNCs remained unchallenged. Real erosion of their dominance has not occurred.

More than thirty years ago, the historian Judd Polk broached the idea of international production, which has since become the economic lynchpin of the globalization paradigm.[62] Since then, scholars have conceptualized several stages of integration. Internationalization is viewed as proceeding in a linear sequential movement. Trade constitutes "shallow" integration because it can be terminated at short notice. The export of goods is complemented by the opening of trading affiliates or distribution outlets in foreign markets. In order to continue drawing on a brand name, forestall local competition, jump a tariff, or benefit from a firm-specific advantage, FDI occurs and gives rise to production on a transnational scale. Simple horizontal strategies involve the opening abroad of affiliates or subsidiaries that replicate the facilities of the parent firm in smaller shape or assemblage (e.g., screwdriver plants). Acting as stand-alone clones of the parent firm, the advantage of affiliates and subsidiaries lies in their close proximity to the market of the host country. Automobile companies such as General Motors and Ford adopted this strategy. Simple integration moves to a higher stage when firms begin outsourcing and subcontracting ("externalization") to their foreign affiliates for some of their inputs. The affiliate produces intermediate goods, not final marketable products, and is, therefore, not autonomous. Simple vertical integration relocates portions of the productive process to the host country, especially labour-intensive tasks. Its main determinant is not the host country's domestic market but lower-cost factors of production, especially labour and export infrastructures such as transportation. With the improvement of communications, management over long distances of fragmented labour-intensive functions becomes possible. Simple vertical integration is often part of an export drive aimed at the international market. It also occurs in accessing location-bound natural resources. For example, Adidas, Nike, and many producers of electronic components rely on this form of asset- or resource-seeking FDI.

With complex integration, all activities are potentially transferable to foreign affiliates operating under the common governance of parent TNCs. The value chain is divided into discrete functions. Production is dispersed geographically according to the criteria of economy and efficiency. Intrafirm linkages are strong, and the level of integration is high. Improvements in communications and information technologies allow central coordination of far-flung interconnected units of the firm. Lower transportation costs and less stringent trade regimes facilitate mobility of inputs and intrafirm trade (internalization of market functions). More uniform consumption patterns, in the sense of demand for similar commodities, favour mass production on a global scale. As trade barriers are lowered, national markets tend to be viewed as part of regional markets.

Deep integration mobilizes FDI towards intangibles or created assets, such as trained human resources, infrastructures, and solid institutions, which are needed to take advantage of changing technologies. The primary motivation of firms changes from seeking markets and natural resources to exploiting competitive advantages.[63] Deep integration is highly oligopolistic and competition-driven, as exemplified by the computer industry. Under this kind of integration, TNCs tend to replace multinational, local-market strategies with global, world-market approaches.[64] Efficiency-seeking, high value-added sectors, such as the biotechnology and pharmaceutical industries, engage in this most recent form of FDI.

Conclusion: From Then to Now

Gross outflow of long-term capital (FDI and portfolio) in the world was 3.3 percent of GDP in 1989-91, which was up from 0.6-1.1 percent in the 1960s and 2 percent in 1984. However, the increase was in fact a recovery. The proportion had been at least 3 percent at the preceding peak in 1913. For the developed Western world, stock of FDI stood at 14 to 19 percent of GDP in 1913 and 12.9 percent in 1996.[65] Rewards stemming from capital flows are still by no means a two-way street, as capital moves mostly from the developed to the developing countries and flows between developing countries are virtually non-existent. The identity of the chief exporters and importers of capital is basically the same. Advanced countries retain skill- and technology-intensive activities; less developed areas are assigned assembly and packaging.[66] In some ways, the international division of labour has not changed markedly from the colonial era. On a world scale, integration remains a hierarchic, top-down process that is closer to continued internationalization by the same developed countries and TNCs than it is to a level global environment.

While the overall picture at the end of the twentieth century is one of structural imbalance, as it was at the end of the nineteenth century, the characteristics and nature of the imbalance are not identical because FDI is now the spearhead of internationalization. The greater importance of FDI, the transnationalization of firms, and international production imply an economic environment at variance with previous phases of internationalization. Developing countries are not formally prevented from partaking in industrial activities. However modest and lopsided, international production is a growing phenomenon. Productive systems are being harnessed and made to intermesh or integrate with each other. Another important change is that industry and services have become more important than natural resources. Reversing nineteenth-century patterns, capital now flows mostly to capital-rich countries. The North-South component in capital flows is proportionately less significant than in the past, as the developing world has become even more marginalized. Capital flows are now mostly a North-North or rich-rich affair, and developed countries are, more than ever, each other's main creditors and debtors. Asset holders have become liability holders, hence the foreswearing of overt protectionism and restrictions.[67] Two-way capital movements, normally considered a hallmark of globalization, are more visible among countries in the North than between countries of the North and the South. In short, North-South integration continues the patterns set in the nineteenth century, but it now takes second place behind North-North integration.

Issues of autonomy appear to have been fairly clear-cut in the past, when insolvent borrower countries that lacked the military means to defend themselves were forced by the hegemonic powers to accept debt-collecting agencies representing foreign creditors. By earmarking specific revenues for servicing external debt, these "money doctors" essentially stripped these countries of their sovereignty. To achieve autonomy meant breaking ties of dependency and widening the range of economic activities, specifically with respect to industry. Today, this type of internal interference has been replaced by the authority of supraterritorial agencies such as the IMF and the World Bank. Autonomy today seems to mean no more than moving up the rungs of the "value ladder" designed by TNCs. Disengagement and even distancing seem to have fallen out of current thinking. A globalizing world skewed to North-North relations faces an issue previously confined to the developing world. Does integration leave room for autonomy? Does autonomy mean setting limits to forces of globalization, such as returning to the management of capital flows or participating fully in them with the hope of bargaining one's way to advantages? Does it mean intensifying capital outflows in order to partake in internationalization and globalization? Are all three avenues recommended? Competition adds an element of friction as the globalizing economy is configured and reconfigured. Like globalization itself, the quest for a meaning to attribute to autonomy is unfinished business.

chapter 7   Global Industrial Enclaves:
               Company Towns and Export-
               Processing Zones Compared,
               1900-2000

               Neil White

Why did people stay in company towns? Some couldn't afford to move ...
Others stayed because the beauty and safety of the rural settings compensated for
the isolation. And still others remained because the remoteness created a sense of
community. For some company towns, that sense of community continued to live
on decades after the towns closed and people scattered around the country.
                                    —Linda Carlson, *Company Towns*
                                           of the Pacific Northwest

Erlinda has worked in the Philippines' Bataan Export Processing Zone for years
and has experienced first-hand the exploitation of the new global division of labour.
Erlinda was harassed on the assembly line and thrown out of work. After work, she
returns to a ramshackle fringe community where families depend on pay that is less
than half the national subsistence wage. When Erlinda organized female workers
harassment increased. In one case, the Filipino military sprayed her and other strik-
ers with red ink so they could be easily identified. In the past few years, Erlinda has
seen the campaign against organized labour turn particularly violent. Assault, ab-
duction, rape, and murder of female activists go regularly unpunished. These are the
"work hazards" in the Filipino enclaves of neoliberalism.
                                    —Adapted from Jane Margold,
                                    "Reformulating the Compliant Image"

EXPORT-PROCESSING ZONES (EPZS) ARE integral to the new global
division of labour and neoliberal capitalism. In the Third World, export-
oriented industrialization and the spread of manufacturing enclaves set

apart from national labour laws and committed to flexible production present a new economic paradigm of development.[1] In 1986 the International Labour Organization (ILO) estimated that there were 166 EPZs with 1.3 million workers worldwide. In 2000 those numbers had ballooned to 845 EPZs with approximately 27 million employees. Those numbers have increased since 2000.[2] "Flexible production" is the corporations' primary rationale for EPZs. In sanctioning flexible production, host governments hope to gain access to foreign investment, encourage industrial development, and reduce poverty, but the flexibility of capital, production, and labour precludes labour unions, job security, and benefits. The transnational corporations (TNCs) that own and contract out to EPZ plants are not responsible for the improvement of the sprawling slum communities that grow in response to instant industrialization, and investment-desperate Third World host governments prefer courting TNCs to spending on social programs. Residents of EPZ communities are left to fend for themselves.

In the early twentieth century the development context of the industrializing West was markedly different. Welfare capitalism that sought to protect workers and communities from the vagaries of the free market was the development paradigm. In terms of industrial enclaves, the welfare capitalist corollary to contemporary neoliberal EPZs was the planned company town. Originally planted on the resource frontiers of Western nations, company towns were laboratories for a variety of practical welfare measures. Resource extractive corporations hoped that the essential workers would settle in the wilderness and stabilize production and profits. Residents of planned company towns, in turn, fostered bottom-up community identities. Despite dependency, residents often achieved a measure of class- and community rights–based autonomy.

Export-producing zones and company towns are expressions of neoliberal and welfare capitalism, but at base both are creations of global capital and experience intense global-local pressures.[3] Comparison of the two highlights a shift in the ways capital enlists political authority for expansion or, more specifically, the temporal acceleration, spatial expansion, and local deepening of the ways capital interacts with political authority to expand neoliberal strategies of production and economic growth. The pace of transnational sourcing, political regimes' openness to plugging portions of their national territories into the global economic web of barrier-free production, and the neglect of citizens' basic needs and rights signals a contemporary convergence of interests between increasingly fetterless capital's heightened ability to enlist state power and Third World states' determination to entice global capital to its shores with promises of state-sanctioned competitive advantages.[4]

Historical comparison also shows how the concept and practice of autonomy has changed over time as well as differences in the ways globalization has been engaged and contested at particular historical moments in dependent industrial enclaves. In company towns, class-based unionism and residents' appeals to shared beliefs in individual and community rights constituted a strategy for achieving autonomy. In EPZs, residents often work out how global-local pressures can be accommodated or resisted in their specific locales through a different array of activist responses that tend to encompass more immediate concerns, such as decent housing and safety from workplace harassment. Also, EPZ residents' conceptions of autonomy tend to stem from cultural and religious traditions, the struggle for gender equality, and perceived relative improvements to social status instead of universalist class and human rights considerations.[5] Put simply, autonomies differ over time and from place to place.

Linked to the question of shifting autonomies, the in situ contestation of globalizing trends over time differs in company towns and EPZs. The autonomies of class and community rights in company towns formed an accepted mode of engagement with agents of global capitalism, while corporate belief in the benefits of socio-economic planning created bargaining power for company town residents. In EPZs, that welfarist bargain is non-existent. Horizontally organized residential self-help associations, more than international labour unions, are the order of the day in the "frontier zones," where international rights discourse is swept away by ineffectual governments, unaccountable corporations, and careening development.[6]

The EPZ experience varies, and there is no single remedy for change. Researchers should be attuned to local realties by conducting more empirical research on the ground. A locally defined measure of autonomy should be encouraged and worked out in specific locales before effective transnational negotiation or resistance can be sought. For a genuine start, we need to relate to workers and residents on their own terms and more readily incorporate local experiences and concepts of autonomy into "hybridized" analyses and programs for change.[7]

Methodological Considerations

Broad comparisons often lead to simplification. The space and time constraints of this study led to a realization that downplaying variation is problematic. Manuel Castells cautions against oversimplification and "grand theory" building and advocates a humble but effective strategy of empirical comparison and critical discussion.[8] Each case in this study has historical and contemporary peculiarities that distinguish it from the others, while development is uneven over time and from place to place. My conclusions are intended primarily to foster debate.

Another concern was to avoid what Arif Dirlik calls "privileging the global," or assuming that global developments, be they TNC penetration or expanding transnational protest organizations, should be the primary focus of analysis.[9] Company towns and EPZs are creations of global capital, but they are not placeless spaces where abstracted global trends intersect. Neither type of enclave could exist without people working and living in them. Researchers view EPZs as analytical borderlands,[10] but for residents they are real communities. Unfortunately, there is a paucity of ground-level studies of mobilizing for autonomy in and around EPZs. Gender analyses constitute the most prevalent and instructive local case studies, but the extant literature is scattered among disciplines. This situation is telling in and of itself. Global sourcing chains are opaque and transnational corporation–host government secrecy regarding EPZs adds a formidable barrier to understanding. Conceptual fragmentation among academic and grassroots commentators makes analysis even harder. There must be a greater attempt to avoid "unnecessary jargon and disempowering obfuscation" in describing the EPZ experience.[11]

Community and Autonomy

The terms *community* and *autonomy* are nebulous and can be used in various ways. In this chapter, community refers to place-based groups of people, or residents, who inhabit the same locality.[12] This is different from space-based communities like networks of activists in NGOs or corporations that operate at a global level abstracted from everyday life. Place-based communities can encompass smaller interest-based groups and be related to and affected by transnational communities, but they are defined by a shared, lived experience.[13] They constitute the immediate experience of global trends played out on the ground in everyday reality. This makes local communities the locus of incipient forms of hegemonic contestation and accommodation.[14] Arif Dirlik qualifies the definition, arguing that local places are best described as ongoing projects.[15] Communities exist in real places but are not autochthonous, static, or linear in development. They are flexible and porous, and residents exhibit shifting practical strategies and tactics for survival.[16]

By extension, community autonomies are the means of securing a decent, locally defined measure of control over or accommodation with outside influences.[17] It is not the intention of this chapter to privilege the local over the global. Local community autonomies are not inherently "good" or progressive. Along with unionization, cooperatives, and other community projects that most would consider positive developments, autonomies can be xenophobic and/or violently exclusionary. Community autonomies are subjective and transient.

Company Towns and EPZs from the Top Down

Canadian sociologist Rex Lucas defines company towns as communities of fewer than thirty thousand inhabitants, in which 75 percent of the workforce is directly tied to one industry and its related services.[18] In the early twentieth century, corporations created single-industry communities on the vast resource frontiers of many Western countries. Planned company towns were primarily a British invention. The popular revolutions that shook the political foundations of continental Europe from 1789 to the second half of the nineteenth century and the growing militancy of British workers instilled a deep fear of social unrest among the British elite, convincing some of the necessity of planning for the well-being of workers. Town-planning experiments by utopian Socialists like Robert Owen provided British capitalists with a model for their own less-than-revolutionary attempts to create quiescent workers.[19] The nineteenth-century liberal project of unregulated global trade and production was replaced haltingly and unevenly by a new emphasis on the social responsibility of businesses and political regimes.[20] From the 1910s to the 1930s, the focus on comprehensively planned industrial hamlets was popularized throughout much of North America and western Europe. It involved a combination of the growing willingness of business and government officials to plan to insulate workers and consumers from the vagaries of the free market, a burgeoning epistemic community of mobile professional planners, government incentives for planning, and cheap building materials.[21]

Most often, planned company towns were designed around extractive industries with isolated resources that required numerous skilled employees permanently on site to maintain production. Vertically integrated extractive corporations often borrowed from popular planning ideas, constructing and administering all aspects of community life from town layout to sewerage and recreation.[22] In Canada alone there were approximately 630 single-industry communities in the early 1970s, with a combined population of nearly one million residents.[23] Many planned towns emerged from a welfare capitalist approach to development. Capitalists, politicians, and planners considered work, family, and community well-being integral parts of prosperous businesses and stable economies. There was an acceptance among all levels of society in most First World nations that social planning was necessary and laudable.

After the Second World War, the protracted Cold War kept welfare capitalist measures in place, but the economic crisis of the early and mid-1970s convinced many economists that the welfare state, state utilities, and regulated economies fostered waste and inefficiencies. Governments in North America trimmed social spending. More generally, political authorities in states around the world — acting on complex combinations of economic coercion by international financial institutions and the proactive enlistment of foreign capital for development and poverty reduction — lowered barriers to foreign trade and investment.[24] Responding to opportunities to attract investment capital in a deregulated business environment, several governments established EPZs.[25] Puerto Rico and Ireland were pioneers after the Second World War. Advisers and managers familiar with these initial forays into export-oriented production helped set up plants in other "developing" nations, resulting in prolonged periods of EPZ growth in Taiwan, Korea, and Mexico during the 1960s.[26]

It was not until the economic downturn of the 1970s, however, that global sourcing and EPZ development became the new paradigm of production for transnational corporations. First World governments began to collectively push for a new liberal global economy during and after the OPEC oil crisis and the concomitant stagflation of their economies. First World governments and global financial institutions like the International Monetary Fund (IMF) and World Bank began lobbying developing Third World nations to institute deregulatory neoliberal policies in order to receive financial assistance. The economic penetration of formerly insulated economies sometimes took the form of outsourcing First World manufacturing to poorer Third World regions in which production was cheaper. As Arjun Appadurai sums it up, there emerged a "common openness to market processes of regimes otherwise varied in their political, religious, and historical traditions."[27] A creeping and uneven socio-economic shift occurred from national welfarism to global neoliberalism, as much as liberalism had been interrupted by economic interventionism in the early twentieth century.[28]

Export-processing zones go by several different names — *maquiladoras* in Latin America and special economic zones (SEZs) in China — but all have comparable traits. Transnational corporations lease plant space directly from host governments or contract production to numerous smaller companies that operate in the zones. A variety of consumer goods, such as clothing, auto parts, and computer hardware, are assembled on production lines and then exported. Considered docile and nimble by employers, females are the preferred labour force in the zones, constituting between 75 and 90 percent of employees.[29] These global commodity chains are designed to be dynamic and flexible so corporations can shop around for the lowest cost production and diversify their assembly contracts.[30] Host governments regularly award sizeable concessions to TNCs and their contractors, and businesses and governments collude to keep labour costs as low as possible.[31]

Physically, EPZs are often fenced compounds of multiple assembly plants. On the ground, flexible production means a lack of concern for employees who work long hours at low wages. As in the company town, EPZ employees and residents are dependent on global capital, but unlike company towns there is a marked lack of planning in EPZs. The residents of EPZ squatter communities often live amidst overcrowding and suffer a near total lack of services. Population growth contributes to unchecked urban sprawl and compounds the problems of neglect.

Many have commented on the state's role in enabling flexible export-oriented production.[32] The state not only played a major role in company towns, it also played a role in EPZ development, but in a different way. It would be impossible for today's offshore industries to exist without state sanction.[33] National governments frame rules in which TNCs operate. Governments encouraged companies to build and administer comprehensively planned communities in the early twentieth century; today's regional and local governments help recruit EPZ workers, while national governments advertise their country's locational and productive advantages in sourcing nations. Third World governments also provide essential physical and communication infrastructure for the zones, while neglecting the lived environment of the very citizens who are essential to the functioning of the zones.[34] This utter lack of social planning represents a new form of capital-political alliance.

In cases of unrest in and around EPZs, the state's role as facilitator for capital is most pronounced.[35] The monopolization of violence by nation-states ensures generally quiescent workforces. This field of contestation is often overshadowed in the literature by a concentration on the seemingly unchecked ability of TNCs to do as they please on the ground. State agency and control are not relics of the past. Capital enlists their all-important support in framing the legislative and practical rules for EPZ growth in particular localities, and it counts on that support to quell unrest. The very legitimacy of corporate penetration and development depends on the collusion of host governments. In most ways, this collusion is not an example of a new bargain between capital and political authority as much as it represents the harder bargain driven by highly mobile capital as it deals with poor, geographically fixed national governments. The *forms* of state collusion in the global, neoliberal economy contrast with those employed in earlier welfare states, particularly in terms of the breadth of support for capital and lack of social planning. Yet state legitimation remains a central organizing principle.

Autonomies in Dependent Industrial Enclaves

Critics frequently portray company towns as little more than labour camps. Isolation, a lack of diversity in employment, and single-company control over work and domestic life have made this notion a prevalent image. However, there was a considerable range of dependence, exploitation, negotiation, and resistance in single-industry communities. Planned company towns were designed to attract and retain a workforce. On the shop floor, companies grudgingly accepted independent trade unions, particularly among skilled employees, when agitation threatened high turnover. For unskilled workers, organizing was difficult because companies considered them easily replaceable. Companies often set up their own unions to deal with some of the concerns of unskilled employees. The company union became synonymous with top-down industrial paternalism and a mask for increased exploitation of labour.

With extensive town and social planning of communities, early twentieth-century company unionism exemplified capital's practical concern with bettering the lives of skilled male workers and their families through planned, top-down measures.[36] An international class-based discourse recognized the importance of unions, and many companies genuinely tried to aid their employees. Company unions in single-industry communities were similar in form but not nearly as cynically employed as subordinate unions in EPZs, provided, of course, that the EPZ administrators allowed unions.

Transnational corporations and allied governments share a manifest lack of concern for the predominantly unskilled female workforces in EPZs. Independent trade union organizing is denied in many localities. In the early stages of South Korea's export-oriented development, unions were outlawed in the zones, and cases of management physically and verbally abusing employees were common. In the mid-1980s, a widespread labour revolt in South Korea brought higher wages and basic shop-floor safety improvements, but companies then began to outsource their Korean operations to new EPZs in Indonesia, the Philippines, and Guatemala, where labour consciousness was not an issue. The possibility of relocation brought renewed employment insecurity and repression to the Korean zones and marginalized attempts at union organizing.[37] Taiwanese EPZ workers had similar experiences.[38] South Korea and Taiwan represent the more developed or "mature" export-processing countries.[39] Despite the claims of host governments that EPZs are a market-driven path to long-run poverty reduction, these cases demonstrate that maturity does not imply a greater willingness to negotiate with or recognize the rights of working families, but rather a net local decline in these hard-won gains.

In the more recent export-oriented economies like Malaysia and Indonesia, governments also deny unions. Labour organizing in Malaysian zones is at the company's discretion. The government enforces that privilege.[40] Like many zones, the Malaysian national government considers EPZs to be geographically separate from their principal customs area. The businesses that operate within the zones are exempt from Malaysian labour laws.[41] In some countries the legal justification is absent, and government labour representatives are simply corrupt. The Indonesian Department of Labour regularly took bribes and ignored safety concerns in EPZ plants in the early 1990s.[42] Organizing along labour lines is nearly impossible in the newer EPZs. What Sassen has termed a "regulatory fracture" is in evidence here in the application of social rights and traditional obligations.[43] Whether by a convenient legal fiction in Malaysia or through blatant corruption in Indonesia, Third World governments' development strategies regularly facilitate a break between widely accepted human and labour rights and the demands of capital.

China and Mexico are two exceptions to the blanket anti-unionism in most EPZS. The majority of workers in China's special economic zones (SEZS) are unionized, and roughly 50 percent of the maquiladora workforce along Mexico's northern border was unionized in the mid-1990s.[44] However, the unions in both Chinese and Mexican zones are state-run, subordinate to the corporations, and have no purpose other than quelling labour unrest. Anita Chan and Zhu Xiaoyang managed to get access to over fifteen hundred Chinese footwear assemblers for their study of work discipline in the SEZs and found that physical coercion, rather than some inherent cultural "cooperative Confucianism," was the primary reason for the much-vaunted "Chinese miracle." One of the main means of controlling Chinese workers is through subordinate unions. They "have no effect on the incidence of penalties [imposed for minor shop-floor infractions] and other forms of control."[45]

Mexican maquiladora trade unions are part of the state apparatus, and, like successive Mexican governments, they support the neoliberal project.[46] Laudatory descriptions of Mexican offshore assembly applaud the fact that unions have little impact on the work process, ensuring greater labour flexibility.[47] Some workers are enrolled in the state unions without their knowledge and without ever meeting union representatives. Those who attempt to install independent trade unions like the Frente Auténtico del Trabajo (FAT) often find state unions and corporations arrayed against them. At a plant in Ciudad Juarez in 1997, three shifts of workers seeking to replace the institutional Confederación de Trabajadores de México with FAT were detained in the plant all day. When time came to vote, workers had to walk a gauntlet of armed thugs and then declare their vote publicly. Not surprisingly, they voted overwhelmingly to keep the state union.[48] Regardless of the age of a state's EPZS, bottom-up, independent union organizing is infrequent and generally repressed violently by corporations and their state allies. Subordinate unionism forms just another layer of control over EPZ workers.

Evidence of transnational union organizing in EPZs is sketchy as well. There are few direct links between unions in Southeast Asia and the First World. There is no tradition of class-based trade unionism throughout much of Southeast Asia, and the few links between transnational and local organizers that do exist seem more concerned with informal net-working to make contacts than with any effective program of support for EPZ workers. This situation corroborates Appadurai's contention that post-1945 theories of benevolent modernization and the Marxist vision of class-based international resistance are exhausted.[49]

Mexican cross-border unionizing has a longer lineage, but the situation does not appear promising for Mexican maquiladora workers. Instances of First World unions colluding with plant management to keep independent Mexican unions like FAT out of the maquiladoras, and the labelling of NGOS as outside agitators by subordinate unions in the more prosperous zones, cast suspicion on cross-border organizing.[50] The San Diego-based Support Committee for Maquiladora Workers and the Mexican Border Region Workers Support Committee train workers to improve the safety of assembly plants in northern Mexico, but there is no support from state representatives or employers. The projects struggle constantly for helpful publicity, while the "asymmetrical character of cross-border labour citizenship" is often viewed by Mexican workers as paternalistic and oriented towards the interests of North American workers.[51] These and similar organizations are not actual unions but educational support networks. Shop-floor reform is left up to individual workers. A serious gap exists between proposals for transnational organizing and actual practice on the ground in EPZS.

In company towns some of the most effective organizing for autonomy centred on community issues. Residents who were not part of the privileged social hierarchy of company towns often mitigated dependence on global capital in small ways by pooling resources to purchase electricity, provide clean water, and petition the government to alter the status of unplanned fringe communities to more effectively collect taxes. Skilled, unskilled, and non-company residents also successfully lobbied companies and governments to build schools and health care facilities and to subsidize various recreational activities.[52] Migrant skilled workers sometimes brought the experience of cooperative movements to the new towns and set up co-ops.[53] Residents of dependent industrial enclaves often realized effective collective agency by organizing around the improvement of community services, while companies were more willing to accede to community initiatives because of their own dependence on maintaining stable workforces on isolated frontiers. Residents of company towns stressed accepted obligations of mutual aid to bring pressure to bear on obstinate employers.

In southern and Southeast Asia today, numerous grassroots organizations successfully help poor communities deal with neglect from above. Nari Udyog Kendra helps construct safe, affordable housing and lobbies for improved transportation for single female garment workers in Bangladesh, while the Self-Employed Women's Association of India helps informal, domestic textile workers set up cooperatives and literacy programs and provides legal advice on employment and business matters.[54] AWARE, an Indian organization for community empowerment, advises residents on how to achieve self-supporting communities and then withdraws when residents feel they have reached a desired level of autonomy. Since 1985 AWARE has withdrawn from over twenty-five hundred settlements.[55] Mumbai's Alliance for the working poor has achieved numerous successes as a federated, horizontally organized, and "patient" grassroots coalition. The Alliance does not engage in partisan politics, seeks transnational assistance cautiously, and focuses on the ways immediate community problems can be resolved through novel, often subversive, means.[56]

Mexico has a long tradition of community organizing around the maquiladoras. The Centro de Orientación de la Mujer Obrera (COMO), while aimed primarily at bettering the lives of female maquiladora employees, entrenched itself in the community of Ciudad Juarez in the 1970s and 1980s.[57] Along with promoting unionization, the COMO focused on education and community issues like child care, women's rights, and the establishment of non-maquiladora cooperatives such as Juarez's garbage handlers. By 1981 it had grown from a handful of concerned plant workers and residents to fourteen thousand members.[58] The FAT applies a similar tactic today. After several setbacks organizing workers along union lines, the FAT shifted direction and appealed directly to the Juarez community by opening the Centro de Estudios y Taller Laboral Asociación Civil (CETLAC).[59] The representatives of CETLAC are community members who seek to educate workers and to improve local living conditions. Though FAT is connected to various international human and labour rights groups, the existence of CETLAC is recognition of the importance of organizing locally for change on a broad community front.[60] These examples provide successful and alternative models for the Third World's working poor to achieve local autonomy and work towards engaging the global from a strong base.

Grassroots community organizing has proven to be the most consistently effective way to gain a measure of control over exploitation in the

EPZs. These local and horizontally linked groups do not always conform to the models of negotiation that were common to welfare capitalism. Instead, they assert different perspectives on what constitutes autonomy and engage in alternative forms of organization.

In EPZs, just as in company towns, union organizing has not been an easy process, but in EPZs the dearth of independent labour unions is nearly total. However, just as in company towns, organizing with a wider community focus can successfully secure relative autonomies. A crucial difference is that, unlike the company town experience, there is little help from governments or corporations for residents of EPZs. They must work out their own ways of accommodating, negotiating, and resisting dependence on global capital. This crucial contrast calls attention to the importance of government traditions that respect law, human rights, and public welfare, and it recognizes that although workers toil with little or no direct aid from authorities in the zones, they have valid and sometimes positive reasons for doing so.

Engaging the Global, Engaging the Local

There are three main, and sometimes linked, approaches to the literature on the prospects for autonomy in EPZs: a focus on class-based resistance, an emphasis on transnational organizations as vehicles of reform, and a concentration on the primacy of grassroots community organizing. Analyzed separately, major difficulties with class- and transnationally centred theories are evident.

Some argue that the best road to change is through class-based organizations like trade unions. Earlier works on the new global division of labour and EPZs place greater emphasis on class resistance than do more recent studies.[61] In these works, the authors understand the outsourcing of manufacturing jobs to Third World countries as creating a working class that, like Karl Marx's nineteenth-century proletariat, needs to organize because of its subordinate position in the mode of production and wrest control from capitalists through strikes and other labour-based actions. Class-centric analyses recognize that resistance to mobile TNCs and complicit governments by independent unions is often ineffective or impossible, so shop-floor control becomes a precursor to the ultimate goal of an international working-class movement capable of overturning capitalism.[62] Community issues in EPZs are peripheral at best and are portrayed as a consequence of the ravages caused by workplace ultra-exploitation.[63] The analytical preoccupation with the struggle of factory workers rarely permits a nuanced analysis in which residents are effective agents of autonomy or which recognizes that EPZ workers' notions of class may not even constitute an impulse for change.

In her case study of Malaysian EPZ workers, Donella Caspersz argues that class is a causal but not centrally located factor in the experience of workers.[64] Class, in the Marxist sense, is normally not part of her subjects' understanding of work and life in the zones. Local research in Malaysian and Indonesian EPZs indicates that many workers, particularly the young, migrant females who compose the bulk of the workforces, often silently suffer the exploitative aspects of their employment because their jobs empower them personally in ways patriarchal village life never did. Relative independence from oppressive gender roles and perceived improvements to social status brought about by disposable income, personal feelings of being "up to date," and the ability to choose romantic encounters should not be discounted as forms of autonomy. Nonetheless, they do not form a basis for opposition to the neoliberal order.[65]

Even when Malaysian and Indonesian workers challenge the conditions of their employment, resistance often takes the form of informal protests that adapt traditional resistance to new situations. The prevalence of individual "spirit possessions" among female zone workers and "stayouts" in which workers stay home en masse to protest the inappropriate behaviour of supervisors are two ways that EPZ workers express resistance in non-class-based ways.[66] A recent Malaysian study demonstrates that the "triggers for these acts of resistance are not class itself," they are everyday and unplanned acts based on traditional and hybridized ways of understanding the world.[67] While such novel forms of autonomy are unlikely to facilitate a broader contestation of neoliberal globalization, discounting them as inconsequential or as false consciousness serves no useful purpose.

In early twentieth-century company towns, there were various cases of company and government suppression of independent local, national, and international unions, but there were successes as well. The history of EPZs is replete with instances when union drives ended tragically in mass layoffs, sudden capital flight, and violence. It is not surprising, therefore, that those most affected by neoliberal industrialization seek other means of achieving autonomy.

Relying on the teleology of class struggle downplays the prevalence, impact, and validity of non-class-based organizations. Moreover, there are glaring historical examples of organized First World labour failing to unify workers against capital. Over the past century, labour drifted to the right on multiple occasions. Class essentialism disempowers those who are not familiar with Marxist discourse and devalues doctrinally unacceptable but successful non-class-based methods of achieving autonomy. As Castells cogently puts it, "although Marxist theory might not have room for social movements other than the historically predicted class struggle, social movements persist."[68] Ronaldo Munck concurs with Castells' position and argues that class essentialism is an obsolete tool for analyzing lived experience under neoliberalism.[69]

Recently, commentators have focused on transnational organizing as a way to empower the victims of the new global division of labour. Formal international organizations were rare in company towns because of geographic isolation, limited communications technologies, and the efforts of companies to keep non-corporate organizations out of the factory and community. Migrant skilled workers, however, brought transnational movement ideas like consumer cooperatives to the towns. The ideas, injected from below in the new settlements, often focused on community improvement rather than on directly challenging company hegemony. The ideas were also not truly global, like today's anti-global NGOs strive to be, but became hybridized, unique parts of the different localities. Contemporary transnational organization, in contrast, implies an ultimate engagement with global capital in global space.[70]

Many who are concerned about the effects of the new global division of labour advocate a "transnational social unionism" to unite numerous shop floors and communities in different cultural contexts in solidarity against neoliberal globalization. Modern NGOs and other transnational activist groups advance the idea that broad coalitions of citizens from the First and Third World can link by way of instant communication technologies like the Internet and through conferences and protests to combat the forces of neoliberalism around the globe. As Jackie Smith says, these new transnational social movements will "cultivate 'imagined communities' beyond nation states" and foster "collective identities that emphasize transcendent values and goals."[71] This approach has a long pedigree in internationalist movements like the anti-slavery campaigns of the nineteenth century, the Communist Internationale, and, more recently, NGOs devoted to promoting human rights. Throughout the 1990s transnational activists regularly targeted meetings of the World Bank, the International Monetary Fund, and the World Trade Organization, a strategy that culminated in the Battle of Seattle riots in 1999. Activists resist neoliberalism while simultaneously establishing global grassroots organizations like the World Social Forum, an "open space" for positive visions of change.[72]

One of the most popular calls for transnational solidarity comes from Naomi Klein's best-selling book *No Logo*. Klein argues that a positive, inclusive resistance, "both high-tech and grassroots, both focused and fragmented — that is as global, and as capable of coordinated action, as the multinational corporations it seeks to subvert" is the best way to engage and contest the contemporary global order.[73] Other commentators advance this position to varying degrees. Labour advocates call for sustained North American cross-border union organizing and a "grand bargain" between workers around the world to coordinate resistance to TNCs, global financial institutions, and allied governments.[74] Still others argue that a global class-based coalition inclusive of feminist and environmentalist perspectives can overturn neoliberal hegemony.[75]

Other writers eschew class essentialism and argue instead for a global social unionism that is not directed by ideological predispositions towards any one form of resistance but is inclusive and practical. Ideally, such movements would resemble the TNCs they seek to counter. Gay Seidman's comparison of massive popular uprisings in Brazil and South Africa in the 1980s and early 1990s provides useful empirical case studies of local-to-national and, ultimately, global organizations that successfully overturned long-standing repressive regimes. According to Seidman, workplace unionization was an element of the struggles in Brazil and South Africa, but wider community involvement that led to mass civil unrest combined with sustained global activism that targeted the general inequality of both countries was the most significant reason for the success of the movements.[76] Along more prescriptive lines, Jeremy Brecher and Tim Costello's numerous works propose a blueprint for globalization from below. Brecher and Costello advocate flexible transnational organizations that are engaged on the ground with local grassroots movements and that can also combat TNCs and financial institutions on a global scale. Political scientist Robert Lambert argues that global social movement unionism "is the only possible alternative to subordination."[77]

The major difficulty with these suggestions is that they privilege resistance in global space when immediate local sites of contestation like EPZs remain largely peripheral to the discourse. Residents who employ new and hybridized forms of local autonomy should be an essential element in defining transnational struggle. As Evans succinctly put it: "Local organizing preceded the formation of a transnational advocacy network and the persistence of local organizing after the network had been formed was essential to achieving its goals. Acting globally enables local organizing that would be 'outside the envelope'; it doesn't replace local organizing."[78] Despite the oft-stated maxim that successful transnationalism can be achieved *only after* affected local communities gain some measure of autonomy, emphasis on organizing locally in EPZs is scanty. This essential local step to organizing translocally and transnationally is undervalued in the rush to resist global capitalism with counter-hegemonic but similarly global institutions. The literature largely ignores the crucial role national governments play in legitimizing the new global division of labour. Governments that allow and encourage corporations to ignore labour laws and flout social obligations are basic obstacles to social justice on the ground. How can working residents build imagined communities before they secure real local communities? Are they even interested in imagined communities of global resistance? On these questions, advocates of transnational struggle and local agents speak in different languages and at cross-purposes.

In their efforts to include Third World perspectives, Brecher and Costello promote subsidiarity. To them, "decisions should be made as close to the locus of the actual activity being decided as possible."[79] However, in 1994's *Global Village or Global Pillage,* Brecher and Costello's only actual EPZ-related example is from mid-1980s Korea, where workers' hard-won gains were eroded when capitalists began to source their operations to other countries.[80] From this case it is difficult to see exactly how subsidiarity can benefit EPZ workers. In other works that concentrate on rural and indigenous local community movements that challenge and refine the dialogue of global resistance, the lack of engagement on the ground in and around EPZs is more pronounced.[81] Nancy Naples, a supporter of transnational resistance, conceded a number of difficulties in the way transnational advocacy groups relate to female EPZ workers, but the emphasis remains on how to include them in those groups without really understanding their specific concerns.[82] Moreover, in a recent paper that critiques the power of the Internet in the organization of transnational networks, Stoecker concludes that social action through the Internet cannot replace face-to-face communication and direct personal relationships in building an effective movement for globalization from below.[83] Communities that struggle to get regular electrical service can really count only on face-to-face activity.

So where do the millions of people directly tied to neoliberal industrial enclaves fit into these prescriptions? Pratt and Yeoh contend that "there is nothing inherently' transgressive or emancipatory about transnationalism."[84] First World programs for resistance to global capitalism often bear striking parallels to neoliberal development schemes in that both are top-down and prescriptive, and both fail to fully incorporate the voices of those most affected by economic exploitation.[85] Munck maintains that abstract internationalism simply does not connect with workers on the ground, while Dirlik argues that "abstract social analysis may serve as impediments to the resolution of questions of everyday life if used inflexibly."[86] If there is no inclusive transnational forum for the local autonomies expressed in EPZ communities, transnational organizations cannot effectively contest the global pressures that are felt most keenly on the ground. In fact, homogenizing movements focused on global counter-hegemony will likely struggle against, rather than incorporate, local autonomies.

Understanding and incorporating individual autonomies and local strategies of community organizing seems most appropriate. Many globalization scholars agree that "the investigation of alternative representations and practices in concrete local settings" in the Third World is under-represented in the literature. They suggest that it is a research priority for understanding the impetus for resistance to — or, I must add, the relative acceptance of — neoliberalism in local, national, and transnational sites.[87] Local cooperative movements, everyday lobbying for basic community services, and the impact of progressive religious and cultural movements in and around EPZs go largely unnoticed. They represent diverse, effective, and new local forms of accommodation, and resistance, to the prevailing socio-economic order.[88] Baruah argues that traditional unionism is one of many tactics in the struggle for the empowerment of workers in the new global division of labour. She also describes cooperatives, skill-training and enterprise-development programs, and marketing aid as some of the various ways textile workers in southern Asia mitigate dependence on global capital.[89] These tactics indicate ongoing and often flourishing local counter-hegemonic moments that do not take the forms most commentators expect.[90] They must be understood if we are to develop a more comprehensive understanding of how local autonomies can, or why they will not, lead to alternative, inclusive globalizations.

Case studies of life in EPZs do have drawbacks. Isolated studies rarely attempt to extrapolate what their local findings mean in the broader context of accommodation to, and struggle against, global neoliberal expansion. Without a wider engagement with the literature, local studies run the risk of portraying local differences as insurmountable obstacles to transnational organization. Leslie Salzinger's gender analysis of Mexican maquiladora workers, for example, indicates that work sites are different even within a single EPZ and, therefore, defy most theoretical categorizations.[91] If difference rules and the chances for broad solidarity and resistance from below are mired in atomized identity politics, what realistic alternatives to neoliberalism are available? In terms of EPZs and autonomy, a greater effort must be made to deepen empirical study into the concrete reality of life in the zones. This work should also be coupled with heightened and ongoing dialogue between those who emphasize autonomy and resistance through local place-based initiatives and those who maintain that constraining neoliberal globalization is best achieved through global space-based organizations. Too narrow a focus on either perspective leads to a skewed interpretation.

Attempts to reconcile the fragmented literature on globalization from below and the potential for autonomy on the ground raise more questions than answers. An understanding of everyday life in EPZ plants and communities, like daily existence in earlier company towns, is central to accurately apprehending the ways ordinary people function under shifting global capitalist regimes. But how *specifically* can varied approaches to local autonomy be integrated into a sustained, coherent challenge to prevailing neoliberal hegemony? How can people and the places they help create, including the ways gender, ethnicity, culture, and class play out on the ground, be inserted into the broader discussion in order to avoid marginalizing the very agents capable of attaining human-centred, alternative globalizations? This question links to another, what does local individual and community acceptance of established order and the emergence of right-wing, violently xenophobic groups say about the likelihood of progressive resistance to globalization?[92] Are those who "buy into" the dominant socio-economic order for understandable, personal reasons, or those who choose to express their resistance in "unacceptable" ways, simply unimportant exceptions in a generally forward-thinking struggle?[93] Labourers who work in the zones to save money or buy status-enhancing consumer goods or to gain social freedoms denied to them in traditional rural communities are expressing forms of personal autonomy, but they are certainly not effective forms of resistance to neoliberalism. Is it possible to incorporate these different, personal autonomies into the study of responses to neoliberal globalization? Finally, how can residents and workers exploit the state's crucial role as facilitator for capital to improve their lives? This issue will benefit from a better understanding of how those who live in the zones view their own situations. An empathetic and more inclusive engagement with global-local dynamics in concrete settings like EPZs promises to overcome First World developmentalist biases and top-down programs for change.

Conclusion

Comparing EPZs to company towns provides a novel historical perspective on how global capital enlists state power, the shifting ways workers and residents of dependent communities conceive and express autonomy, and the potential methods for engaging and contesting globalization that spring from those autonomies. The basic way capital enlists political authority for the creation of EPZs is the same way it gained contracts to exploit First World resource frontiers: negotiating with governments. In early and mid-twentieth-century welfare states, negotiations for frontier development generally assumed some measure of social planning by companies and/or governments. This approach was not found in the laissez-faire nineteenth century, and it is clearly not the case today. Today, mobile capital and its agents have increased their ability to drive a hard bargain and avoid the costs of planning through technological improvement and an openness to neoliberalism among Third World governments.

A simple top-down account of transnational corporate economic exploitation and government collusion does not accurately capture the experience of dependent industrial enclaves. The people who inhabit EPZs are neglected and exploited, but they are not powerless victims. Like company towns, EPZs are real communities in which local grassroots agents strive for personal and collective autonomies. They negotiate, resist, and accommodate the global hegemonies of profit-centred capitalism and government collusion in a variety of ways that differ over time and from place to place. Residents of EPZ communities focus their attempts at local autonomy on immediate concerns: personal concerns of social status and collective issues of basic sanitation and freedom from outright abuse at home and work. Their wider justifications for these attempts have more to do with adapted traditional obligations and gender issues than with international class and human rights considerations. Often these autonomies are experienced as intensely personal, but new forms of group organization and effective tactics for engaging the global can also spring from everyday experiences.

While central to the wider struggle to engage, contest, and overturn neoliberal globalization, transnational networks are powerless in EPZs if they do not adapt themselves to the locality in question and speak to the concerns of residents, not the other way around. Every EPZ community has its own historical and cultural peculiarities that defy reductionist analysis, and their improvement remains a central issue in today's search for alternative globalizations. More effort is required to understand daily life on the ground in EPZs. Greater study of local autonomies can only improve the abstract and fragmented understanding of the lives of Third World workers and residents in the new global division of labour. Integrating the dialogues of First and Third World academics and activists into hybridized strategies for altering current development paradigms is essential.[94] Recognizing unexpected and non-progressive local counter-hegemonies is one step towards re-imagining EPZs as places. Another is an understanding that autonomies are achieved through accommodation as well as through resistance. Visions for change originate in personal experiences and local sites. They cannot be implemented from above.

chapter 8   Freedom of the Ether or the
                  Electromagnetic Commons?
                  Globality, the Public Interest,
                  and Multilateral Radio
                  Negotiations in the 1920s

                  Daniel Gorman

> *Regulation of traffic upon the channels of the ether is as essential as the*
> *regulation of traffic upon our crowded streets, but equally in both cases*
> *the purpose must be to expedite movement, to stimulate progress, and*
> *not to retard it.*
> —Herbert Hoover, International Radiotelegraph Conference,
> Washington, 1927[1]

AS THE AMERICAN OCEAN-LINER SS *Leviathan* sailed through the
English Channel on 24 June 1924, nearing the end of a long transatlantic
passage, the ship's onboard radio broadcast a musical program followed
by a speech from the captain. The passengers no doubt appreciated the
diversions as they neared the end of a tiring trip. The British government, however, was less amused. In response to this seemingly innocu-
ous action, it launched an official protest against the United States. The
British claimed that the ship's "frivolous" transmissions posed a potential
danger to other vessels in the area. The *Leviathan* case was by no means
unique. Indeed, the United States filed similar protests on several occasions, such as when transmissions from the Japanese SS *Kinkasan Maru* interfered with distress signals from the burning SS *Everet* on Point Gorda,
California, in 1926.[2] While no one on the *Everet* was hurt, that was certainly not the case fourteen years earlier when the *Titanic* hit an iceberg
off the coast of Newfoundland. Her transmissions for aid went unheard,
and 1,490 people drowned. The radio operator of the closest vessel, a

mere twenty miles away, was asleep, and there was no one else on board who could operate the equipment.

The supranational regulation of the radio frequency spectrum in the 1920s was a significant global development. The electromagnetic spectrum, also known as "the airwaves" or "frequency band," is a renewable, though limited, natural resource. Frequencies (wavelengths in the older usage) refer to the number of times a periodic occurrence (such as the cycle of a carrier wave) occurs within a given interval of time.[3] The use and regulation of the band has become an issue of great, and global, importance. The global use of the spectrum was a problem first identified in the early 1920s, as the advent of radio broadcasting led to mutual interference. At best, such interference threatened to curtail the cultural and financial potential of broadcasting; at worst, it was a threat to public safety, drowning out distress and navigation transmissions. The frequency band differed from other, established, forms of property because it was an "invisible" entity with no analogous predecessor.

The problem of mutual interference was addressed at the seminal 1927 International Radiotelegraph Conference (IRC) in Washington, a decisive moment in the history of global communications. The United States spearheaded the conference, and its initiative was an early indication of the paramount role that the United States would play in globalization's subsequent development (see Hedetoft, this volume). The delegates achieved a workable compromise between conceiving of frequencies as a property like any other, best left to the laws of supply and demand, and conceiving of frequencies as an international commons, as a public good to be regulated for the use and benefit of all. By defining the electromagnetic spectrum as a *res communis* domain, which belongs to no one and may be appropriated as private property, the delegates averted what the ecologist Garret Hardin once termed "the tragedy of the commons," namely, abuse through overuse of a shared property.[4] In an interwar environment marked by political confusion and mutual antipathy, especially during the 1930s, the global agreement on frequency rights stands out as a notable triumph.

The regulation of the frequency band was one of the earliest global articulations of a non-tangible entity as property. Global regulation occurred not through the dissolution of national borders and boundaries, but by transcending them, drawing on both the exogenous nature of late nineteenth-century European empire building and the commercial spirit of the United States. Mutual frequency interference constituted a coordination problem that could only be solved through international cooperation.[5] The mutual benefit each participating state received was the common ability to develop and use the new technology of radio. The 1930s are often depicted as a period of deglobalization, a categorization that has overshadowed the real steps taken in global integration, both in the 1920s and during the Second World War (see Pruessen, this volume).[6] The globalization of radio rights through the IRC created a supraterritorial organization at both the political and conceptual level. This transition furthered a transworld consciousness and encouraged greater efforts to build collective autonomy by reasserting or creating both national and local identities.[7] The regulation of the frequency band was thus a case of globalization assisting, rather than hindering, autonomy.

The Emergence of the Technology and Early Steps towards Regulation

As the examples of the Leviathan, Everet, and Titanic show, radio's early importance was as a tool of nautical communication. The Royal Navy, in particular, developed wireless technology to communicate at sea without detection, installing Marconi radio sets on all its dreadnoughts.[8] The first calls to regulate radio came from ship-to-shore and ship-to-ship operators who, frustrated with the Marconi Company's monopoly of wireless telegraphy, organized an international conference in Berlin in 1903. The Berlin conference, focusing only on maritime usage, established the guiding principle of global radio regulation: "wireless telegraph stations should operate, as far as possible, in such a manner as not to interfere with the working of other stations."[9]

This principle was reconfirmed in 1906 by the first International Radiotelegraph Convention, which also established specific frequencies (then measured in wavelengths) for use by maritime and service stations (such as military use) and obliged signatory nations to send technical data, including frequencies used, to the International Bureau of the International Telegraph Union (ITU). The ITU, formed in 1865 to regulate the new telegraph industry (see Stolow's chapter in this volume for another global aspect of this technology), is the world's oldest international body of its kind, illustrating the centrality of communications to globalization.[10] Although the ITU, informally known as the Berne Bureau, had no formal jurisdiction, it became an international clearing house for telecommunications information and the predecessor of the modern International Telecommunications Union. The practice of reporting frequencies to the ITU informally established vested rights for the station or service that first used a given frequency. Countries that did not adhere to the regulations of the Berlin agreements, particularly those concerning non-interference, found negotiating with signatory nations over radio rights more difficult.[11] Thus, while the early radio conventions did not constitute international law per se, they did establish norms for future multilateral radio negotiations.

The 1912 London International Radiotelegraph Conference was convened in response to the *Titanic* disaster and concentrated on maritime radio regulation. The London Convention further codified the principle of non-interference, stating that "the operation of radio stations must be organized as far as possible in such a manner as not to disturb the service of other stations of the kind."[12] The London delegates planned their next conference for Washington in 1917. However, progress towards a broader international radio agreement was curtailed by the First World War, despite technological improvements that were driven by military strategy.[13] Combatant nations, especially the Allies, used the wireless to transmit codes, because landlines were vulnerable. The Inter-Allied Signal and Wireless Transmission Commission oversaw matters of operation, while the Inter-Allied Radiotelegraphic Commission administered technical issues such as wavelengths and equipment.[14]

Although a regulatory framework had emerged before the First World War, it was only after improvements in transmission technology that multiple over-the-air uses became possible, including broadcasting, a term that was adapted from the farming phrase for spreading seed over a field.[15] Broadcast signal power before 1920 was weak and unreliable. The chief operator of the US government radio station in Santo Domingo told the American legation in the Dominican Republic in 1916 that he had difficulty receiving and transmitting messages.[16] A year earlier, an American signal officer told his commander that "I know of no radio stations in Haiti capable of transmitting messages, except those operated by the American Forces ... The only receiving set known to be in operation is the small set at the College St. Louis, Port-au-Prince."[17] Most early wireless broadcast stations, especially international ones such as that between Lyons, France, and Annapolis, Maryland, handled the traffic of diplomatic or press services.[18] There were signs, however, that broadcasting was the wave of the future. Japan had twenty-two wireless stations by 1920, although they faced time restrictions; for instance, the Funabashi station was limited to nine hours a day for commercial purposes.[19] In the United States, restrictions of the Radio Act of 1912 were relaxed in 1918 to allow companies to produce radio equipment for the government without paying patent fees, thus resulting in a broadcasting boom. Westinghouse's KDKA was the first public station, debuting with a broadcast of the Harding-Cox presidential election returns on 2 November 1920. In Detroit, WWJ made the first commercial broadcast, also in 1920.[20] Radio companies almost immediately sought to expand overseas. The Radio Corporation of America (RCA) was formed in 1919 at the behest of the acting secretary of the navy, Franklin Delano Roosevelt. The RCA wanted to consolidate US wireless ownership to combat the British Marconi monopoly, and it investigated the prospects for building wireless stations in Venezuela. The Argentine Marconi Company purchased exclusive rights to transmit and receive internationally in Cuba, a country that US officials had identified as posing a potential interference threat. Other countries, such as Ecuador, prohibited the use of wireless telegraph and telephone apparatuses by private persons, effectively giving the state a broadcast monopoly.[21] The European powers followed a similar path, establishing the central conflict in later broadcast frequency negotiations: private ownership versus public rights.

The Inter-Allied Radiotelegraphic Commission, formed in 1919, drew up draft proposals on both international radio and maritime communication. These proposals became the EU-F-GB-I Protocol, signifying the assenting powers by their French acronyms (the United States, France, Great Britain, and Italy). The protocol called for international radio and maritime service regulations, including the "establishment of an International Communication Office and the amalgamation of the various conventions which affect international communication."[22] Building on these proposals, the five Allied nations met in Washington in 1920 to establish regulations until such a time as the next Radiotelegraph Convention could meet. Three questions dominated the gathering: what to do with captured German cables; whether extant copyright agreements applied to radio; and how to minimize the forecasted problem of broadcast interference. One senior US official spoke of "the backwardness of development of international electrical communications." The British delegate, voicing European sentiments, wanted "to see if the international co-operation to which they have been accustomed, cannot be extended."[23] The delegates sought to "draw up the modifications necessary to make the 1912 convention conform to progress made in the radio art, it being intended to impose these modifications on the central powers after the approval of the neutrals had been secured."[24] Their vehicle was to be a newly created Universal Electric-Communications Union, which would administer all forms of electrical communication. Despite the initial optimism, the proposed union proved stillborn. The first divisive issue was over who should control undersea cables.

The Allies took control of German cable lines under the Treaty of Versailles (part VIII, article 244, annex VII). The British believed they deserved the lion's share of cables, as they had incurred great expense during the war and "seizure was [a] legitimate exercise of the use of sea power."[25] Japan wanted all German cables in the Pacific, while France and Italy proposed joint ownership agreements with the United States over German-owned, cross-Atlantic cables joining their countries. The Americans wanted all transatlantic cables open to leasing, as they feared the British would expand their "all Red Route" cable domination into the realm of wireless. The cable issue influenced radio discussions because radio transmissions still required cables for long-distance messages, especially overseas.[26]

Britain was the first country to realize the global potential of radio, if only for secondary purposes. The journalist Charles Bright wrote in 1909 that "it seems not unlikely that wireless telegraphy may, in due course, be turned to considerable account in this direction for comparatively unimportant, or non-urgent, messages, as well as for the simultaneous transmission of news to different parts of the Empire." He added, "In such cases, economy is really more important than celerity or efficiency."[27] Two years later Bright noted that "the immediate question in connection with this new invention is how we can get it under control from a single centre."[28] This quest for centralized control drove Britain's desire to organize wireless along public lines. In contrast, the United States favoured a private model for a proposed trans-Pacific cable. Despite the acknowledged benefits of wireless, such as its greater resistance to weather and sabotage, the cable remained a valued resource, not the least because it was more amenable to property ownership along state lines.[29] President Wilson's optimistic vision of the "internationalization of cables" came to naught. Like the League of Nations, which the US Senate never ratified, a global solution to the cable issue was thwarted by conflicting views on the national interest. The result was an uneven pattern of public and private ownership across the globe.

The Allies were further confounded by how to apply extant copyright law to radio broadcasting. In 1886 the Berne Convention for the

Protection of Literary and Artistic Works had established international copyright legislation. The treaty's signatories pledged to respect the copyright legislation of other signatories, creating an ersatz global understanding of intellectual property for creative work. It became unclear, however, if the convention applied to radio broadcasting. As one US official told a group of radio industry leaders, "No one seems to know whether the existing copyright agreements protect material that is radioed."[30] It was difficult, for one thing, to regulate access to radio broadcasts. Broadcasting implies the broad and scattered dissemination of transmissions to many receivers. Contemporaries compared broadcasting to either "an infinitely extended concert hall" or "the phonetical reproduction *longissima manu*."[31] How could copyright holders ensure that their material would not be used without their consent? Was the copyright holder or the broadcaster the creator of the material? Could broadcasting even be monitored at all? The United States was a party to neither the Berne Convention nor the ITU, making international agreement on broadcast copyright nearly impossible. The British-led proposal to fuse the ITU and the International Radiotelegraph Convention, which would potentially provide a global forum in which copyright issues might be addressed, thus failed.

The United States, spurred by its private radio industry, was more concerned with broadcast rights themselves. Commercial interests in the United States favoured an open market.[32] In contrast, the European radio industry had developed along strictly state lines and thus supported firm global regulation of what it deemed a public property. The key question was, as the US delegate put it, "should international communication be authorized, call it license or whatever you want — or should any Tom, Dick or Harry, without a license, be permitted to conduct international communications?"[33] It was this threat of unfettered access that led to the global regulation of radio. The problems — ownership and access — were apparent to all. Businessmen argued that "commercial companies want to know that in spending a large amount of money on a certain service, they will have a certain band of wavelengths that they can use." Government officials worried about cross-border interference: "Suppose you have two countries that are not contiguous, that do not belong to the convention, and they exchange radio with utter disregard to any of the provisions of the convention ... They may muss up everybody else." The stumbling block was "the stock argument that the country owned the universe [meaning the air above its territory]."[34] Charles Neave, of the RCA, believed that "if there is any international arrangement it should be limited to getting uniformity in only certain things and preventing interference of power stations and allotment of wavelengths and technical matters of the sort."[35]

In 1912 the London Convention had allocated some wavelengths for strictly government use, including maritime usage, but it could not address broadcasting, which did not then exist. In 1920 the Washington Convention broached issues of copyright and broadcast allocations, including the "classification of services and of radio sending stations, distribution of wavelengths, conditions to be fulfilled by mobile stations, and the use of the 600 metre wavelength [the established maritime distress frequency]."[36] The Washington meeting went no further though because of disputes over cables, copyright, and broadcasting, as well as the absence of Germany, Russia, and many smaller nations at the convention. Had subsequent radio conventions followed the model of the Universal Electric-Communications Union negotiations, the global regulation of radio would likely have been severely curtailed.

Developments in radio technology in the 1920s, however, made long-range broadcasting a reality, resulting in a radio boom and a state of frequency chaos that cried out for global regulation. The regenerative receiver circuit and the vacuum tube oscillator, both invented during the war, allowed for the generation of continuous waves and made continuous radio broadcasting possible. The high-frequency alternator, produced in the General Electric labs, allowed for overseas radiotelephone broadcasting by 1917. President Wilson used the technology to communicate with Washington while en route to the Paris Peace Conference in 1919. Broadcasting was given further impetus by the lack of privacy in early radio telephony conversation and the invention of a tuning device to allow multiple waves to be tuned in on a single receiver.[37]

Radio grew especially quickly in the United States. By 1922, 690 separate stations had federal licences to broadcast on one of only two frequencies, 833 or 750 khz.[38] Adding to the confusion was the growing number of radio hams — short-wave home-station operators who used short-wave transmitters developed by the RCA in 1924 — who could relay clearer signals over longer distances. Patent disputes, which had plagued the industry in the 1910s, had been obviated in the 1920s by the economy of scale achieved by the RCA, a union of several competing radio interests. Furthermore, the United States' vast geography, and its widely distributed population, meant that a national radio station was impractical.[39] Washington's attempts to regulate radio as a form of inter-state commerce were stymied by several successful lawsuits brought by private industry.[40] Frequency interference soon reached epidemic pro-portions. Almost two hundred new stations appeared in 1926, prompt-ing the government to create the Federal Radio Commission (FRC) in 1927. The FRC, the forerunner of the Federal Communications Com-mission, which was formed in 1933, licensed and regulated stations and also banned telegraph, telephone, and radio companies from owning or building one another's infrastructure.

Frequency interference was also rampant in Europe. European sta-tions, with the exception of those in the USSR, operated public broad-casting. They were compact states that required limited frequency space to cover the whole nation. Many were multi-ethnic, lending strength to the argument that the state must run broadcasting in the name of the public interest — in this case, to satisfy ethnic diversity. Interference was, thus, less a domestic issue than an international one. The public nature of European broadcasting gave it some advantages of scale. Reuters, for instance, was the world's only truly global news agency in the 1920s (AP and others were domestic services), and it gave the British an advantage in shaping news coverage abroad.[41]

The International Radiotelegraph Conference of 1927: Globalism and Nationalism

The 1920s were a period of great flux for the development of interna-tional communication. The transition from telegraph to wireless was still incomplete, but the expansion of radio, and broadcasting in particu-lar, was truly astounding. This transition was swift and uneven enough to pose a serious challenge to the international system. Given the limi-tations of previous conferences, a new solution was needed. The Lon-don Convention of 1912, which had ninety-seven adherents by 1927, was indicative of the growing importance of radio, but the agreement was silent on the issue of broadcast rights. The Conference on the Limita-tion of Armament, held in Washington in 1922, addressed wartime radio use, but, like the 1920 Washington radio conference, it remained an Al-lied initiative of limited scope.[42] France lobbied to hold a conference on electrical communications in 1925 that would unite radio and telegraph conventions, but this idea was rejected by the United States, Canada, and several Latin American nations. The American countries, which did not sign the ITU, opposed the state-run nature of European telegraphy and sought to protect their private telegraph industries by avoiding international agreements. The philosophical difference between public and private ownership would colour negotiations over radio as well. Many countries submitted radio proposals to the 1925 ITU conference in Paris. These proposals, collated by the Berne Bureau, became the basis for the 1927 International Radio Conference (IRC).[43] While adhering to earlier ideas, such as national sovereignty and technical compatibility, the proposals for the 1927 IRC represented a new model of global communications regulation, which allowed broadcasting to develop as both an industry and a cultural entity.

The decisions reached in 1927 continued to influence the global radio industry, and none was more important than the global allocation of frequency rights. The conference recognized that "there is a limited number of channels through the ether on which radio communication may be conducted" and that mutual interference would result if adequate international regulation was not achieved.[44] Representatives of thirty-six countries came to Washington for the conference. Unlike previous conferences, many industry and private organizations were also invited, including government broadcasters such as the BBC, Compagnie Radio France, and Dansk Radio Aktieselskab; private users groups like the International Amateur Radio Union; and wireless companies such as Western Union Telegraph Company and the Société Belge Radio-Electrique.[45] The delegates toured radio-broadcasting sites on the eastern seaboard and relaxed with trips to Mount Vernon, the Smithsonian, and a Duke-Navy football game. Delegates were well aware of the conference's historic significance, as their identification cards featured a photo of "Benjamin Franklin flying his kite in his early experiments in drawing electricity from the clouds, many years before the use of radio but significantly anticipatory of that means of communication."[46]

The seventeen hundred proposals brought forward in the Berne Book of Proposals formed the conference's framework. The most important of these pertained to article 5 of the conference's regulations, which dealt with wavelengths. The philosophical difference over private and public stewardship of radio was solved by a notable compromise. The Convention's regulations were divided into general regulations, to which everyone agreed, and supplemental regulations dealing with telegraph rates, to which Canada, the United States, and Honduras did not agree because of commercial and diplomatic rivalries.[47] As Manon Davis of the RCA warned, "the British already control the cables ... would they not be in good position to dominate a combined radio and wire telegraph conference."[48] American and Canadian delegates wanted questions of national sovereignty to be kept separate from management issues, which they believed should be governed by each state, and they wanted proposals to be agreed upon by all participants rather than just a majority. Delegates initially resisted an international agreement — "there must be much delay when top hats, morning coats and brass bands foregather from the ends of the earth before governments can begin formal discussion" — but they also realized that broadcasting was a realm in which global regulation was needed to structure market dynamics.[49] Indeed, both domestically and internationally, radio was one of the few industries to ask for regulation. Some companies were farsighted in their understanding of the potential of the new medium. Davis, for example, told the delegates: "I do not know how long it will be, but all of you gentlemen doubtless realize that at some time in the future the transmission of messages by radio will not be by dots and dashes, but by the facsimile reproduction of the message as it was originally written."[50]

Press releases of the IRC gave notice of both the conference's broad scope and the key issue of frequency allocation.[51] They also publicized the variety of radio services the conference would cover, including commercial, press, governmental, amateur, experimental, broadcasting, beacon, navigational, and distress services.[52] The delegates faced one overriding philosophical problem. Were frequencies "property," and, if so, how were they to be distributed? The United States argued that frequencies should be distributed by service rendered and that no station should be able to own a frequency. Others, such as Germany and Latvia, favoured allocation by priority of established service. As one delegate observed: "The wavelength is like an island discovered by a citizen of some particular country; the island would belong to the country whose citizen discovered it. In the same manner the wavelength belongs to the country whose citizen first used it." Other delegates disagreed: "Radio grew up like Topsy ... we will find that some people have squatted on wavelengths which should have been allocated to some other purpose ... If you cannot get a squatter to move for reasons of good will, you may have to buy him off."[53] The abortive 1921 conference had considered allocating frequencies on the basis of the wave type emitted, but that idea had become obsolete by 1927, when continuous waves had overtaken damped waves. In pre-conference discussions, a consensus emerged "that due consideration should be given to the station first using any given frequency in public service when engaged in international service."[54] Thus, a de facto priority right was established, even though the conference did not codify this principle.

Broadcast rights dominated the IRC deliberations because broadcasting was inherently political. Broadcasting quickly became a tool of nationalism, especially in Europe, where the state owned the airwaves. As a result, many proposals in the Berne Book advocated the allocation of frequencies on a country-by-country basis. Germany especially favoured this option, perhaps because it was surrounded on all sides by rival broadcasters.[55] Even states that proposed allocation according to service type used nationalist arguments.

The Irish Free State was a vocal proponent of service allocation. In 1926 it established the world's first national broadcaster, the Irish Broadcasting Company (later Radio Éireann), based on a white paper that emphasized the cultural potential of radio. The efficacy of such a public policy was immediately debated. D.J. Gorey, leader of the conservative Farmer's Party, believed that radio content should "be carefully revised from the moral and national standpoint. We do not want the minds of our youths contaminated with some of the stuff that the youths of other countries have been imbibing."[56] Others, such as Unionist MP Bryan Cooper, resisted the majority's nationalist stance: "I am afraid that if we are to have wireless established on an exclusively Irish-Ireland basis, the result will be 'Danny Boy' four times a week, with variations by way of camouflage."[57] In proposing a service allocation, Ireland made the nationalist argument that "broadcasting is the only means by which scattered rural settlements rapidly receive information of capital importance" such as weather and stock prices, anticipating later satellite services such as Sky and CNN.[58] The Irish example also reveals the paramount importance of radio for nation building, especially for small or emerging nations or national groups that did not have their own state.

While western Europe was nearly unanimous in its support for service allocation, such a scheme was not unproblematic. Service frequencies, especially for non-essential services, differed across the Continent. Proposals to regulate international communication, such as traffic along the Danube, seemed to challenge the country-based European model. A potential breakthrough appeared when France and Britain proposed that fixed stations transmitting internationally (that is, across at least one national border) should be allowed to use any frequency within the range agreed upon for that service, provided no interference was caused. If there was interference, they suggested that a multilateral agreement be reached.[59] This proposal coincided sufficiently with the US plan to lay the framework for a global solution.

Private interests in the United States were leery of any binding, nationally-based allocation scheme. They especially opposed measures that would compel the United States to accept foreign transmissions, preferring self-interest as the motivating force. With these considerations in mind, the US delegation proposed that each government oversee internal management issues. International communication would be governed by the principle of non-interference: "Any high contracting party may assign any frequency to any radio station under its jurisdiction on the sole condition that it does not interfere with any communication of any other country." The frequency allocation table would thus apply solely to those transmissions that "by their nature are known to be capable of causing material international interference."[60] In other words, countries would retain autonomy over internal broadcasting as long as no mutual interference occurred. This arrangement might be termed "globalization where necessary."

Perhaps because the global agreement achieved at the 1927 IRC was accomplished through indirect means, it raised issues of sovereignty and freedom of the proposed international communications commons. Some, especially poorer countries in which the cost of moving stations was more onerous, hesitated to give up priority rights. Poland, for instance, complained that it would have to shift a station on 1111.1 m to its new band.[61] Delegates were also concerned over access. The most important IRC decision on this point was to affirm 500 kilocycles per second (kc/s) (600 metres) as the international calling and distress frequency.[62] Proposals by Sweden and Hungary to establish broadcasting in the 520-60 kc/s (580-45 m) band were defeated by Canada and the United States, which warned that "it is not wise to make a compromise between security of human life at sea and the needs of broadcasting. Human life must be considered first." The IRC accepted the Dutch proposal that "[we] must have a 'No Man's Land' where no one is permitted to enter. We owe that to our sailors and to our shippers."[63] Safety at sea was an especially resonant issue because the Italian ship *Principessa Mafalda* sank off the Brazilian coast while the conference was in session. Wireless distress calls saved over seventeen hundred lives, as ships from six different nations arrived within an hour to rescue people.[64]

If some European countries wanted expanded broadcasting rights, the United States undervalued the importance of other international services. Washington opposed Europe's wish for specific meteorological bands, preferring instead to rely on its own system. Europe saw meteorology as an international issue, as interference to such synoptic messages posed a global danger for ship and air traffic that relied on these weather reports. The conference eventually allotted space for synoptic weather reports, as well as aircraft calling and distress service, time signals, radio-direction finding stations, and other point-to-point service messages.[65] These essential international services were addressed under article 5, which provided for freedom of international communication.[66] The delegates thus agreed upon a global system of emergency and information services, another example of limited globalization.

International broadcasting also raised issues of sovereignty and autonomy. While the principle of non-interference was to guide domestic broadcasting that might overlap international borders, long-distance broadcasting was more difficult to regulate. Long-distance broadcasting, or relay broadcasting, used higher frequencies than regular short-distance stations and was more sensitive to environmental influences. The representative of the International Radio Union stressed the importance of long wavelengths for broadcasting because they allowed for transmissions in mountainous regions and over great distances in rural districts.[67] Colonial powers, notably the British and the Dutch, were most concerned with relay broadcasting as a means of uniting their far-flung empires. The Dutch argued that their long-distance broadcasts should have priority on higher frequencies.[68] Tropical states, where static is more prevalent, also supported the separate allocation of short-wave frequencies for relay broadcasting.[69]

Although Washington was lukewarm towards the use of long waves, long-distance broadcasting had friends in US private industry. Radio engineer consultant Alfred Goldsmith argued that relay broadcasting was "not a mere communication from one individual to another, but is in a sense a message addressed by the people of one nation ... and it therefore partakes of the nature of a quasi-national activity."[70] While the Dutch, like other colonial powers, wanted separate bands for relay broadcasting, they also opposed any provision that threatened their sovereignty in international waters. The final provisions on relay broadcasting were thus voluntary, allowing the regional regulation of limited broadcasting rights in long wavelengths where they already existed.[71]

Questions of national autonomy also influenced the final convention's split between the general regulations (featuring the allocation table, service regulations, and point-to-point transmissions), which all signatories supported, and a voluntary appendix, covering contested issues, such as telegraph communication rates, upon which nations were divided. The dual nature of the convention reflected the split over private or public ownership of broadcasting rights: "In Europe where the countries are relatively small in size and large in number, where languages differ and where customs and degree of technical progress vary greatly there seems to be a necessity for comprehensive and detailed agreements among *nations*." While "on the North American continent, where the countries cover a wide area and the same language is spoken there is no paramount need for a comprehensive and detailed international convention." Indeed, the United States argued that the market would reduce interference on its own and that to regulate broadcasting was "not only detrimental to the advance of science but also economically unsound."[72]

The European desire to link the IRC and ITC was also opposed by the United States and Canada, which both wanted the autonomy to set their own telecommunication prices.[73] While European states, which owned their own broadcasting stations, could implement regulations immediately, North American governments needed to pass separate domestic laws compelling private interests to adhere to any new international regulations. Western European officials also wanted the International Technical Committee in Berne to act as a final arbitrator for disputes, a proposal rejected by the United States on the grounds of state sovereignty. As a result, the Berne Bureau assumed its present role as a technical advisory board and information clearinghouse. Despite the agreement reached on sharing the frequency band, the split structure of the convention reveals the limits of global thinking in the late 1920s, when nationalism and demands for national autonomy were ascendant.

The existence of regional agreements also attenuated the convention's global reach. With the Berne Bureau denied punitive powers, the IRC was, in effect, a voluntary agreement. Signatories were to work out multilateral problems in a multilateral fashion. This structure is less surprising if the global radio regulations are seen as contemporaries saw them — as an unusually broad multilateral agreement. Consequently, the IRC delegates encouraged the use of regional agreements, many of which predated the IRC, to ensure that the convention would function effectively. The North American Radio Broadcasting Agreement provided a forum for Canada, the United States, and Mexico to arbitrate disputes. The British-inspired International Broadcasting Union performed a similar function for European broadcasters. On an operational level, the outcome of the IRC represented the amalgamation of these regional agreements and itself encouraged the creation of further bilateral and multilateral agreements to uphold the principle of non-interference. The global radio rights established in 1927 were thus a result of extended multilateralism. Internationalism functioned as a midwife of globalization.

Consolidating and Expanding Global Rules

The IRC codified several other minor issues. The challenge of rapidly changing technology, for example, was addressed with the banning of spark sets, which transmitted damped waves that caused interference. Additionally, the IRC established acceptable levels of variance from the allocated band, a British-inspired international code of signals, minimal standards for mobile radio operators, a system of station call signals, and space for amateurs on the frequency table.[74]

The IRC's main achievement, however, was the establishment of frequency rights through the frequency allotment table. The table was displayed in a document of almost mystical complexity, occupying an entire wall of an expansive Department of Commerce boardroom. The table was largely silent, however, on the regulation of high frequencies (short-wave). These bands, which were only beginning to be exploited, were used mainly for international traffic (such as diplomatic communication) by maritime and aviation services and by amateurs. Short-waves were exploited in the 1930s for broadcasting to the developing world, a decisive step in reducing the conceptual and experiential divide between the industrial and colonial world.[75] The limitations of the IRC agreement were evident in the 1930s, when "jamming," the intentional interference of another broadcast, became widespread. Jamming is hard to prevent, especially as the IRC's principle of mutual consent was based on preventing unintentional interference. Austria was probably the first practitioner of this art, using it by 1934 to counter Nazi propaganda. In 1936 the League of Nations International Convention Concerning the Cause of Peace attracted thirty-seven signatories who pledged not to jam or use radio for political purposes. Germany was a notable absentee, and, in practice, by the late 1930s all European powers jammed except Britain, which feared that the practice would compromise its military and imperial strength.[76]

The regulation of high frequencies was debated at the 1938 Cairo radio-telegraph conference, but no agreement was reached on the issue until after the war. As in the earlier example of the Irish government using radio broadcasting to build a sense of national consciousness among its population, the practice of radio jamming for political purposes reveals how deeply entwined radio was with nationalism. Given these diverging national interests, the cooperation shown in the negotiation of the IRC is even more noteworthy.

The 1927 IRC was followed five years later by the Madrid Conference. While not as revolutionary, the Madrid agreement produced some nota-ble institutional advances. For example, it fused the Radio and Telegraph Conventions, reflecting an institutional transition from the international approach of the nineteenth century to the global approach of the twenti-eth century. Madrid also established the International Telecommunica-tions Union (ITU), an organization that remains at the forefront of global telecommunications administration.[77] These institutional developments embedded the property rights agreements reached at Washington within the emerging framework of global governance, which had begun to take shape in the interwar years, and which, as Adrian Jones shows in a dif-ferent context in his chapter on Nuremberg, flourished after the Second World War.

The IRC agreement has been modified many times, notably in re-sponse to lobbying at the ITU's World Administrative Radio Conference by developing nations for greater frequency access. Its property princi-ples, however, still hold force. The Washington model reflected an ideo-logical compromise borne of the debates over public and private use of the spectrum. The frequency table was devised to prevent global anarchy through mutual interference, a classic potential case of Hardin's tragedy of the commons. The table, however, created an artificial scarcity, with domestic regulators granting limited frequency rights to a small num-ber of interests, thus foregoing huge potential public profits and prevent-ing the general public from fully utilizing the airwaves. Nevertheless, the IRC did set a precedent. Although the international community has continued to use the national regulatory model to address other emerg-ing property types, it has followed the IRC compromise that some auton-omy must be given away and pooled to create a global commons. Such "globalism" has taken the form of information sharing, harmoniza-tion, and the increasing importance of technological change in relation to political difference, all factors central to the continued work of the

ITU. This compromise has helped to attenuate some, though not all, of the endemic friction between nation-states in general and between the Global North and the Global South in particular.

Conclusion

Regulation serves a gatekeeping function. Frequency regulation brought some order to a deterritorialized field and demonstrates that the nation-state, far from always preserving its autonomy, can sometimes be complicit in fostering globalization. Just as Internet Service Providers wield enormous power in the current world of electronic media, "owning" a space on the frequency band was tremendously important in the radio era, and continues to be so today. The radio regulatory model was adopted by subsequent international agreements for land-based television broadcasting. Satellite broadcasting seemed initially to pose a fatal blow to international communications regulation, as broadcaster and receptor would no longer necessarily be in the same country. The delegates to the 1971 World Administrative Radio Conference on space telecommunications, however, agreed that satellites should be construed as "high-flying aerials," and thus satellite broadcasting was incorporated into the IRC model. Satellite transmissions were only blocked between nations, such as the United States and Cuba, that did not politically recognize one another.[78] A more radical interpretation, known as the "Bogsch theory" after its proponent Arpad Bogsch, the former head of the World Intellectual Property Organization, stresses the autonomy of both satellite broadcaster and receptor and holds that the legislation of all receptor countries should be applied to satellite broadcasting cumulatively.[79] The Bogsch theory thus stresses the global and cosmopolitan over the national, represents a decisive break from the older de facto understanding of radio as an element of the nation-state, and anticipates the regulatory uncertainties created by the advent of new "virtual communities."

These new virtual communities are united not "by geographic proximity but by shared values, goals or experiences."[80] They potentially threaten the global equilibrium promoted, if not in practise always secured, by the principles of the IRC. As Leslie Pal details in his essay on Internet governance, a private entity — the Internet Corporation for Assigned Names and Numbers (ICANN) — rather than a multilateral agreement plays the largest regulatory role for the Internet.[81] Like the IRC, ICANN is an American-led initiative that, to a great degree, reflects the philosophy of private ownership. Unlike the IRC, ICANN allows little non-American input into its decisions. It is thus unaccountable to the global audience it serves. Perhaps the World Summit on the Information Society, a coalition of global information technology actors also discussed by Pal, will point the way to a more globally inclusive structure for Internet governance in the spirit of the IRC. Whether these new virtual communities will be subsumed under existing global regulatory models, create new arenas for autonomous expressions free from global homogenizing forces, or produce new and unpredictable scenarios are pressing current questions.

The sociologist Clive Kessler suggested in 2000 that globalization is "now arguably creating, for the first time in human history, the detailed social infrastructure of a single unified humanity, a universal human community: a network of mutual human interdependence and of worldwide involvement in one another's fate."[82] The radio negotiations of the 1920s and 1930s formed part of this process. Although radio quickly became a state tool of information management, it also created a new and profitable medium for dissent, resistance, and the preservation or creation of autonomy. The IRC negotiations signalled a change from international coexistence to international cooperation and interdependence.[83] The inherently "global" nature of radio necessitated a global means of regulation. This process was certainly uneven, especially in its tendency to favour industrial over underdeveloped states, yet it nonetheless deterritorialized the medium.[84] While the IRC delegates initially pursued competing national interests, they were forced to solve the problem of mutual interference by thinking globally. This process of growing global awareness both reified national interests, as delegates sought to locate their arguments within pre-existing boundaries (both geographical and cultural), and helped create a new, global, arena of shared endeavour.

Chapter 9   A Globalization Moment:
Franklin D. Roosevelt in
Casablanca (January 1943)
and the Decolonization/
Development Impulse

Ronald W. Pruessen

22 JANUARY 1943: Franklin D. Roosevelt is hosting a dinner for the
Sultan of Morocco, Prime Minister Winston Churchill, and other guests
in a villa on the outskirts of Casablanca. The president was about to return to Washington after a week of talks with Churchill about important war issues, including the timing and location of a "Second Front."
Given the battles raging on multiple fronts not so many miles away, security was tight around the villa. There had been a German air raid on
Casablanca three weeks before and Harold Macmillan later wrote that
as he approached the president's quarters he realized he had "never seen
so many sentries armed with such terrifying weapons." Around the dinner table, the atmosphere was lighter, almost celebratory for most of the
guests — in spite of the fact that deference to the Muslims present meant
an absence of alcohol.

    At one point in the evening, Roosevelt began chatting with the Sul-
tan "about the wealth of natural resources in French Morocco and the
rich possibilities for their development."

They were having a delightful time, their French — not Mr.
Churchill's strongest language — easily encompassing the question
of the elevation of the living standards of the Moroccans and — the
point — of how this would of necessity entail an important part of
the country's wealth being retained within its own boundaries.

> The Sultan expressed a keen desire to obtain the greatest possible aid in securing for his land modern educational and health standards ...
>
> [Roosevelt] remarked cheerfully enough that the postwar scene and the prewar scene would, of course, differ sharply, especially as they related to the colonial question ... dropping in a remark about how the past relationship between French and British financiers combined into self-perpetuating syndicates for the purpose of dredging riches out of colonies.[1]

The description of the above conversation is Elliot Roosevelt's (the president's son, who had been flown in from his posting in Algeria to see his father), and the memories of others present confirm its substance. Perennial diplomat Robert Murphy noted that British and French guests seemed either "outraged" or "perturbed," for example, at what they might have seen as "subversive" remarks. The president himself later recounted the story with relish, recalling how Churchill went "very red in the face" and began to "splutter."[2]

As is suggested by other chapters in this volume, a fully rounded understanding of globalization — and its impact on autonomy — requires attentiveness to impulses, initiatives, and patterns that long predate the application of the now pervasive label. Franklin D. Roosevelt's dinner with the Sultan of Morocco — as well as other aspects of the president's journey to North Africa in January 1943 — can serve as one useful example of a globalization moment not often recognized in later narratives.

Barely one year after the United States' entry into the struggle against the Axis powers, Roosevelt was clearly demonstrating a passionate interest in *postwar* planning — and his ideas and policy inclinations were precisely related to core features of what has come to be called globalization. On the one hand, for example, a presidential vision was emerging in which emphasis was placed on the creation of a literally global economic system, complete with liberal trade regulations and currency transactions. Vivification of the vision would require many reforms of traditional practices, very much including moves towards the breakup of established empires as well as the subsequent economic, social, and political development of former colonial regions. The combination of "decolonization" and "development" would be of great importance to the development (so to speak) of the concept of globalization that has proven so important to the history of subsequent decades.

On the other hand, Roosevelt's efforts on behalf of his vision — before, during, and after his visit to Casablanca — provide an early example of the special role to be played by the United States in the movement towards the practices and values associated with globalization. Indeed, given the shared convictions and powerful impact of his Washington successors, it seems appropriate to see Roosevelt's journey to Morocco as an episode in the deeper history of imperialism — particularly with respect to the issue of linkages between globalization and neocolonialism. The question underlying the latter term is whether the heteronomy to which many societies were subjected under classical imperialism would give way to collective autonomy or new structures of heteronomy. In short, the tensions between globalization and autonomy were already in evidence that mid-winter evening in Casablanca.

Continuing the Progressive Wilsonian Tradition

By 1943 Roosevelt saw the United States as being surrounded by a grievously troubled world. Although the bloodshed and destruction of the Second World War might alone have been responsible for these troubles, movement towards such a perception had actually been underway for more than two decades. In particular, Roosevelt's first exposure to Washington responsibilities had come during the Great War, and clear memories of earlier devastation greatly amplified the resonance of the subsequent struggle against the Axis powers. As well, it is almost needless to say that the president's worldview had been profoundly affected by the crisis of the Great Depression. He was convinced that years of grave economic difficulties had helped prepare the ground for a second world conflict.

Like other American leaders of the early 1940s, Roosevelt twinned his perception of a troubled world with a determination to build a better and safer one — and postwar planning became a major preoccupation long before an end to fighting drew near. Like these leaders, as well, Roosevelt put special emphasis on his own country's role when he thought about the future. He believed the United States had the wisdom and the power required to reform the international order in ways that would bring lasting peace and prosperity.

Sensitivity to problems and dangers beyond American borders was as old as the nation, of course — and then some, indeed, given the nation's birth by way of a break from the British Empire. In earlier times, though, a sense of superiority concerning the noble building project underway in the United States often prompted a tendency to see aloofness as a desirable posture. Economic and cultural ties with Europe could actually be very dense, but maxims such as "no entangling alliances" and pronouncements like the Monroe Doctrine demonstrated the attractiveness of an alternative vision.[3] American self-admiration took a more determined route around the turn of the twentieth century. The Progressive movement, which focused on the solution of domestic problems, combined with a consciousness of burgeoning us power to produce greater interest in using American insight and ingenuity to reform a flawed international order. Theodore Roosevelt, FDR's "Bull Moose" cousin, was an early exemplar. For all his reputation for bellicosity, the White House's first Roosevelt was also anxious to moderate at least some of what he saw as dangerous excesses at home and abroad. He worked to calm roiling imperial struggles during the Russo-Japanese War and at the Algeciras Conference, for example, and approved of the establishment of a Permanent Court of Arbitration at The Hague in 1907. William Howard Taft was enamoured of an American-style dollar diplomacy that promised to produce — he thought — a more peaceful international arena by "substituting dollars for bullets." Taft and his secretary of state, Philander Chase Knox, also hoped to persuade traditional imperial powers that a neutralization scheme for Manchurian railways would be a more modern and reasonable alternative to a classic struggle for spoils. And in the fire of a Great War — the conflict that powerfully demonstrated how systemic weaknesses greatly overpowered the tentative, early efforts of Progressives — Woodrow Wilson developed a much more ambitious American blueprint. Although most often associated with the founding of the League of Nations, Wilson's crusading zeal generated a sweeping agenda that also proposed liberal alternatives to what he (and others) saw as a long list of dangerously atavistic habits and practices. Imperialism, colonialism, militarism, and secret diplomacy, Wilson urged, should be replaced by self-determination, disarmament, open covenants, and open door trade practices.[4] The notion here of self-determination refers to the replacement of heteronomy with collective autonomy, in which nations would give themselves their own laws.

Franklin D. Roosevelt was a fully subscribed heir to the Progressive reform impulse. He was in his first term in the New York State Senate when he began supporting Wilson's presidential ambitions, and his loyalty led to an appointment as assistant secretary of the navy in 1913.[5] Work with this commander-in-chief left a permanent mark. There is an obvious linkage, for example, between FDR's defence of the League of Nations as vice-presidential candidate in 1920 and his key role as builder of a new international organization more than two decades later.

But Roosevelt both inherited and *extended* the Wilsonian enthusiasm for international reform. Designs for the United Nations Organization, which replaced the League of Nations, did not emerge from a simple dusting off of older templates, for instance. The passage of time and an accumulation of failures generated sometimes quite different plans — for the US president and many others — and Roosevelt certainly envisioned detailed and complex possibilities in which his predecessor had shown little or no interest. (One case in point: FDR's death prevented any real experimentation with his Four Policemen notions, but the articulation of the concept demonstrated the presence of an energetic — and typical — experimental streak.) The New Deal's foreign policies from beginning to end also evidenced enthusiasm for international economic reform — *and* a readiness to push beyond the more limited steps taken during Wilson's presidency. The Reciprocal Trade Agreements Act of 1934 and the grand-scale designs encapsulated by the term *Bretton Woods* (the International Monetary Fund, the World Bank, and so on) built expansively on Progressive interest in a more open and flexible world economy.[6]

FDR and Imperial Reform at Casablanca

Roosevelt's experiences in connection with the January 1943 Casablanca Conference reveal some of the specific foci encouraged by Wilsonian reform thinking *and* how that thinking evolved over time. In particular, Casablanca highlights the way in which decolonization had become an important feature of the president's postwar planning — and the way decolonization then served as a springboard to the emergence of development concepts.

In Roosevelt's case, imperial reform had emerged as an identifiable theme even before the United States entered the Second World War. British sensitivities meant that the subject was initially approached somewhat gingerly — which entailed a degree of vagueness — but neither London nor Washington leaders would have been under illusions about the direction of the president's thinking, particularly when it came to autonomy. Churchill, for example, was aware enough to explicitly exempt the British Empire from the August 1941 Atlantic Charter's pledge to "respect the right of all peoples to choose the form of government under which they will live; and the wish to see sovereign rights and self-government restored to those who have been forcibly deprived of them."[7] During the prime minister's visit to Washington shortly after Pearl Harbor, the theme of decolonization surfaced very precisely when the president urged the desirability of reform in India. Roosevelt couched the matter in the context of strengthening the anti-Japanese war effort, but Churchill knew perfectly well that it would be impossible to rebottle the genie of independence and angrily resisted discussion of the issue. At a White House dinner, Roosevelt nodded down the table in Churchill's direction and told the guest sitting next to him, "You know, my friend over there doesn't understand how most of our people feel about Britain and her role in the life of other peoples ... It is in the American tradition, this distrust, this dislike and even hatred of Britain — the Revolution, you know, and 1812; and India and the Boer War, and all that ... We're opposed to imperialism — we can't stomach it."[8]

Although Roosevelt saw nothing he would have regarded as progress with respect to India in the immediate aftermath of this Churchill visit, he did not stop fleshing out his own thoughts on decolonization. In a fashion particularly relevant to the role of decolonization and development strategies in the evolution of globalization, he began to couple references to imperial reform with speculation about trusteeship. When Russian Foreign Minister Vyacheslav Molotov visited Washington in May 1942, for example, he seems to have been taken aback when one conversation found the president sketching in a plan for international control of the Pacific islands that had been turned over to Japan as mandates by the League of Nations. Roosevelt warmed to his theme by also speculating about the fate of "colonial possessions" in general: "The President took as examples Indochina, Siam, and the Malay States, or even the Dutch East Indies. The last-mentioned would some day be ready for self-government, and the Dutch know it. Each of these areas would require a different lapse of time before achieving readiness for self-government, but a palpable surge toward independence was there just the same, and the white nations thus could not hope to hold these areas as colonies in the long run."[9] Although it is rarely noted in traditional accounts, the Casablanca Conference provided a significant new opportunity for the articulation and advancement of Roosevelt's thoughts on decolonization.

Ordinarily, the conference is seen as one knot in the string of top-level Anglo-American consultations concerning the conduct of the war against the Axis. In Morocco in January 1943, Roosevelt, Churchill, and a clutch of key military advisors went through another round of deliberations on the timing and location of a second front — and tried to defuse likely Moscow suspicions about delays by pronouncing the unconditional surrender policy for the common enemy. They also struggled to sort out and manage the shifting intricacies of the French political situation by arranging what was referred to as a "shotgun marriage" between Henri Giraud and Charles de Gaulle.[10]

But there were also moments in Casablanca that revealed how much Roosevelt looked beyond current battles and problems. Like Churchill and the British-American military team, he knew how important the second front and French political arrangements would be to an Allied victory. More than most of his colleagues in Casablanca, however, his mind would regularly focus on the world he hoped would emerge on the other side of that victory. Like Woodrow Wilson before him, Roosevelt continued to think about reforming the global structures and systems that had generated two world wars and a devastating economic crisis — with special emphasis on decolonization.

The nature of Roosevelt's Casablanca itinerary may explain why he regularly shared thoughts about imperial reform during his weeks away from Washington. The president's journey to and from Morocco required stops in Trinidad, Belem (Brazil), Bathurst (Gambia), and Dakar (Senegal). Literal immersion in the colonial world could easily have made issues that had long been of interest to him especially vibrant. There is evidence of conversations about imperialism (and its future) with his son Elliot, his confidante Harry Hopkins, and his British, French, and Moroccan interlocutors in Casablanca; with US Vice Consul Kenneth Pendar during an expedition to Marrakech; and with Liberian President Edwin Barclay and Brazilian President Getúlio Vargas during stopovers on the way home. While the frequency of Roosevelt's references might alone make it clear that such thoughts were not casual in nature during this journey, his subsequent behaviour and earlier interests make it even clearer. The thoughts and words do not figure in the standard literature dealing with the Casablanca Conference — but then previous accounts were often written with an eye to the military and political history of the Second World War rather than the evolution of decolonization and development policies (or the origins of globalization, for that matter).

It also deserves mention that Roosevelt's early 1943 journey into the colonial world was extremely unusual for him. His expedition to Africa had a unique and even dangerous character that is hard to appreciate more than six decades later. It is not too difficult to imagine that the memorable nature of his travels gave the episode an extra jolt of resonance as far as the president's thoughts and planning concepts were concerned.

The journeys to and from Casablanca saw Roosevelt's first air travel as president, for example — the first air travel undertaken by any president while in office, in fact. And what journeys they were. Both the state of technology and wartime conditions meant that it took the president three days to get from Washington to Morocco. Nor was the prospect of enemy attention the only danger in the air. Roosevelt's sometime fragile health was also a real issue: his doctor was a member of the presidential party, for example, and his awareness of the problems inherent in maintaining cabin pressure led him to insist on longer flight routes that would avoid trickier altitudes above 11,500 feet.[11]

Some of Roosevelt's comments and conversations during his complex itinerary touched old bases — such as his overarching concern for colonial reform. As he told the Sultan of Morocco (during the dinner described at the beginning of this chapter), "the postwar scene and the prewar scene would, of course, differ sharply, especially as they related to the colonial question." In discussions with his son Elliot, he was even more emphatic. "When we've won this war," he told him at one point, "I will work with all my might and main to see to it that the United States is not wheedled into the position of accepting any plan that will further France's imperialistic ambitions, or that will aid or abet the British Empire in its imperial ambitions." Indeed — and this point is certainly confirmed in other sources — the president made it clear that he had no intention of waiting until the end of the conflict to make this point to Churchill: "First at Argentia, later in Washington, now here at Casablanca," Roosevelt told his son, "I've tried to make it clear to Winston — and the others — that while we're their allies, and in it to victory by their side, they must never get the idea that we're in it just to help them hang on to their archaic, medieval Empire ideas."[12]

Roosevelt also returned to his interest in trusteeship during his Casablanca journey. He wanted Robert Murphy to keep this in mind during evolving conversations with the French, making sure to avoid any apparent American commitment to "guarantee the return to France of every part of her empire."[13] The president gave a clear example of what he had in mind during a conversation with Brazilian President Vargas on the return journey to Washington. He spoke about the need to make new arrangements for French colonies and possessions in Africa and the Americas. With respect to Dakar, in particular, Roosevelt said it "should be left after the war in some sort of trusteeship: three commissioners, perhaps: one from United States, one from Brazil and one from some other American country, perhaps."[14]

Casablanca also revealed a distinctive new twist in Roosevelt's reform thoughts — one perhaps inherent in his overall worldview and his experience, but not previously elaborated in the way that became more common and influential from this point on. It was during his expedition to Morocco that Roosevelt first pushed his interest in decolonization towards a specific concern for development issues. And, as his son later noted, development went on to become "one of his favorite topics."[15]

Many of Roosevelt's previous references to colonial reform and trusteeship had either been of a relatively sketchy and abstract nature or had limited elaboration to essentially *political* matters relating to collective autonomy. The Atlantic Charter referred to restoring "sovereign rights and self-government ... [to] those who have been forcibly deprived of them," for example — and the president's 1942 ruminations to Molotov referred to self-government as the end result of a period of colonial trusteeship.[16] During his journey to and from Morocco, however, Roosevelt began to discuss what he saw as the significant *economic* and *social* dimensions of a trusteeship–self-government sequence. His sensitivity to such dimensions is not at all surprising given the decade of New Deal experience that predated the Casablanca Conference, but its specific and first-time application to decolonization suggests that this is an important moment in the evolution of development (and, again, globalization).

Roosevelt articulated these new themes repeatedly in January 1943. Shortly after his arrival in Casablanca, for example, he told his son about the future role of a revived international organization in the reform of traditional imperialism: "France, for example. France will have to take its rightful place in that organization. These great powers will have to assume the task of bringing education, raising the standards of living, improving the health conditions — of all the backward, depressed colonial areas of the world."[17] When Roosevelt hosted his dinner for the Sultan of Morocco, living standards, health care, and education were again specifically identified as key gauges — and in a conversation with a skeptical

US vice consul the following day, the president argued that there was a real chance for New Deal approaches to have an impact on Morocco.[18] Nor was this a momentary Moroccan fancy. Liberian President Edwin Barclay later said that "world social and economic problems" figured in his conversation with Roosevelt during a Monrovia stopover on the way back to Washington, perhaps as something of a backdrop to specific discussions of US assistance with a harbour expansion project. Another stopover in Brazil found Roosevelt discussing Brazilian industrial development with President Getulio Vargas.[19]

Roosevelt actually began to use the specific term *development* at this point, as well, and he used it in a way that would be thoroughly recognizable by the experts and advocates of later years. During a conversation with the Sultan, for example, the Moroccan leader bemoaned the fact that a shortage of qualified scientists and engineers in his country would hamper efforts to improve health care and education. In reply, the president "suggested mildly that Moroccan engineers and scientists could of course be educated and trained under some sort of reciprocal educational program with, for instance, some of our leading universities in the United States ... He [also] mentioned that it might easily be practicable for the Sultan to engage firms — American firms — to carry out the development program he had in mind, on a fee or percentage basis."[20] If his journey to Casablanca reveals Roosevelt's evolving thoughts on decolonization and development, his conversations were also numerous and expansive enough to illuminate the logic that drove his intellectual movement. Several threads are discernible, each separate but ultimately complementary, with a range that suggests a complex mind and a determined will.

At times, for example, Roosevelt voiced what might have been taken for abstract ethical concerns. As Harry Hopkins put it in a conversation with the Sultan's vizier, the president believed "that many peoples of the world have not had their rightful share of the good things of the world." Imperialism was to blame: "Powerful countries have exploited smaller countries," with "wealth and resources" being "siphoned out for the benefit of the powerful country."[21] Roosevelt's impression had been dramatically reinforced by his stopover in the Gambia on the way to Casablanca. His son's memory of his father's description is vivid:

At about eight-thirty, we drove through Bathurst to the airfield. The natives were just getting to work. In rags ... glum-looking

... They told us the natives would look happier around noontime, when the sun should have burned off the dew and the chill. I was told the prevailing wages for these men was one and nine. One shilling, ninepence. Less than fifty cents ... A day! Fifty cents a day! Besides which, they're given a half-cup of rice ... Dirt. Disease. Very high mortality rate. I asked. Life expectancy — you'd never guess what it is. Twenty-six years. Those people are treated worse than the livestock. Their cattle live longer![22]

Two months later, the memory lingered. In a half-joking but biting letter written to Churchill while Anthony Eden was visiting Washington, Roosevelt mentioned a recent bout of the flu: "I think I picked up sleeping sickness or Gambia fever or some kindred bug in that hell-hole of yours called Bathurst."[23]

Roosevelt was not simply moved by abstract idealism, however — anymore than Woodrow Wilson had been before him. Both presidents could be naive at times, to be sure, but each also had a hard-headed practicality that is missed by those who focus on their supposed lack of realism. In January 1943, for example, Roosevelt's sense of the unfairness of traditional imperialism was never really separate from his conviction that a whole range of global reforms was a pragmatic and vital necessity. War and economic crisis would otherwise remain on the horizon. During one Casablanca discussion of the French empire, for example, the president could not have been clearer in his articulation of national interest:

Why does Morocco, inhabited by Moroccans, belong to France? Or take Indo-China ... Why was it a cinch for the Japanese to conquer that land? The native Indo-Chinese have been so flagrantly downtrodden that they thought to themselves: Anything must be better, than to live under French colonial rule ... I'm talking about another war ... about what will happen to our world, if after this war we allow millions of people to slide back into the same semi-slavery! ... Don't think for a moment ... that Americans would be dying in the Pacific tonight, if it hadn't been for the shortsighted greed of the French and the British and the Dutch.[24]

Not that the logic behind Roosevelt's decolonization/development enthusiasm was solely negative in tone. In keeping with his ebullient personality — and a New Deal–spawned interest in using economic growth to solve severe problems — his sensitivity to ethical or geopolitical issues could also pull him in the opposite direction. His son later described a Casablanca conversation that touched on North African geography and terrain. In words whose spirit might easily have figured in some earlier dialogue about the Tennessee Valley Authority, the president recalled that rivers beginning in the Atlas Mountains disappeared under the Sahara: "Divert this water flow for irrigation purposes," he said. "It'd make the Imperial Valley in California look like a cabbage patch ... The Sahara would bloom for hundreds of miles!"[25]

Decolonization, Development, and Globalization

If his journey to Casablanca reveals the way Roosevelt's long-established Wilsonian interest in *decolonization* could spawn attentiveness to economic and social development, why does it deserve to be seen as a *globalization moment*? What is there about this decolonization/development combination — or, perhaps more precisely, about Roosevelt's particular uses of the concepts of decolonization and development — that illuminates the earlier history of globalization and autonomy?

Two features of the combination deserve to be highlighted here. On the one hand, Roosevelt's 1943 behaviour can be seen as an early example of key intellectual shifts in thinking that led the way to the eventual coining of the term *globalization* — a concept that invites a distinctive way of thinking and looking at the world. On the other hand, Casablanca also reveals Roosevelt's interest in the kind of actions and policies that would figure prominently in a globalization agenda.

Roland Robertson's study of globalization points to the way in which the compression of the world in the twentieth century — engendered especially by technological and economic developments — can produce an "intensification of consciousness of the world as a whole" or "consciousness of the global whole."[26] Franklin Roosevelt revealed exactly this pattern as a literally global thrust became characteristic of his thinking. By 1943 he routinely spoke — not at all carelessly — of the need to build a better "postwar *world*." In the 7 January 1943 State of the Union address given just days before he left for Casablanca, he could not have been clearer:

Victory in this war is the first and greatest goal before us. Victory in the peace is the next. That means striving toward the enlargement

of the security of man here and *throughout the world*. It is of little account for any of us to talk of essential human needs, of attaining
security, if we run the risk of another World War in ten or twenty
or fifty years. That is just plain common sense. Wars grow in size,
in death and destruction, and in the inevitability of engulfing *all
nations*, in inverse ratio to *the shrinking size of the world* as a result of
the conquest of the air. I shudder to think of what will happen to
humanity, including ourselves, if this war ends in an inconclusive
peace, and another war breaks out when the babies of today have
grown to fighting age.[27]

Such conceptualization and phrasing also precisely demonstrate a related
reference in Martin Albrow's work on globalization's distinguishing features — that is, to the way "the globe serves as a focus for, or a premise
in shaping, human activities."[28]

Of course, it might be argued that Roosevelt's emphasis on "the
world" was really just a variation on what has long been labelled "internationalism." As a child, the future president maintained a stamp collection that intrigued him through its glimpses of far off lands: Was this not
akin to the inclinations that had led many rulers and statesmen, business
leaders and missionaries, writers and artists to interests in the wider (and
wider) world throughout history? But Roosevelt as president can legitimately be seen as possessed of both an internationalist and a more dis-
tinctly global vision. In particular, his thoughts on decolonization and
development took the breadth of internationalism and added an intensity
and depth that are more appropriately linked to globalization. And this
global vision included a new perspective on autonomy in its emphasis on
the end of classical imperialism.

The distinctions between breadth, intensity, and depth become clear-
est when the actions emerging from intellectual perceptions are considered. Policy commitments linked to decolonization, for example,
were strikingly in tune with the emphasis on integration and perme-
ability within late twentieth-century globalization. The literature on
globalization is consistent in pointing to these characteristics, in spite of
many variations in analyses of sources and consequences. In a now classic account, Thomas L. Friedman described "the inexorable integration
of markets, nation-states, and technologies to a degree never witnessed
before — in a way that is enabling individuals, corporations, and nation-states to reach around the world farther, faster, deeper, and cheaper

than ever before."[29] Two variations on the same theme are offered by Jan Aart Scholte when he refers to the "process of removing government-imposed restrictions on movements between countries in order to create an 'open,' 'borderless' world economy" — and by Anthony Giddens when he surveys the "reconfiguration of geography, so that social space is no longer wholly mapped in terms of territorial places, territorial distances and territorial borders."[30]

When Roosevelt conceptualized the reform of traditional empires, he envisioned concrete steps that would lead in exactly these directions — steps without which, indeed, the integration and openness described could almost surely not have been achieved. Like Woodrow Wilson before him and like many American policy makers after him, he envisioned progression towards a liberalized international environment in which the prying open of doors to vast colonial realms would push the world towards the deterritorialization and supraterritoriality so much associated with globalization.[31] Where Roosevelt as an internationalist may have been content to have thoughts and concerns touch down in different parts of the world — in the way his plane landed again and again on his way to Casablanca — the Roosevelt who evolved towards an early vision of globalization wanted to enfold those different locales into what he believed would be a profoundly new world-system. (In the process, as will be discussed below, he was also imagining steps towards at least a partial reconceptualization of collective autonomy.) If the essence of internationalism can be captured by picturing the fingers of a hand being splayed to span separated points, a Roosevelt-like globalism requires appreciation for the hand's ability to hold the whole.

All by itself, Roosevelt's vision of decolonization increased the intensity or degree of internationalism towards thoughts, goals, and practices much associated with globalization. His interest in development — so evident at Casablanca in early 1943 — makes his relevance to an understanding of globalization's historical roots even more striking.

The logic behind the president's desire for imperial reform is particularly revealing here. As is suggested above, Roosevelt believed that a transition away from colonialism would eliminate one of the perennial causes of international conflict: competition among imperial powers for control of territories, resources, and markets. However, Roosevelt explicitly identified an additional source of global conflict: the resentment of colonial peoples against their imperial masters. It was his consciousness of such resentment that generated his remarks at Casablanca about the way British, French, and Dutch greed had prepared the ground for Japanese actions and a measure of broader Asian support for them.[32]

Roosevelt believed that the potentially explosive anger of colonial populations might be tamed, however, if steps were taken to avoid their slip back into "semi-slavery" — and the articulation of development possibilities in Casablanca was part of an intellectual process in which Roosevelt was essentially feeling his way towards the delineation of such steps. In this respect, as he did so often during the Second World War, the president was once again applying New Deal experiences and insights to the international arena. His own country had been in crisis when he was elected in 1932, and he had stumbled towards programs that would hopefully foster sufficient measures of rationalization and growth to avoid both a total collapse from and brutal conflicts over a redistribution of shrinking resources. Domestic trial and error — as well as an overlay of Keynesian logic — eventually made growth a central tenet of what became known as "vital center" liberalism: enough expansion of the economy to benefit all sectors and classes (even if all would not benefit in equal measure).[33]

Roosevelt's interest in development in 1943 makes it clear that he was contemplating the application of this liberal, reformist strategy to the colonial world. In doing so, he offers another example of the way globalization impulses are evident in his thinking and behaviour. Taking off from the speculations of Adam Smith, many recent theorists have been emphatic about the positive impact of an open and permeable world on prospects for economic growth. It was Smith who argued, for example, that the discovery of America and a passage to the East Indies were the most important events in recorded history: ships were able to bring together distant corners of the globe, "enabling them to relieve one another's wants ... increase one another's enjoyments ... encourage one another's industry." Jeffrey Sachs summarizes one strand of more current economic theory by underlining the way it stresses "that long-term growth depends on increased productivity and innovation, and that the incentives of both depend (as Smith conjectured) on the scope of the market. If innovators are selling into an expanded world market, they will generally have more incentive to innovate."[34]

In a variety of ways, then, Roosevelt's interest in decolonization and development connect with intellectual and policy patterns of central significance to an understanding of globalization. His combined interest in decolonisation *and* economic and social advancement, it might be added, also makes Roosevelt an important and often unappreciated transitional figure in the history of development: on the one hand, his evolving and multifaceted vision put him intellectually in front of his contemporaries among world leaders; on the other hand, his calculations and conceptualizations clearly predated the more familiar 1950s-60s formulations concerning growth and modernization.[35]

Though he had not much more than two years to live after returning from Casablanca, the president certainly worked to push his interests towards the kind of concretization that became more and more evident in subsequent decades. Anthony Eden had an early hint of momentum in Roosevelt's views a few months after the North African meeting — while the British foreign secretary was visiting Washington — when Roosevelt elaborated further on trusteeship concepts. (At one point, the president suggested that London might want to give up control of Hong Kong as a vigorous reform gesture.)[36] This early hint of staying power then found many subsequent echoes — in ongoing efforts to shape the trusteeship role of what became the United Nations Organization, for example, and in the conceptualization of the International Bank for Reconstruction and Development.[37]

The Problematic Nature of the Progressive Impulse

If Roosevelt's interest in decolonization and development help illuminate the early history of globalization, some aspects of the style with which he pursued his interests also illuminate later developments. A number of the more problematic features of latter-day globalization — including the way it has affected the autonomy of many actors in the international arena — were already evident in the 1943 moment being explored in this chapter.

Like other analysts of recent times, for example, Ulf Hedetoft argues — in his contribution to this volume as well as elsewhere — that the post-Cold War international order we have come to associate with globalization was "largely ... forged in the cauldron of US interests." Instead of an open world-system in which all have the potential to compete and grow and thrive, it has been regularly suggested that Americans have succeeded in creating a global arena in which they themselves enjoy significantly more wealth and power than anyone else (see Ulf Hedetoft's contribution to this volume). Countless references to American hegemony or the United States as a hyperpower testify to this — and while neither of these characteristics was especially discernible in the early

1940s, Roosevelt's thinking and behaviour certainly offer hints of what was frequently noted in later years.

The days surrounding the Casablanca Conference are revealing in this respect, as in others. Sometimes the suggestive moments were quite personal, reflective of the special power or style of this particular president. One member of Roosevelt's entourage recalled coming upon him in the salon of a Marrakech villa, shortly before a group would be gathering for pre-dinner drinks. He was "stretched out on one of the couches ... As I came up to him, he put out his hand to me, and said with an engaging smile: 'I am the Pasha, you may kiss my hand.'"[38] There is humour here that is quintessentially Roosevelt — but there is also a touch of what Harold Macmillan (who was at the Casablanca Conference) called "the Emperor of the West."[39] At other times, early 1943 moments are more suggestive of the dimensions of national power, which was clearly evident by this time. On 21 January, for example, Roosevelt, Harry Hopkins, and others travelled the eighty-five miles from Casablanca to Rabat to visit the US Fifth Army training there. In a vast North African field, the president lunched with twenty thousand American soldiers, eating boiled ham and sweet potatoes, fruit salad, and bread, butter, and jam; the Third Division Artillery Band could be heard in the background playing songs, "Chattanooga Choo Choo" and "Deep in the Heart of Texas," where they had probably never been played before. [40]

Such images can be seen as harbingers of the more blatantly obvious and essentially unique influence that would be exercised by the United States over the evolution of globalization processes and institutions — not to mention the limits to collective autonomy implicit in the conception of decolonization.[41]

The scale of American power is often seen as the backdrop to a tendency towards arrogant self-perceptions and condescending attitudes towards others. Here too Roosevelt in 1943 is suggestive of strains that are shared by both US behaviour and globalization. One key link in this case is the judgmental thrust inherent in many chartings of the development philosophy. As Gilbert Rist makes clear in his path-breaking work, superciliousness was often at the very core of the zeal that drove colonial enterprises long before the United States assumed a major international role: imperial powers saw themselves as keepers of the "sacred trust of civilization," charged with the mission of guiding backward peoples up from the Dark Ages. Policy makers in the United States had no trouble catching up with such attitudes. Indeed, the eventual determination to twin decolonization and development priorities — so strongly represented by Franklin Roosevelt — made an especially crucial contribution to the intellectual trajectory associated with globalization. American thinking and practice from the 1940s onward made it possible to shift from colonizer/ colonized conceptualizations and terminology to dichotomies in which underdevelopment and modernization were controlling concepts.[42]

Though hardly unique in this sense, Roosevelt could certainly send off signals of hauteur. These could be accompanied by a virtual wink — as in the "you may kiss my hand" moment — but there was enough deep-seated patrician self-confidence in this president to make it clear it was not simply humorous. At times, certainly, he could give voice to an almost magisterial paternalism. In a meeting with Charles de Gaulle in Casablanca — immediately after dinner with the Sultan — Roosevelt spoke of "his view that the Allied nations fighting in French territory ... should hold the political situation in trusteeship for the French people. In other words ... France is in the position of a little child unable to look out for and fend for itself and that in such a case, a court would appoint a trustee to do the necessary."[43] If this was the president's way of envisioning the state of one of Europe's traditionally great powers, it requires little effort to imagine a strong element of noblesse oblige in his thinking about those colonial peoples deserving of development opportunities and how much autonomy they might be able to handle.

Paternalistic presumptions are also clearly related to at least two other tendencies. On the one hand, particular styles of acting out the modernization and development impulse have relevance for the emerging literature on gender issues in international relations. A key link here — whether the focus is on Roosevelt in 1943 or globalization in its later forms — is the way that paternalism emerges in patriarchal contexts. A theoretical literature that dates back to Hobbes and Machiavelli as well as centuries of male-dominated governing structures have certainly generated language and assumptions about "male" responsibilities to protect and make advancements.[44]

On the other hand, many analysts would argue that the paternalist impulses of Roosevelt and globalization enthusiasts are essentially grounded in imperialist traditions and mindsets. When Rist suggests that US development programs allowed Washington to "deploy a new anti-colonial imperialism," for example, he is clearly highlighting innovation in style as opposed to the continuity of substance.[45] This theme also figures prominently in other contributions to this volume: Yassine

Essid grapples with the relevance of imperialist legacies to the continuation of development problems in North Africa; Stephen Streeter sees US efforts to win "hearts and minds" in Guatemala and Vietnam during the 1960s as "thoroughly infused with notions of empire and imperialism"; and Ulf Hedetoft locates "the bedrock of the global turn" in "imperial-cum-globalizing endeavours on the part of America."

For all his Wilsonian reform passion, it is not unreasonable to question just how far Roosevelt would have gone beyond an essentially formal decolonization process. When one twins this process with development, how much scope for collective autonomy is actually present? Even on this front, it has been shown that evolving circumstances had a way of affecting his sense of how earlier intentions might be executed — as with his early 1945 reconsideration of Indochina's future in the face of revised calculations concerning France's likely importance in postwar Europe.[46] Was this a special case — or would it have become a template? Would his liberal reform values have kept him more generally on track — and would even his approach to Indochina have evolved further (or again) when wartime pressures were lightened? Questions about the implementation of development visions might also be reasonably raised. Would Roosevelt's New Deal interest in encouraging a measure of equitable growth have translated into concrete results on the international level? Would the results have been more expansive in reach — more congenial to the autonomy of the United States' interlocutors — than concepts of neo-imperialism suggest, for example?

These are not merely rhetorical questions. Both domestically and internationally, Roosevelt revealed an ability to go beyond conventional or traditional categories — and not simply as an intellectual game. The Four Policemen concept he saw as a complement to plans for a new and inclusive international organization, for example, certainly suggested a capacity for thinking both idealistically and pragmatically — or even cynically. This capacity has generated much discussion about whether he would have been able to manage postwar relations with Moscow in such a way as to have prevented or significantly altered the Cold War that emerged so soon after his death.[47] Alternative scenarios for a post-1945 era in which Roosevelt continued to occupy the White House cannot persuasively posit a presidential style lacking in imperial character, however. It was only *four* policemen that he envisioned, after all, and an interest in cooperation among great powers would not have automatically promised much for those not in the club. This pattern is yet another tendency that links US policy impulses of the early 1940s with the globalization of more recent years.

Conclusion

It is, ultimately, impossible to determine all of the characteristics or implications of Franklin Roosevelt's decolonization/development impulse — since he died before he had an opportunity to fully translate ideas into practice. The presence of the impulse alone, however, gives the president's Second World War planning a real measure of substantive relevance to any charting of the roots of globalization and its impact on autonomy in the formerly colonized world. All by itself, it is important that Roosevelt *desired* Wilsonian, liberal reforms — and that his pursuit of objectives like decolonization and freer trade purposefully envisioned a permeable international system substantially more like what we see around us in the early twenty-first century than anything that preceded his tenure in the White House.

Among other things, the timing of Roosevelt's globalization moment at Casablanca suggests the need to somewhat stretch the chronology highlighted in other contributions to this volume. Yassine Essid, Ulf Hedetoft, and Stephen Streeter all persuasively demonstrate that the calculations and pressures of the Cold War era generated policies of relevance to globalization — and to the impact of globalization on autonomy. Consideration of the decolonization/development impulse in 1943, in contrast, leads attention to earlier currents as well. (If Roosevelt's wartime planning demonstrates some of the ways in which pre-Cold War events influenced the patterns and processes predominant at the start of the twenty-first century, it echoes thoughts informing Samir Saul's chapter in this volume.)

There was a moment at the end of the Casablanca Conference that hinted nicely at the longer-term relevance of Roosevelt's reform vision. As the president's plane taxied down the airport runway, Winston Churchill rapidly climbed back into a limousine and said he hated to watch planes take off. "It makes me far too nervous," he remarked, adding, "If anything happened to that man, I couldn't stand it. He is the truest friend; he has the farthest vision."[48] Despite his words on this occasion, Churchill often demonstrated his resistance to the thrust of Roosevelt's vision. In some respects, this resistance makes it all the more interesting that he could both prize the friendship and ruminate about who might be more in touch with the world of the future.

chapter 10   **Paradigm Shift and the Nuremberg Trials: The Emergence of the Individual as a Subject and Object of International Law**

Adrian L. Jones

At a casual glance, the proceedings at the International Criminal Tribunal for the Former Yugoslavia (ICTY) in The Hague, Netherlands, may have seemed rather underwhelming, given the modest courtroom setting and the exhaustive and mundane procedural matters. These trivialities do not diminish, however, the enormous social implications of that internationally sanctioned judicial process. Among those indicted by the ICTY was Slobodan Milosevic, the former president of Serbia and Yugoslavia, who sat approximately twenty metres away from the public and press gallery, buttressed by a soundproof glass barrier that enveloped the courtroom. Although he unexpectedly died during the latter stages of his trial in March 2006, the proceedings, as the first indictment (and subsequent trial) of a sitting head of state for alleged acts committed in that capacity, were a precedent-setting development in international criminal justice. The names of leaders such as Slobodan Milosevic and Charles Taylor, the former Liberian president, have become notorious in the global arena, but the prosecution of their alleged international crimes are comparatively recent developments. Accordingly, the novelty and significance of contemporary advances in international criminal justice must be appreciated in historical perspective. Within this context, the Nuremberg trials serve as the proper historical point of departure. Without discounting the significance of the subsequent Tokyo trials, the Nuremberg proceedings are widely considered to represent a watershed in international law because the International Military Tribunal for the

Far East essentially followed the Nuremberg tribunal's jurisprudence when it applied its own charter.[1]

Nuremberg typically conjures certain emotions and understandings, but it is generally not recounted in popular circles with any degree of detail. Its significance more broadly lies in catalyzing a fundamental shift in norms, expectations, and understandings of individual human worth, dignity, and responsibility, which came to be enshrined and developed within international law. In elevating or affirming the distinct situation of individual persons as direct *subjects* of regulation by international law, and as ultimate *objects* of the law's protection, the Nuremberg trials constituted a decisive departure — a paradigm shift — from previous eras of international law.[2] Here, the term *paradigm* refers to the prevailing and fundamental ontological premises upon which the world is understood. After Nuremberg the conventional image of an international system of sovereign states was eclipsed by a more complex view of global society that encompassed individuals, as such, through the principles and objectives of international criminal law. These conceptual understandings and sentimental connotations came to be globalized through international norms, treaties, institutions, and political discourses.

This account is not merely about crucial developments in international law. More fundamentally, a global normative awakening occurred in the wake of the Second World War, one of the most devastating conflicts in human history that encompassed atrocities of unprecedented dimension and gravity. The nature and magnitude of this globalization moment was underscored by the Nuremberg trials, which altered fundamentally the contours and provinces of international law. The proposition that individuals, including state officials, could be held accountable outside of the state for acts committed during armed conflict and for acts committed against their own citizens departed from conventional norms of insulated sovereign authority. The inverse proposition, also novel, was that all individuals are entitled to basic protections, irrespective of their citizenship and residency status. Indeed, the unique nature of what have come to be known as international human rights is that they are principally held by individuals in relation to their own governments. In bypassing sovereign states and attaching rights to all persons individually, these twin vertical dimensions constitute a striking directional exception within the broader horizontal ordering of the conventional international law of states.

This chapter focuses on the ongoing friction between ideals of personal autonomy on the one hand and the sovereignty and collective autonomy of states on the other, a friction that is foreshadowed in John Weaver's chapter in this volume. By the start of the Second World War, many critics had articulated the view that when certain aspects of personal autonomy, often formulated as "rights," are denied by states, individuals should have legal recourse or protection beyond states. In reaction to the large-scale atrocities committed in the Second World War, the Allied powers set up the legal framework for the Nuremberg trials, in part to address these rights issues. This fundamental change in thinking about the limits of state sovereignty represented a shift in the paradigm of the relations between individuals, their personal autonomy, and the states to which they belonged. This progression ultimately formed the basis for the permanent International Criminal Court (ICC), which entered into force in 2002. The ICC embraces and institutionalizes a dual notion of personal autonomy that transcends the collective autonomy of the state but also entrenches an extended exercise of collective autonomy at the level of global responsibility and governance.

Historical Foundations: Continuities and Discontinuities

Although the immediate physical destruction, human suffering, and atrocious wrongdoings committed against combatants and civilians in the Second World War were the proximate causes for the Nuremberg trials, the proceedings had deep social foundations and historical antecedents. Indeed, the ancient Stoic philosophical tradition conceived of a "natural law" that was premised upon fundamental notions of ethics and virtue and that encompassed concern for an extension of one's self to one's kin and to all of humanity.[3] These sentiments resurfaced within the classical revivals of the Renaissance and the Enlightenment.[4] Embryonic forms of human rights enactments such as the French Declaration of the Rights of Man and the Citizen and the American Bill of Rights, however, further reinforced the fusion of citizenship, patriotism, and nationhood.[5] These proclamations did not contemplate enforcement through scrutiny external to the state, much less invite formally sanctioned global accountability.

One of the oldest international crimes is piracy. However, efforts to punish and deter piracy through international law constituted more of a loosely coordinated response to a practical problem than a collective resolve fuelled by normative condemnation. The law came to deem piracy an international crime because the boundaries of its commission were international, on the high seas. The given crimes were essentially domestic wrongdoings — theft, hijacking, and so on — which happened to be committed in international settings. In contrast, what was unique about the Nuremberg trials was the introduction or affirmation of international, or "global," crimes with transcending normative resonance. The Nuremberg tribunal authoritatively deemed such offences as an inherent violation of global standards of conduct, quite apart from their direct transborder effects or lack thereof. International crimes do not encompass all infractions of humanitarian or human rights law: they include only those atrocities "characterized by the directness and gravity of their assault upon the human person, both corporeal and spiritual."[6] As reflected in the ICC's jurisdiction, discussed below, they have the "strongest 'peace and security' element or the strongest link to 'the collective conscience of humanity.'"[7] These crimes directly and fundamentally threaten the "ideal, attainable and urgent autonomy" of individuals.[8]

Governance of the conduct of armed conflict also predated the Second World War. Informally, the norms associated with "the warrior's honour" in combat are timeless: "Wherever the art of war was practiced, warriors distinguished between combatants and noncombatants, legitimate and illegitimate targets, moral and immoral weaponry, civilized and barbarous usage in the treatment of prisoners and the wounded. Such codes may have been honored as much in the breach as in the observance, but without them war is not war — it is no more than slaughter."[9]

Henri Dunant, who helped found the International Red Cross and Red Crescent movement and was the first recipient of the Nobel Prize, helped initiate the modern codification of these principles in international humanitarian law. The 1864 Geneva Convention, which introduced basic protections for war victims, was succeeded by the 1899 and 1907 Hague Conventions, which distinguished between combatants and civilians. But both conventions were otherwise very conservative relative to contemporary legal principles. The nature and scope of international humanitarian law — what it was designed to accomplish and how — changed dramatically after the total war and home front experiences of the Second World War. Mirroring the codification of international human rights, international humanitarian law took a progressive, individual-focused turn. The standards set by the 1949 Geneva Convention "represented a shift from the methods of warfare to the protection of the victims of war," including civilians.[10]

The most direct antecedent to the Nuremberg and Tokyo trials was the post-First World War Commission on the Responsibility of the Authors of the War and on Enforcement, which proposed that the peace treaties envisaged at the Paris Peace Conference of 25 January 1919 confer criminal jurisdiction over individual persons.[11] Indeed, the International Military Tribunal (IMT) at Nuremberg specifically referenced that commission as a crucial precedent for the principle of individual criminal responsibility under international law.[12] Part VII of the Treaty of Versailles, entitled "Penalties," was intended to deal with such questions. In particular, Wilhelm II of Hohenzollern, formerly the German kaiser, was to be tried for "a supreme offence against international morality and the sanctity of treaties."[13] However, in the interests of promoting stability within the Weimar Republic, the Allies simply requested that Germany prosecute a limited number of war criminals before its Imperial Supreme Court in Leipzig.[14] According to one legal scholar, this episode also highlighted the political uncertainties and anxieties associated with international trials: "It can become a political contest over historical truth or political responsibility and this can prove embarrassing for the prosecuting State or organization. Austen Chamberlain anticipated some of these problems when he cautioned against plans to prosecute the Kaiser after the Great War by remarking that 'his defense will be our trial.'"[15] In any event, these early attempts to impose individual criminal responsibility ultimately failed in an era that continued to adhere to strict understandings of national sovereignty, as questions of individual accountability were overtaken by considerations of political expedience and convention.[16] The Allies' intent to prosecute Turkish officials under the Treaty of Sevres for committing mass atrocities — now widely recognized as genocide — against the Armenians also succumbed and deferred to half-hearted national proceedings.[17] The Armenian tragedy and its aftermath eerily foreshadowed events to come. One legal historian has observed: "Many see the lack of attention following the Armenian genocide as an important precedent for the subsequent Holocaust of World War II. Indeed, it has been reported that, in trying to reassure skeptics of the viability of his genocidal schemes, Hitler stated, 'Who, after all, speaks today of the annihilation of the Armenians?'"[18]

Formal international law remained rigidly state-centric prior to the Nuremberg trials. Indeed, the organizational principle of state sovereignty perhaps reached its zenith in the decades leading up to the Second World War, when there was generally conceived to be a sharp demarcation between the internal and external affairs of states. States understood that direct and indirect interference in their domestic affairs was unequivocally proscribed. Within this context, the law deemed individuals to be subsumed by states. The individual had no formal standing under international law and minimal visibility within broader realms of global politics. Individuals were subjects and objects of international law only indirectly, by virtue of their citizenship and residency status within states. The historical precursors surveyed above demonstrate, however, that the ascendance of the sovereign state in formal international law was, nonetheless, accompanied by a normative undercurrent that acknowledged the transnational status of the individual. Although discussions after the First World War failed to fuse these disparate legal and normative trajectories, those precursory developments helped set the stage for the legal breakthrough at Nuremberg.

Legal and Political Dimensions

As victory for the Allies in the Second World War became imminent, widespread reports of mass atrocities raised the issue of responsibility for such wrongdoings and the mechanisms by which justice would be administered. In October 1943, the United States, the United Kingdom, the Soviet Union, and China signed the Joint Four-Nation Declaration. It stated that national prosecutions would be conducted pursuant to the laws of free governments in the liberated countries, but "without prejudice to the case of German criminals whose offenses have no particular geographical localization" and who would be prosecuted by the joint declaration of the Allies.[19] This agreement led to the Trial of the Major War Criminals before the International Military Tribunal (IMT) at Nuremberg.

In August 1945, France, Great Britain, the Soviet Union, and the United States signed the "Prosecution and Punishment of the Major War Criminals of the European Axis," an agreement that formally established the Charter of the International Military Tribunal.[20] The charter, which provided for the constitution, jurisdiction, and functions of the IMT, recognized three crimes against international law: crimes against peace, war crimes, and crimes against humanity (art. 6). Other significant principles included the following: individual criminal responsibility (art. 6);

irrelevance of official position for considerations of responsibility or miti-
gation of punishment (art. 7); superior orders would not excuse, but would
perhaps mitigate, criminal responsibility (art. 8); defendants would receive
a fair trial (art. 16); the tribunal's judgment would be final and not subject
to review (art. 26); and convicted persons would face death or other just
punishment (art. 27). That all the judges and prosecutors were appointed
by the original four powers constituted perhaps the major drawback of the
proceedings.[21] Nonetheless, the willingness of the other nineteen Allied
states to sign the charter bolstered the IMT's international legitimacy.[22]

In addition to their respective legal traditions, the Allied powers each
brought specific concerns to bear on the political debates surrounding the precise charges to be laid.[23] Genocide, as such, was not included
in the Nuremberg indictments because of French and Soviet concerns
about the domestic persecution of their own populations.[24] Accordingly,
the charge of crimes against humanity was adopted, which was more
closely linked to crimes against peace.[25] The IMT declared: "The persecution of Jews at the hands of the Nazi Government has been proved
in the greatest detail before the Tribunal. It is a record of consistent and
systematic inhumanity on the greatest scale."[26] In contrast, the atrocities
committed against the Jews preceding the outbreak of war were found
to rest outside of the tribunal's jurisdiction, not having been committed
"in execution of, or in connection with" any of the crimes listed in the
charter.[27] Nonetheless, the Nuremberg trials catalyzed the enactment of
the 1948 Convention on the Prevention and Punishment of the Crime of
Genocide, which, according to one scholar, "ensured that the Holocaust
was 'the' defining event of the twentieth century."[28] Genocide is now
firmly established as a distinct atrocity under international criminal law,
although the first international conviction did not occur until a 1998 case
before the International Criminal Tribunal for Rwanda (ICTR).[29] Hence
the paradigm shift ultimately did not forestall the so-called age of genocide in the twentieth century.[30]

The IMT demonstrated a progressive view of international law and
the social ills with which it should be properly concerned: "The law of
war is to be found not only in treaties, but in the customs and practices
of states [and] from general principles of justice. This law is not static,
but by continual adaptation follows the needs of a changing world."[31] In
perhaps the most oft-cited passage delivered by the IMT, the notion of
sole state responsibility was rejected: "Crimes against international law
are committed by men, not by abstract entities, and only by punishing

individuals who commit such crimes can the provisions of international law be enforced."[32] This articulation of individual criminal responsibility was a striking departure from conventional understandings of state sovereignty and the legal immunity of state leaders. Individualized guilt did not, however, detract from the trials' broader social objectives of re-educating the German population and European societies more generally."[33] In rebuking the superior orders defence, the IMT declared: "That they [the accused] were assigned their tasks by a dictator does not absolve them from responsibility for their acts. The relation of leader and follower does not preclude responsibility here any more than it does in the comparable tyranny of organized domestic crime."[34]

Practical considerations limited the number of defendants who could be tried. Also, several top Nazi officials had not survived the war, including Adolf Hitler who had committed suicide. Twenty-four defendants were selected from the most senior ranks of the Nazi apparatus and charged. One committed suicide, and one was determined to be unfit to stand trial. Twenty-two were tried, one *in absentia* (Martin Bormann). The trial lasted ten months. Three defendants were acquitted. Of the nineteen convicted, twelve were sentenced to death (including Bormann), three received life sentences, and four received lesser terms of imprisonment.[35]

The IMT's core judicial pronouncements were affirmed by the UN General Assembly and then formulated by the UN International Law Commission as the seven Principles of Law Recognized in the Charter of the Nuremberg Tribunal and in the Judgment of the Tribunal (the Nuremberg Principles): (I) individual responsibility for crimes under international law; (II) internal laws do not relieve such responsibility; (III) irrelevance of official capacity; (IV) irrelevance of government or superior orders, provided a "moral choice" was available; (V) right to fair trial; (VI) crimes punishable under international law: crimes against peace, war crimes, crimes against humanity; and (VII) complicity in the commission of such crimes is a crime under international law.[36] As one law professor has explained, these principles established a "new relationship between the individual, the State, and the international community [joining with the Charter of the United Nations] as part of the revolution in public consciousness."[37]

Given the IMT's judicial and prosecutorial composition, as well as the departure from strict principles of legality or established legal convention, some critics derided the proceedings as victors' justice and retrospective law.[38] Unease with the proceedings lay not only with those before the tribunal but also with many legal experts in Britain and the United States who were divided on the right of the victorious to bring the German leaders to trial.[39] These concerns have endured, notwithstanding that the IMT directly addressed such charges.[40] Nonetheless, the prevailing legacy of Nuremberg was the legal establishment of the individual as a distinct subject and object of international law. Moreover, one scholar has found it "historically remarkable that after the most destructive and uncivilized conflict in human history, there should have been resort to the civilized institutional drama of a trial at law."[41] This legal outcome is particularly striking when one considers that Winston Churchill had reportedly invoked the "outlaw" principle, thereby proposing that enemy leaders should be summarily executed upon their capture.[42]

The UN General Assembly resolution of 1946 that endorsed the Nuremberg Charter envisaged that some more permanent arrangement would be made.[43] There were a range of institutional proposals, but efforts to this end became fragmented and half-hearted in the Cold War political climate.[44] Nonetheless, the International Law Commission continued to work on a design for a tribunal, as did several prominent public intellectuals, including Benjamin Ferencz, a member of the US prosecution team at Nuremberg. Meanwhile, the Nuremberg legacy continued to manifest itself, helping to catalyze the enactment and progressive development of international human rights standards and the modernization of international humanitarian law.

In sum, the Nuremberg trials punctuated underlying and more fundamental evolutionary dynamics within global legal, social, and political systems. Nonetheless, the proceedings were not purely the culmination of linear trends in these domains. As Anthony Hopkins has observed, stages of globalization typically coexist with their predecessors and successors, whether symbiotically or competitively.[45] In this case, the elevation of the individual as a distinct subject and object of international law and as a global social concern introduced a novel tension, or friction, within the state-centric paradigm of international affairs. In the aftermath of unprecedented suffering and destruction, a current of postwar internationalism fuelled a determination for reconstruction and improvement.[46] Nuremberg's significance is properly considered within this broader historical context. The trials reflected and reinforced normative foundations of individual worth and dignity, and they validated not only global concern for such ends but also global responsibility. These sentiments were derived from a broader foundation of globality, or the notion of a "world society." As the historian Akira Iriye has explained, the term *global consciousness* can be used to suggest "the idea that there is a wider world over and above separate states and national societies, and that individuals and groups, no matter where they are, share certain interests and concerns in the wider world."[47] Although such sentiments existed prior to the Second World War, they were nonetheless fundamentally transformed by the experience of atrocities during this war and their prosecution at Nuremberg.

Globalizing the Nuremberg Legacy: Evolving Norms and Practices of Autonomy

The contemporary international human rights regime reflects the same normative concerns that founded the Nuremberg proceedings and their embodiment of respect for the worth and dignity of all persons. Its major components include the 1948 Universal Declaration of Human Rights, the 1948 Convention on the Prevention and Punishment of the Crime of Genocide, the 1966 International Covenant on Civil and Political Rights, and the 1966 International Covenant on Economic, Social and Cultural Rights. States agreed to the establishment of global institutions such as the UN Office of the High Commissioner for Human Rights and significant regional bodies such as the European Commission of Human Rights and the Inter-American Commission on Human Rights, which were charged with promoting respect for these principles and protections. Encouraging respect for human rights is also listed in the founding Charter of the United Nations as one of its fundamental principles and purposes (art. 1[3]). The charter also mandates the UN to promote universal respect for, and observance of, human rights and fundamental freedoms (art. 55[c]) and requires that all members take joint and separate action for the achievement of such purposes (art. 56).[48] In practice, these prescriptions have awkwardly contended with the charter's proscription against intervention in matters that are essentially within the domestic jurisdiction of any state (art. 2[7]). Nonetheless, the charter authoritatively distinguishes between individual autonomy and states' prerogatives.

Although the legitimacy of human rights has achieved widespread acceptance, scholarly debates continue over the precise theoretical basis of these rights. In the prevailing view, they are "inherent in the very idea of being human [and] have force whether or not they are explicitly recognized."[49] Their express recognition and enumeration after 1945 has, however, generated heightened respect for individual liberties and fundamental freedoms. The interrelated nature of such rights and protections for the autonomy and well-being of individuals and groups has also been increasingly acknowledged. The 1993 Vienna Declaration and Programme of Action recognizes that "all human rights are universal, indivisible, and interdependent" (art. 5). The UN Millennium Declaration echoed these sentiments: "Only through broad and sustained efforts to create a shared future, based upon our common humanity in all its diversity, can globalization be made fully inclusive and equitable."[50]

Although these developments within international law and institutions reflected broader evolutions of social identities, affiliations, and allegiances, sovereign statehood has remained the "grundnorm" of international law and politics.[51] Indeed, heightened preference for the state form of polity was evidenced by formal decolonization and the disintegration of the Soviet Union, which nearly quadrupled the number of UN member-states between 1945 and 2005. This ascendance of the sovereign state was somewhat paradoxically accompanied by new constraints upon the exercise, scope, and exclusivity of the state's authority. Acceptance and approval by other states was increasingly contingent upon a state's conduct towards its own citizens and residents, signifying a "new legitimation environment."[52] Infringing governments risked losing the requisite "legitimacy capital" for full and equal participation in international organizations and aid programs, as the government of apartheid South Africa demonstrated.[53]

This shifting social and political context had internal and external dimensions. Internally, human rights groups and social activists followed progressive normative trends by more boldly challenging the monopoly of state control and accountability. These practices referenced or embodied the very individual human rights protections that states themselves had erected. Dissenters and activists increasingly made their formal and informal appeals and grievances known not only to the subject state but also to external governments, international intergovernmental organizations, non-governmental associations, and the collective conscience of the global community.[54] In response, these external actors became emboldened in confronting states for their impugned *internal* actions. Complaints about human rights violations and state oppression were no longer confined to the insular diplomatic channels of interstate relations, but became increasingly manifest in global arenas, as advocacy groups and networks effectively championed the claims of domestic opposition groups.[55] Subsumed within such tactics were the now-familiar practices of "name and shame" politics.[56] As the political scientist Cecilia Lynch observes, "legal norms do not arise in a vacuum, but are socially contested, promoted, and legitimized."[57] These developing practices and concepts of autonomy rested within the shadow of globalization, and they continue to reflect and reinforce an emerging globality. State sovereignty was not always challenged per se, but core features of individual and collective autonomy — identity, community, and allegiance — were less presumptively or simplistically equated with state-based citizenship and residency.

Thus, the long-standing proscription against interference within states' sovereign affairs steadily began to yield to a more nuanced dialogue with normative concerns for the security and well-being of vulnerable individuals and groups. Sovereignty was increasingly seen as a "product of the recognition of the international system itself, rather than as a pre-existing trait inherent in States."[58] UN Secretary-General Kofi Annan declared in 1999: "States are now widely understood to be instruments at the service of their peoples and not vice versa."[59]

These evolving norms and practices of social concern and agency represent an embryonic manifestation of *global citizenship*. Traditionally, citizenship has been understood to involve a singular, bilateral relationship between the individual and the state.[60] As a feature of broader globalization trends, however, individual self-conceptions and expressions of citizenship have become increasingly variable, multi-faceted, and infused with a cosmopolitan ethic, thus having a "pluralizing impact on identity formation."[61] The concept of global citizenship permits a reconsideration of individual rights and responsibilities. The implication is that while states may remain the primary nexus of formal citizenship, they have become a less exclusive frame of reference for individual identities and allegiances. According to the human rights scholar Michael Ignatieff, "Human rights create extraterritorial relationships between people who can't protect themselves and people who have the resources to assist them. The rights revolution since 1945 has widened the bounds of community so that our obligations no longer cease at our own frontiers."[62] Accordingly, active global citizens condemn not only "first order violations of the law" by oppressive governments but also "second order violations" by bystander states that ignore such violations or refuse to enforce international law.[63]

Explicitly or implicitly, the concept of individual *human security* has emerged in tandem with global citizenship in activist, academic, and even policy-making discourses. Both notions reflect the promise that there are common bonds that unite all of humanity. These concepts also suggest that gross human rights violations should be of fundamental global concern. Typically, the most widespread and systematic atrocities since the Second World War have been directed by the state apparatus. Paradoxically, then, states have come to serve as both the ultimate pro-tectors and potential violators of human security, as they still possess at least a virtual monopoly over the means of violence. In this sense, the concept of human security transcends the state by casting the physical, psychological, and spiritual well-being of the individual as a pressing im-perative of global society, one that is separate and distinct from conven-tional matters of international peace and security. As such, individual autonomy is fundamentally recognized in the policy orientation of in-ternational criminal law, which situates individuals as the essential or ul-timate objects of its transnational protective mandate.

The development and evolution of safeguards in human rights and humanitarian law, and in related political and social struggles, has fol-lowed a trajectory that corresponds to increasingly popularized sen-timents and expressions of globality. One prominent legal scholar has drawn a loose analogy between the legal and normative consolidation of human rights and the growth of a "secular religion."[64] The widen-ing and deepening of these aspects of international law that focus on the individual reflect notions of "extensionality" (the extent to which so-cial relationships become more global) and, the inverse, "intensionality" (the extent to which global phenomena affect peoples' daily lives).[65] As such, they demonstrate evolving norms and practices of autonomy, and they imply new and expanding domains of social concern. Accordingly, although dimensions of an incipient globality predated the Nuremburg trials, a transformative historical rupture occurred: a legal and normative tipping point whereby individuals and other non-state actors became de-cidedly more visible, aware, and active.

Regrettably, consistent judicial enforcement of international crimin-al law was wanting in the decades that followed the Second World War. Hence, the proposition of a paradigm shift may need to be tempered with a more sobering view of the post-1945 era, which one pair of schol-ars has called the "fifty years' crisis."[66] These views are not incompatible, and their differences may be explained as a disjunctive clash between normative understandings and political rigidities. In the wake of the Nuremberg trials, the global normative framework progressed towards a "Kantian" model with transnational ideals. Political realities still largely resembled the conventional "Groatian" paradigm of minimalist rules for the coexistence of otherwise self-contained and autonomous states.[67] Kriangsak observes: "Compared to other branches of law, international criminal law has been slow in crystallization as a viable legal system. Foremost among the reasons hindering the development is the shield of state sovereignty and its attendant ramifications."[68] State prerogatives in relation to those of citizens and residents, including matters of criminal justice, rest at the core of traditional sovereign statehood. Thus, even with the progressive development of human rights and humanitarian law standards, a permanent, independent, and universalistic international tribunal was not politically viable. As the introduction to this volume suggests, new ideas may engender friction over contested meanings and implications. Nuremberg's legacy endured, but the powerful rhetoric of sovereignty and human rights was often selectively distorted for political advantage in the great power struggle of the Cold War.[69]

Finally, in the 1990s the normative imperatives of international criminal law began to coexist more equally with conventional understandings of state sovereignty, which led to the establishment of the ICTY in 1993 and the ICTR in 1994. It is particularly noteworthy that, in establishing these ad hoc tribunals, the UN Security Council characterized the Bosnian and Rwandan conflicts as threats to international peace and security (as it did with the Darfur, Sudan, crisis, which it referred to the ICC in March 2005). The jurisprudence produced by these tribunals has reflected a progressive view of the principles and objectives of international criminal law. The decline of international armed conflict relative to the increased incidence and gravity of internal civil wars has posed unique legal challenges. Especially telling was the ICTY's definitive clarification that war crimes may occur in internal or non-international conflict situations.[70] The ICTY has also clearly established that crimes against humanity exist as self-standing crimes, even in the absence of an armed conflict.[71] Moreover, the ad hoc tribunals have progressively acknowledged and condemned specific gender-based international crimes and recognized the particular vulnerabilities of women and children within the actual administration of justice.[72] Most fundamentally, the ad hoc tribunals contributed to the essential perception of international criminal justice as a viable governance enterprise. They provided a normative impetus and practical guidance for a renewed discussion of an old idea: a permanent international criminal court.[73] Within this context, a relatively large number of states established the ICC as a "direct descendant" of the IMT at Nuremberg.[74]

The International Criminal Court:
Institutional Fulfillment of the Nuremberg Legacy

The proposition of a permanent tribunal regained momentum in diplomatic and activist circles in the early 1990s, culminating in a decisive showing of state support for the final Rome Statute of the International Criminal Court in July 1998. The number of ratifying states reached sixty in April 2002, and the Rome Statute then entered into force on 1 July 2002. The ICC, which is permanently located in The Hague, Netherlands, represents a substantial fulfillment of the Nuremberg legacy. It institutionalizes the principle of individual criminal responsibility for serious international crimes, while also addressing the shortcomings of the Nuremberg model and more recent ad hoc experiments.

The global project represented by the ICC is expressed in the Preamble to the Rome Statute: "Conscious that all peoples are united by common bonds, their cultures pieced together in a shared heritage, and mindful that this delicate mosaic may be shattered at any time."[75] Within this context, the statute proposes a number of wide-ranging and laudable goals: to achieve justice for all; to end impunity; to help end conflicts; to remedy the deficiencies of ad hoc tribunals; to take over when national criminal justice institutions are unwilling or unable to act; and to deter future war criminals.[76] These objectives recognize that international trials serve a variety of legal, social, and political functions, including deterrence, punishment, establishing a factual or historical record, and promoting respect for the rule of law.[77] However, these objectives may exist in tension: "Remembrance and amnesia compete for dominance in the way different sectors of a population choose or are forced to respond to the problem of crime and atrocity."[78] Accordingly, the ICC and other prosecutorial options within the broader emerging program of international criminal justice enforcement efforts coexist with alternative mechanisms for achieving justice, truth, and social reconciliation.

The ICC is *complementary* to national criminal justice systems, and thus it will generally not directly administer justice unless states are "unwilling or unable" to genuinely conduct investigations and prosecutions.[79]

As a distinct type of supranational format, its central aim is to facilitate legislative and capacity-building measures to enhance the vigilance and effective functioning of national justice systems. Moreover, as a "territorially disembodied institution," when the ICC does proceed directly, it will rely heavily upon cooperation and judicial assistance from states.[80] These duties include arresting and surrendering persons to the court, protecting victims and witnesses, and preserving evidence.[81] Thus, the ICC stands out prominently among new types of supraterritorial organizations that distinguish the postwar era. Its subject-matter jurisdiction is limited to the most serious crimes of concern to the international community as a whole: genocide, crimes against humanity, and war crimes.[82] The ICC will also have jurisdiction over the crime of aggression, if and when a definition is adopted in accordance with the Rome Statute's amendment provisions.[83]

The final resolve to overcome the practical hurdles of negotiating a treaty of such sophistication testifies to the breadth and depth of support for the Nuremberg legacy. As of 1 March 2008, there are 105 States Parties, each having signed and ratified the Rome Statute.[84] The integration and contributions of non-state actors within the ICC initiative also illuminates novel concepts and practices of autonomy and social agency. In particular, the Coalition for an International Criminal Court, an umbrella association of over twenty-five hundred non-governmental organizations worldwide, brought significant technical expertise and political influence to bear upon the ICC negotiations. Its members continue to coordinate global strategies with state and non-state actors to promote ratification, implementation, and adherence to the Rome Statue. The ICC also transcends the states system by its embodiment of global citizenship. As Nigel Dower observes: "If one way of thinking of citizenship is in terms of a citizen having certain legally established rights and duties, then what the establishment of the Court does is provide a formalization of the duties individuals have in relation to one another in the world qua members of the global legal community."[85]

The Nuremberg Principles are prominently embedded in the Rome Statute. Thus, the court's jurisdiction is restricted to individual criminal responsibility of natural persons.[86] The law shall be applied without any distinction based on official capacity (art. 27). Military commanders may be held responsible for crimes committed by subordinate forces because of a failure to exercise proper control (art. 28). Duress may exculpate an accused, but acting pursuant to superiors orders is not a defence per se (art. 33). In other respects, however, the Rome Statute progressively diverges from the Nuremberg model. Pursuant to the legal maxim of *nullum crimen sine lege* (no crime without law), a person cannot be held criminally responsible under the Rome Statute unless the impugned conduct was, at the time of its alleged commission, a crime within the ICC's jurisdiction (art. 22[1]). Further, to foreclose pre-emptively any suggestions of retroactivity, persons may not be held criminally responsible by the ICC for conduct that occurred prior to the Rome Statute's entry into force (art. 24[1]). These provisions attempt to alleviate the concerns raised about the Nuremberg legacy, which is consistent with an evolving emphasis from substantive justice towards strict legality.[87] Unlike the judicial composition of the IMT, ICC judges are elected by a two-thirds majority of the Assembly of States Parties (art. 36[6]). Also, unlike the IMT, no trials may be conducted *in absentia* (art. 63), the maximum penalty is life imprisonment (art. 77[1][a]), and there are extensive appeal provisions (arts. 81-84). Given these and other departures, Nuremberg was, in one scholar's opinion, a "provocation to action but not a direct precedent."[88]

Conclusion: Contesting Globalization and Autonomy within International Law

The concepts and ideals articulated at Nuremberg introduced a novel and fundamental tension within international law between individual and collective forms of autonomy. In this sense, some incongruence or friction remains between the *vertical* order of international criminal justice and the broader *horizontal* regime of international law.[89] Although conceptions of individual worth, dignity, and accountability have gained widespread acceptance within global society, this core tension remains today. These struggles have been evident over the years in debates about strengthening international human rights enforcement. Beyond international criminal justice, they are also evident in continued proposals towards a more consistent and effective legal framework to govern humanitarian intervention.[90] The "responsibility to protect" has emerged as a powerful and expansive normative maxim within these discussions, if not as a fully crystallized principle of customary international law.[91] That the Nuremberg Principles and their corollary individual protections continue to rest uneasily within the sovereign states system does not diminish their legal, historical, and social significance. Rather, it attests to the rigidity of international law, which, compared to other areas of global governance such as trade, has been markedly resistant to globalization challenges and opportunities.

An added complication is that state and non-state actors vary in their capacity to attain autonomy. On the one hand, certain individuals and non-state collectivities possess the political freedom and resources to assert claims of individual or personal entitlements of autonomy, either for themselves or for those whose interests they seek to protect and promote. Other individuals and groups, particularly in autocratic states, remain marginalized in the realization or assertion of personal autonomy. On the other hand, powerful states have the disposition and the capacity to resist transnational pressures for the expression and implications of individual autonomy, including the purview of global institutions. For example, the US abstention and obstruction of the ICC has further fuelled debates about contemporary US hegemony or empire, as Hedetoft's chapter in this volume suggests. It is noteworthy, however, that US influence was ultimately overwhelmed at the Rome negotiations by the concerted diplomatic stance of the approximately sixty "like-minded" states and their progressive vision of an independent and effective court. Thus, the most important story of the ICC is that so many states have converged to create an unprecedented judicial body. This institution reflects enlightened connotations of what state sovereignty entails or implies, and it highlights the necessity for more formalized and robust spheres of individual autonomy within international law and global institutions. The ICC negotiations may have broader implications for the relative role and capacity of the United States to determine the substantive governance agenda and project its preferences within multilateral settings. In David Wippman's view, "For the United States in particular, Rome represents a relatively unusual form of international law-making, in which other states, acting without US consent, can fashion an international institution and international legal rules that could constrain US power."[92] In fact, the United States has softened its rhetorical tone towards the ICC in recent years, in contrast to its starkly oppositional stance following the initial negotiations. Though prospects for full American participation remain uncertain, its willingness to allow the Security Council to refer the Darfur crisis to the ICC suggests that the United States may eventually adopt a more constructive posture that acknowledges the court's legitimate role and existence.

In sum, this fundamental tension within international law between individual and collective forms of autonomy reflects a broader engagement and contestation of globalization and globality. Individual autonomy, as embodied by the Nuremberg trials, competes with the collective autonomy of states to define the rules by which they themselves shall be governed. As a feature of globalization, the struggle concerns the degree to which individual autonomy is recognized and celebrated as an inherent feature of humanity and, thus, the extent to which states must share with global institutions the responsibility for safeguarding this transnational ideal. In fact, states possess the unique capacity to express and uphold these novel dimensions of individual autonomy by joining and cooperating with ICC preceedings and preventing and prosecuting international crimes at the national level. In practical terms, therefore, states are vital intermediaries in the ICC-individual relationship. By a progressive reading of this three-dimensional juxtaposition, the ICC simultaneously advances individual and collective forms of autonomy. States substantially reaffirm their sovereignty as the front-line guardians and administrators of justice, while also acting in concert through the ICC as a unique expression of collective autonomy at the global level.

The ICC is a significant institutional fulfillment of the Nuremberg legacy, reflecting a broader progression of cosmopolitan morality within the formal structure and normative fabric of international law. As such, its final establishment marks a significant historical development within the broader context of globalization and globality. The ICC is a significant institutional feature within a broader globalization "narrative which seeks to reframe human activity and entrench it in law, rights and responsibilities."[93] As a decisive globalization moment, the Nuremberg trials represented the crucial normative and legal paradigm shift, which ultimately provided the foundations for the ICC initiative. Nuremberg established the novel parameters of individual autonomy and responsibility that transcend the international law of states and bind individuals with the global community as a whole. Although the full impact of the Nuremberg legacy was delayed, the trials fundamentally challenged previously sacrosanct global norms about state sovereignty and personal autonomy, thereby distinguishing the post-1945 era from prior periods of the modern state system.

chapter 11   The US-Led Globalization
Project in the Third World: The
Struggle for Hearts and Minds
in Guatemala and Vietnam in
the 1960s

Stephen M. Streeter

STUDIES OF GLOBALIZATION OFTEN fail to incorporate adequately the
developing world, especially Asia and Latin America. Probing the homologies of the Vietnamese and Guatemalan revolutions offers one way
to explore how globalization and autonomy connected with the ideas of
imperialism and empire during the Cold War era.[1] The conflicts in Vietnam and Guatemala represented important challenges to the emerging
US-led globalization project. Beginning in the 1960s, the United States
began promoting liberal capitalist forms of national development to
counter Socialist models of development that threatened to gain appeal
in the Third World.[2] President John F. Kennedy alerted Congress in 1961
that the "whole southern half of the world — Latin America, Africa, the
Middle East, and Asia — are caught up in the adventures of asserting
their independence and modernizing their old ways of life." Failure to
help these countries to develop rapidly, Kennedy warned, would be disastrous because "widespread poverty and chaos lead to a collapse of existing political and social structures which would inevitably invite the
advance of totalitarianism into every weak and unstable area." Communists, in particular, were engaged in subversive activity "to break
down and supersede the new — and often frail — modern institutions"
under construction by the developing countries. The president then invoked Manifest Destiny (referring to special US "obligations" ten times)
to justify the creation of a vast foreign assistance program that would
mark the 1960s as a "Decade of Development."[3]

President Kennedy presented his proposal as a "dramatic turning point in the troubled history of foreign aid to the underdeveloped world," but the "Decade of Development" speech may also be treated as a decisive globalization moment.[4] According to the scholar Jan Aart Scholte, accelerated globalization blossomed in the 1960s because of advances in communications, the spread of markets, innovations in financial transactions, the proliferation of international organizations, the invention of new global production systems, rising transworld ecological problems, and the emergence of a truly global consciousness.[5] How globalization unfolded was also greatly influenced by decolonization, or the emergence of dozens of new Third World nations as Old World empires disintegrated after the Second World War.[6] Whether globalization would proceed along capitalist or Communist lines would be determined, in part, by the development model these countries adopted. Indeed, Kennedy's 1961 foreign aid speech can be seen as a riposte to Soviet Premier Nikita Khrushchev's prior pledge to champion national "wars of liberation."[7] For either side, the collective autonomy of the new states was welcomed and was to be promoted, as long as the new states fit in with the favoured model of development (see also Pruessen, this volume).

The US-Led Globalization Project

The contest between the United States and the Soviet Union for influence in the Third World became known in the 1960s as the battle for "hearts and minds." By providing development assistance to Third World countries, US officials hoped to persuade them to join a liberal capitalist world order that embraced private enterprise, open markets, and free trade. The idea that other nations could and should replicate the developmental experience of the United States, with little autonomy to forge their own path, has been described by the historian Emily Rosenberg as the "myth of liberal developmentalism."[8] When Kennedy administration officials promoted this myth, they conveniently forgot or ignored that the US government had historically subsidized the private sector and erected tariff barriers to protect local industry. According to one economic historian, by the nineteenth century the United States had become the "bastion of modern protectionism."[9]

The roots of liberal developmentalism can be traced back to the Open Door policy of 1899, or even earlier, but the myth evolved in significant ways after the Second World War, when modernization theory gained popularity in US academic circles.[10] Modernization theory offered a solution to the dangers facing the United States in the Third World. Walt W. Rostow, a Kennedy administration adviser and an important proponent of modernization theory in the 1960s, postulated that all societies evolved through sequential economic stages of growth. According to Rostow's scheme, "traditional societies" in the Third World were struggling to enter the "take-off" stage that would ultimately propel them into an era of high mass-consumption.[11] The transition between traditional society and the take-off stage, Rostow warned, could be highly destabilizing as "individual men are torn between the commitment to the old familiar way of life and the attractions of a modern way of life." Communists who preyed on weaker nations during their transition were, in Rostow's memorable phrase, "scavengers of the modernization process."[12]

Modernization theory provided the rationale for shaping US development assistance programs that would enable newly developing nations to speed through the early stages of modernization and avoid Communist subjugation.[13] Policy makers and journalists in the United States frequently referred to this counter-insurgency strategy as "nation building." In areas where Communism threatened, US officials considered it essential to provide a military shield for development assistance projects. Otherwise, Communist guerrillas would gain the support of the rural masses either through intimidation or with promises to end class exploitation and poverty.[14]

The concepts of modernization and nation building are thoroughly infused with notions of empire and imperialism.[15] During the Cold War US government officials and academics frequently described Third World peoples as "primitive" or "childlike" and in need of up-lift by the "advanced" cultures of the West.[16] Gender also figured prominently in US conceptions of the struggle against Communism, as the historian Robert Dean has explained: "Counterinsurgency became a kind of bureaucratic cult in the Kennedy administration, serving as an institutional expression of the masculine ideals embraced by the president and many members of his national security staff."[17] These biases helped justify the repression of global popular resistance to a liberal capitalist world order that greatly benefited US economic interests. Just as Great Britain had demanded free trade of its colonies during the heyday of its empire, so too the United States championed liberal developmentalism when it could benefit most from open markets.

The US-led globalization project was cleverly disguised through the hearts and minds metaphor, which implied that the United States was primarily interested in competing peacefully for the allegiance of Third World peoples. In practice, "nation building" proved a violent affair that undermined the sovereignty of many Third World countries and, thus, their autonomy.[18] US modernization efforts interfered with collective autonomy in several ways. First, US development assistance programs failed to acknowledge that many societies emerging from colonialism required drastic measures to overcome racial and class barriers. In agriculture, for example, US advisers focused on increasing production through improved technological methods instead of pressing for badly needed land reforms. Second, the US development assistance programs almost always took a back seat to military counter-insurgency strategies that decimated the very civilian populations that supposedly needed protection from the guerrillas. Third, Washington treated Communism as a monolith and opposed any nationalist group that wanted to pursue state-sponsored development strategies. Fourth, US officials frequently viewed peasants and indigenous peoples as prehistoric savages who needed to be "integrated" into modern society.[19]

Guatemala: Another Vietnam?

The quintessential example of nation building during the 1960s was the Vietnam War. As one of the most destructive military conflicts in modern history, the Vietnam War epitomized the US approach to counter-insurgency. The war also stood as a powerful example of how formerly colonized peoples attempted to resist the globalization project of the world's greatest economic and military power. The rebel leader Ernesto Che Guevara called Vietnam "the great laboratory of Yankee imperialism" and urged Latin American revolutionaries to "follow the Vietnamese road" to create "a second or a third Vietnam."[20]

The Latin American country that most closely resembled Vietnam in the 1960s was Guatemala.[21] The similarities are, at first glance, striking. Vietnam and Guatemala shared a similar class structure: at the top, an oligarchy of wealthy landlords, businessmen, and military officials; in the middle, a small sector of professionals and labourers who resided in the capital city; and at the bottom, a very large peasantry (campesinos), which constituted 80 percent or more of the population. As underdeveloped countries, Vietnam and Guatemala exemplified classic economic dependencies. While the masses barely survived through subsistence agriculture, the export of raw materials — rice, rubber, and tin in Vietnam, and bananas, coffee, and sugar in Guatemala — provided the major source of foreign exchange.

The historical paths of Vietnam and Guatemala, as Che Guevara astutely observed, temporarily diverged in 1954.[22] In Vietnam, the successful siege at Dien Bien Phu by the Vietminh led to the Geneva Accords, which ended the French occupation and divided Vietnam temporarily along the seventeenth parallel.[23] In Guatemala the Dwight D. Eisenhower administration engineered a coup that overturned a leftist government that had sponsored a decade of reform known as the "ten years of spring." The political direction of the two countries converged again by the 1960s, as Washington installed and propped up dictators who soon provoked popular protest. Resistance eventually coalesced around guerrilla organizations led by Marxist nationalists and loosely supported by popular organizations such as labour unions, student groups, religious organizations, and peasant leagues. Although US officials wildly exaggerated the control that the Soviet Union and Cuba exerted over the Vietnamese and Guatemalan revolutions, rebels received economic and military assistance from Communist allies.[24]

The structural similarities between the conflicts in Vietnam and Guatemala led some observers to overlook crucial differences. Although both Guatemala and South Vietnam were run largely by dictatorships in the 1960s, Vietnam's indigenous bourgeoisie was extremely weak and lacked nationalist cohesion because of its displacement by Chinese merchants and long association with the French colonialists.[25] By contrast, Spain had left Guatemala more than a hundred years earlier, allowing a local oligarchy to solidify its power.[26] Guatemala's social structure was deeply divided by two major competing ethnic groups: Maya and Ladino. The term *Maya* is used to represent the indigenous peoples (Indians) who survived the Spanish conquest in Guatemala. The Maya constituted at least one-half of the population in 1960, and they were divided into twenty-three language groups who suffered extreme poverty and discrimination. The term *Ladino,* which is equivalent to *mestizo,* refers to individuals of mixed ancestry who speak Spanish, wear Western clothes, and generally embrace Western culture. By comparison, at least 85 percent of Vietnam's population was ethnically Vietnamese. Minority peoples figured marginally in the outcome of the Vietnam War.[27]

The similar class structure of Vietnam and Guatemala has understandably led scholars to describe the conflicts in these countries as peasant revolutions. But the historical background explains why the Vietnamese were far better positioned than the Guatemalans to launch a successful revolution. The legacy of the First Indochina War gave the Vietminh valuable organizational experience when they confronted the Americans. Guatemala's first guerrilla leaders, mostly middle-class army officers and late converts to Marxist-Leninism, committed many strategic and tactical errors that undermined their ability to build a popular base. Despite philosophical and tactical differences between the North Vietnamese government (Democratic Republic of Vietnam, or DRV) and the South Vietnamese National Liberation Front (NLF), the Vietnamese revolutionaries were relatively united behind Ho Chi Minh. The Guatemalan guerrillas, by contrast, splintered into squabbling Marxist sects.[28]

Geography influenced these conflicts differently. The NLF was closely tied to the DRV, which managed to obtain Chinese and Soviet economic and military aid that enabled the guerrillas to keep pace with the increasingly sophisticated weaponry of the United States. The NLF was also able to retreat at key junctures in the war to sanctuaries in Laos and Cambodia. Although the Guatemalan guerrillas received some training in Cuba, nearly all of their weapons had to be captured from the enemy or bought with ransom money obtained through kidnappings. In the early 1960s, the Guatemalan guerrillas tried to form several fronts *(focos)* in the southern and eastern parts of the country, but these efforts fared badly, and by the middle of the decade the rebels fled to Guatemala City. Washington never dispatched US combat troops to Guatemala, whereas American forces numbered over half a million at the peak of the US intervention in Vietnam.[29]

In brief, the Vietnamese revolutionaries defeated the Americans and unified the country in 1975 because of their long history of resisting invaders, ingenious approaches to guerrilla warfare, support from other Communist countries, and, perhaps most important, their legitimate claim as authentic Vietnamese nationalists. The Guatemalan conflict, by contrast, dragged on for decades, ending in a stalemate in 1991, when the guerrillas and the government signed a peace pact that transferred the contest into the electoral arena. Aside from numerous logistical and geographical difficulties, ethnic divisions severely hampered the Guatemalan guerrillas. The early guerrilla movement was led by Ladino army officers who misread the ethnic question because of their dogmatic adherence to Marxist models of class struggle. The Guatemalan revolutionaries eventually learned from their mistakes and tried to expand among the Maya in the 1970s. But the Guatemalan army and internal security forces, heavily fortified by US military equipment and counter-insurgency training, retaliated by conducting a scorched earth campaign in the highlands that killed more than two hundred thousand Guatemalans before the civil war ended.[30]

The Struggle for Hearts and Minds

To implement the Decade of Development, President Kennedy consolidated various US foreign assistance agencies in late 1961 under a new body called the US Agency for International Development (AID). Although AID depended on funding from Congress, the agency was placed under the jurisdiction of the State Department, where it served as an important instrument of US counter-insurgency strategy. Under the influence of modernization theory and liberal developmentalism, AID approached the problems of poverty and development the same way throughout the Third World. The operations of AID demonstrate how empire promoted the rise of supraterritoriality, as the US foreign aid bureaucracy and its programs became easily transferable from one part of the globe to another.

The advances in transportation and communications systems that accelerated globalization also enabled the United States to wage technowars against the foreign Other in regions far removed from the imperial centre.[31] Both Guatemala and Vietnam were discussed on a regular basis by Kennedy's Special Group (Counterinsurgency), which included the chiefs of the US Central Intelligence Agency, Joint Chiefs of Staff, US Information Agency, and AID. Economic aid from the United States was channelled to Guatemala through a $20 billion development assistance program for Latin America called the Alliance for Progress. President Kennedy, who considered Latin America "the most dangerous area in the world," announced the Alliance with great fanfare as a "vast co-operative effort, unparalleled in magnitude and nobility of purpose, to satisfy the basic needs of Latin American people for homes, work and land, health and schools."[32] In Saigon, the US Military Assistance and Advisory Group (MAAG) grew more than tenfold during the Kennedy administration to house more than ten thousand economic and military advisers.[33] To

Kennedy, Vietnam represented "the cornerstone of the Free World in Southeast Asia, the Keystone to the arch, the finger in the dike."[34]

The US-led globalization project in Vietnam and Guatemala rapidly ran into numerous obstacles. The establishment of such large aid missions, for example, created what critics called "shadow" or "parallel" governments.[35] The assignment of US officials to Vietnamese "counterparts" in the South Vietnamese government (Government of Vietnam, or GVN), for example, made it difficult to maintain that home governments inspired development projects. The South Vietnamese dictator Ngo Dinh Diem complained in 1963 that, because of the legacy of a "colonial mentality," many villagers "believe that the Americans are now the government" and "disregard the authority of my local officials."[36] Diem's enemies capitalized on this relationship by dubbing the GVN "My-Diem," which translates to "the US-Diem clique."[37] Despite appearances of collusion in both Vietnam and Guatemala, US advisers and government officials clashed over how to implement development programs. The Guatemalan regime of Enrique Peralta Azurdia declared several AID officers *persona non grata* for demanding that all AID contracts be drawn up in English.[38] In South Vietnam, Diem insisted in 1963 that US aid be sent directly to GVN instead of to the US aid mission, as was formerly the practice.[39]

Given their common ideological origin, AID's "hearts and minds" programs differed little in form and function from country to country. In fact, several dozen AID and embassy officers serving in Guatemala during the latter half of the 1960s had previously been stationed in Vietnam.[40] Prior to 1960, US economic aid to developing countries went mostly to large infrastructure projects such as highways, water ports, airports, and irrigation systems. Beginning with the Kennedy administration, AID expanded US development assistance to encompass agriculture, health, education, housing, community development, public administration, and police training. The US Information Service publicized these programs through pamphlets, newspapers, movies, and radio and television programs. A detailed review of these programs illustrates how the US-led globalization project interfered with local autonomy.

Because struggles over land helped spark both the Guatemalan and the Vietnamese insurgencies, agrarian reform could be considered the single most important nation-building strategy.[41] US officials feared that a land-hungry peasantry would be vulnerable to revolutionary promises to exact social justice, but they adamantly refused to pursue land reforms that would violate the sanctity of liberal developmentalism. Instead, AID provided technical assistance to spur agricultural production, and it sponsored various land colonization schemes.[42] Following the 1954 coup in Guatemala, US officials guided the reversal of the largest land reform in Guatemalan history (Decree 900) and began to support colonization projects that relocated campesinos from overcrowded regions to remote sections of jungle.[43] In South Vietnam, Diem's "reverse land reform" of the late 1950s had actually exacerbated peasant grievances, so Kennedy administration officials turned to the "strategic hamlet" program to counter the recruiting efforts of the NLF. The plan called for moving peasants from their ancestral homelands to fortified villages, mostly in the Mekong Delta, where they could be "protected" from the NLF.

The land colonization projects in Guatemala and the strategic hamlet program in Vietnam failed miserably. Guatemalan agricultural settlements remained isolated and lacked basic services; even more important, they were simply too small in size and number to alleviate the demand for land by hundreds of thousands of campesinos displaced by the expansion of agro-export agriculture. According to one study, the rate of land distribution from 1952 to 1954, when Decree 900 was in effect, was eighteen times greater than the rate of land distribution from 1955 to 1970. Whereas Decree 900 had benefited more than half a million campesinos, the colonization projects of the 1960s benefited less than 10 percent of the landless population.[44]

In South Vietnam the strategic hamlet program failed because it expanded too rapidly and alienated peasants who were forcibly uprooted from ancestral lands. The Diem regime conscripted peasants into building the hamlets without pay and then permitted corrupt village officials to charge exorbitant taxes. The NLF managed to defeat the program by penetrating the hamlets at night, intimidating the administrators, removing barbwire fences, and luring recruits with promises of land. The strategic hamlet program faded after the 1963 military coup because it lacked support from South Vietnamese leaders and because US authorities judged the program a failure.[45] In 1969, AID created the "land-to-the-tiller" program, an ambitious project to redistribute land through legal expropriation. Yet this scheme also failed to affect the outcome of the war. Powerful landlords influenced the courts in order to evade the law, and the land issue receded as the war intensified. After the Tet Offensive of 1968, Vietnamese society had become so polarized that most villagers had to choose sides, thus negating the political goal of land reform.

Civic action and community development projects designed to win hearts and minds in the countryside fared little better than land reform efforts. In Guatemala, us-sponsored cooperatives, literacy campaigns, rural leadership training, and small-scale development projects disrupted social relations in the countryside by empowering Indians in highland villages that had long been dominated politically and economically by Ladinos. When the Peace Corps and AID introduced cooperatives that enabled highland Indians to use fertilizer and pesticides on their subsistence plots, yields increased so rapidly that fewer Indians had to descend to the coast to work on coffee and sugar plantations. Increasing literacy among the Maya also made it more difficult for labour contractors to entrap peasants in debt peonage. Angry at having to raise wages to reduce the labour shortage, wealthy planters encouraged vigilantes to attack the organizers of the cooperatives and literacy projects. These "vigilantes" were actually paramilitary squads organized by the internal security forces, which were in turn trained and equipped under AID's Public Safety Program and the us Military Assistance Program. us officials insisted that strong police and military forces were needed to combat the guerrilla threat, even though they understood that "counter-terror" undermined nation building. The fixation on "law and order" eventually doomed AID's hearts and minds programs in Guatemala because, in supporting corrupt dictatorships, the police and the military protected the oligarchy from popular dissent.[46]

Civic action and "revolutionary development" projects in South Vietnam resembled the AID development assistance programs in Guatemala. Early civic action teams in Vietnam constructed wells, irrigation ditches, roads, and schools; provided medical supplies and agricultural extension services; and strengthened rural agricultural cooperatives.[47] These programs were eventually incorporated into the pacification effort, which was coordinated by a joint civilian-military unit known as Civil Operations and Revolutionary Development Support (CORDS). Under the direction of Robert Komer, CORDS dispatched anti-Communist cadre teams to live and work in the villages so they could infiltrate the NLF infrastructure. Pacification caused the NLF enormous difficulties, but not because peasants were suddenly swarming to the GVN side. In fact, villagers distrusted government cadres, whom the peasants regarded as city slickers with little understanding of country living. Inadequately trained and riddled with corruption, cadre teams often proposed projects that were ill suited for a given region.[48]

The inability of US officials to fathom that support for the internal security forces was undermining nation building in Guatemala or that pacification was not going to win the war in Vietnam reveals a major clash between the US-led globalization project and the autonomy of Third World peasants. Officials in the United States could not understand their failures, which they often attributed to the inability of Third World peoples to govern themselves, because that would have challenged the myths of modernization theory and liberal developmentalism.[49] President Lyndon B. Johnson's desire to transform the Mekong Delta into a "Tennessee Valley" demonstrated more than simple ignorance. The assumption that a gigantic development project based on the Tennessee Valley Authority model would win hearts and minds in Vietnam reflected a belief that the world could be made over in the American image.[50] Cultural stereotypes of peasants permeated the US civilian and military bureaucracy. In both Guatemala and Vietnam, AID officials blamed the failures of nation building on a supposed lack of nationalism among the domestic population. "At the core of the problem of poverty are the Indians," asserted one US report from Guatemala, "whose traditions lead them to avoid social integration and modernization."[51] Roger Hilsman, who helped implement the strategic hamlet program in South Vietnam, believed that peasants in Southeast Asia "have little or no sense of identification with either the national government or Communist ideology."[52]

These views of the peasantry reflected a major assumption of modernization theory, that peasants were primitive, passive, and isolated. One official with the United States Information Service compared the minds of Vietnamese peasants to the "shrivel[l]ed leg of a polio victim whose understanding of the world remains at the level of a six-year old." Matchbooks inscribed with Vietnamese flags and strategic hamlet slogans were useless, he declared, because peasants did not know how to strike matches. Nor did they understand the meaning of democracy, Communism, or any other political ideology; they were even ignorant of their own history.[53] Such prejudices bolstered a common interpretation of the wars in Guatemala and Vietnam, which cast peasants as innocent bystanders caught in the crossfire between two armies. One observer likened Vietnamese villages to the wind: "When the Viet Cong enters, the population turns pro-Communist; when the Government troops arrive, sentiment shifts to the Government."[54] According to one RAND Corporation study, Vietnamese peasants described their wartime experience as being on the "anvil and under the hammer," or as "living under two yokes."[55] The anthropologist David Stoll has used similar metaphors to relate how many Mayans experienced political violence in Guatemala.[56]

These portraits capture the difficult decisions that individuals have to make in wartime; they also strip peasants of much historical agency. That some Vietnamese would voluntarily choose to join revolutionary forces was so unthinkable to most US officials that they resorted to Cold War stereotypes of peasants as Communist "dupes." The truth, as the historian David Hunt has suggested, was far more complicated: some "villagers saw the guerrillas as intruders, others joined the NLF, while still others sat on the fence." It should not surprise us that "peasants often reassessed their options, moving from support for the Front to neutrality to the government side and back again."[57] This kind of oscillation is evident in the testimony of Le Ly Hayslip, who grew up in a contested South Vietnamese village in the 1960s: "I sang and danced for the South Vietnamese army. I killed chickens and ducks and cooked for them, but they didn't pay. At night we sang and danced for the Viet Cong. We sang to Uncle Ho that he would bring love to our village. So we played both roles. But our hearts and minds were at night with the freedom fighters."[58]

Tantalizing scraps of evidence suggest that the peasants had a more sophisticated understanding of the world at large than most analysts have recognized. Globalization in the 1960s was not simply a top-down affair in which imperial powers such as the United States or the Soviet Union imposed their way of life onto *tabula rasae* in the Third World. Just as globalization enabled the United States to project its power across the planet in the 1960s, so too it helped Third World revolutionaries imagine a world connected in ways that enhanced their autonomy. The friction generated by these clashing visions explains, in part, the unevenness of globalization during the Cold War era.

Because US officials had little grasp of peasant life, they were baffled as to why their nation-building strategies failed. To General Maxwell Taylor, one of the great mysteries about the war was the NLF's ability to maintain high morale and rebuild its units despite very heavy losses. In order to uncover the miraculous "recuperative powers of the phoenix," the State Department hired the RAND Corporation, a non-profit think tank, to interview NLF defectors and prisoners of war. The RAND interviews offered revealing glimpses into a reality that many US officials were loath to acknowledge because it clashed with their own beliefs about modernization. Some RAND investigators were amazed to learn that peasants were not Communist robots and could offer quite sophisticated explanations of why they joined the Front.[59] Factors that pushed peasants towards the NLF included the blatant corruption of the GVN, fear of conscription into the Army of the Republic of Vietnam, lack of job opportunities, anger over the American bombing and shelling of villages, resentment caused by such failures as the strategic hamlet program, and hatred of the American-backed Diem regime, which was often equated with the former French colonial government. To gain support in the villages, the NLF carried out an informal land reform and reduced or eliminated land rent in zones under its control. Some families sided with the NLF because they had a son or daughter who had gone north to join the revolution, while others joined the Front because they predicted that it would emerge as the winner in the long run. The interviews also revealed that, contrary to the notion in US circles that the South Vietnamese lacked a sense of nationalism, many peasants backed the southern revolution as a genuine expression of the popular national will that would secure Vietnam its autonomy.[60]

So startling and unacceptable were these findings, that Washington mostly ignored them.[61] Policy makers instead fell back on explanations that exaggerated infiltration from the north and overemphasized the NLF's coercive tactics as a method of recruitment.[62] Worse, the failures of the hearts and minds programs were used to justify an escalation of violence. Some RAND researchers portrayed peasants as rational self-maximizers who would do anything to avoid pain. By this logic, they reasoned that the US counter-insurgency emphasis should be on coercion rather than on development assistance programs, which were a waste of time and money.[63] "If you don't break their military machine," one US military officer declared, "you might as well forget winning the hearts and minds of the people."[64]

While heavy bombing and pacification programs wreaked havoc with the NLF's infrastructure, heavy-handed tactics proved to be counterproductive because their very harshness provided a fresh supply of NLF recruits who preferred to die in a blaze of glory than spend the rest of their lives in a refugee camp.[65] The NLF also gained supporters by proselytizing to peasant communities, which were, in the words of one cadre, "like a mound of straw, ready to be ignited."[66] The cosmopolitanism that the Front promoted in the villages, moreover, meant that peasants were quite capable of forging their own opinions about world events.[67] The Front's diplomatic branch waged a brilliant campaign to gain the respect and admiration of solidarity movements all over the globe. Vietnamese revolutionaries became famous throughout the Third World, especially where similar liberation struggles to achieve autonomy were unfolding.[68]

The obvious fallacies of the domino theory should not prevent us from acknowledging that Third World revolutionaries developed bonds of solidarity that enabled them to challenge liberal developmentalism. These movements naturally turned to each other as they strove for autonomy in a world increasingly dominated by US hegemony. The fascination that Vietnam held for the Guatemalan guerrillas, for example, illustrates the ways in which Third World revolutionary movements became globalized in the 1960s.[69] Members of Guatemala's first guerrilla movement, Rebel Armed Forces (FAR), frequently described their struggle in a global context. Yon Sosa, a former Guatemalan military officer who had helped form FAR, claimed to be greatly inspired by the success of Cuba, China, North Vietnam, and North Korea. "All you have to do is look around and see what's happening in the world," he told one reporter. "How could we not be for socialism?"[70]

The Vietnamese revolution also shaped the strategies and tactics adopted by the Guatemalan guerrillas. After travelling to North Vietnam and witnessing the Tet Offensive, FAR commander César Montes decided that developing a winning strategy in Guatemala was not merely a question of having superior arms, training, and experience, but of building a unified people's war.[71] Consequently, the Guatemalan guerrillas adopted many of the same techniques as the NLF to mobilize peasant villages. Local village committees were established, for example, to settle local disputes and discuss political issues.[72] The newspaper *Revolución Socialista* was widely read and discussed in every guerrilla camp, as members were eager to keep informed about Vietnam.[73] To honour the great leader of the Vietnamese revolution, Guatemalan guerrillas named one of their fronts after Ho Chi Minh.[74]

Attempts to model the Guatemalan revolution on other successful revolutions in the Third World was not without its drawbacks. Guatemalan guerrillas frequently quarrelled with each other over the proper "political line" their revolution ought to be following. These breaches spilled over into the Tricontinental Conference in Havana, where different factions lined up on either side of the Sino-Soviet split. Fidel Castro and FAR commander Turcios Lima, for example, denounced Yon Sosa for having fallen under Trotskyist influences.[75] Romanticization of the struggle in Vietnam also lured the Guatemalan rebels into a false sense of optimism about the chances for a worldwide Socialist triumph. After boasting of imminent victory in the early 1960s, FAR units were nearly wiped out by the military, and the guerrillas had to fight for two more decades before agreeing to a peace settlement that only marginally achieved their initial goals.

Conclusion: From Modernization to Neoliberalism

The US attempt to "modernize" Third World countries in the 1960s did not initially succeed, at least in the sense that neither Guatemala nor Vietnam followed the path envisioned by Walt Rostow. Yet, since the end of the Cold War, many Third World countries, including Guatemala and Vietnam, have embraced neoliberal reforms built on the foundations of liberal developmentalism, thereby leaving the dreams and aspirations of revolutionaries largely unfulfilled. As one student of global poverty has observed, although Third World liberation movements successfully "asserted the autonomy of the world's majority," they merely "reframed" exploitation rather than ending it.[76] Guatemala, for example, developed a large export maquila manufacturing industry and promoted agro-export agriculture, while Socialist Vietnam began loosening state controls over its economy in the 1980s through the "Doi Moi" reforms.[77] Given the "global turn" referred to by Ulf Hedetoft in this volume, it may be tempting to conclude that the struggles of the 1960s against the US-led globalization project were largely in vain.[78] During his visit to Hanoi in 2000, President Bill Clinton compared globalization to a force of nature, "not something we can hold off or turn off."[79]

The determinism invoked by neoliberal pundits in the twenty-first century seems about as warranted as the premature speculation by Francis Fukuyama in 1989 that the end of the Cold War marked the end of history.[80] The consequences of globalization continue to play out in unexpected ways in the lesser-developed countries. As a result of the autonomy won by Guatemalan revolutionaries, Mayans now have formal political representation in the Guatemalan government. Globalization has also spawned a vibrant pan-Mayan movement that has formed part of the global indigenous rights movement in favour of self-government, as described by Ravi de Costa in this volume.[81] The US military defeat in Vietnam gave the Vietnamese some autonomy to regulate the pace of their integration into the world economy.[82] The US-led globalization project did not completely triumph in the 1960s, but the axes of resistance have shifted from Communist states to populist governments and non-government organizations that continue to challenge US hegemony.[83]

chapter 12

A Globalizing Moment: The United Nations' Decades for Development and the North African Countries

Yassine Essid

Fourth, we must embark on a bold new program for making the benefits of our scientific advances and industrial progress available for the improvement and growth of underdeveloped areas. More than half the people of the world are living in conditions approaching misery. Their food is inadequate. They are victims of disease. Their economic life is primitive and stagnant. Their poverty is a handicap and a threat both to them and to more prosperous areas. For the first time in history, humanity possesses the knowledge and skill to relieve suffering of these people. The United States is pre-eminent among nations in the development of industrial and scientific techniques. The material resources which we can afford to use for assistance of other peoples are limited. But our imponderable resources in technical knowledge are constantly growing and are inexhaustible. I believe that we should make available to peace-loving peoples the benefits of our store of technical knowledge in order to help them realize their aspirations for a better life.
—President Harry S. Truman's inaugural address,
20 January 1949

But the mysteries of outer space must not divert our eyes or our energies from the harsh realities that face our fellow men. Political sovereignty is but a mockery without the means of meeting poverty and illiteracy and disease. Self-determination is but a slogan if the future holds no hope.

That is why my nation, which has freely shared its capital and its technology to help others help themselves, now proposes officially designating this decade of the 1960s as the United Nations Decade of Development. *Under the framework of that Resolution, the United Nations' existing efforts in promoting economic growth can be expanded and coordinated. Regional surveys and training institutes can now pool the talents of many. New research, technical assistance and pilot projects can unlock the wealth of less developed lands and untapped waters. And development can become a cooperative and not a competitive enterprise — to enable all nations, however diverse in their systems and beliefs, to become in fact as well as in law free and equal nations.*
—President John F. Kennedy's address before the General Assembly of the United Nations, 25 September 1961 (emphasis added)

THE WAY WE SPEAK about globalization has led some people to think that it is a new, indeed inexorable, phenomenon that marks a sharp rupture from all past events, imposing its form on all societies. In this perspective, any attempt on the part of countries on the southern shore of the Mediterranean to protect themselves from this sweeping force or to carve out spaces of autonomy in the face of its onslaught are efforts in vain. A closer look reveals, however, that globalization is not just a recent phenomenon brought about by revolutions in transportation, the advance of information and communications technologies, and the rise of the transnational corporation. This most recent phase of the spread of transplanetary connections began to be nurtured during the Second World War. As Pruessen's chapter indicates, the framework was put in place in the late 1940s with the Bretton Woods institutions and nourished by economic theories of development already discussed between the British and the Americans. Accordingly, contemporary globalization may be seen as the culmination of the ideology of development that began to be articulated as early as the 1940s and 1950s (see Pruessen and Streeter, this volume). The contemporary discourse about globalization, although presented discursively as a process freely consented to by all countries in the world in their pursuit of the ideals of freedom and prosperity, is really a hegemonic one linked to early postwar-era thinking. Globalization is seen to follow the same unifying logic and reproduce the same arguments as the discourse on development in the 1940s, 1950s, and 1960s. Likewise, its proponents envisage a homogeneous international system in which a large portion of humanity living in difficult circumstances is encouraged to believe that a Western model of growth and development is the only path to end poverty. Similar to this older discourse, globalization is pushing the whole world to endorse the idea that no other approach to the social or political regulation of an economy is possible or desirable. A fully functioning globalized economy is beyond the control of any state wishing to opt for an alternative vision or to impose its authority on economic processes.

The economy-centred development models of the mid-twentieth century that were followed by the countries along the southern shores of the Mediterranean Sea in the hope of finally securing their autonomy have failed. This chapter examines the hopes and disappointments in the postwar period of decolonization by reviewing the three decades of development. Promoted by the United Nations with strong backing from the United States, the pursuit of development was supposed to lead, finally, to the integration of newly independent, less-developed countries into the world economy. Our starting point is John F. Kennedy's speech of 25 September 1961 to the UN General Assembly, when he designated the 1960s as "the United Nations Decade of Development." Kennedy's speech itself is significant, not because the Decade of Development was a success, for it was not. Rather, it allows us to reflect on how contemporary discourses of globalization follow in the wake of the ideology of development that emerged in the postwar period. Development thinking dominated debates in less wealthy countries for at least three decades, and in each decade the political, economic, and cultural autonomy of peoples came into question in different ways. The history of development and/or underdevelopment brings into light the whole problem of the complex links that societies maintain with their history, culture, and intellectual heritage.

Contemporary globalization had its wellsprings in the same Western ideology that underpinned President Harry S. Truman's foreign aid program and inspired President Kennedy's pledge to the developing world. These development initiatives grew out of a strategy that constituted the beginning of a highly conceptualized and rationalistic vision of a new world economic order.[1] The fruits of that vision ripened recently with the emergence of a globalized order that advanced at great speed. In the process, the issues of development and underdevelopment appear to have been swept aside, leaving behind the question of whether the poverty of so many will ever really be addressed.

The "globalizing" enterprise launched by the United States to combat underdevelopment had clear ideological motives in the early postwar period (see Pruessen, this volume, for elaboration). To contain Soviet expansionism, the Truman administration took four steps. First, US officials developed a nuclear deterrent. Second, they attempted to rebuild western Europe through the Marshall Plan. Third, the United States sought to establish a new world economic order based on the Bretton Woods agreement and its enforcement institutions — the International Monetary Fund (IMF), the World Bank, and the General Agreement on Tariffs and Trade (GATT). Fourth, the Truman administration provided economic assistance to underdeveloped countries with the aim of promoting Western development models that would provide the best protective shield against the temptations of Socialism and Communism. The United States and other Western countries wanted to use development assistance to bring decolonizing movements under their control, thus ensuring that, once independence was achieved, local leaders would not embark upon a Socialist revolution. This final step helps explain why the United States tolerated so many of the authoritarian regimes that emerged in the early Cold War.

Beginning in 1949, US officials suggested to newly liberated developing countries that they could achieve in ten years what the industrialized countries had struggled to achieve over the previous three centuries. As is discussed in the chapter by Stephen Streeter, Westerners — and Americans in particular — were often prone to confuse the economic and political evolution of their own societies with a universal path that the rest of the world would necessarily follow. This myth of liberal developmentalism spread to the peoples of the Third World, who came to believe that through the technical assistance and financial support promised by the industrialized countries they would quickly "catch up" and enter an era of enhanced well-being and guaranteed prosperity. They believed this in vain.

If the term *globalization* is defined as the "extending of trade (goods and capital) and the favouring of [the] movement of people from Europe to all parts of the planet," then the last quarter of the nineteenth century is an earlier globalizing era, as Saul demonstrates in his chapter.[2] The intensification of exchanges among the industrialized countries occurred simultaneously with their imperial reach into regions now known as the Global South. These movements of people and exports of capital reinforced and complemented the domination of Europe over

underdeveloped societies by disturbing their socio-economic equilibrium and keeping them underdeveloped. Forced to reorient production
to meet the needs of metropolitan centres, the economies in colonized
lands responded to the requirements of world capitalist markets, leaving little, if any, capacity to address their own internal domestic needs.
The world's agricultural systems shifted in response to Europe's industrial growth: the cultivation of indigenous food crops declined, while
handicraft and artisan production in regions such as Morocco and Tunisia dwindled or vanished. Traditional economies gave way to structures
of production that emphasized the mass production of primary products that could be exchanged for a wide range of manufactured goods.
This shift from a domestic, food-oriented agriculture to an export-
focused agricultural and natural resource economy catered primarily to
the needs of hegemonic imperial centres, as Egypt's cotton boom and
Lebanon's burgeoning silkworm-breeding industries demonstrated. The
development of capitalist property relations controlled by large landowners (Tunisia, Morocco) during the colonial period worsened the plight of
local artisans and the salaried classes, thus disrupting traditional patterns
of social stratification.

In short, imperialism at the end of the nineteenth century was economically successful for the first time in developing a global market
that was not based on the laws of supply and demand but on relations of
power and force. While it introduced modernizing advancements, industrial capitalism undermined the autonomy of colonized countries'
economies, setting in train processes that created and perpetuated the
countries' own underdevelopment.[3]

Prior to Western imperial incursions, some countries were not so
"backward" or completely outside modernity and world capitalism as
some observers have assumed. As early as the nineteenth century, certain countries had introduced significant reforms designed to provide
the foundation for modernization and industrialization. Colonization
brought these attempts to a brutal halt, however, by blocking the emergence of any industries that might compete with those at the imperial
centre. Examples of these effects include Egypt under Mohamed Ali,
Tunisia under Khaireddine, and the Ottoman Empire. The economic
policies of these regimes might have brought about modern transformations in economically self-sustaining societies if the European powers
had not stifled autonomy through military force and the "weapon" of
"free trade."[4]

The emergence of independence struggles signalled the failures of colonial Europe, which had subjugated so many societies through forced integration and territorial occupation. Many local elites adopted the universal Enlightenment values touted by Westerners to protest human rights violations committed in the periphery. Eventually, the colonizers realized that it would be more profitable to deal with politically free peoples, so long as the potential for opening markets in the future could be preserved. In ceasing to practise formal imperialism, however, European metropoles found themselves facing cutthroat competition from the United States, which was bent on becoming the world hegemon after the Second World War.[5] As Pruessen's chapter indicates, us leaders believed that direct colonization had become obsolete and costly. They sought to install a system of liberalized trade across the world that would provide them with the natural resources they needed and markets for their own products. It is no mere accident that as soon as independence became a reality, the call for development addressed to Third World countries came mainly from the United States.[6]

Accordingly, Kennedy's speech in 1961 signalled the replacement of colonialism by a new global project, one initiated by an international authority, the United Nations, and backed by a great power, the United States, allegedly the very incarnation of a free market economy. The aim of this project was to get all nation-states in the world to adopt economic and political systems based on liberal capitalism and representative democracy. All the countries in the world would achieve success by following the same economic and social development path, thereby erasing their heterogeneity. The very use of the concept "underdevelopment" automatically implied the employment of an existing development model as a reference or as an ideal goal to be achieved. The biological metaphors and other adjectives commonly used when discussing development reveal the narrow vision of Western ideology. Many accounts of underdevelopment began by speaking of "primitive" societies, "backward peoples," and "nations in the making." Some countries were allegedly suffering from a state of *"mal développement,"* while others were supposedly "on their way to development." Finally, there were "developing countries," "emerging" countries, and "developed and advanced" countries. Under this growth model, all underdeveloped countries were seen as lagging far behind industrialized countries. Development was therefore conceived as a matter of "catching-up." Poor countries would erase their weak position by following the same evolutionary "path" as the advanced capitalist ones, drawing upon technology and capital provided by the latter states.

In this context, the decolonization era represented a decisive moment. Newly acquired autonomy, which elites hoped to use to shore up cultural and religious values that had been repressed under colonialism, had to be restricted in use in order to face the demands of the development project. In the push to develop that followed independence, political leaders of the underdeveloped countries made immense use of the metaphor of delay as a slogan to mobilize the masses. Leaders reminded their citizens that it was vital to catch up and "join the convoy" that had already started off (Bourguiba *aliltihaq bi l-rakb*). It became a matter of accelerating the pace of growth. So the pursuit of economic adjustment legitimized delays in the rebuilding of political institutions, in looking towards economic self-sufficiency, in enriching social institutions such as schools and universities, or in reviving repressed cultural practices; in short, the pursuit of economic adjustment put building a fully sovereign nation-state on hold. Only economic growth was seen as necessary for development. Accordingly, when the West reminded underdeveloped countries of their obligations, political leaders felt free to emphasize economic development, even if it came at the expense of building democracy and recognizing and respecting human rights.

The First Development Decade, 1961-70: Certitude

Following their independence, the Maghreb countries (Morocco, Algeria, and Tunisia) were all confronted with the same question: What do we do to overcome underdevelopment? "Economic growth" was the answer of the industrialized countries. Only through economic growth, they insisted, could these countries catch up and narrow the gap that separated them from fully developed Western countries. With the financial and technical help that would be provided by the industrialized countries, ten years was thought to be sufficient time to achieve this goal. In 1960 the US economist Walter Rostow proposed that underdeveloped countries could follow the same main stages of economic growth that the West had followed, beginning the process with takeoff (*al-iqlâ'* for the Arabs) and ending as societies of mass consumption. This essentially economic vision of development glossed over socio-cultural and other non-economic factors. Rostow identified 1783 as the takeoff year for industrialization in England, and he maintained that helping the underdeveloped countries was simply a matter of recreating and simulating the conditions that made the British takeoff possible. Rostow was not alone. Many Western historians joined together with political scientists and economists to try to explain the determining factors of economic development from a historical perspective. For example, in 1963 the historian Paul Bairoch studied the economies of France and England before and after 1790, roughly the period when their economies took off. He tried to show that, after an increase in agricultural productivity, both countries followed a path of ever-expanding industrialization. So, agricultural modernization was seen as having a multiplier effect and, thus, as a diffuser of progress across the whole economy. Bairoch ignored social and cultural factors on the grounds that even though "economic factors are not the only ones to be taken into consideration, they remain sufficiently important to explain development and underdevelopment in their own right."[7]

This concept of development assumes that the world's populations all share the same needs. In the words of one critic, "Being underdeveloped means, therefore, both a lack of key material goods and the impossibility of filling that gap."[8] Conceived of in this way, development appears to be the key to satisfying everyone's needs and to achieving this goal. Colonization hampers development because it prevented some Arab countries from becoming integrated into the world market.[9] In extreme cases like Algeria, for example, colonization deprived people of all forms of liberty and control over their economic resources, thus delaying development. In this sense, compared with the rationality of development and later globalization, colonization blocks economic progress and is, therefore, opposed to the principle of economic freedom. Hence, decolonization will be a step towards progress, bringing underdeveloped states closer to development.

The delay thesis assumes that underdevelopment can be explained essentially with reference to endogenous factors: a transition from a traditional society to a modern one brings development. It becomes imperative, therefore, to give up all traditional cultural and social practices because they act as stumbling blocks to development. According to this model, Western education plays a key role in helping underdeveloped nations emulate the developed countries. Hence, there is no need to fret about the past or to instruct citizens about their national heritage, as this knowledge (and related factors) only creates another obstacle on the path to development. As soon as one accepts that the Western model is the most advanced, there is no point in considering any others. The claims of universality, so cherished in the field of economics, state that there is no rationality but that of the West. The proponents of modernity see no other possible economic rationality but that of the West, be it a Socialist or a capitalist economy.[10] Following any other set of ideas or rationalities is harmful and to be discouraged.

Although they gained independence at different times (1956 for Tunisia and Morocco; 1962 for Algeria) and under circumstances that differed from one country to another, the conditions of decolonization in the Maghreb countries largely explain the varying choices open to these societies and, thus, significant differences in their economic policies. State Socialism was preached in Algeria in the service of great causes, including avocations for a new international order based on equitable relations between North and South and the promotion of non-alignment. In Algeria the distribution heavily favoured the wealthy over the poor, which helps us understand why a Socialist model was favoured before independence. Already in the Western camp, liberalism was favoured in Morocco. The essentials of this strategic focus have remained, but they have been marked by variations over time in the country's relationships with the United States and France. Finally, Tunisia has been distinguished by a broader public sector than the other two countries, and it has opted consistently for a pro-Western position in order to ensure that its territorial integrity and sovereignty are protected from threatening neighbours.

Despite the different paths that the countries took when they chose an economic model, the three economies of the Maghreb remained tightly linked with that of their former metropolitan centre, France. As poor countries, they had a high rate of illiteracy and lacked local elites who could take over, as was evidenced by the large number of French managers and teachers called upon, particularly during the 1960s, to assist the three countries to establish programs for economic and cultural development and ensure the future of the French language.[11] The major goal of national independence, therefore, had to expand beyond the recovery of formal sovereignty to include full control of the respective national territories and natural resources. The assumption was that, with these assets, these countries would be able to recover all their "belongings," including the use of their "mother" tongue both vis-à-vis the West and the Near Eastern Arab countries of the Machrek.[12]

While the end of colonization might have brought peace and freedom to the people of the Maghreb, there nevertheless remained many obstacles to development: high illiteracy rates, shortages of persons with professional or skilled trade qualifications, and a lack of local markets. Great efforts would be required to secure the necessary housing stocks, food, and education to achieve wealth and welfare for all. On the economic side, the countries would have to engage in significant accumulation of capital in order to lay the foundations for a national industrial infrastructure. To many, it appeared that the state and *only the state* could lead the way. Just as the state played a crucial role in the creation of the welfare states in developed countries, so too the state came to be seen in the Maghreb as essential for regulating the economy and, in the process, bringing about social reforms.

After independence the Maghreb countries rapidly became one-party states. The Neo-Destour Party (rebaptized the Socialist Destourian Party) ran Tunisia, and the FLN (National Liberation Front) controlled Algeria. In 1963 the Tunisian Communist Party was outlawed, and all political parties were banned in Algeria, except for the FLN, thus forcing opposition movements underground. A monarch took advantage of the rivalry between the Istiqlal or Independence Party and the Socialist Union of Popular Forces (USFP) to assume power in Morocco. Thus the socio-political organizations of the state in the Maghreb countries were frozen at the time of independence into an authoritarian form when it came to managing the decolonization process.[13]

As authoritarian states came to dominate the region, government authorities spied on citizens, weakened trade unions and civil organizations, and took full control of the mass media. A decade of state-controlled economic growth began under a burgeoning public sector that succeeded in establishing community welfare. The Maghreb countries also attempted to pursue import substitution industrialization that involved locally produced manufactured goods.[14] These development strategies failed even though Morocco in 1956 and Tunisia in 1969 tried to strengthen the private sector through protective legislation. Encouraged largely by international investors and American businesses, there was a substantial increase in the export of capital goods from developed countries to underdeveloped countries, thus increasing the economic dependence of the latter.[15] The outcome was similar in Algeria, where President Houari Boumédienne attempted to launch a triple revolution in agriculture, industry, and culture in 1965. Governments first tried to build an industrial infrastructure (a policy known as "industrializing industrialization"). This strategy, however, increased the technological dependence of the given country on the West and gradually led to a deterioration in the national balance of trade. Excessive state control through self-managed estates and cooperatives disrupted agricultural production. The "cultural revolution" boiled down to a "re-Arabization" of education, which in the absence of secular qualified teachers led to a surge of Islamic fundamentalism. Communal struggles between the fundamentalists and their opponents in the state eventually cost Algeria many thousands of human lives. Red tape inherent in the one-party system left little room for political pluralism or freedom of expression in any of the countries.

To varying degrees, the three countries proved incapable of establishing an industrial policy that would generate a coherent and integrated production system. From their inception, these governments relied on the transfer of Western technology rather than developing the capacity to produce capital goods and intermediary consumer goods that would enhance economic autonomy.[16] The coercive institutional climate also blocked freedom of expression and stifled innovation. By the end of the 1960s, the development project had surrendered not to market forces but to an entrepreneurial and developmental state that over-regulated most transactions, thereby denying autonomy to private economic actors.

The Second Decade of Development, 1970-80: Doubt

On 25 October 1970, the United Nations General Assembly outlined a new approach for the second Decade of Development. The average target growth rate for gross domestic product was increased to 6 percent, and the resolution included a social dimension that emphasized the goal of creating a more equal redistribution of income and wealth.[17] The failure of development strategies based on import-substitution and the increase in the debt of underdeveloped countries led the development paradigm for the "Third World" to expand from the economic field to the political and cultural domains.

Unfortunately, the term *Third World* can be a confusing concept, especially in relation to globalization. The term *Third World* refers to countries that stood between developed, industrialized, "Western" nations on the one hand and the Soviet Union and its satellites on the other. As underdeveloped countries that were neither totally liberal and capitalist nor Socialist and Marxist, Third World countries sought autonomy in a development process that transcended economic factors. Their position was less an attempt to set up a specific model for change than a cultural critique of capitalism and imperialism. In this respect, the Third World rejected a linear conception of development and relied on political and cultural means to build solidarity among the countries of Africa, Asia, and Latin America in opposition to the "West" (primarily the United States, western Europe, and Japan), which was sometimes referred to as the "Free World" or the "First World."

"Third Worldism," as the movement came to be known, generated a heated debate about growth models and development theories. At the outset, many in the underdeveloped countries believed that the path to development that western Europe had followed was not reproducible. It appeared utopian to suggest that the Third World could cover the same distance in a decade or two that the Western countries had taken three centuries to transverse. It did not make sense to define underdevelopment through the notion of delay or being late. Rather, underdevelopment should be seen as a structural blockage to growth that followed from the effects of domination by the advanced capitalist countries, which distorted and prevented integration of a national economy. Thus, underdevelopment came to be viewed as a global issue that had to be dealt with at the national level, taking into account the special circumstances of each country. This intellectual approach to the problem of underdevelopment eventually culminated in the formation of dependency theories based on centre-periphery analysis and notions of unequal development.[18]

Pessimism about the prospects of catching up to the West led the historian Paul Bairoch to speculate that, even assuming that the Third World could grow at a rate that surpassed that of developed countries, it would still take the Third World 270 years to achieve parity.[19] According to Bairoch and other critics, the causes of underdevelopment were not endogenous but rather exogenous factors, including economic phenomena outside the range of state policies and linked closely to the international division of labour. Development theories based on modernization and Westernization were wrong because they failed to acknowledge economic dependency, lack of opportunities for development, cultural dimensions, and social alienation. In the eyes of these Third World theorists, underdevelopment was not, as was so often claimed, the result of a heavy burden caused by indigenous cultural traditions; nor could it be blamed on the absence of Western education or a lack of foreign investments. Rather, underdevelopment was the consequence of an ever-increasing dependence on the countries of the capitalist West, which exploited Third World resources and practised cultural and social imperialism.[20] These critics began to see cultural autonomy as one way to change the direction of globalization. They rejected the idea that the West had the right to project its own values as universal ones. In their view, all cultures were valid and Third World countries needed assistance to celebrate their respective national heritages.[21]

Consistent with this critical interpretation, the dichotomy between the developed and the underdeveloped countries became known as "Third World versus the West," a phrase that signalled opposition to political and cultural imperialism. Western academics were by no means indifferent towards this interpretation. In fact, the debate about the Third World generated an impressive literature and sparked considerable analysis by Western social scientists, particularly in the disciplines of ethnology, anthropology, and history. Some of these scholars came to blame the West for the deplorable situation of Africans, Arabs, Indians, South Americans, Asians, and oppressed peoples generally across the globe. At the same time, Third World intellectuals challenged old interpretations, raised new questions, and denounced the harmful impact of colonialism. They also tried to resurrect old traditions among peoples long denigrated in the name of modernity, even exalting local cultures to the point of creating new mythologies about these cultures.[22]

The economic crisis of the 1970s raised further questions about the supposed benefits of the world capitalist system.[23] Until the early 1970s, the economies of the advanced industrialized countries appeared to function perfectly as "growth" touched every sector of society. The protests of 1968 challenged this alleged success, however, by demonstrating that the mere abundance of material goods did not ensure happiness; many apparently did not want to live by bread alone. These protests in effect represented a spiritual rejection of the "affluent society" model that had served as the main reference point for countries all over the world. Beginning in 1970 the world balance of power began to shift, as the United States experienced an economic slowdown while Japan and western Europe grew spectacularly. The 1973 oil crisis further aggravated the economic problems of the industrialized countries, which suddenly had to divert increasing amounts of their assets to pay for energy. The rise in oil prices and the birth of the Organization of Petroleum Exporting Countries (OPEC) demonstrated to many Third World countries that primary resources could be used to reduce economic dependence and promote development. This situation was favourable to the revival of the idea of an Arab Socialist state adapted to the entire region. Through such a model, the Arab people would gain control over the means of production and secure the economic development of all Arab countries. To this end, all local wealth should be socialized for the benefit of all Arabs. Nonetheless, Arab Socialism, which had Nasser's Egypt as its model, would be state Socialism, backed up by authoritarian economic planning, thereby leading to an Arab Union of Socialist Republics, which would have a central government strong enough to "socialize" every means of production across the entire region. All local particularities would be discouraged in favour of building national Arabic pride; priority was to be given to fast and prestigious economic development in harmony with the values of the Arab man. "Since Arabic nationality is said to be essential for the Arab man, socialism in the Arab Near East is Arabic in its essence. Moreover, as the Arab nation is one, there can be only Arab socialism, and not a series of local socialist experiments. Consequently, Bourguiba's socialism is, in fact, a false socialism."[24]

During this decade of economic crisis, some Westerners expressed doubts about the organization of the economic system and the individual's place within it. In the Mediterranean Arab world, however, the emphasis shifted to demands for autonomy through traditional Arab culture. The rediscovery and valorization of national cultural and intellectual heritage, couched as a legitimate demand for the affirmation of a national or Arab identity, was supposed to lead to the erasure of the divisions separating independent Arab nations. For the exponents of pan-Arabism, especially in the Near East, language and culture were considered the most perfect expressions of the Arab nation and its celebrated past. For these exponents of Arabism, looking back to the pre-Islamic Babylonian, Chaldean, Roman, and Byzantine eras appeared to be the best way to prepare for the future. The excavation of archaeological sites revived the tourist industry. A vainglorious myth about the Arab past emerged, as historians searched for Arab antecedents to nearly every European invention or discovery. The attempt to confirm for an apologetic purpose the existence of authentic and original Arabic thinking became known as *al-tûrâth al-fikrî al-'arabî* (the cultural heritage of Arab thought).[25] The attempt to replace Orientalism with an authentic Arab voice took an extreme turn when some intellectuals began to discredit universal values such as freedom, democracy, and respect for the individual on the grounds that these concepts were tainted by their European origins.

Third World leaders treated criticisms of their governments as acts of unwarranted interference and imperialism and used them to justify the further building of authoritarian and corrupt regimes. In response, Western commentators, rejecting the long-standing taboo against questioning romantic views of the Third World, asked not, what is underdevelopment? but rather, what is development?[26] Some defenders of Third Worldism offered rejoinders by invoking the old paradigm of exploitation: development equalled the wealth plundered from the Third World.[27] According to this view, inequalities in the terms of trade fostered an economic dependence that underwrote the power of the West. To put it simply, if the developed world was rich, it was because the underdeveloped world was poor. Unfortunately, the crude division of nations into "rich" and "proletarian" helped very little to understand the causes of underdevelopment. By attempting to explain all the hardships and misfortunes of the Third World as the consequence of exogenous factors, Third World leaders tried to exempt themselves from responsibility for some of the ills of their respective countries.

Despite these many efforts, the gap between developed countries and the Global South has not been reduced. Very often, underdeveloped countries are invited to adopt a particular development model before the previous model has had time to bear fruit. Today, many proponents of globalization applaud the homogenization of cultures and lifestyles when most underdeveloped countries have yet to resolve the identity crises generated by the adoption of previous development models. In the words of one prominent French sociologist, "the history of each country slips away from its culture, its identity, its aspirations, its values. Powerful institutions such as the IMF, World Bank, and World Trade Organization (WTO) can impose an economic rationale on the States, but the private actors empowered by this rationale need take no cognizance of political or social objectives of the given country."[28]

Third Decade of Development and Beyond, 1980 to the Present: Rebirth of the Political

When the second Decade of Development came to an end in 1980, UN targets for the developing world had not been achieved and Third Worldism was losing steam. Some countries did manage to grow at a rate that exceeded expectations, permitting them to join the ranks of the "emerging" nations. But most underdeveloped countries actually experienced a worse financial situation because of an explosion of foreign debt and negative economic growth rates. Development efforts failed to touch the lives of the masses, which became even further marginalized, while elites in their own countries reaped the benefits of globalization and modernization.

Yet the United Nations pushed on. Admitting that the development objectives of the previous two decades had not been met, it proclaimed yet a third Decade of Development. The announcement was met by indifference by governments and the media because many were now resigned to the idea that countries in the Global South were responsible for their own development. Some argued that the time had arrived to implement a new international economic order. Given that the critics of capitalism had failed to propose a viable revolutionary alternative, the new catchphrase became "adjustment," meaning compliance with a standard. Implicitly, all other alternatives to capitalism were no longer worthy of consideration, and the debate over how to promote development took place within the logic of the triumphant liberal market economy.

The 1980s thus became the decade of "structural adjustment," as international financial institutions attempted to implement a series of reforms that would force the economic and financial structures of the developing countries to conform to neoliberalism. According to the IMF and the World Bank, economic crises were no longer to be attributed to external factors but to a structural disequilibrium in the economy caused by certain forms of production, trade, social organization, and bad governance. The short-term solution was to achieve stabilization by correcting the imbalance between resources and employment, while the long-term solution called for restructuring the economy to permit increased private investment and the opening further of external markets. As debt servicing mounted and exports dwindled, the IMF and World Bank introduced structural adjustment programs (SAPs) that required governments to reduce public spending, devalue local currencies to promote exports, remove obstacles to imports, and reduce, if not eliminate, state intervention in order to achieve a greater liberalization of the economy.

Although SAPs improved the macro-financial accounts, they hurt many countries socially by increasing already intolerable unemployment levels, reducing the standard of living, and eroding educational and health services. Temporary welfare programs designed to offset the SAPs did not prevent serious social disturbances from erupting in Casablanca, Cairo, and Tunis. Despite having applied the same reforms, but

227

independent of the IMF, Algeria did not escape their social effects, which were expressed in the riots of 1988.[29]

North African leaders were forced to acknowledge the failures of three decades of development. Some were so pessimistic about the lack of economic growth and industrialization that they simply gave up and announced the "end of development."[30] Other signs of failure included weak national identities, Arab disunity, and the states' inability to build integrated societies based on common values and norms. True, Morocco, Tunisia, and Algeria all experienced a substantial drop in public deficits, but social services in health and education deteriorated while unemployment skyrocketed. In short, neoliberal globalization had effectively worsened the already deep-seated inequalities of the previous era.

Partially as a consequence of these failures, the North African region witnessed a remarkable ideological transformation, which was set in motion by the Iranian revolution of 1979. The rise of a militant Islam, whether radical (Algeria) or moderate (Tunisia and Morocco), which had hitherto been confined to the Middle Eastern context, offered a new refuge from despair and attracted many educated youth who lacked future prospects and were looking for alternatives to the failed secular or pan-Arab ideologies of the 1970s.[31] The old nationalist model based on a unified Arab nation that was essentially anti-Islamic yielded to fantasies of creating an Islamic unity. Such unity, it was alleged, had been blocked by Western imperialist policies that had divided Muslims into separate, secular nations. On the cultural level, the decline of nationalist Arab modernist movements led to a rejection of Arab nationalism. Rather than encouraging people to identify with their Arab ancestors, radical Muslims led a fight on various fronts against pre-Islamic cultures that had been tied, wrongly, to Western cultures. Totalitarian regimes blocked democracy so effectively that any form of political protest against the political regime and its social values had to be done outside formal political institutions.

Neither Third Worldism nor neoliberalism succeeded in providing Arabs or followers of Islam with a clear-cut cultural identity. This disenchantment is all the more frustrating because of the widespread perception that a rapidly expanding Western model of civilization is being forced culturally upon everyone, even as the material benefits of Westernization are less and less accessible to most of humanity. In the Maghreb, authorities attempted to redefine cultural identity with slogans such as "getting back to the source," "Arabization," and "authenticity" *(hawiyya, ta'rîb,* and *'asâla).*[32] These barely disguised Islamic fundamental-ist efforts to rally the masses around a religious alternative to nationalis-tic Arab ideologies meant that identity was no longer to be rooted in the nation, as was common in Western cultures. Rather, it arose out of ad-herence to the *umma,* the worldwide community of Muslims.

Conclusion

The SAPs implemented in the third Decade of Development did not suc-ceed because they failed to consider the vital role that public institutions, including social and educational policies and good governance, play in ensuring the effective functioning of markets. Once again, we are re-minded of the lessons of the 1960s: development is not simply a mat-ter of economic growth, it must be embedded within social policies and institutions that permit society to adjust and rebound from economic shocks. The relative failure of structural adjustment policies resulted in a return of political concerns to the debate over development. According to some, globalization was little more than a way to rationalize relations of domination based on a new growth model.[33] When the adjustment decade ended, several historic events guided globalization.

After the collapse of the Soviet Union in 1989, the United States be-came the unchallenged master of the world. The US government began promoting a "New World Order," which later became known as the "Washington Consensus." Initially, the Washington Consensus stood for a series of policy reforms deemed essential for the development of Latin America. The "Ten Commandments," as cynics dubbed them, required the state to disengage from the economy to permit market forces and the private sector to guide economic development. Although its first propon-ent, economist John Williamson, devised these principles for a specific geographical region in a particular historical context, the formula was soon applied to all underdeveloped countries, where it became identi-fied with neoliberalism and market fundamentalism. As we have seen, this "one size fits all" approach inspired the focus on development since the 1950s. As Williamson later observed: "My version of the Washington Consensus can be seen as an attempt to summarize the policies that were widely viewed as supportive of development at the end of the two de-cades when economists had become convinced that the key to rapid eco-nomic development lay not in a country's natural resources or even in its physical or human capital but, rather, in the set of economic policies

that it pursued."[34] Unfortunately, a program that reduces state intervention to a minimum and permits the "market" to reign supreme cannot
reduce poverty or lead successfully to a long-lasting development that is
just and democratic. One of the major advancements of the 1990s was
the acknowledgement that the transition from a Communist or underdeveloped economy to a capitalist one required building the proper institutional infrastructure. In the presence of weak political institutions,
otherwise beneficial economic policies usually come at the expense of
social institutions.

Then came the 11 September 2001 attack on the World Trade Center,
which jolted the United States out of its complacency about Islamic terrorism. Following the attack, domestic security concerns became Washington's major preoccupation. A second kind of Washington Consensus
emerged as the George W. Bush administration began to radically revise
US relations with the rest of the world, particularly Muslim countries. In
one decade, powerful and violent movements of a political nature had
globalized under the flag of an ideological Islam that was divorced completely from the universal and humanitarian values associated with Islam
as a religion. The surge of anti-Western Islamic fundamentalism and its
extremist offspring can be traced to the failure of modernity; regressive
cultural and social policies of autocratic and corrupt regimes; poverty
and frustration, aggravated further by population growth; and the liquidation of secular opposition groups.

In early 2004 the Bush administration circulated a plan among the
Group of Eight (G8) to reform the Middle East. The "Greater Middle East
Initiative" looked all too familiar to those in the Third World: promote
democracy and good governance, build a knowledge society, and widen
the scope of economic opportunities. According to this formula, democracy and good governance constitute the framework within which development will occur.[35] Unfortunately, as one observer has pointed out,
economic development and liberal democracy do not always go hand in
hand, and totalitarian regimes can benefit from economic growth while
evading pressures for reform.[36] Even worse, economic growth could,
in certain cases, consolidate and reinforce the authoritarian and repressive features of these regimes. The slow pace of democratization in the
Arab and Muslim world, so frustrating for Europe and especially for the
United States, reinforces the lessons learned from the decades of development: encouraging economic growth has rarely, if ever, led to democracy and pluralism. Moreover, many leaders have learned how to use the

rules of this development policy game to their own advantage. They manipulate institutions and put democracy off indefinitely while claiming to be highly liberal. The autocrats in the Maghreb countries now use the fundamentalist threat as an argument against democracy: democratic reform would lead, they say, to a landslide victory by Islamic fundamentalists.

The decade of independence in the postwar period promised an era of economic, political, cultural, and social autonomy. But the successive economic models — capitalism, Third Worldism, and structural adjustment programs — failed to secure the integration of the North African countries into the global economy. The agents of development, nationalist and autocratic political regimes, did not understand the social consequences of these policies, and this failure led to the hegemony of single-party rule accompanied by worsening social conditions. Under more recent economic, cultural, and political globalization, the situation in these countries is continuous, in one key respect, with the decades of development. Autonomy comes in the form of resistance to liberalizing political life. In the independence era, this reluctance was justified as necessary if the development agenda was to be given top priority. More recently, this reluctance is recast as a matter of resisting Western-led globalization and the imposition of Western values in the form of democracy, human rights, and good governance. The nation-state, political leaders argue, is the only vehicle for guarding and preserving social cohesion and equality in the face of the globalization juggernaut. The real question that remains is, which juggernaut — global capitalism or global Islam?

chapter 13   Snakes That Are Rainbows:
Indigenous Worldviews and the
Constitution of Autonomy

Ravi de Costa

GLOBALIZATION AND AUTONOMY HAVE special importance for the
world's indigenous peoples, who have often been and still are subject to
the globalizing effects of colonization. In keeping with this volume's efforts to convey ideas through selected moments, the following account
seeks to explore indigenous views on the meanings and potentialities of
globalization and autonomy. It uses three distinct episodes from the history of indigenous Australia, including the building of an embassy on the
grounds of the Parliament, and binds them with an Aboriginal account of
the making and remaking of the world. The purpose of these recurring
moments is to remind us that the different ways the natural world has been
understood are significant for humans' collective autonomy. As we will see,
a people's understanding of autonomy arises out of the interplay between a
particular cosmology or worldview and the social and natural environment
in which those people live. Aboriginal cosmologies predated the arrival of
Europeans, and those cosmologies both authored and authorized indigenous societies' social orders and understandings of human freedom. When
colonization assaulted their social and natural environment, such worldviews were profoundly challenged. These challenges, however, did not result in a complete assimilation of European ideas. Rather, an indigenous
worldview was brought to bear on relations with Europeans and shaped
indigenous peoples' responses to the destructive forces of colonization. A
notion of autonomy as survival in the face of cataclysm emerged in the
late and post-imperial periods, and it was shaped largely by the growing

sense of indigeneity that arose from connections with and understandings of other indigenous peoples in the world.

The earth has become so hot that it can hurt people's feet to walk on bare soil. The wind is blowing from the south-east — hot, dry, and dusty. The country is parched, the animals have grown thin, the waterholes and billabongs are drying up. The sun, which is necessary to life, is beginning to destroy life ... as the blossoms dry up, the flying foxes move to the river, roosting in the trees along permanent waterholes. When the Rainbow snakes see the flying foxes, their Dreaming allies, hanging above them, they know it is time to move.[1]

Autonomy and the Revealing World

The story of the Rainbow Snake that weaves through this chapter tells of the changing of the seasons and its consequences for the world that the Yarralin community in Australia's Northern Territory calls home. It invites the reader to consider the complex connections between the dynamic geographies we inhabit, the philosophical meanings we ascribe to these spaces, and possible structures of human action.

The *Oxford English Dictionary* defines *autonomy* as "the possession or right of self-government; freedom of action." Though often applied to states and institutions, this definition privileges purposive action, intentions, and plans by relying on a discrete and unified subjectivity akin to the ideal of the individual. But related terms, like *autonomic,* hint at another dimension. Taken from physiology, the term describes processes like circulation and respiration that are not consciously directed. The philosopher John Searle suggested that humans assign to these autonomic processes functional meanings. As we have become aware of how physical systems function, humans have imposed frameworks of values and intentions onto those systems.[2] The function of circulation and respiration is to enable life; life is good; therefore, our social order should promote the flourishing of life.

As the introduction to this volume suggests, we can think of this process as establishing the basic criteria for collective autonomy. The assignment of laws, rules, norms, and values that reflect human understanding of the physical world, as it is inhabited, is indeed an imaginative act. Consequently, a priori assumptions about the status of the world, not least those that are grounded in culture, become implicated in our autonomy. This approach propels us towards a fundamentally intersubjective account of the landscape in which autonomy must be experienced. Because humans can and do adopt particular dispositions towards the world, investing it with meaning and shared dispositions, social constructions such as property, money, sovereignty, or the family emerge. Such an analysis suggests that human identities, interests, and the meanings ascribed to actions are similarly subject to construction; they are endogenous to the social circumstances in which such interests and identities are formed, because they rely on collective intentions.[3]

A further explanation can be found in "constitutive rules," which create "conditions of possibility" by bringing the game, or landscape of action, into being. There is no game of chess until it is constituted by the rules.[4] Scholars in numerous fields have sought to explain particular social or political subjectivities as reliant on conditions of possibility, or epistemes.[5] These philosophical insights motivate the following analysis of three distinct periods in the history of indigenous Australians: a pre-contact cosmological era, the modern era of British colonization during the nineteenth century, and the decolonization era beginning after the Second World War. The findings suggest that constructions of autonomy are significantly influenced by particular human understandings of the world as a totality. What are here called *worldviews* encompass not only the nature of reality but also the ways in which we know that we can and *should* act within that totality. Consequently, this chapter stresses a feature of human autonomy that recurs throughout vastly different historical periods. Worldviews, including what we have latterly called "globality," provide practical and everyday knowledge about the world that both enables and legitimizes certain forms of autonomy. Worldviews act as blueprints on which human beings may locate themselves and plan their lives in ways that help them to manage difficulties, resist oppression, and reconstruct identities.

Adopting this approach enables us to begin to bridge the gap in the sociology of knowledge between intellectual and practical accounts of the worlds of action, thereby arriving at a new synthesis of human experience appropriate to the global human condition. In the late 1960s, the sociologists Peter Berger and Thomas Luckmann directed scholarly attention towards the knowledge-producing aspects of everyday human activity and life. They suggested this line of inquiry, in part, as an antidote to an excessive preoccupation with ideological analyses, in which knowledge was theorized as the consequence of world-historical forces such as class. What really needed to be understood was the process of objectification of subjective sense impressions and meanings, by which the "*inter*subjective commonsense world is constructed."[6] Global conditions invite us to renew an interest in processes of ideation, and to examine the role of those processes in constructing formulae for legitimate and meaningful action. Contemporary forms of autonomy now arise both within global networks and in the diffuse and mediated representations of the global public sphere. Here, ideas like neoliberalism and ecological crisis jostle and commingle with individual experience, making the "everyday" and the "practical" seem elusive.

This chapter shows that it is in our consciousness and explanations of *totality* that legitimation of the social order is grounded and that human intention is made meaningful. The three worldviews considered here — cosmology, modernity, and indigeneity — allow us to better understand indigenous peoples' accounts of autonomy. We see indigenous peoples living in a difficult natural environment, confronting the global expansion of European empires and their paternalistic policies and identifying themselves within a globally networked and mediated post-imperial order. Even though the contents of the world differ greatly across these three periods, indigenous experiences reveal that autonomy relies on the conditions of possibility provided by worldviews.

Now the rainbow is young and restless. It gets up out of the water, opens its mouth, and shoots out lightning and saliva. The saliva is rain and it contains tadpoles. The first rain alerts the lightning people. Lightning women flash their lightning with increasing frequency, aroused by the Rainbow snake. The rain brings steam up from the hot earth; steam collects into clouds which carry more rain. The wind shifts, coming now from the north-west ... These early rains arouse other species. Various grubs, as well as frogs, are "boss" for rain: they call on the rainbow to bring more. As the rains increase, the floodwaters rise, signalling the presence of the mature rainbow.

Cosmology and Autonomy

Cosmology serves to orient a community to its world, in the sense that it defines, for the community in question, the place of humankind in the cosmic scheme of things. Such cosmic orientation tells the member of the community, in the broadest possible terms, who they are and where they stand in relation to the rest of creation.
—Freya Mathews, *The Ecological Self*

For many indigenous Australian communities, the story of the Rainbow Snake provides such a function because it unifies all moments, all beings, and all places in its travels and transformations.

Creation myths have long fascinated scholars seeking to understand indigenous worldviews. For example, in his study of Aboriginal religions, L.R. Hiatt observed "a genre, a suite of fleeting forms" that involved variations on the Rainbow Snake image that indigenous Australian philosophers used to explain the origin of the world and the fundamental nature of reality. In far-flung parts of the continent, the Rainbow Snake embodied indigenous explanations of the two regions inaccessible to human experience: the sky and the underground. "Rainbows appear in the former, and snakes emerge from the latter. Their unification in the concept of the Rainbow Snake constitutes not merely an imaginative connection between the two domains of mystery impinging on the everyday world but a theory of an external source of the latter's Being."[7]

In their major study of indigenous Australia before European contact, the anthropologists Ronald and Catherine Berndt described the realm of mythology as the "precedent for all human behaviour from that time on … This was the past, the sacred past; but it was not the past in the sense of something that is over and done with."[8] On the contrary, religious tradition was frequently the basis on which distant tribes interacted. Widely shared sacred narratives of origins underpinned what the Berndts called the "collective enterprise" of social identification and solidarity.[9]

Ian Keen's comparative anthropology of seven indigenous communities found that cosmology "framed regional orders of 'law' [and] provided the foundations of social order," including basic accounts of the physical properties of the world and the "precepts and practices" that informed human social existence.[10] For the indigenous peoples of the Kimberley region of Western Australia (Ngarinyin, Wunambal, and Worrora), the creator-being dreamt the ancestors *(wanjina)* into existence during the mythical creation era *(lalan)*. Wanjina took various forms, particularly clouds, which encountered other beings as they travelled across the country, shaping landscapes and literally moulding the physical space in which people would find food and water.[11] Wanjina also came to govern the Wunambal institutions of exogamy (marrying outside the group) and social avoidance laws, such as those between a wife's mother and a daughter's husband.[12]

The Pintupi of the Western Desert in central Australia hold similar beliefs. According to the anthropologist Fred Myers, the visible world of the Pintupi depends on "the noumenal dimension of Being out of which everything emerges, in which all life forms are steeped, but which people must be taught to see."[13] As Myers explains, "the constitution of the world by The Dreaming must be treated phenomenologically as a given condition of 'what there is,' an endowment of being and potential that defines for Pintupi the framework of human action."[14] Humans create nothing, not even their own children, which are understood to result from the independent transformations of autonomous spirits.[15] For the Pintupi, the term *ngurra* means variously country, camp, and place, or it can refer to the people who live on the country, that is, the Pintupi themselves.[16] Thus Pintupi identity exists within a framework of social order that emphasizes the embodiment of human sociality in a mythologized landscape.

The Arrente people of central Australia provide another example of how cosmology can shape the indigenous social order. According to the linguist T.G.H. Strehlow, in this community they see "autonomy" as being conferred on patrilineal clans by mystical links with sacred sites on their own territories; centralized authority thus did not emerge, nor did large-scale warfare to control territory. Consequently, "men and women lived in a state of freedom and social equality ... male elders subjected novices to religious disciplines in order to transform them into free and autonomous men."[17]

As these studies suggest, cosmology explains the origins of the world for indigenous peoples, and developing a mature understanding of creation stories can reveal the parameters of acceptable and meaningful social behaviour. Freedom is not the capacity to act within the web of "human alliances, creation and choices, but is seen as imposed by an embracing cosmic order."[18] This ordered worldview, however, enables activities that would otherwise be impossible in the precarious environs of the Australian desert. Fred Myers observes:

The sources of what Westerners would think of as autonomy and authority are considered by the Pintupi to exist "outside" the self, projected outward into The Dreaming and onto the landscape, where they are available as social artifacts. This projection of a domain "outside" of society overcomes two constraints that impede certain kinds of coordinated social action: (1) the web of mutual obligation and relatedness between people in this society of former hunter-gatherers, which is based on their need for help from each other; and (2) the value placed on equality or personal autonomy, such that no one is prepared to be told by others what to do.[19]

The water becomes dark and muddy, forming whirlpools which are the rainbow in action. Careless people and animals can be sucked into these pools, drowned and perhaps eaten by rainbows.

Modernity and Autonomy

The colonization of Australia during the nineteenth century coincided with the resurgence of evangelical Christianity.[20] Of the various experiences that Aboriginal peoples had with colonial modernity, coming to understand notions of humanitarianism that were characteristic of this form of Christianity was common, and Aborigines used them to resist the colonizers. They articulated and developed new notions of autonomy that permitted them to engage with and challenge imperialism. Historians have offered several explanations for the rise of evangelicalism and its humanitarian mission, including Protestant alarm at the proselytizing achievements of Catholicism and a widely felt need to reassert faith in the face of ascendant scientific explanations. An important source of momentum for the rise of evangelicalism in the nineteenth century was the passionate desire of many Christians to end the abhorrence of slavery and to realize an "empire of good."

In this evangelical vision, "a reformed and revitalized Christian Britain could offer leadership to the globe." Widespread support for humanitarian ideas was based on their dissemination through an emerging network of publications prepared by church missionary societies for domestic congregations. These publications often satisfied a prurient fascination with the "barbarism" of other peoples and reflected puritanical obsessions with alleged cannibalism, depraved sexualities, and general savagery.[21] The global expansion of missionary practice also required the opening of "areas of social and family life which had previously been policed by tribal elders and custom, rather than fixed religious codes."[22] Through the extensive regulation of indigenous peoples' lives, imperialists sought to dominate not just more territory but also the human experience.

The evangelical worldview in its humanitarian mode promoted a particular kind of autonomy. Humanitarians sought a universal framework of principles in which slavery was unacceptable and emancipation was understood as the liberation of God's children. Hence the missionary mind became linked with conversion.[23] Faith in a universal brotherhood in Christ was required, because many evangelicals understood that the logic of emancipation made it "no less incumbent on them to befriend other victims of colonising enterprise who, though not actually slaves, were exposed to treatment as bad as the state of slavery involved."[24]

Christian humanitarians, and the Aborigines Protection Society in particular, persuaded the Colonial Office to establish reserves in southeastern Australia beginning in the 1830s.[25] Historian Bain Attwood, who has studied the initial response of indigenous survivors to the first wave of European settlement in southeastern Australia, notes that after the periods of sustained frontier violence and the spread of epidemics, fragmented indigenous communities regrouped on small reserves run by missionaries. Many Aborigines became interested in engaging with the newcomers, not least so their children could have access to education, "one of the principal sources of agency and power in the white man's society."[26] Evangelicals believed that the social benefits they offered on the reserve would lead to moral and spiritual improvement. But many, if not most indigenous people, viewed the mission and reserve regimes as invasive and destructive because they suppressed indigenous traditions severely in their attempt to assimilate tribal people and bring "Truth to those living in darkness."[27]

Attwood's close observation of one Moravian mission in Victoria called Ramahyuck (1862-1908) reveals the concerted and all-encompassing effort by missionaries "to change the indigenes in spatial and temporal terms."[28] In the mid- to late nineteenth century, missions were built and managed according to rational and utilitarian models established by the religious and intellectual networks of the imperial world. Mission design of the Victorian era established physical boundaries and rules that enforced European notions of individuality, gender, and family. The missions also imposed rigid routines of schooling and labour to instill regularity and responsibility.[29]

Many indigenous people came to understand that mission doctrines offered a significantly different account of power and authority than did those that dominated colonization. Attwood identifies three spurs to politicization created by indigenous encounters with these doctrines: first, Christianity relied on the inclusive concept of universal brotherhood; second, it insisted on a higher authority, under which colonists and indigenous people were equals; finally, it offered millenarian deliverance from the injustice of the present.[30]

Many indigenous Australians were able to take solace from the right-eousness that knowledge of scripture offered. Mona Burton, a self-described "full blood," gently encouraged white people to read "the second book of Corinthians, the tenth chapter and the seventh verse which says: 'Do ye look on things after the outward appearance? If any man trust in himself that he is Christ's let him of himself think this again, that, as he is Christ's even so are we Christ's.'"[31] David Unaipon, perhaps the first published Aboriginal author, felt especially blessed by the arrival of Christianity and thought he had entered a "new mental world."[32] In later years numerous indigenous leaders found their political voice at the pulpit, including Don Brady, Cedric Jacob, and Doug Nicholls, who had a distinguished career in several fields before becoming governor of South Australia.

The humanitarian reserves policy created a firm conviction among indigenous peoples across southeastern Australia that they had entered into a direct relationship with the Crown. Many saw this step as recognition of their priority and sovereignty, and it gave them the means to reconstruct their own identities in a wider social order that included Europeans.[33] Later colonial actions, such as the opening of reserve lands to white settlers, thus created a sense of betrayal and inspired new phases of resistance. Petitions protesting against the encroachment of settlers or the abuse of authorities flowed from reserves and missions to the Crown.[34]

On 17 February 1846, the indigenous inhabitants of Flinders Island, off the coast of Tasmania (then known as Van Diemen's Land), petitioned Queen Victoria for assistance in their plight. Flinders Island was not the traditional home of these people but a reserve granted to those Aborigines who had survived dispossession and years of officially condoned violence on Van Diemen's Land. The governor of New South Wales had created their sanctuary, Wybalenna, as a compromise and as an inducement for those surviving Aborigines to abandon the mainland. Having agreed to be removed from the colonists' preferred lands, Aborigines found themselves living in a desperate and oppressive environment. The petitioners described themselves in terms that asserted the origins of their relationship to the Crown as active and decisive agents: "We Your Majesty's Petitioners are your free Children that we were not taken prisoners but freely gave up our country."[35]

Throughout southeast Australia over the next seventy years, reserve-based communities, seeking the fulfillment of the "wishes of Her Most Gracious Majesty Queen Victoria," petitioned colonial authorities.[36] The best-documented campaign is that of William Cooper, who spent the 1930s struggling to present a petition to the British monarch.[37] Much like earlier petitions, Cooper's petition appealed to imperial morality both in its use of language and its goals. The problem presented in his petition was that whites either did not realize that they were not living up to their *existing* obligations or they did not care to. In these moments, we see that indigenous political actors relied on a worldview that colonists could understand in order to claim the autonomy enjoyed by white subjects, including those universal obligations and responsibilities granted and overseen by an imperial Christian authority. Their claims for specific civil entitlements and social justice (including land) showed that they craved inclusion as full human subjects in an existing normative order.

Attwood seeks to recover the politicizing effects of humanitarianism, which heightened indigenous peoples' consciousness of themselves as Aborigines. Those who were forced away from missions developed a stronger sense of difference and of being oppressed. Those who sought to retain traditional lands and to oppose their relocation developed a sense of commonality with other Aborigines outside their own communities. These common experiences, in turn, came to shape Aborigines' understandings of their own history and came to be held as beliefs or myths that were used to explain who they had come to be in the present.[38] Heather Goodall has argued that such assertions show the continuity of indigenous claims within a new context of settlement that acknowledged Europeans and their colonial presence.[39] Although their cosmological worldviews had been badly damaged, indigenous peoples adapted their claims to the new accounts of totality and universalism familiar to white settlers.

By the end of the nineteenth century, this type of universalism was almost entirely obscured by the "cynicism of empire," in which scientific racism became ascendant.[40] This combined with the burgeoning desire of settlers to conduct their own affairs without interference from the metropole. Although humanitarianism was pushed aside, evangelical Christianity with its global program of humanitarian mission had an enduring impact on the politics of the indigenous question, especially in discussions about how colonial imperatives could be restrained. More to the point, it constituted new rules for colonization that repositioned indigenous peoples in a global moral order that enabled new forms of autonomy. Christianity was a doctrine of salvation, one that consoled and galvanized while promoting a morality of caring about others that showed the hypocrisy of settlers. Missions and reserves challenged colonists by contradicting their unfettered right of expansion. Spaces reserved for indigenous communities allowed them to regroup and develop new and broader identifications, including the widely held view of a direct and formal indigenous relationship with the Crown. Finally, the humanitarians offered the possibility of more effective participation in the settler polity by expanding indigenous literacy. The worldview of humanitarians assisted indigenous people to reconstitute their status in a normative global order dominated by Europeans.

After a few months the rainbow has expanded its influence enormously: floods abound, the sky has been cloudy for a long time; the sun has been eclipsed by the rain. The flying foxes are said to have gone underwater to join the rainbow, and frogs stop calling for rain. The rainbow has been roaming abroad and is becoming "old and tired."

Indigeneity and Autonomy

In the twentieth century and especially after the Second World War, the European ordering of the world according to peoples' alleged level of civilization became increasingly untenable. Settler colonies achieved independence, while elites in resource colonies developed ideologies of liberation. Imperial centralization became too costly to maintain as world wars and depression exhausted European nation-states (see chapters by Pruessen and Essid). New global networks of communications and transportation linked diasporic identities and experiences and international institutions grew in number, not only to manage new networks but also to articulate and confront global problems.

The autonomy of indigenous peoples both suffered and advanced as the world was transformed. More indigenous peoples were pulled into the capitalist system, damaging further indigenous economies with new incursions such as large-scale mining operations and the settler communities that grew to support them (see White, this volume). But in many settler colonies, the postwar era was influential in two related ways. First, developments, such as the 1951 amendments to the Indian Act in Canada or the range of reforms in Australia during the 1960s, ensured the formal extension of liberal and civil rights protections to indigenous peoples.[41] Second, by building on these new political freedoms, indigenous Australians joined the new currents of anti-colonial politics and portrayed their circumstances as subject to the same global forces that operated not only in other settler states but also in resource-rich states.[42] The global phenomenon of decolonization offered indigenous peoples a new way to see the world, one that combined grievance and resistance with solidarity among all those subject to the marginalizing effects of colonialism while, at the same time, asserting cultural difference.

The Aboriginal Tent Embassy, set up on the lawn in front of the Parliament House in Canberra on Australia Day, 26 January 1972, embodied this new worldview and represented a new mode of indigenous autonomy in Australia. The participants in the demonstration — young, angry, articulate, urban Aborigines — re-imagined the global order at the same moment that they appealed to it. Indigenous Australians called for new relations with the nation-state and represented themselves in a political action that was a novel blend of existing modes of petition, demonstration, and occupation. Moreover, they understood that their actions were aimed at bringing about a global order that was inclusive of all human beings, indigenous and non-indigenous alike.

The establishment of the embassy was a spontaneous reaction to the Conservative federal government's inadequate response to claims for indigenous land rights in Australia during the 1960s. In 1971, in the first legal assessment of the claims of Native title, the Federal Court finally ruled that the plaintiffs (the Yolngu of northeastern Arnhem Land) did not hold any form of title justiciable under Australian law. Embarrassed, government officials felt obliged to make new policy. Just before Australia Day 1972, they granted forms of alienable leasehold to approved traditional groups. Young, urban indigenous leaders rejected the concession and accused the government of having "reduced Aboriginals to the same level as flora and fauna by saying that we belong to the land but the land doesn't belong to us."[43]

The American Indian Movement's occupation of Alcatraz in 1969 was a major source of inspiration for the Australian protest. One of the Tent Embassy demonstrators later recalled that "the Indians had taken over Alcatraz at the same time and I wanted to put our plight into the eyes of the world."[44] A central protagonist, Roberta Sykes, described the embassy's rationale as exposing "the global conspiracy of silence about the expropriation of Australia from the Aboriginal people ... It was up to us to inform the outside world on the specifics of our predicament. We realised the effort would require a great deal of imagination and ingenuity from a people with no resources."[45]

The materials used to construct the embassy were rudimentary. In the late evening of Australia Day, four young Aboriginal men set up camp on the open ground immediately in front of the seat of Australian power, the Commonwealth Parliament building in Canberra. Their camp appeared initially to be little more than "a beach umbrella and placards."[46] Gary Foley, one of the four original protestors, was not discouraged: "This is an embassy: the Prime Minister's statement yesterday effectively makes us aliens in our own land, so like the other aliens we need an embassy."[47] The demonstration grew rapidly as indigenous people arrived from Sydney and Melbourne, as well as from Yirrkala and the islands of Arnhem Land.[48]

Photographs reveal the protest's humble and demotic character, as indigenous people and their supporters sat on the ground, cooked and ate in the open, and slept in half a dozen tents. Politicians dressed in suits who emerged from the Parliament House to negotiate with the leaders appeared in sharp contrast to the barefooted demonstrators draped in peace symbols.[49] Local ordinances did not proscribe such temporary and transient dwellings, so the government was unable to remove the embassy legally.[50] The protestors thus gained time to show the world how indigenous peoples were forced to live their entire lives in shacks and lean-tos. By demonstrating the absolute failure of Australia's self-proclaimed egalitarianism, the Tent Embassy protest redrew the contours of the Australian public imagination about indigenous lives. As Greg Cowan has noted, through the "expression of its heterogeneous contributors and of the mixing of spaces and materials," the Tent Embassy "symbolises a great deal about place-making."[51]

The Tent Embassy protest also stimulated a striking rethinking of indigenous representations of selfhood, which helped consolidate a new form of autonomy for Aboriginal peoples. This form included an intersubjective awareness and solidarity that was drawn from a shared experience of dispossession and cultural difference. Conceived and enacted by the more militant parts of the urban indigenous community in southeastern Australia, the embassy remains highly regarded, even by indigenous activists who advocate more orthodox methods of struggle. Faith Bandler, an Islander woman and a significant leader in the Federal Council for Aboriginal and Torres Strait Islander Affairs, claimed that the embassy "brought everybody together and strengthened ties between the black people."[52]

The impact of the embassy protest was not simply confined to Australia. As one historian of the event noted, the visitors to the embassy "included Soviet diplomats, a representative of the Canadian Claims Commission, and a cadre from the Irish Republican Army who donated a linen handkerchief to the cause."[53] Several protest organizers also tried to establish a permanent international base to promote the indigenous struggle on a global scale.[54] The Aboriginal Information Centre, for example, served as an indigenous political and cultural embassy to draw support from sympathetic international governments and leftist European social movements.

Indigenous peoples now saw themselves as both prepared and obliged to conduct international relations. The broader reformulation of indigeneity led to greater pressure on international institutions and eventually resulted in an ongoing campaign for the universal recognition and protection of indigenous rights (see the volume *Indigenous Peoples and Autonomy* in this series). As part of this global political history, the embassy revealed the way that the autonomy of indigenous peoples had been reconceived by the 1970s. As a media-savvy way to create new pan-indigenous identifications, it juxtaposed indigenous social reality with symbols of national power. But this autonomous action took place in a social milieu that was infused with an awareness of the global effects of imperialism and colonialism. The conclusion for indigenous peoples was that they had to reconstitute their politics to challenge the dominant worldview — the normative order of nation-states.

The sun now asserts itself, burning the rainbow. At the same time, the wind shifts to the east and breaks the rainbow's back. Burnt and broken, it retreats to the rivers. The east wind clears the skies and brings the cold weather. Dingos have their litters, kangaroos and turkeys become fat; the whole emphasis of the world shifts from water to land, from rain to sun, from river resources to land resources. When the country dries out, the white gum trees blossom and the flying foxes return. Cold weather recedes as the sun takes over the sky and heats up the earth, and the whole cycle begins again.

Conclusion

How should we think about autonomy on a globalized landscape? Is an overarching political philosophy the only answer, as Thomas Friedman and others continue to suggest, because the collapse of Communism "allowed us to think of the world as a single space"?[55] How significant were the first images of Earth made available by human travel in orbit? Do ideas of globality require knowledge of totality to include, at minimum, an appreciation that the world is a spherical mass of minerals orbiting the sun, a post-Copernican worldview? The debate so far has explicitly excluded eras and worldviews that predate that breakthrough, while Jan Aart Scholte's discussion of supraterritoriality advances a critique of strictly materialist accounts of geography.[56]

Accounts of globalization and autonomy that stress human interactions are, without question, important. This chapter has suggested, however, that we must take into account the cultural and philosophical commitments that connect particular understandings of totality or globality with structures of human agency and autonomy. Worldviews, which make possible, sensible, and desirable all kinds of exchanges between people, are in turn shaped by new forms of autonomy in what may be the most fundamental dialectic of the human condition.

It can be said that indigenous peoples are more amenable to this type of reasoning than to others. They have been subjected to the imposed worldviews of European modernity, and in the classical formulations of indigenous Australia the autonomy of humans was something prescribed by mythologized explanations of a socio-physical order. In fact, thinking about indigenous experiences may assist all of us to understand how our own autonomy is bound up with prevailing accounts of the global order of things, revealing connections that in less condensed communities may be more difficult to observe. Worldviews make certain kinds of human activity possible, meaningful, valuable, or necessary. The planet hurtling towards ecological catastrophe may be the most compelling example of a contemporary worldview that, for a growing number of people, is shaping autonomy and motivating action. Worldviews also make certain forms of autonomy redundant, inefficient, or unacceptable. The global visions of neoliberals and neoconservatives, like those of imperialists and colonizers in earlier times, continue to make this clear.

Chapter 14   Globalization and US Empire:
              Moments in the Forging of the
              Global Turn

              Ulf Hedetoft

THE SETTING: Hofdi House, outside of Reykjavik, Iceland, 11 and 12
October 1986. A cold, windy, and rainy weekend — the atmosphere
is bleak, and the residence has a reputation for being haunted. *The protagonists:* the heads of the two rival superpowers, Ronald Reagan and
Mikhail Gorbachev. *The occasion:* a seemingly modest, informal, and
haphazardly planned "pre-summit meeting" between the two leaders to
discuss relations between their countries, especially the state of the nuclear arms race, and to prepare for a proper summit meeting later.

   In spite of the meeting's failure to produce any agreement, it should be
regarded as the pivotal moment in the superpower confrontation that we
usually refer to as the Cold War — and the pivotal moment in the United
States' effort to overcome the last constraints of bipolarity to further its
global hegemonic ambitions to fully harness globalization to American
imperial sovereignty. This seemingly inconsequential, and in many ways
unsuccessful, two-day encounter between the heads of state in fact contains and condenses the past history of salient conflicts between the two
superpowers' "incommensurable systems" in an almost ideal-type way.[1] It
also points ahead to their final resolution in the form of Soviet capitulation
to the interests and power of the United States. As Jack Matlock, US ambassador to the Soviet Union between 1988 and 1991, has astutely noted:
"Reykjavik was the hinge summit; it was a breakthrough — probably the
most important summit we had. What was decided there ... eventually became the [Intermediate-Range Nuclear Forces (INF)] treaties. So to look

at it as a failure is to look at it in a very superficial way."[2] This evaluation is echoed by Henry Kissinger in a statement that, typically, blends realism and deception: "Gorbachev's last opportunity to bring about a rapid end to the arms race, or at least to magnify the strains on the Alliance, passed at Reykjavik."[3] Kissinger, correctly, notes the importance of the occasion, but he does so in a way that allows for the possibility that, had Gorbachev only been a defter statesman, the meeting might have led to an "end to the arms race" due to the alleged "vulnerability of the American negotiating position."[4] George Schultz, the secretary of state, is less prone to beating about the bush: "We should give them the sleeves from our vest on SDI [Strategic Defense Initiative — "Star Wars"] and make them think they got our overcoat. [And in retrospect,] I knew that the genie was out of the bottle: the concessions Gorbachev made at Reykjavik could never, in reality, be taken back. We had seen the Soviets' bottom line."[5] Paul Nitze, chief US arms negotiator, agrees: "It was the best Soviet proposal we have received in twenty-five years."[6]

1986-90: Overcoming the Constraints of Bipolarity

And so it was, though hardly for reasons of incompetent diplomacy on the Soviet side. The concessions made by the Soviets — comprising "a 50% reduction in all strategic weapons, a total elimination of Soviet and American intermediate-range missiles in Europe, strict compliance with the ABM Treaty ... American terms for on-site verification ... drop[ping] the previous Soviet demand that French and British missiles be included in any agreement ... limit[ing] the USSR's missiles in Asia to 100 warheads ... recogniz[ing] human rights as a legitimate part of future superpower negotiations," and quite a lot more — had a more realistic, and imperative, basis.[7] This was ever-widening asymmetries of military and economic power between the superpowers, produced not least by the gigantic military armament of the early Reagan years, which was noted cynically by Kissinger when he was in a less deceptive and more triumphal mood. "From Angola to Nicaragua, a resurgent America was turning Soviet expansionism into costly stalemates or discredited failures, while the American strategic buildup, especially SDI, posed a technological challenge which the stagnant and overburdened Soviet economy could not begin to meet. At a moment when the West was launching the supercomputer microchip revolution, the new Soviet leader watched his country slip into technological underdevelopment."[8] Economic, technological, and military forms of superiority joined forces in the American strategy of the 1980s — the so-called Second Cold War.[9] It was a strategy for which Kissinger's native language coined a fitting term, *Todrüstung*. The strategy involved arming the enemy to death, first, by forcing it to divert huge economic resources from domestic to military use, which would drain production, infrastructure, and popular consumption, and second, by exerting massive and continuous competitive pressure on the enemy's military sector in its own right, which would eventually highlight the insufficiency of giving exclusive financial and organizational priority to the means, above all others, of maintaining superpower status. In the early 1980s, this debilitating negative synergy between the two main sectors of the Soviet economy was beginning to make a visible impact on the formulations of its foreign and security policies.

This strategic context and the success of the American strategy added new meaning to Kissinger's description of the race between two "incommensurable systems." By the mid-1980s, the two superpowers were not simply beyond comparison in terms of political, economic, or ideological *structure* but, more importantly, with respect to economic, political, technological, and military *power*. George Kennan and President Harry S. Truman's anti-Communist strategy of the 1940s had been successfully implemented. The "containment" of the enemy had been completed; now it was a question of its "rollback" and eventual annihilation.[10]

The "evil empire's" entitlement to the superpower label had come to reside in one attribute and one attribute only: a vast quantity of nuclear warheads fitted onto intercontinental and medium-range missiles that pointed towards European and American targets. And although this military potential, allied to the comprehensive conventional forces of the Warsaw Pact countries, would be sufficient to wreak significant havoc in a third world war, it was no longer an adequate match for the military capabilities of the United States and its European allies. The SALT (Strategic Arms Limitation Talks) negotiations of the 1970s had served their function. They had once again made war on even the grandest scale *calculable* for the political and military elites of the Western superpower. Or, in Kissinger's somewhat euphemistic phrasing, "arms negotiations were becoming a device for applying pressure on the rickety Soviet system."[11]

By the mid-1980s, these "arms control" negotiations no longer struck the United States, bargaining from a position of new-gained strength, as very useful. Rather, it started regarding them as "an abstruse subject involving esoteric fine points that even with the best intentions would take years to resolve."[12] The US armaments program of the early 1980s, including the threat of a future SDI program, had the objective of stepping up — beyond all diplomatic finesse and all idealistic Soviet discourse on peaceful coexistence — the relentless pressure on the Soviets. The goal: to render their nuclear potential — the only remaining bargaining chip they still possessed — "impotent and obsolete," as Reagan chose to phrase it, even if the president, for public propaganda purposes, presented the threat in the form of an idealistic desire to rid the world of *all* nuclear weapons.[13]

In fact, however, Reagan was "proposing to erase everything that the Soviet Union had propelled itself into bankruptcy trying to accomplish."[14] At Reykjavik, therefore, Gorbachev, being at the receiving end of overwhelming American superiority, did not allow himself to be seduced into unconditional and immediate capitulation by Reagan's idealist rhetoric: "Excuse me, Mr. President, but I do not take your idea of sharing SDI seriously. You don't want to share even petroleum equipment, automatic machine tools or equipment for dairies, while sharing SDI would be a second American Revolution."[15] This statement also reveals the dire economic and technological plight of Soviet civil society at the time. The following example of power talk by Reagan, in response to Gorbachev's question of whether Reagan was no longer in favour of the "zero option [you] proposed regarding medium-range missiles," speaks volumes about the asymmetries of the Reykjavik meeting: "No, I like it very much, but only with a global resolution of the issue. If the zero is on a global scale, then this would be fabulous. But if intermediate-range missiles are eliminated only in Europe ... I could not agree to that. Your missiles [in Asia] could reach Europe from there, after all, and in addition, they could be moved suddenly to other places."[16]

Straight talk: We *now* demand that you eliminate *all* your nuclear weapons; only then will we be satisfied. The statement suggests a replay of the zero option showdown of 1981, but with one or two significant differences. When the Soviet Union refused to remove its SS-20s in Europe, the United States deployed Pershing and Cruise missiles, gaining an additional advantage in the "European theatre" that not only neutralized any credible Soviet threat but also constituted a potentially deadly first-strike capacity. At Reykjavik, therefore, Reagan was able to raise the stakes and play the trump card by threatening the Soviet Union once more with a not-yet-deployed (not-yet-developed) system (SDI), which could render the entire Soviet nuclear capability useless and nullify any advances and recognition the country had gained internationally as a rival superpower. Reagan's demand boiled down to a rather fateful either/or option: either you dismantle your nuclear potential voluntarily (the global zero option), or we will make it useless by further developing and subsequently deploying SDI.[17] Gorbachev's response, lame as it was, clearly manifested the weakness of the Soviet position: "But you have nuclear weapons in South Korea as well, aboard forward-based weapon systems, not to mention other nuclear arms ... We have already opted to leave aside the strategic arsenals of Great Britain and France, and this is a concession on our side. Nor are we raising the issue of forward-based systems. Why has the United States not taken any steps in return?"[18]

This is the discourse of a man already defeated but scrambling to save face. In Kissinger's brutal formulation, Reagan was putting the "Soviet leadership on notice that the arms race they had started so recklessly in the 1960s would either consume their resources or lead to an American strategic breakthrough."[19] Since no lifeline was offered, and after countless Soviet concessions, the ultimate face-saver consisted of standing firm on the least realistic demand, namely that the United States abandon all plans to deploy SDI technology. In other words, the United States was to forget about its most powerful (though still fictitious) bargaining chip, the one that, above all, had brought it all the concessions from its opponent. So, on the one hand, "Gorbachev could not go home and tell his people that he had agreed to eliminate all ballistic missiles while allowing the Americans to develop a space-based defense system."[20] On the other, there was no way that Reagan could be persuaded to budge on SDI. Indeed, given the strength of his position and the ideological conviction that carried American interests, why should he?

So Reykjavik broke down, but the dénouement was in sight and almost all of the Soviet concessions came to be included in the INF Treaty signed the following year in Moscow, including the destruction of *all* intermediate missiles, though "the Soviets had nearly three times as many intermediate missiles as the US Pershing inventory."[21] Within a few years, Gorbachev had abandoned the Brezhnev Doctrine and the right of the Soviet Union to the east European sphere of influence.[22] The last significant constraint on a conflation of US imperial sovereignty and globalization — what George Bush Sr. termed the "New World Order" — was being removed. The United States was overcoming bipolarity and constructing the necessary conditions for the next phase of globalization — a thoroughgoing reconstitution of the global order under US leadership.[23]

In order to spell out how it came this far, some reflections on neo-imperialism, the international order, and the global turn are called for.

US Empire and the Global Order

Canadian historian Samir Saul has succinctly argued that "globalization per se is not imperialism or empire, but it creates material conditions that allow imperialism or empire to attain global dimensions." He notes that "imperialism and empire predate globalization historically and conceptually" and that "although globalization is an ongoing cumulative process with roots reaching far into the more or less distant past, it is only very recently that it has emerged as a discernible reality. Incrementally, greater interconnectedness unified the world to the point of making it possible to approach it as a single unit. As imperialist control and imperial rule extended geographically, they established ties between areas formerly unrelated to each other or transformed existing relations between them."[24]

Empire (in the colonial sense) and globalization are not identical concepts and should not be conflated. Colonial empire is deeply tied to territoriality, geopolitical fragmentation, and the existence of multiple, competing political orders. In contrast, globalization contains a supraterritorial dimension, is linked to the material and ideational attainment of global singularity, and bases itself on the power of economic and technological processes.[25] Between the two lies the putty of the nation-state and the international system.[26] In this sense, globalization can provide the conditioning context for what should be conceived as a neo-imperial political order.[27] In this chapter, the terms *neo-imperial* and *neo-imperialism* are used to refer to the aggregate capacity to project power and interest beyond one's formal sphere of sovereign authority in such a way that other political units, other autonomies, are induced or coerced into pursuing choices in keeping with the interests and preferences of the neo-imperial sovereign, accommodating it in multiple ways by adapting to its agenda, and, more often than not, taking this road because it is viewed to be the lesser evil or the most beneficial way to protect and defend national interests.[28] The implication is that neo-imperialism rests on the ability to behave in a sovereign manner beyond the confines of one's immediate and legitimate sovereign space — while applying a range of different instruments on a continuum between coercion and diplomacy, between hard and soft power.

There are three core differences between colonial empires and neo-imperialism. First, where the former are based on territorial conquest and domination, the latter relies on a wider and usually more "indirect" palette of instruments for the achievement of control and compliance. Second, the causal and reflexive relationship between globalization and empire has been reversed: colonial imperialism created — economically, geopolitically, technologically, institutionally, and culturally — many of the necessary conditions for postwar globalizing processes, whereas today it is globalization that provides the basis for new forms of imperial politics. Third, whereas colonialism consisted of a curious mélange of imperial and national, state-driven and substate political and cultural processes that were largely uncoordinated and unorchestrated by any one central agency (though clearly with European powers in the driver's seat), the state of affairs today is different. The "unipolar" structure of the world — the power and global reach of US interests — not only makes globalization a more coordinated process, it also increasingly conflates globalization and (American) empire.[29] Since the Second World War, a peculiar creature has thus been born, one that weds powerful nationalism, ultimate sovereign control, and "homeland security" policies to global hegemonic ambitions and liberal-cosmopolitan agendas.

The prudence of observing the analytical distinction between globalization and empire should not obscure the reality of their very substantial overlap in this age of accelerated or postcolonial globalization.[30] Globalization can no longer be approached as a set of forces that operate independently from, or set limits on, the projection of American power in the world, as an ideal that has been distorted and abused by American power, or as an indication of the "false promise of globalization."[31] Latter-day global structures must primarily be analyzed as results of more or less felicitous political engineering by representatives of American political preferences, which have consistently been aimed towards harnessing, shaping, and reconstituting the international order for their own neo-imperial purposes. They have astutely taken account of factual conditions at different junctures, pragmatically forging new "doctrines" and instruments along the way and repeatedly breaking down or sidestepping obstacles and constraints.[32] For that reason, globalization today bears the indelible imprint of the American imperial steamroller of the twentieth century and is largely the product of more or less liberal ideologies, preferences, and practices on the part of the United States — with all the paradoxes and contradictions this entails.[33]

Hence, where it makes sense to point, on the one hand, to the paradoxical relationship between discourses of a borderless, virtual, and supraterritorial world beyond the control of human or national agency and, on the other, to institutional mechanisms and legislation that run counter to such visions, it is an analytical and normative *impasse* to deal with such questions as a problem of incomplete globalization or "inadequate governance."[34] Admittedly, the intellectual property system of the World Trade Organization (WTO), the disparities between the possibilities for capital and labour mobility in national and international regimes, and the protectionist measures, or most-favoured-nations categories, designed to stem and regulate free trade militate against utopian imaginaries of a borderless world working in favour of increasing numbers of people across the globe. The situation, however, is that glossy representations of what globalization ought to be like collide, more or less mercilessly, with its reality. That reality, in turn, is one in which global processes are simultaneously engendered and harnessed by the interstate system, where the units of that system will all try, to the best of their ability, to reduce threats and maximize opportunities that derive from the global order. It is the reality of this globalization that needs to be scrutinized, not the one we might have had.

The Reykjavik debacle illustrates this contention. It symbolically crystallizes — into one moment and one place that was suspended between the two hemispheres while belonging unequivocally to the American one (the setting, Keflavik Airbase, being sufficient evidence) — all of the systematic, pragmatic endeavours of the United States to achieve global supremacy and all of the illusory politics of the USSR to catch up with and be recognized by its ideological adversary. This moment points irrevocably forward towards the pivotal turning point, 1990, and the abdication of the Soviet Union from the aspirations it once harboured for (equal) superpower status.

Accordingly, contemporary unipolarity cannot be divorced from the factual structure of globalization, nor from American imperial design, which has proved itself adept at "dispens[ing] with all sentimentality," as George Kennan, the father of the containment doctrine, put it in 1948.[35] For the same reason, American design is very unsentimental about the means it uses to achieve objectives, even when it implies different attitudes to the same political values. Where Kennan thought that the maintenance of American prosperity and supremacy meant ceasing to "think about human rights, the raising of living standards and democratization," these standards are currently being widely, albeit selectively, deployed as key instruments to legitimate the advances of US interests on a global scale.[36]

Until the 9/11 attack, after which even "neo-conservative commentators have begun to talk with pride and promise of the 'new American empire,'" this line of reasoning would most likely have been either rejected by most scholars of international relations or, at best, accepted as applicable only to the 1945-71 period.[37] Bruce E. Moon, for instance, argues that "at the end of World War II, the United States exhibited the two most important characteristics required of a candidate to champion global liberalism ... it possessed the dominance that affords a hegemon both the greatest incentive and the greatest capacity to advance globalization."[38] The Bretton Woods system is here seen to express "the combination of American hegemonic credentials and fortuitous circumstances [that] were sufficient to meet the delicate balance between national and systemic needs."[39] Since then, however, the United States has supposedly abandoned its global role to pursue increasingly nationalistic, unilateral, and isolationist policies. This is a narrative of decline, of narrow nationalism, and of skewed global structures — of a powerful country taking unreasonable and self-serving advantage of its pre-eminent power.

The alternative reading offered in this chapter demonstrates that the United States has pursued a consistent neo-imperial line of policy and action since the Second World War and the Bretton Woods agreement. Thus the institutions, commitments, and instruments put in place in the early postwar period are as explicable in terms of American policy goals as was, for instance, the abandonment of Bretton Woods in the 1970s (see separate section below) or the unilateralism of American foreign policy after 9/11 (see the last section).[40] But this reading also shows that it is primarily the interaction of such continuity of purpose and shifts of instruments that has produced the kind of "accelerated globalization" we factually take account of when we discuss such issues, "confirming the fears of all those who have suspected that much celebrated 'globalisation' actually means a system of open economies dominated by US and corporate interests."[41] Globalization in its contemporary phase comes not à la carte, but à l'Américaine.[42]

In line with Kennan's realism and the military logic that culminated at Reykjavik, the key question, therefore, is the one formulated by Robert Hunter Wade: "How do you exercise statecraft to bolster the pre-eminence of your country, allow your citizens and only your citizens to consume far more than they themselves produce, and keep challenges down, without having to throw your military weight around more than occasionally?" This is a more incisive way of posing the moot question of how to balance hard and soft power in the exercise of imperial dominance.[43]

Before this interplay of economics, military might, and cultural influence can be explored, the following question must be addressed. Why, if there is such sustained continuity in (American) intentions, do we need to think of the developments that culminated at Reykjavik, or other events such as the fall of the Berlin Wall or the disintegration of the Soviet Union, as a global *turn* — and not simply as the natural and logical *continuation* of a consistent policy process?

Conceptualizing the Global Turn

To answer this question requires rethinking the traditional dichotomy between continuity and rupture. In historical reality, developments are rarely either peacefully evolutionary or dramatically revolutionary, although exceptions do exist. Mostly, however, and certainly in this case, we witness a specific interweaving of gradualist processes, which, because of incremental quantitative expansion or the addition of new constitutive elements (or both), end in a qualitatively new condition that is often highlighted by pivotal events, unexpected developments, or unforeseen social and cultural impacts. What is really the result of a gradual buildup — interacting causalities that spark off reactions and effects that impinge on handed-down, socio-political structures and cultural ways of life — is often perceived as a sudden rupture. Quantitative developments engender qualitative changes, which manifest themselves in specific moments and coalesce around socio-political turning points.[44] Sometimes "moment" and "turning point" conflate into one; at other times they play out as temporally separate and thematically discrete phenomena.

I refer to this gradual (and highly engineered) buildup of developments and events that culminated in a dramatic turning point, the end of the Cold War, as the global turn. A turn is not a rupture, but a change of direction undertaken more or less abruptly. The global turn is obviously not to be conceived of as a U-turn. We are not heading back down the same old familiar avenue, though this is the image championed by many global skeptics, neo-medievalists, or world-systems theorists.[45] Rather, we should think of it as an increasingly sharp curve that takes us along a trajectory that stands at a ninety-degree angle to the original line of approach. This is a very different direction from the one originally taken, but it allows important baggage to be shifted from one direction to the next without being totally dislocated or thrown off. The past — containing all the necessary seeds of change in embryonic form — is carried recognizably into the future. But the future — nursing and developing those seeds to full fruition — is nevertheless configured differently and holds novel threats, opportunities, and goals. The old order has been transformed by having had a new one — one that grew out of the frictions and antagonisms of the past — superimposed on it.

Applying this metaphorical representation to the global turn requires that three points be highlighted. First, in travelling along the avenue of the past, signifying moments of great import and impact can be identified. This avenue is not a completely straight line either; it contains imperceptible, though still important, shifts of direction. One such moment in the evolution of the United States' relationship with the rest of the world happened between 1971 and 1973 — the revamping of the Bretton Woods institutional structure (see below), which completed the subordination of the international financial system to US preferences.

The second point relates to the distinction between the international and the global order. It makes no sense to imagine this distinction as one in which, almost overnight, the international order prior to 1986-90 was supplanted by a global American order in the 1990s. Nor is it reasonable to see the global order and its institutions as being ushered suddenly in after 1990, imposing themselves on the old structure and nullifying its nature and effects. The turn is subtler and more complex. First, the international order that came into being after the Second World War was already geared to and largely engineered by American interests, while some international institutions (e.g., the World Bank and International Monetary Fund, but also the General Agreement on Tariffs and Trade) represented early attempts at global governance.[46] And second, proper international institutions and organizations (for instance, sovereignty and the United Nations) did not disappear after 1990 but underwent a process of transformation and adaptation. [47]

How then should the global turn be conceived in the context of the international-global binary? I suggest tracing it along three axes: primacy, outreach, and the quantity/quality problem. *Primacy* implies the order of dominance between US-dominated liberal globalization and the international order. The rather symmetrical balance of influence between the two shifted markedly in favour of "American empire" after 1990. This asymmetry allowed the United States to abrogate the principle of non-intervention in the affairs of sovereign states in the following instances: (1) to create an institution for the global liberalization of trade and services (the WTO), in large measure geared to and supportive of American interests, such as the intellectual property system; (2) to introduce the principle and goal of global "full spectrum dominance"; (3) to proclaim the clash of civilizations and the war on terror as the next (last?) barrier to be overcome; and, in line with all this, (4) to launch the principle and right of preventive strike as the guiding principle of US foreign policy for the future.[48]

Outreach refers to the geopolitical expansion of American empire after 1990 — a quantitative change with far-reaching qualitative implications for the structure of American military roles; the presence, institutional collaboration, and deployment of economic resources; and the general freedom of action of US power and "public diplomacy."[49] With the constraining influence of the USSR gone and bipolarity overcome, all other states gravitated — not necessarily voluntarily or without friction — towards the US centre and its combined financial and military supremacy. In the process, these states had to accept a dramatic transformation in their ability to exercise their sovereign powers.[50]

Finally, the *quantity/quality problem* means that the very quality and depth of globalization are impacted as a consequence of this spatial expansion and the *domain*-related intensification of global trends and interconnectedness (e.g., in and by means of new communications technology in environmental policy arenas, global migration patterns, and so forth). These transformations call for new policy responses and new institutional forms of governance. Transformations of the global political scene paved the way for economic liberalization after 1990 — but these transformations, in turn, have demanded a qualitative rethinking of political governance and a reconstitution of sovereignty.

The third, and in one sense most important, point is that the carefully prepared and consciously engineered process of transforming the relative symmetries of the international order into the much more conspicuous asymmetries of the global condition has, for the United States, taken the form of overcoming obstacles to and forging synergetic connections between three related processes or developments: (1) the freedom of "dollar diplomacy," for which the decisive moment was the abandonment of the gold standard; (2) military predominance, for which the decisive moment was Reykjavik; and (3) ideological and cultural hegemony, for which the decisive moment was 9/11.[51] These pivotal moments, which climaxed at Reykjavik, all represent transit points along the curvature of the global turn — points that connect Kennan's realism with the blend of imperial arrogance and post-constructivist epistemology that was uttered by a senior White House aide in an interview with Ron Suskind: "We're an empire now, and when we act, we create our own reality. And while you're studying that reality ... we'll act again, creating other realities, which you can study too, and that's how things will sort out. We're history's actors ... and you, all of you, will be left to study what we do."[52]

Confident statements such as these are, incidentally, quite difficult to square with Niall Ferguson's thesis of US world power being an "empire in denial."[53] Of course, many American politicians and academics deny the fact of neo-imperial policies, sometimes for purely propagandistic purposes. More often, however, they do so in order to pre-empt historical analogies between the territorial rule of colonial empires and the US system of global influence, which is pre-eminently "informal": direct rule is used only as a temporary and last-resort instrument for the enforcement of compliance.

I have already dealt at length with the pivotal *military* moment in the series of events that led up to this new type of US political discourse. However, as many commentators have pointed out, hard power is a necessary but not sufficient precondition for sustaining neo-imperial domination on a global scale. As logic dictates and the historical sequence of postwar developments have demonstrated, economic power precedes and bolsters military predominance, while, conversely, military predominance creates new conditions for the expansion of economic and financial interests. The pivotal institutional factor here is undoubtedly Bretton Woods — its initiation and implementation, certainly, but, just as importantly, its alleged breakdown and failure in the early 1970s.

1971-73: Overcoming the Constraints of Bretton Woods

The most common evaluation of these events is that they represented a weakening of the United States' position in the world. However, the abandonment of the gold standard and the par value system meant that American political and business communities had additional freedom to manoeuvre. The argument here is *not* that it was in the early 1970s

— and only then — that the international financial system came to be harnessed to American interests.[54] Rather, the argument is that both Bretton Woods and its successor system were largely determined by and geared to US preferences. Differences between the two systems reflected two different international political and economic contexts.[55]

During the Bretton Woods period, in which the reconstruction of a workable international system and the prevention of grievous mistakes that had been made in the interwar decades were main concerns, a number of universal monetary and financial functions were allocated to the United States, functions that this country alone could assume in the postwar period. The United States received unprecedented benefits and opportunities, but it also faced constraints and obligations that became increasingly apparent over the course of the 1960s.

The main advantage for the United States was the "privilege of financing deficits with its own currency," which "effectively freed [the United States] from external payments constraints ... to promote objectives believed to be in the national interest," but these benefits and opportunities also harnessed the IMF and the World Bank to US interests.[56] The obligations connected with this global monetary predominance consisted of monitoring and being responsible for monetary stabilization and a sustainable form of international economic development that would not be ruinous to any of the major players. This role was predicated on the free convertibility of all national currencies into greenbacks, on the free convertibility of greenbacks into gold, on pegging currencies to this dollar/gold standard within narrow "bands," and on granting others the right to pursue national trade interests, even in forms that might not always be in sync with US interests.

Benjamin Cohen correctly concluded that the Bretton Woods system rested on an "implicit bargain" as "America's allies acquiesced in a hegemonic system that accorded to the United States special privileges to act abroad unilaterally to promote US or collective interests. The United States, in turn, condoned [even encouraged, as in the case of the Marshall Plan and the Organisation for European Economic Cooperation] its allies' use of the system to promote their own prosperity, even if this happened to come largely at the short term expense of the United States."[57] The United States also accepted that, although the system militated against the use of monetary policies to regulate national trade and currency imbalances, countries were still able to use capital control mechanisms, because the capital account remained within the purview of national sovereignty.

The bargain was not made, however, among equals, with benefits and drawbacks evenly distributed. This was a regime that was formally multilateral, but in terms of substance, structural properties (e.g., the system of IMF voting rights), and modes of functioning it was heavily weighted in favour of the United States. This advantage can be seen in the system's early form (i.e., what was arrived at in 1944), and even more so in 1946-47, when the United States, without audible objections, assumed responsibility for making it work because the original conditions had proved to be inadequate and overly optimistic. It was, in fact, a system of licensed competition: the United States granted other nations the ability to trade and almost unlimited access to its national currency, on the condition that they open their markets and their currencies to US interests and refrain from exploiting traditional possibilities for currency adjustment to "beggar thy neighbour."

At least for a time, by combining the political struggle of the United States against the USSR with the imposition and management of a liberalized economic regime in the Western hemisphere, the system managed to balance the world's trading nations' interest in the reconstruction and expansion of their industrial capacities with the United States' interest in global political-economic predominance. Thus, all other states (except the second superpower and its allies) were subjected to American terms, allowing the United States itself to smoothly export its capital surpluses abroad and to partake in the expansionary successes of other countries through their dependence on its national currency.

Since this ingenious system was asymmetrically weighted against those other countries, they soon felt its sting in the form of complaints about a "dollar glut" in the 1960s, whereas earlier complaints, in a different phase, had sung a song about dollar shortages. American balance of payments deficits started to show up because of the greenback's role as universal money. In turn, this result led to a drop in the value of the American dollar. When the first phase of economic reconstruction was over, the huge dollar holdings that had accumulated in national banks led to a serious and continuous reduction in the value of national wealth. This reduction had relatively minor consequences for the United States itself, since it is not primarily a trading nation but rather a capital-exporting nation that can make good on its deficits by printing dollars, boosting domestic production and productivity in the process. The effects were more severe, however, for the dependent nation-states (Europe, Japan, and the OPEC countries, in particular), which could not compensate for this de facto devaluation by increasing exports precisely because of the increased value of their national currencies. Nor could they compensate by devaluing their currencies, since this too would run counter to the Bretton Woods regime. These dependent states thus found themselves in a situation in which the system of liability financing was starting to work against them, and the asymmetries were becoming intolerable.

What these countries could and did do was minimize their losses by demanding that their dollar holdings be converted into gold. This demand was never what the engineers of the project had intended, and since the United States had already started to become impatient with the more "altruistic" components of system, its response was swift. The dollar/gold convertibility option was suspended by Nixon in August 1971 and was followed by the abrogation of the adjustable peg system in early 1973.[58] These steps formally meant the demise of the Bretton Woods currency system, although, in fact, its main institutional structures and normative assumptions have persisted to the present day.

What really changed was the relationship between the system and its major promoter and beneficiary. Freed from the constraints that even "its own" system had imposed on it, the United States was left with almost exclusive benefits and only one remaining constraint: in the ultimate resort, even the dollar must be measured against the real standard of value in the world, even though convertibility had been abandoned. For the same reason, the United States still jealously guards Fort Knox and its national gold reserves, and it has not thrown them to the wind.[59]

Although, at the time, much talk and many analyses focused on enhanced "interdependence" in the world and the reliance of the United States on others, the evidence points in a different direction.[60] From the perspective of the United States, Bretton Woods had served its purpose and could be ditched with impunity. The US dollar's role as the prominent global reserve currency and the one used in the vast majority of international transactions continued, in spite of intermittent value fluctuations. For the US dollar was backed by the proliferation of American global business advances and the country's military predominance. Formal responsibility for the institutional system (IMF, World Bank, and GATT) was discontinued, leaving the United States free to exploit it in a more ruthlessly self-interested manner. It did so by successfully influencing the following in its favour: IMF conditionalities and limitations on accessibility to foreign capital accounts, World Bank debt-servicing arrangements, and GATT/WTO agreements on free trade, agriculture, and permissible protectionism.[61]

Finally, the end of Bretton Woods freed the United States from the responsibility of making sure that its partners (mainly European countries) enjoyed prosperity and progress at the (very limited) expense of the Americans through cheap loans or donations handed out "for free" or in return for political allegiance. In purely market-oriented terms, these partners had managed to recuperate. The asymmetries, if measured against standard economic variables, had seemingly lessened, and the Allies apparently had become more self-sustaining, having converted access to the *conditions* to compete into the *capacity* to compete.

This process of levelling-out, however, concealed new forms of dependence on the US centre, which was never much dedicated to or dependent on competing with the others as just any other trading nation. And at the time (the early 1970s), the United States had other priorities and objectives. It is little wonder, then, that in the international relations literature on the United States, theories of complex interdependence were soon supplemented by theories of hegemonic stability.[62] In practical politics, the so-called Washington Consensus — the institutional stamp of approval on neoliberal globalization of the US kind — made the same point.[63]

Many scholars no doubt still prefer to see the global order as one in which mutual dependence explains significant processes and outcomes, and one in which the United States is as dependent on others (for markets, resources, and alliances) as these others are dependent on the United States. The core question is the extent to which US power (projection) can be reasonably compared to that of other countries or regions. This chapter demonstrates that we cannot grasp the quality and extent of American world power by employing the same criteria and variables that we would normally apply to other nation-states to assess, for instance, trade figures, national debt statistics, or foreign direct investment. The interplay between military, economic, cultural, and political-institutional power and resources in the United States makes for its qualitative uniqueness rather than simply its quantitative superiority. Accordingly, if we must think of international affairs in terms of interdependence, then we should not do so by placing interdependence in opposition to empire. We are, after all, facing very uneven forms and levels of mutuality, ones in which the global freedom to manoeuvre, the power to set agendas, and the possibility of exerting pressure on others are distributed extremely asymmetrically. The United States is not all-powerful (let alone invulnerable) by any means. Nor can it do without partners and alliances. But its capacity for synergetic power projection is both superior to and qualitatively different from that of any other country. Others, therefore, gravitate willy-nilly towards the American centre while trying to take the fullest possible benefit of either going along with or balancing against the leading world power.[64]

Thus, the shifts of power implied by changes in the superpower show-down and the extra freedom of manoeuvre provided to the United States by the formal collapse of Bretton Woods are more appropriately conceptualized in terms of increased (though still curtailed) predominance than of mutual dependence. The rationale for this argument lies neither in American dollar supremacy nor in the country's military predominance but in the fruitful and mutual *synergy* between them; the same kind of synergy is found in domestic politics and summarized in the concept of the military-industrial complex.[65]

In essence, the liberation from financial constraints that took place between 1971 and 1973 and the transgression of geopolitical obstacles to worldwide political supremacy that occurred between 1986 and 1990 are two sides of the same process of imperial-cum-globalizing endeavours on the part of the United States, which remains the bedrock of the global turn. The freedom provided by having most economic transactions in the world conducted in its currency was a prerequisite for gigantic military armaments programs, or the acquisition of incomparable instruments of political pressure, coercion, and extortion. Conversely, those military resources functioned as the umbrella of power, under which American economic and financial interests come to global fruition, aided and abetted by diplomatic bargaining ploys inside and outside institutional contexts.

Events in the early 1980s demonstrate the first of these propositions. Reagan's gargantuan armaments buildup was made possible by deficit spending and the attraction of foreign investors to US government bonds at a historic level; this spending program would not have been feasible without the position and strength of the US dollar. The American economic production and consumption boom of the 1990s illustrates the second proposition. The global expansion of the American military presence and the sheer knowledge of what American force could achieve paved the way for American investments in the former

Communist world and elsewhere. It also was responsible for the gravitation of increasing numbers of cooperative regimes to the American centre, and for ensuring continuous American access to natural resources, especially Middle Eastern oil.

By the late 1990s, the American project of harnessing globalization to the sovereignty of American empire had been advanced considerably. The major building blocks were in place for supremacy in the soft area of the economic "invisible hand" and also for "hard power."[66] The latter in turn engendered a vision of military full spectrum dominance on land, on the seas, in the air, and in space, which was formulated during Clinton's second term. The remaining limitations to the full conflation of American empire and global structures were related to the cultural problem of ideological and normative hegemony on a global scale.[67] In the West, this problem has been articulated through the fierce debates that surround Samuel Huntington's clash of civilizations thesis, the rise of the neocon hardliners to ideational prominence since the presidency of George H.W. Bush, and the intra-Western cleavages attendant on the Iraq intervention.[68] In the rest of the world, the issue has taken the shape of terrorism in the name of Islam and of widespread cultural resistance to the imposition of American values on local identities. The events of 9/11 exposed this tear in the fabric and, in addition to displaying US societal (not military) vulnerability to "asymmetric threats," provided the Bush administration with an opportunity to complete the global turn by converting neo-imperial *domination* into *hegemony,* while settling some old scores in the process.[69]

9/11 and the Completion of Empire: Overcoming the Constraints of Culture?

The synergetic relationship between "dollar" and "gunboat" diplomacy constitutes both the necessary and, in a sense, the sufficient condition for American global domination, but not for ideological and cultural hegemony.[70] The present phase of completing the link between empire and globalization by means of their ideological, cultural, and normative dimensions nevertheless is not indispensable. It does, however, constitute a logical — and from an American perspective desirable — step in the process of achieving full spectrum dominance. The ideological dimension is not without important historical precedents, and, therefore, it should not be seen as a new invention by neoconservative Republicans, but rather as a core constitutive element in the entire postwar period. The struggle to overcome bipolarity, for instance, was centrally predicated on the distinction between freedom and unfreedom and, hence, on the objective of disseminating the values of the free world to people held in subjugation by the "evil empire." The difference between then and now is mainly that ideology was clearly subordinate to military and political objectives in the earlier phase, whereas today it is — at least according to the public discourses of neoconservatism — the opposite relationship that applies.

The struggle *against* terrorism, fundamentalism, and other kinds of insurgency and *for* the global dissemination of freedom, democratic rule, and civilizational values is aimed ideally at providing the best possible framing conditions for American predominance in economic, political, and diplomatic areas — a culturally frictionless and globally accepted *Pax Americana*.[71] The downside has two dimensions. First, since this goal presumes regime change and nation building of a thoroughgoing nature in other parts of the world, it cannot be achieved through the deployment of soft instruments of public diplomacy, but only through violence and war. Second, the cultural push not only defies other ("alien") cultural norms, but openly — through the doctrine of pre-emption and the measures taken to implement it — violates principles of national sovereignty and territorial inviolability. What is projected as the peaceful completion of American Manifest Destiny engenders a series of divisive consequences (see Streeter's contribution to this volume).[72]

When the United States decides to depict other civilizations (read: Islamic fundamentalism) and their "terrorism" as "rogue states" that threaten Western values, this activity demonstrates the freedom with which the United States can act unilaterally. It also exposes the degree to which global domination has already been achieved. Thus, when the United States focuses first on using soft power and then turns the problems that these areas engender into an argument for all-out *military* alertness and mobilization, it shows a hegemon freed from any need to maintain consistency between freedom and action.[73] With the closure of the Cold War, all essential economic, political, and military obstacles to us predominance had been overcome, with the exception of a few remaining insubordinate states and rulers. What was still lacking was widespread support by peoples around the globe for the values of the free world and the presumption that the United States is "bound to lead."[74] The remaining bastion to be conquered, therefore, is civilizational: the values, loyalties, political cultures, and hearts and minds of ordinary people outside the United States. For this reason, many current international relations debates in the United States have orchestrated a battle of values and power, one in which America/the West is portrayed either as on the defensive and in potential decline or as a benevolent "empire lite," which is necessary if the world is to become a democratic place.[75]

This way of framing the question of cultural hegemony highlights two important factors. The first is that reprehensible — but not mindless — acts of atrocity such as 9/11 do not pose a threat to US global dominance. Depending on one's perspective, they can be seen as desperate acts of religiously inspired revenge, as attention-grabbing political initiatives to get media exposure around the world, or as protests against the encroachments of Western civilization on certain countries and their traditional sources of income, ways of life, and religious beliefs. But a menace they are not, which was reflected in the conspicuous asymmetries of the battle scene, where sophisticated, high-tech weaponry and attendant economic, political, and cultural resources encountered crude forms of savagery and emasculated forms of civic protest.

The second factor is to remember that the causative factors of globalization have a Western origin, and terrorism perpetrated in Allah's name is reactive. The "war on terror" constantly produces the hostility against which it is directed and dedicated to stamping out. Over and above the general conflicts and disgruntlements that economic and political globalization engenders around the world, the practical manifestations of the American ideological "crusade" breed their own discontents and open new fault lines and battlefronts.[76]

The United States is both the chief catalyst and protagonist of the global march of modernity. Whether it engenders economic expansionism and "McDonaldization," territorial occupation and informal empire, nuclear threat and ubiquitous military presence, or ideological confrontation and cultural export initiatives, it cannot but produce political counter-reactions, cultural discontents, and hostile images of the West. The civilizational offensive rhetorically spearheads an effort to bring reason, democracy, freedom, and humane values to the rest of humankind, yet it is unthinkable without, and it may well strengthen, the barbarism it purports to fight. In this sense, the United States represents its own kind of fundamentalism.[77] The American struggle for ideological hegemony on a global scale is predicated on the conviction that the civilizing mission is morally justified beyond a doubt, something which, at least in formal terms, more than equals the high-sounding rallying cries of "Islamic fundamentalism."[78] President George W. Bush's cultivation of his born-again Christian faith is a personal reflection of this larger ideological battleground.

Thus, the stated objective of US foreign policy contravenes both its immanent logic and the means it employs. The battle for democratic values in order to compel non-Western peoples' conversion to Western universalism and acceptance of the American global presence cannot be peacefully resolved. The inherent expansionism of modernity per se creates the basis for dissatisfaction with it, and the chosen instrument — warfare of various kinds — belies the allegedly humanitarian objective. Nor can the conflict be resolved militarily, though it can possibly be contained in its most dysfunctional manifestations, but only by means of constant military alertness, global surveillance of an unprecedented kind, and an ever more intensive securitization of the global condition.

This permanence of military mobilization brings us back to Hofdi House, the usefulness of imperial instruments of dominance and expansion, and the historical lesson of the Reykjavik narrative. As Kenneth Waltz has convincingly argued, even global nuclear proliferation poses no serious threat to the United States. The best that other nation-states can hope for is to acquire a few nuclear devices, which might have a regional deterrent or balancing effect (as in the case of India and Pakistan), but they cannot alter the global power structure.[79] Only Russia possesses the immediate technological prerequisite, intercontinental means of nuclear delivery, and no state possesses the total political, scientific, and economic resources to make a real challenge possible — or, for that matter, rational. When the comprehensive nuclear arsenal of the USSR could not, or did not dare to, match US power, how could others hope to do so in the contemporary world?

The early 1990s saw a proliferation of hopeful debates about the post-Cold War period as the "end of history," the age of universal democracy, and a time containing the seeds of "perpetual peace" among civilized political entities interacting within a liberal, market-determined framework on the world stage.[80] On that backcloth, neoconservative and neo-realist discourses and think tanks currently advocating the "war on terror" and the struggle for US normative hegemony strike a shriller note. They are trying to legitimate a reality typified by perpetual war and never-ending vigilance by conjuring up the utopia of universal freedom that awaits us at the end of the journey.[81] This discursively constructed world of moral emergency represents no perpetual peace, but rather a precarious stability vitally dependent on the counter-image of its always-imminent destruction at the hands of evil forces plotting to substitute freedom, order, and morality with a return to the Dark Ages. It is evident, then, that there are important differences and tensions among the three different levels of American imperial objectives — economic-financial, political-military, and cultural-normative.

The first two (and the synergetic link between them) have reached the point where there is little doubt that the United States is globally dominant and that full spectrum dominance has been virtually achieved. They complement each other well; threats at one level can be addressed at another. The Iraq case illustrates this interaction. Far from being caused by American worries about either terrorist links to the Hussein regime or fears about weapons of mass destruction — these were mere marketable justifications — the operative trigger was something else. The United States was cognizant of the potent linkage between its desire to obtain control of a conflict-ridden but strategically important region and its considerable concern that Saddam Hussein, in 2000, had started to conduct oil transactions in Euros rather than US dollars.[82] The global dominance of the United States is seriously threatened by political responses of this nature, particularly if the country sets an example for others to follow.

The question of cultural-normative domination, in contrast, plays out according to a different logic and is much harder to achieve, as earlier and more formal empires have found at more modest scales. Ideational hegemony cannot be politically ordered, imposed, or manipulated at will. It challenges deeply held beliefs in the benefits of ethnic, national, and local cultural autonomy, which is a direct product of the international order and works increasingly as compensation for the dramatic changes this order is undergoing. Furthermore, and despite rhetoric to the contrary, ideational hegemony is not an independent array of autonomous cultural or value-oriented goals, it is intimately wedded to the maintenance of predominance (and hopefully the achievement of hegemony) at the other two levels.[83] Notwithstanding repeated presidential assurances to the contrary (see, for instance, George W. Bush's second inaugural address, January 2005), regimes that freely and democratically choose to pursue policies that run counter to American preferences have little chance of achieving enthusiastic support. Nor can they expect financial assistance from Washington, in spite of their adherence to the values of the open society.[84]

Accordingly, the present phase of attempts to overcome cultural resistance to the American empire represents, if nòt the most important, certainly (in many ways) the toughest test for American global power. It is a process replete with contradictions, setbacks, partial victories, and perhaps even retreat, and its conclusion is questionable. The process also provides grounds for theories of imperial overstretch that are more plausible than those in much of the current international relations and globalization literature that, more often than not, build their case on doubtful historical analogies and fail to take into account structural differences and the capacity of political actors to learn from historical mistakes.[85] Although their impact cannot be planned or engineered with any degree of accuracy, it must be granted that powerful cultures spread and cross-fertilize with local cultures in a variety of unpredictable ways; consequently, it would be foolish to deny that American culture has enjoyed considerable global successes since the Second World War.[86] For that reason, too, historical examples may not teach us very much about the present condition and future consequences of US global ambitions. Determinism should be shunned in favour of the realization that the nexus between American empire and globalization is a *sui generis* phenomenon, understandable exclusively on its own terms.

Epilogue

Since 2006 international developments have underscored the risks, paradoxes, and tensions that US global ambitions increasingly face. The economic recession in the United States is not in itself a sign of an empire in retreat. Rather, it comes as the result of a combination of factors: financial crisis, a decline of global confidence in the US dollar as an international currency (with the consequence that a larger proportion of international trade is now conducted in Euros), soaring energy prices, a booming Chinese economy, and a Russia reinvigorated in both economic and military terms. In addition, the results of policies to combat religiously legitimated terrorism and build stable and secure nation-states in the less-developed world have been questionable and have highlighted the precarious nature of the neoconservative project of the Bush administration.

These developments have been accompanied around the world by a visible loss of identification with the American civilizational mission, trans-Atlantic disagreements in the NATO alliance (e.g., burden sharing in Afghanistan), and concerted efforts in many countries to resist further encroachments on their historical identities by trying to maintain, if not their traditional sovereignty, then at the very least their political independence and cultural autonomy.

These various developments do not mark the end of American global domination, but they do underline a growing disjuncture between the United States as a military, economic, and financial superpower and the United States as an ideological and intellectual force of questionable status. The three levels of dominance complement each other less well as 9/11 fades from view in the rear-view mirror. Harnessing globalization to us preferences may have to be abandoned in favour of more realistic goals, and hegemony now seems to be little more than a distant utopian vision. In this light, the legacy of the neoconservative era may in fact prove to be one of imperial overstretch, informed by the arrogance of power and the intention to seek quick and effective revenge on Islamic insurgents. What cannot be determined at this point is whether the consequences of this regime will be permanent or temporary. But it is beyond doubt that the challenges facing the successors to George W. Bush will be formidable when it comes to advancing domination further.

Abbreviations

AID	Agency for International Development
CBMA	cross-border mergers and acquisitions
CETLAC	Centro de Estudios y Taller Laboral Asociación
COMO	Centro de Orientación de la Mujer Obrera
DRV	Democratic Republic of Vietnam
EPZ	export-processing zone
FAR	Rebel Armed Forces
FAT	Frente Auténtico del Trabajo
FDI	foreign direct investment
FLN	National Liberation Front
FRC	Federal Radio Commission
GATT	General Agreement on Tariffs and Trade
GFCF	gross fixed capital formation
GVN	Government of Vietnam
ICANN	Internet Corporation for Assigned Names and Numbers
ICC	International Criminal Court
ICTR	International Criminal Tribunal for Rwanda
ICTY	International Criminal Tribunal for the Former Yugoslavia
ILO	International Labour Organization
IMF	International Monetary Fund
IMT	International Military Tribunal
INF	Intermediate-Range Nuclear Forces

IRC	International Radio Conference
ITU	International Telegraph Union/International Telecommunications Union
MAAG	Military Assistance and Advisory Group
NLF	National Liberation Front
RCA	Radio Corporation of America
SAP	structural adjustment program
SDI	Strategic Defense Initiative
TNC	transnational corporation
USFP	Socialist Union of Popular Forces
SEZ	special economic zone
VOC	Dutch East India Company (Verenigde Oostindische Compagnie)
WTO	World Trade Organization

Notes

Introduction

1 Karl Marx and Friedrich Engels, "Manifesto of the Communist Party," in *The Marx-Engels Reader*, 2nd ed., ed. Robert Tucker (New York: W.W. Norton, 1978), 476-77.

2 Paul Q. Hirst and Grahame Thompson, *Globalization in Question: The International Economy and the Possibilities of Governance* (Cambridge: Polity Press, 1996), 60.

3 Anthony Giddens, *Runaway World: How Globalization Is Reshaping Our Lives,* 2nd ed. (New York: Routledge, 2003), 28.

4 See William D. Coleman and John C. Weaver, eds., *Property Rights: Struggles over Autonomy in a Global Age* (Vancouver: UBC Press, forthcoming) for further elaboration on this question.

5 Jan Aart Scholte, *Globalization: A Critical Introduction*, rev. ed. (New York: Palgrave Macmillan, 2005), 54.

6 Ibid., 59.

7 Robert Latham and Saskia Sassen, "Digital Formations: Constructing an Object of Study," in *Digital Formations: IT and New Architectures in the Global Realm,* ed. Latham and Sassen (Princeton, NJ: Princeton University Press, 2005), 2.

8 Scholte, *Globalization,* 61.

9 Roland Robertson, *Globalization: Social Theory and Global Culture* (London: Sage, 1992), 8.

10 Ulrich Beck, *Power in the Global Age: A New Global Political Economy* (Malden, MA: Polity, 2005).

11 Len Doyal and Ian Gough, *A Theory of Human Need* (New York: Guilford Press, 1991), 55.

12 Ian Gough, "Lists and Thresholds: Comparing the Doyal-Gough Theory of Human Need with Nussbaum's Capabilities Approach" (WeD Working Paper 01, ESRC Research Group on Wellbeing in Developing Countries, Bath, United Kingdom, 2003), 8, http://www.bath.ac.uk/econ-dev/wellbeing/research/workingpaperpdf/wed01.pdf.

13 Doyal and Gough, *Theory of Human Need,* 55-59.

14 Ibid., 187.

15 For an elaboration of the rights needed to fulfill this particular condition, see David Held, *Democracy and the Global Order* (Stanford, CA: Stanford University Press, 1995), 159–88.

16 Cornelius Castoriadis, *Philosophy, Politics, Autonomy* (New York: Oxford University Press, 1991).

17 Ibid., 164.

18 Ibid., 165.

19 For discussions of "instaneity" and "simultaneity," see Scholte, *Globalization*, 59–61, and for "timeless time," see Manuel Castells, *Rise of the Network Society* (Cambridge, MA: Blackwell, 1996), 174–97.

20 Timothy Brook, "Time and Global History" (paper presented at the fourth meeting of the Globalization and Autonomy Research Project, Munk Centre, University of Toronto, September 2005), 6.

21 Frederick Cooper, *Colonialism in Question: Theory, Knowledge, History* (Berkeley: University of California Press, 2005), 13.

22 Ibid., 18.

23 Scholte, *Globalization*, 84.

24 A.G. Hopkins, "Globalization — An Agenda for Historians," in *Globalization in World History*, ed. A.G. Hopkins (New York: Norton, 2002), 1–10.

25 Anna Lowenhaupt Tsing, *Friction: An Ethnography of Global Connection* (Princeton, NJ: Princeton University Press, 2005), 5.

26 See John Darwin, *After Tamerlane: The Global History of Empire* (London: Penguin Books, 2007).

27 Alfred W. Crosby, *Ecological Imperialism: The Biological Expansion of Europe, 900-1900,* Canto ed. (Cambridge: Cambridge University Press, 1993), 70–103.

28 Richard Drayton, "The Collaboration of Labor: Slaves, Empires, and Globlalizations in the Atlantic World, ca. 1600-1850," in *Globalization in World History*, ed. A.G. Hopkins (New York: Norton, 2002), 99–115.

29 John C. Weaver, *The Great Land Rush and the Making of the Modern World, 1650-1900* (Montreal and Kingston: McGill-Queen's University Press, 2003), passim.

30 Caroline Elkins, *Imperial Reckoning: The Untold Story of Britain's Gulag in Kenya* (New York: Henry Holt, 2005), passim.

31 Angus Maddison, *The World Economy: A Millennial Perspective* (Paris: Development Centre of the Organisation for Economic Co-operation and Development, 2001), 113–18.

32 Richard A. Pierce, *Russian Central Asia, 1867-1917: A Study in Colonial Rule* (Berkeley: University of California Press, 1960), 141–52.

33 C.R. Boxer, *Portuguese India in the Mid-Seventeenth Century* (Delhi: Oxford University Press, 1980), 50.

34 Lauren A. Benton, *Law and Colonial Cultures: Legal Regimes in World History, 1400-1900* (Cambridge: Cambridge University Press, 2002), passim.

35 Chistopher Bayly, quoted in C.A. Bayly et al., "On Transnational History," *American Historical Review* 111, 5 (2006): 1450.

36 On the American dominance in the establishment of the postwar international institutions, see Stephen C. Schlesinger, *Act of Creation: The Founding of the United Nations* (Boulder, CO: Westview Press, 2003), passim; Georg Schild, *Bretton Woods and Dumbarton Oaks: American Economic and Political Postwar Planning in the Summer of 1944* (New York: St. Martin's Press, 1995), passim; Ngaire Woods, *The Globalizers: The IMF, the World Bank, and Their Borrowers* (Ithaca, NY: Cornell University Press, 2006), 15–64. See also Barry J. Eichengreen, *Globalizing Capital: A History of the International Monetary System* (Princeton,

NJ: Princeton University Press, 1996) and Robert Gilpin, *Global Political Economy: Understanding the International Economic Order* (Princeton, NJ: Princeton University Press, 2001).

37 Robert J. McMahon, "The Republic as Empire: American Foreign Policy in the Twentieth Century," in *Perspectives on Modern America: Making Sense of the Twentieth Century*, ed. Harvard Sitkoff (New York: Oxford University Press, 2001), 80-100.

38 Odd Arne Westad, *The Global Cold War: Third World Interventions and the Making of Our Times* (New York: Cambridge University Press, 2005).

39 Peter M. Haas, "Introduction: Epistemic Communities and International Policy Coordination," *International Organization* 46, 1 (1992): 3.

40 Tsing, *Friction*, 7.

41 See the essays in David M. Anderson and David Killingray ed., *Policing the Empire: Government, Authority, and Control, 1830-1940* (Manchester, UK: University of Manchester Press, 1991), passim.

42 Julie Evans et al., *Equal Subjects, Unequal Rights: Indigenous Peoples in British Settler Colonies, 1830-1910* (Manchester, UK: University of Manchester Press, 2003), passim.

43 Sankar Muthu, *Enlightenment against Empire* (Princeton, NJ: Princeton University Press, 2003), 263.

44 Tsing, *Friction*, 9.

45 Jürgen Osterhammel, *Colonialism: A Theoretical Overview* (Princeton, NJ: Markus Wiener, 1997), 16-17.

46 Tsing, *Friction*, 6.

47 Cátia Antunes, *Globalisation in the Early Modern Period: The Economic Relationship between Amsterdam and Lisbon, 1640-1705* (Amsterdam: Askant, 2004), 187-88. For an extensive use of these variables, see David Held et al., *Global Transformations: Politics, Economics and Culture* (Stanford, CA: Stanford University Press, 1999).

48 Arjun Appadurai, "Grassroots Globalization and the Research Imagination," *Public Culture* 12, 1 (2000): 7.

49 Charles Taylor, *Modern Social Imaginaries* (Durham, NC: Duke University Press, 2004), 5.

50 Anthony Giddens, *The Consequences of Modernity* (Stanford, CA: Stanford University Press, 1990), 52-53.

51 Saskia Sassen, *Territory, Authority, Rights: From Medieval to Global Assemblages* (Princeton, NJ: Princeton University Press, 2006), 328-29.

52 Aihwa Ong, *Neoliberalism as Exception: Mutations in Citizenship and Sovereignty* (Durham, NC: Duke University Press, 2006).

53 Arif Dirlik, *Global Modernity: Modernity in the Age of Global Capitalism* (Boulder, CO: Paradigm, 2007), 6-9.

54 Arjun Appadurai, *Modernity at Large: Cultural Dimensions of Globalization* (Minneapolis: University of Minnesota Press), 1-26.

Chapter 2: Tibet and the Chinese World-Empire

1 "Récit de João Cabral (1628)," in Hugues Didier, trans., *Les Portugais au Tibet: Les premières relations Jésuites (1624-1635)* (Paris: Chandeigne, 2002), 236.

2 Ippolito Desideri, *An Account of Tibet: The Travels of Ippolito Desideri* (London: Routledge, 1932), 133.

3 Peter Perdue, *China Marches West: The Qing Conquest of Central Eurasia* (Cambridge, MA: Harvard University Press, 2005), 20.

4 Christopher Beckwith, *The Tibetan Empire in Central Asia: A History of the Struggle for Great Power among Tibetans, Turks, Arabs, and Chinese during the Early Middle Ages* (Princeton, NJ: Princeton University Press, 1987).

5 On the eastward expansion of the Cossacks, see Perdue, *China Marches West*, 84-89, 161-73.

6 Galbi [Ge'erbi], "Pingding Xizang beiwen" [An epigraphic record of the pacification of Tibet], in *Qing zhengfu yu lamajiao* [The Qing government and lamaism], ed. Zhang Yuxin (Xuchang: Xizang renmin chubanshe, 1988), 290.

7 Desideri, *An Account of Tibet*, 168, 171. On Desideri, see Sven Hedin, *Southern Tibet, 1906-1908* (Stockholm: Lithographic Institute of the General Staff of the Swedish Army, 1917), 1:278-79, 3:10-14. Desideri's account may be "one of the best and one of the most reliable ever written on Tibet" (1:279), and Desideri is "a sharp and conscientious observer" (3:14), but his political observations are unreliable, as Luciano Petech has noted in his *Selected Papers on Asian History* (Rome: Istituto Italiano per il Medio ed Estremo Oriente, 1988), 218-19. See also Luciano Petech, *China and Tibet in the Early 18th Century* (Leiden: Brill, 1950), 50, 54.

8 For the concept of national geo-body, see Thongchai Winichakul, *Siam Mapped: A History of the Geo-Body of a Nation* (Honolulu: University of Hawaii Press, 1994), 16-18.

9 Kangxi wanted better military intelligence, including new maps of "all the countries which are immediately submitted to the Grand Lama": Hedin, *Southern Tibet*, 1:263, citing Jean-Baptiste du Halde, *The General History of China* [1741], 4:459. When the delegation returned from Lhasa, they handed over the geographical data they had collected to a Jesuit cartographer in Beijing, but he found them inadequate. A second survey in 1715-17, which used two Tibetan lamas trained in geometry, produced better results. Jesuit cartographers included these data in their atlas of the Qing empire. They presented a copy to Kangxi in 1718 and to Louis XIV, which he kept in his private library in Versailles.

10 The Manchus and Russians concluded the Treaty of Nerchinsk in 1689 in order to oppose rising Zunghar power in the region. The Manchus followed this diplomatic initiative with a military campaign that sidelined the Zunghars for two decades. This history is reconstructed in Perdue, *China Marches West*, 139-208; see also Thomas Barfield, *The Perilous Frontier: Nomadic Empires and China, 221 BC to AD 1757* (Cambridge: Blackwell, 1989), 277-94.

11 *Qing shengzu shilu* [Veritable records of the Kangxi emperor], 259:4b, quoted in Gu Zucheng, ed., *Ming-Qing zhi Zang shiyao* [Historical outline of Ming and Qing policies to control Tibet] (Lhasa: Xizang renmin chubanshe, 1999), 136.

12 That winter (1717-18), the Zunghars stripped the Lhasa plain of every tree, which they burned as firewood. When the Manchus arrived three years later, they completed the deforestation by digging up the stumps for the same purpose.

13 Memorial of 23rd day, 3rd month, 58th year, in *Kangxi manwen zhupi zouzhe quanyi* [Complete translation of Kangxi's vermilion rescripts in Manchu] (Beijing: Zhongguo shehui kexue chubanshe, 1996), doc. 3366. The translation is my own.

14 Shortly before the second Manchu invasion, Emperor Kangxi declared himself satisfied that the boy was a true incarnation — yet he hedged his bets by sending the young Dalai Lama a seal of office inscribed with the title of Sixth Dalai Lama, not Seventh. The slip allowed the emperor to sidestep the theological conundrum as to which lama was legitimate, an issue that could be sorted out later.

15 Reprinted in Zhang, *Qing zhengfu yu lamajiao*, 290.

16 Desideri, *An Account of Tibet*, 170; for consistency I have altered his spelling of names.

17 Galbi, "Pingding Xizang beiwen," 290. Desideri believed that Dhondup died in flight, whereas, in fact, he made it back to Zungharia. A Russian envoy visiting Zungharia some years later found Tsering to be a powerful Zunghar leader — and on bad terms with Tsewang Rapten, the cousin who had sent him into Tibet: Petech, *China and Tibet*, 34n4. The Zunghars were destroyed by a Manchu military campaign in the mid-eighteenth century, following a devastating smallpox epidemic that reduced their numbers by half.

18 Desideri, *An Account of Tibet*, 170.

19 Louis Schram, quoted in Warren W. Smith Jr., *Tibetan Nation: A History of Tibetan Nationalism and Sino-Tibetan Relations* (Boulder, CO: Westview Press, 1996), 125.

20 On the campaign of 1728, see Shu-hui Wu, "How the Qing Army Entered Tibet in 1728 after the Tibetan Civil War," *Zentrale-Asiatische Studien* 26 (1996): 122-38.

21 Immanuel Wallerstein coined the term *world-system* to identify a unit of analysis above the state. A world-system need not include the entire globe, although that possibility is always latent in any world-system; rather, it is a system that constitutes a world unto itself. See his *World-Systems Analysis: An Introduction* (Durham, NC: Duke University Press, 2004), 16-17. Despite criticisms of the concept, I have found it heuristically useful for exploring the gap between Chinese and Western assumptions about Tibet.

22 Dalai Lama XIV, *The Spirit of Tibet: Universal Heritage*, ed. A.A. Shiromany (New Delhi: Allied Publishers, 1995), 135.

Chapter 3: Litigating for Freedom in the British Empire, 1815-22

1 *Papers Relating to the Manumission of Steyntje and Her Children with an Appendix* (Cape Town: George Greig, 1827), 6. The only extant copy is in the National Library of South Africa, Cape Town. It includes the copies of petitions, pleadings, and depositions, appearing as *In the Privy Council, George Anderson, Appellant, against Steyntje and her Children, Respondents*, Treasury Solicitor (TS), TS 11, 212, War Office (WO), WO 12, 9590, the National Archives (United Kingdom).

2 James N. Rosenau, *Distant Proximities: Dynamics beyond Globalization* (Princeton, NJ: Princeton University Press, 2003), 4.

3 Jerry H. Bentley, "Cross-Cultural Interaction and Periodization in World History," *American Historical Review* 101, 3 (1996): 749-70; A.G. Hopkins, "The History of Globalization — and the Globalization of History?" in *Globalization in World History*, ed. A.G. Hopkins (London: Pimlico, 2002), 11-36.

4 A.G. Hopkins, "Introduction: Globalization — An Agenda for Historians," in *Globalization in World History*, ed. A.G. Hopkins, 5-6.

5 Jan Aart Scholte, *Globalization: A Critical Introduction*, rev. ed. (Basingstoke: Palgrave Macmillan, 2005), 120.

6 Jonathan Israel, *Empires and Entrepots: The Dutch, the Spanish Monarchy, and the Jews, 1585-1713* (London: The Hambledon Press, 1990), x. On the Dutch economy, see Jan de Vries and A. Van der Woude, *The First Modern Economy: Success, Failure and the Perseverance of the Dutch Economy* (Cambridge: Cambridge University Press, 1997), 665-722.

7 Jonathan Israel, *The Dutch Republic: Its Rise, Greatness, and Fall, 1477-1806* (Oxford: Clarendon Press, 1998), 934-46.

8 Notes Collected from the Colonial Placcards since 1652 upon the Subject of Slavery, Guardian of Slaves Office (SO), SO 17/1, National Archives of South Africa, Cape Town.

9 Ibid., 131.

10 Extracts from the *Statutes of India* [enclosure], Sir John Cradock to Lord Bathurst, 25 January 1813, in George McCall Theal, ed., *Records of the Cape Colony from October 1812 to April 1814* (London: William Clowes and Sons, 1901), 9:131-32. It is not stated whether Cradock's action had retroactive effect. Subsequent references refer to Theal and the volume number.

11 Nigel Worden, *Slavery in Dutch South Africa* (Cambridge: Cambridge University Press, 1985), 50-51; Robert Carl-Heinz Shell, *Children of Bondage: A Social History of the Slave Society at the Cape of Good Hope, 1652-1838* (Hanover/Lebanon: Wesleyan University Press/University Press of New England, 1994), 112-13.

12 To give local effect to ordinances, the Cape authorities normally printed and distributed them for posting in the colony's towns. There is no trace of the 1770 ordinance in the records of the postings: *Kaapse Argiefstukke, Kaapse Plakkaatboek, Deel III (1754-1786)* (Kaapstad: Cape Times, 1949), 76-87.

13 Petition of the Slaves of the Late Widow Schmidt [undated], SO 12/16, National Archives of South Africa, Cape Town.

14 Cradock to Bathurst, 25 January 1813, Theal, 9:130.

15 Shell, *Children of Bondage,* 379. Shell reports that the 1770 statutes allowed for the "possible manumission if one parent was of European descent."

16 Cradock to Bathurst, 15 April 1814, Government House (GH), GH 23/4, Cape Repository.

17 Watson, *The Slave Question,* 26-29. Watson points out that Somerset was reluctant to antagonize slaveholders but anxious to report his amelioration measures as successful. I am grateful to Peter Burroughs for the information about Somerset's mother. Somerset thought slavery had to be ameliorated immediately and emancipation introduced gradually. An initial measure was a proclamation on 26 April 1816 that required the registration of all slaves. In 1823 Somerset issued another proclamation intended to greatly improve the conditions of slaves: Neville Thompson, *Earl Bathurst and the British Empire, 1762-1834* (Barnsley: Leo Cooper, 1999), 202.

18 Names are notoriously confusing. Many Dutch patriarchs had large families and used first and middle names common in previous generations. Spellings of first and middle names are variable: "Johann" can be "Johan" or "Jan"; "Roedolph" can be "Rudolph." To sort out family connections and establish consistent spellings, I used C.C. De Villiers, *Geslagsregister van die Kaapse Families: Geheel Omgewerkte Uitgawe Hersien en Angevul de C. Pama,* 3 vols. (Kaapstad: A.A. Balkema, 1966), 3:919.

19 *Papers,* 6.

20 Marcus Wood, *Slavery, Empathy, and Pornography* (Oxford: Oxford University Press, 2002), 398-427.

21 *Papers,* 7.

22 J.A. Truter, "Treatise on the Origin, Progress, and present State of the Orphan Chamber at the Cape of Good Hope, Compiled for the Use of His Majesty's Commission of Inquiry," 1824, Court of Justice (CJ), CJ 3663, National Archives of South Africa, Cape Town.

23 Truter, "Treatise on the Origin," 100.

24 *Papers,* iii.

25 Ibid., 7.

26 Ibid., 19.

27 De Villiers, *Geslagsregister van die Kaapse Families,* 1:322.

28 Return of Applications and Complaints for Freedom Which Have Been Made to the Guardian of Slaves in Cape Town from the 1st August to 25 Dec. 1826, Theal, 30: 52-72, see 55.

29 *Papers*, 45.

30 Ibid., 24.

31 De Villiers, *Geslagsregister van die Kaapse Families*, 1:140-42.

32 Henricus Cloete, *Theses Philologico-Juricae* (Lugduni: Batavorum, 1811), 12, copy in the National Library of South Africa, Cape Town.

33 *Report of the Proceedings in the Case of His Majesty's Fiscal versus L. Cooke, W. Edwards, and J.B. Hoffman for Alleged Libel* (Cape Town: G. Greig, 1824), 1-4, copy in the National Library of South Africa, Cape Town. Cooke and Edwards claimed the collector of customs sold an apprenticed freed slave as a slave. Hoffman was accused of preparing a petition for publication. Cloete represented Cooke.

34 Frederick Cooper, *Colonialism in Question: Theory, Knowledge, History* (Berkeley: University of California Press, 2005), 21.

35 De Villiers, *Geslagsregister van die Kaapse Families*, 1:28.

36 Die legul gehoord tot inleggende acte van Mr Edward Gerrard, 8 May 1815, Rynier Beck's Notarial Deeds, Notarial Records, Cape District, NCD 36/25, National Archives of South Africa, Cape Town.

37 Michael Andrianus Smuts, *Specimen Iuridicum Inaugurale Specimen* (Lugduni Batavorum, 1807), 73, copy in the National Library of South Africa, Cape Town. De Villiers, *Geslagsregister van die Kaapse Families*, 3:905.

38 Kort Register op de Civile Notul von Primo Jan 1800 Tot Ultimo Dec 1821, 223, MS B85, Manuscript Division, National Library of South Africa, Cape Town. This volume is an index; however, the minutes have not survived.

39 *Papers*, 23.

40 Proclamation by Lord Charles Somerset, 26 April 1816, Theal, 11:102-5.

41 Proclamation, Theal, 11:105; Walter Harding, ed., *The Cape of Good Hope Government Proclamations from 1806 to 1825, as Now in Force and Unrepealed and Ordinances Passed in Council from 1825 to 1838* (Cape Town: A.S. Robertson, 1838), 1:16, copy in the National Library of South Africa, Cape Town.

42 *Papers*, 6.

43 Ibid., 38.

44 Ibid., 21.

45 Ibid., 17. It is likely that the missing formality related to Weeber's belief that he purchased her freedom.

46 GH 48/2/40, 26.

47 *Papers*, 16.

48 R.L. Watson, *The Slave Question: Liberty and Property in South Africa* (1990; repr., Johannesburg: Witwatersrand University Press, 1991), 5.

49 *Papers*, 64.

50 Ibid., 65-66.

51 Ibid., 24.

52 Ibid., 31.

53 Chester W. New, *The Life of Henry Brougham to 1830* (Oxford: Clarendon Press, 1961), 281-304; S.M. Waddams, *Law, Politics and the Church of England: The Career of Stephen Lushington, 1782-1873* (Cambridge: Cambridge University Press, 1992), 63-99.

54 *Papers*, 90.

55 Ibid., 117.

56 Ibid., 25-26.

57 Ibid., 23.

58 On Brougham and Tindal, see *Dictionary of National Biography* (Oxford: Oxford University Press), 2:1358, 19:887.

59 *Papers*, 93.

60 Ibid., 104.

61 Ibid., 141.

62 Ibid., 146.

63 Ibid., 162.

64 Minute of 2 November, Notule van Hof van Appek vir Sivilie Sake, GH 48 1/2, National Archives of South Africa, Cape Town.

65 Ibid.

66 Somerset to Bathurst, 31 March 1823, Theal, 15:354-56.

67 Douglas Hay and Paul Craven, eds., *Masters, Servants, and Magistrates in the British Empire, 1562-1955* (Chapel Hill: University of North Carolina Press, 2004), 1-58.

68 Seymour Drescher, "The Long Goodbye: Dutch Capitalism and Antislavery in Comparative Perspective," *American Historical Review* 99, 1 (1994): 60-69.

69 Arthur Stinchcombe, *Sugar Island Slavery in the Age of Enlightenment: The Political Economy of the Caribbean World* (Princeton, NJ: Princeton University Press, 1995), 199-200.

70 Leonard Thompson, *A History of South Africa* (New Haven, CT: Yale University Press, 1995), 111-12.

71 Philip D. Curtin, *The World and the West: The European Challenge and the Overseas Response in the Age of Empire* (Cambridge: Cambridge University Press, 2000), 276.

72 Wendy Harcourt, "Rethinking Difference and Equality: Women and the Politics of Place," in *Places and Politics in an Age of Globalization,* ed. Roxann Prazniak and Arif Dirlik (New York: Rowman and Littlefield, 2001), 300.

73 Eric Hobsbawm, *On History* (New York: The New Press, 1997), 254. A careful defence of claims like Hobsbawm's declaration, including a recognition of flaws, is provided by Martha Nussbaum, "Human Functioning and Social Justice: In Defense of Aristotelian Essentialism," *Political Theory* 20 (May 1992): 202-42.

74 Arif Dirlik, "Place-Based Imagination: Globalism and the Politics of Place," in *Places and Politics in an Age of Globalization,* ed. Roxann Prazniak and Arif Dirlik (Lanham, MD: Rowman and Littlefield, 2001), 49.

75 Debates over human rights, initiated by assorted critics of individualism and responded to by human rights advocates, are extensive. See Rhoda Howard, *Human Rights and the Search for Community* (Boulder, CO: Westview Press, 1995), 51-74. On the difficulty of establishing who speaks for place, see Robert K. Hitchcock, "Human Rights and Indigenous Peoples in Africa and Asia," in *Human Rights and Diversity: Area Studies Revisited,* ed. David P. Forsythe and Patrice C. McMahon (Lincoln: University of Nebraska Press, 2003), 205-23: "Indigenous peoples in Africa and Asia often reject the argument that cultural values should override universal human rights standards" (221).

76 Richard Elphick, *Khoikhoi and the Founding of White South Africa* (Johannesburg: Ravan Press, 1985), 237-38.

Chapter 4: Ottoman Military and Social Transformations, 1826-28

1 See Virginia H. Aksan, *Ottoman Wars, 1700-1870: An Empire Besieged* (Harlow: Pearson Education, 2007), chaps. 8-9, for a fuller discussion.

2 Timothy Brook, "Time and Global History" (paper presented at the fourth meeting of the Globalization and Autonomy Research Project, Munk Centre, University of Toronto, September 2005), 8.

3 Bernard Lewis set the standard for this story in *The Emergence of Modern Turkey* (Oxford: Oxford University Press, 1968). A recent version, which argues that state security concerns prohibited the development of a free multi-party system under Atatürk, is Ersel Aydınlı, "The Turkish Pendulum between Globalization and Security: From the Late Ottoman Era to the 1930s," *Middle East Studies* 40, 33 (2004): 102-33.

4 The Ottomans could be said to be experiencing an "imperial revival," which "denotes the reemergence of a hub-like structure between the core and either all or some of its former peripheries": Alexander J. Motyl, "Why Empires Reemerge: Imperial Collapse and Imperial Revival in Comparative Perspective," *Comparative Politics* 31, 2 (1999): 128. Motyl's intriguing metaphor for empire is a wheel with a hub and spokes but no rim. The re-emergence requires "an ideologically defined rationale for reimperialization" and "sufficient state capacity to make imperial reconstitution possible" (127).

5 See particularly, Selim Deringil, *The Well-Protected Domains: Ideology and the Legitimation of Power in the Ottoman Empire, 1876-1909* (London: I.B. Taurus, 1998) and Benjamin Fortna, *Imperial Classroom: Islam, the State and Education in the Late Ottoman Empire* (Oxford: Oxford University Press, 2002).

6 Virginia Aksan, "Breaking the Spell of Baron de Tott: Reframing the Question of Military Reform in the Ottoman Empire, 1760-1830," *International History Review* 24, 2 (2002): 253-77. I have described this in further detail in *Ottoman Wars*.

7 Helmuth von Moltke, *Lettres d'Maréchal de Moltke sur l'Orient,* trans. Alfred Marchand, 2nd ed. (Paris: Librairie Fischbacher, 1872), 111-12; Cengiz Kırlı, "The Struggle Over Space: The Coffeehouses of Istanbul, 1700-1845" (PhD diss., SUNY Binghamton, 2000), 262-68.

8 Ahmed Cevdet, *Tarih* (Istanbul, 1858-83), 4:2203. Cevdet is the foremost nineteenth-century historian of the Ottomans.

9 Avigdor Levy, "The Military Policy of Sultan Mahmud II, 1808-1839" (PhD diss., Harvard University, 1968), 53-56. I have followed Levy's summary of the events here and below, as he consulted all the contemporary accounts.

10 Aydınlı, "The Turkish Pendulum," 104.

11 Levy, "The Military Policy," 62-63.

12 Ibid., 65-83.

13 İ. Uzunçarşılı, *Osmanlı Devleti Teşkilatindan Kapukulu Ocakları* (Ankara: Türk Tarih Kurumu, 1943), 622-23.

14 *Kanunnâme-yi asâkir-i mansure-yi Muhammadiye* (Istanbul: n.p., 1829), 133-41.

15 Helmuth von Moltke, *The Russians in Bulgaria and Rumelia in 1828-1829, During the Campaigns of the Danube, the Sieges of Brailow, Varna, Silistria, Shumla, and the Passage of the Balkans,* trans. Marshal Diebitch (London: John Murray, 1854), 13.

16 Dror Ze'evi, "*Kul* and Getting Cooler: The Dissolution of Elite Collective Identity and the Formation of Official Nationalism in the Ottoman Empire," *Mediterranean Historical Review* 11, 2 (1996): 177-95. While Mehmed Ali's military reforms in the 1820s and 1830s

have received considerable attention, few historians have attempted a comparable study of the sources and social ramifications of those of Mahmud II. See Khaled Fahmy, *All the Pasha's Men: Mehmed Ali, His Army and the Making of Modern Egypt* (Cambridge: Cambridge University Press, 1997).

17 Esad Efendi, *Üss-ü Zafer* (Istanbul: n.p., 1927), 103ff. It is important to note that this story of the elimination of the Janissaries was printed and circulated widely.

18 Howard Reed, "The Destruction of the Janissaries by Mahmud II in June, 1826" (PhD diss., Princeton University, 1951), 245. The performance reputedly brought the listeners to tears.

19 Amira Bennison, "Muslim Universalism and Western Globalization," in *Globalization in World History*, ed. A.G. Hopkins (London: Pimlico, 2002), 90.

20 Aksan, "Breaking the Spell of Baron de Tott," 270.

21 As discussed in Tony Ballantyne, "Empire, Knowledge and Culture: From Proto-Globalization to Modern Globalization," in *Globalization in World History*, ed. A.G. Hopkins (London: Pimlico, 2002), 124-31.

22 Birgit Schaebler, "Civilizing Others: Global Modernity and the Local Boundaries (French/German, Ottoman and Arab) of Savagery," in *Globalization and the Muslim World: Culture, Religion and Modernity*, ed. Birgit Schaebler and Leif Stenberg (Syracuse: Syracuse University Press, 2004), 22.

23 Fully explored in Hakan Erdem, "Recruitment of 'Victorious Soldiers of Muhammad' in the Arab Provinces, 1826-1828," in *Histories of the Modern Middle East: New Directions*, ed. Israel Gershoni, Hakan Erdem, and Ursula Woköck (Boulder, CO: Lynne Rienner, 2002), 189-204.

24 Kemal Karpat, "The *Hijra* from Russia and the Balkans: The Process of Self-Definition in the Late Ottoman State," in *Muslim Travellers: Pilgrimage, Migration and the Religious Imagination*, ed. Dale F. Eickelman and James Piscatori (Berkeley: University of California Press, 1990), 131-52; Justin McCarthy, *Death and Exile: The Ethnic Cleansing of Ottoman Muslims, 1821-1922* (Princeton, NJ: Darwin, 1995). The latter is not without its critics.

25 For fuller description, see Erik J. Zürcher, "The Ottoman Conscription System in Theory and Practice," in *Arming the State: Military Conscription in the Middle East and Central Asia, 1775-1925*, ed. Erik J. Zürcher (London: I.B. Tauris, 1999), 79-94, and H. Zboiński, *Armée ottomane: Son organisation actuelle telle qu'elle résulte de l'exécution de la loi de 1869* (Paris: Librairie militaire de J. Dumaine, 1877).

26 Viorel Panaite, "The *Re'ayas* of the Tributary-Protected Principalities: The Sixteenth through the Eighteenth Centuries," *International Journal of Turkish Studies* 9, 1-2 (2003): 83.

27 Ibid.

28 Ruben Safrastjan, "Ottomanism in Turkey in the Epoch of Reforms in XIXC: Ideology and Policy I," *Etudes Balkaniques* 24 (1988): 75.

29 Butrus Abu Manneh, *Studies on Islam and the Ottoman Empire in the 19th century, 1826-1876* (Istanbul: Isis Press, 2001), 89.

30 Aydınlı argues precisely that in "The Turkish Pendulum," 106.

31 Carter Findley, "The Advent of Ideology in the Islamic Middle East (Part I)," *Studia Islamica* 55 (1982): 159-63.

32 Fatma Müge Göçek, *Social Constructions of Nationalism in the Middle East* (Albany: SUNY Press, 2002), has considerable detail on all aspects of the non-Muslim communities.

33 Deringil, *The Well-Protected Domains*, passim; Schaebler, "Civilizing Others," 18.

34 The best short explanation of the significance of 1841 is to be found in Roderic Davison, "Britain, the International Spectrum, and the Eastern Question 1827-1841,"

New Perspectives on Turkey 7 (1992): 15-35. Recent studies of the nature of late Ottoman colonialism include Ussama Makdisi, *The Culture of Sectarianism: Community, History, and Violence in Nineteenth-Century Ottoman Lebanon* (Berkeley: University of California Press, 2000); Eugene Rogan, *Frontiers of the State in the Late Ottoman Empire: Transjordan, 1850-1921* (Cambridge: Cambridge University Press, 1999); see also Deringil, *The Well-Protected Domains*.

35 Roderic Davison, "Foreign and Environmental Contributions to the Political Modernization of Turkey," in *Essays in Ottoman and Turkish History*, ed. Roderic Davison (Austin: University of Texas Press, 1990), 83. The date of the conversation is not given.

36 The Public Debt Administration has been likened to the International Monetary Fund. Feroz Ahmad, *Turkey: The Quest for Identity* (Oxford: Oneworld, 2003), 56. Present-day Turks point with pride and bitterness to the fact that republican Turkey acquired and subsequently paid off the Ottoman debt by the 1950s. Aydınlı, in "The Turkish Pendulum," argues that state security concerns primarily prevented the full application of the rule of law.

Chapter 5: Wired Religion

1 This chapter draws in part on material published in my essay, "Salvation by Electricity," in *Religion: Beyond a Concept*, ed. Hent de Vries (New York: Fordham University Press, 2008), 669-86. Ann Braude has commented on the difficulty of measuring adherence to Spiritualism, given the movement's markedly acephalous nature: no formally recognized leadership and no clear protocols for defining one's status within the cause. See Ann Braude, *Radical Spirits: Spiritualism and Women's Rights in Nineteenth-Century America* (Boston: Beacon Press, 1989), 25-26. The porous boundaries dividing Spiritualism from other religious categories — especially with regard to the difference between Spiritualists and "ordinary" Christians, or, for that matter, between Spiritualists and adherents to a variety of indigenous religions practised in West Africa, Brazil, the Caribbean, and elsewhere — make it difficult to produce meaningful statistics. Nevertheless, there is a broad consensus that Spiritualism enjoyed precipitous growth over the second half of the nineteenth century. Some estimates suggest that 3 million Americans were at least peripherally engaged with the movement by the end of the 1850s and that, by the 1870s, the number of participants rose to more than 11 million. See Werner Sollors, "Dr. Benjamin Franklin's Celestial Telegraph, or Indian Blessings to Gas-Lit American Drawing Rooms," *Social Science Information* 22, 6 (1983): 991.

2 On Spiritualist influences on British, Canadian, American, French, and British-colonial literary production, see, *inter alia,* Jann Matlock, "Ghostly Politics," *Diacritics* 30, 3 (2000): 53-71; Stan McMullin, *Anatomy of a Seance: A History of Spirit Communication in Central Canada* (Montreal and Kingston: McGill-Queen's University Press, 2004); Pamela Thurschwell, *Literature, Technology and Magical Thinking, 1880-1920* (Cambridge: Cambridge University Press, 2001); Gauri Viswanathan, "The Ordinary Business of Occultism," *Critical Inquiry* 27, 1 (2000): 1-20. On links between Spiritualism and the birth of cinema, see Simon During, *Modern Enchantments: The Cultural Power of Secular Magic* (Cambridge, MA: Harvard University Press, 2002); Tom Gunning, "Phantom Images and Modern Manifestations: Spirit Photography, Magic Theater, Trick Films, and Photography's Uncanny," in *Fugitive Images: From Photography to Video,* ed. Patrice Petro (Bloomington: Indiana University Press, 1995), 42-71. On the relationship between Spiritualism and the development of various nineteenth-century human sciences, such as experimental psychology, psychiatric

medicine, psychoanalysis, sexology, and anthropology, see Adam Crabtree, *From Mesmer to Freud: Magnetic Sleep and the Roots of Psychological Healing* (New Haven, CT: Yale University Press, 1993); Ian Hacking, "Telepathy: Origins of Randomization in Experimental Design," *Isis* 79, 3 (1988): 427–51; Molly McGarry, *Ghosts of Futures Past: Spiritualism and the Cultural Politics of Nineteenth-Century America* (Berkeley: University of California Press, 2008); Janet Oppenheim, *The Other World: Spiritualism and Psychical Research in England, 1850-1914* (Cambridge: Cambridge University Press, 1985); Peter Pels, "Spirits and Modernity: Alfred Wallace, Edward Tylor and the Visual Politics of Facts," in *Magic and Modernity: Interfaces of Revelation and Concealment*, ed. Birgit Meyer and Peter Pels (Stanford, CA: Stanford University Press, 2003), 241–71; Jennifer Porter, "The Spirit(s) of Science: Paradoxical Positivism as Religious Discourse among Spiritualists," *Science as Culture* 14, 1 (2005): 1–21; George Stocking, "Animism in Theory and Practice: E.B. Tylor's Unpublished 'Notes on Spiritualism,'" *Man* 6, 1 (1971): 88–104; Ann Taves, *Fits, Trances and Visions: Experiencing Religion and Explaining Experience from Wesley to James* (Princeton, NJ: Princeton University Press, 1999); Elisabeth Wadge, "The Scientific Spirit and the Spiritualist Scientist: Moving in the Right Circles," *Victorian Review* 26, 1 (2000): 24–42.

3 Braude, *Radical Spirits,* 56–82, and passim. Cf. Diana Basham, *The Trial of Woman: Feminism and the Occult Sciences in Victorian Literature and Society* (London: Macmillan, 1992); Alex Owen, *The Darkened Room: Women, Power and Spiritualism in Late Victorian England* (Philadelphia: University of Pennsylvania Press, 1989). On transnational feminist movements in the nineteenth century, see Sandra Stanley Holton, "'To Educate Women into Rebellion': Elizabeth Cady Stanton and the Creation of a Transatlantic Network of Radical Suffragists," *American Historical Review* 99, 4 (1994): 1112–36; Margaret H. McFadden, *Golden Cables of Sympathy: The Transatlantic Sources of Nineteenth-Century Feminism* (Lexington: The University of Kentucky Press, 1999).

4 See David Armitage, "Three Concepts of Atlantic History," in *The British Atlantic World, 1500-1800,* ed. David Armitage and Michael J. Braddick (London and New York: Palgrave, 2002), 11–27; Joseph Roach, *Cities of the Dead: Circum-Atlantic Performance* (New York: Columbia University Press, 1996).

5 Armitage, "Three Concepts," 11–27. See also Jorge Cañizares-Esguerra, *How to Write the History of the New World: Histories, Epistemologies, and Identities in the Eighteenth-Century Atlantic World* (Stanford, CA: Stanford University Press, 2001); Donna Gabaccia, "A Long Atlantic in a Wider World," *Atlantic Studies* 1, 1 (2004): 1–27; Paul Gilroy, *The Black Atlantic: Modernity and Double Consciousness* (Cambridge, MA: Harvard University Press, 1993); Daniel T. Rodgers, *Atlantic Crossings: Social Politics in a Progressive Age* (Cambridge, MA: Belknap Press of Harvard University Press, 1998).

6 Jean-François Bayart, *Le gouvernement du monde: Une critique politique de la globalisation* (Paris: Fayard, 2004); J.R. McNeill, "The End of the Old Atlantic World: America, Africa, Europe, 1770-1888," in *Atlantic American Societies from Columbus through Abolition, 1492-1888,* ed. Alan L. Karras and J.R. McNeill (London: Routedge, 1992), 245–68.

7 These examples are culled from the first ten years of *La Revue Spirite* (1858-68), when the journal was run by its founding editor, Allan Kardec. A complete archive (in French) of the first decades of the journal can be found at http://www.espirito.org.br/portal/download/pdf/fr/index.html.

8 Peter van der Veer, *Imperial Encounters: Religion and Modernity in India and Britain* (Princeton, NJ: Princeton University Press, 2001).

9 Benedict Anderson, *Imagined Communities: Reflections on the Origin and Spread of Nationalism,* 2nd ed. (London: Verso Books, 1991), 53–58.

10 On the growth of Spiritism in western Europe, see Lisa Abend, "Specters of the Secular: Spiritism in Nineteenth-Century Spain," *European History Quarterly* 34, 4 (2004): 507-34; Nicole Edelman, *Voyantes, guérisseuses et vissionnaires en France, 1785-1914* (Paris: Albin Michel, 1995); Thomas Kselman, *Death and the Afterlife in Nineteenth-Century France* (Princeton, NJ: Princeton University Press, 1993); John Warne Monroe, *Laboratories of Faith: Mesmerism, Spiritism, and Occultism in Modern France* (Ithaca, NY: Cornell University Press, 2007); Lynn L.Sharp, *Secular Spirituality: Reincarnation and Spiritism in Nineteenth-Century France* (Lanham, MD: Lexington Books, 2006). On the transplantation of Kardec's ideas to Brazil and, more generally, the syncretism of African and European religions and their sustained interaction in the New World, see Marion Aubrée and François Laplatine, *La table, le livre, et les esprits: Naissance, évolution et actualité du mouvement social spirite entre France et Brésil* (Paris: Lattès, 1990); Roger Bastide, *Les religions africaines au Brésil: Vers une sociologie des interpénétrations de civilisations* (Paris: Presses Universitaires de France, 1960); Sylvia Damazio, *Da elite ao povo: O espiritismo no Rio de Janeiro* (Rio de Janeiro: Bertrand, 1994); Emerson Giumbelli, *O cuidados dos mortos: Acusação e legitimação do espiritismo* (Rio de Janeiro: Arquivo Nacional, 1997); David Hess, *Spirits and Scientists: Ideology, Spiritism, and Brazilian Culture* (Philadelphia: University of Pennsylvania Press, 1991); J. Lorand Matory, *Black Atlantic Religion: Tradition, Transnationalism, and Matriarchy in the Afro-Brazilian Candomble* (Princeton, NJ: Princeton University Press, 2005); João Vasconcelos, "Espíritos clandestinos: Espiritismo, pesquisa psíquica e antropologia da religião entre 1850 e 1920," *Religião e Sociedade* 23, 2 (2003): 92-126. On the development of Kardecismo in the Spanish-speaking Caribbean, especially Cuba and Puerto Rico, see George Brandon, *Santería from Africa to the New World: The Dead Sell Memories* (Bloomington: Indiana University Press, 1993); Armando Andres Bermudez, "Notas para la historia del espiritismo en Cuba," *Etnología y Folklore* 4, 1 (1967): 5-22; Stephan Palmié, *Wizards and Scientists: Explorations in Afro-Cuban Modernity and Tradition* (Durham, NC: Duke University Press, 2002).

11 Sérgio de Oliveira Birchal, "The Transfer of Technology to Latecomer Economies in the Nineteenth Century: The Case of Minas Gerais, Brazil," *Business History* 43, 4 (2001): 48-67; Todd Diacon, *Stringing Together a Nation: Cândido Mariano da Silva Rondon and the Construction of a Modern Brazil, 1906-1930* (Durham, NC: Duke University Press, 2004); Laura Antunes Maciel, "Cultura e tecnologia: A constituição do serviço telegráfico no Brasil," *Revista Brasileira de História* 21, 41 (2001): 127-44; Nicolau Sevcenko, "A capital irradiante: Técnica, ritmos, e ritos do Rio," in *História da Vida Privada No Brasil*, vol. 3, ed. Fernando Novais (São Paulo: Companhia das Letras, 1998), 513-619; Flora Süssekind, *Cinematograph of Words: Literature, Technique and Modernization in Brazil* (Stanford, CA: Stanford University Press, 1997).

12 Quoted in Tom Standage, *The Victorian Internet: The Remarkable Story of the Telegraph and the Nineteenth Century's On-line Pioneers* (New York: Berkley Books, 1998), 90.

13 James W. Carey, *Communication as Culture: Essays on Media and Society* (New York: Routledge, 1989), 203-4.

14 For discussion of the array of inventors, investors, and intermediary agents implicated in the "birth" of electrical telegraphy, see Standage, *Victorian Internet*, 22-56; Ken Beauchamp, *History of Telegraphy* (London: Institution of Electrical Engineers, 2001), 20-101. Here, it should also be noted how hazardous it is to refer to the telegraph as a singular technology. Morse's electromagnetic apparatus was only one of a diverse group of nineteenth-century devices associated with the practice of distance writing (tele-graphy), which encompassed different methods of encoding and deciphering messages and different possibilities of human interface (e.g., machines that required attention from human

operators as opposed to those that could relay signals automatically). One must also guard here against the temptation to rely upon heroic narratives of technological invention, which typically repress the cultural, financial, and technical contingencies involved in establishing a viable market for new technologies. For more nuanced accounts of the commodification of information, the establishment of new systems of circulation through telegraphy, and the integration of this technology into the emerging industrial infrastructure of railways, shipping lines, and postal services in such disparate places as the United States, Britain, and the Ottoman Empire, see, *inter alia*, Yakup Bektas, "Displaying the American Genius: The Electromagnetic Telegraph in the Wider World," *British Journal for the History of Science* 34, 2 (2001): 199-232; Daniel R. Headrick, *The Tentacles of Progress: Technology Transfer in the Age of Imperialism, 1850-1940* (Oxford: Oxford University Press, 1988); Daniel R. Headrick, *The Invisible Weapon: Telecommunications and International Politics, 1851-1945* (Oxford: Oxford University Press, 1991); Iwan Rhys Morus, "Currents from the Underworld: Electricity and the Technology of Display in Early Victorian England," *Isis* 84, 1 (1993): 50-89; Iwan Rhys Morus, "The Electric Ariel: Telegraphy and Commercial Culture in Early Victorian England," *Victorian Studies* 39, 3 (1996): 339-78.

15 Carey, *Communication as Culture,* 202.

16 Ibid., 201-30; Menahem Blondheim, *News over the Wires: The Telegraph and the Flow of Public Information in America, 1844-1897* (Cambridge, MA: Harvard University Press, 1994); John Steele Gordon, *A Thread Across the Ocean: The Heroic Story of the Transatlantic Cable* (New York: Walker and Company, 2002); Annteresa Lubrano, *The Telegraph: How Technological Innovation Caused Social Change* (New York: Garland Publishing, 1997); David Paull Nickles, *Under the Wire: How the Telegraph Changed Diplomacy* (Cambridge, MA: Harvard University Press, 2003).

17 For a vivid account of the structure and organizational culture of telegraph offices in late nineteenth-century America, see Gregory J. Downey, *Telegraph Messenger Boys: Labor, Technology, and Geography, 1850-1950* (New York: Routledge, 2002).

18 As described, for instance, in Manuel Castells, *The Rise of the Network Society* (Oxford: Blackwell, 1996).

19 For a useful summary of the history of international cabling initiatives, see http://atlantic-cable.com.

20 This is exemplified by the simultaneous growth of the submarine telegraph industry and the scientific disciplines of oceanography and hydrography, which were fed by a shared desire for reliable and detailed knowledge about the ocean floor. Indeed, beginning in the 1850s and 1860s, rapid innovations in deep-sea sounding technologies helped to transform the seabed of the Atlantic from an unknown (and largely unconsidered) entity into a new frontier: an uncivilized space, ripe for conquest and exploitation. See Helen M. Rozwadowski, "Technology and Ocean-Scape: Defining the Deep Sea in the Mid-Nineteenth Century," *History and Technology* 17 (2001): 217-47.

21 John Durham Peters, *Speaking into the Air: A History of the Idea of Communication* (Chicago: University of Chicago Press, 1999), 142.

22 See, for example, Christoph Asendorf, *Batteries of Life: On the History of Things and Their Perception in Modernity* (Berkeley: University of California Press, 1993); Laura Otis, *Networking: Communicating with Bodies and Machines in the Nineteenth Century* (Ann Arbor: University of Michigan Press, 2001).

23 Allan Kardec, *The Book on Mediums, or, Guide for Mediums and Invocators,* trans. Emma A. Wood (1861; repr., York Beach, ME: Samuel Weiser, 1970), 116-17.

24 See, for instance, Morus, "The Electric Ariel," 375; Braude, *Radical Spirits,* 23-24; Jeffrey Sconce, *Haunted Media: Electronic Presence from Telegraphy to Television* (Durham, NC: Duke University Press, 2000), 50-55; Sollors, "Dr. Benjamin Franklin's Celestial Telegraph," 996. On the intangibility of the "wires" enabling spirit communication, see Richard J. Noakes, "Telegraphy is an Occult Art: Cromwell Fleetwood Varley and the Diffusion of Electricity to the Other World," *British Journal for the History of Science* 32, 4 (1999): 446, 450-59.

25 See especially Owen, *The Darkened Room,* 202-34.

26 As detailed, for instance, in Noakes, "Telegraphy Is an Occult Art." See also Richard J. Noakes, "'Instruments to Lay Hold of Spirits': Technologizing the Bodies of Victorian Spiritualism," in *Bodies/Machines,* ed. Iwan Rhys Morus (Oxford: Berg, 2002), 125-63.

27 See Peter Lamont, "Spiritualism and a Mid-Victorian Crisis of Evidence," *Historical Journal* 47, 4 (2004): 897-920.

Chapter 6: The Internationalization of Capital

1 Jean-Claude Debeir, "Le problème des exportations de capitaux français de 1919 à 1930: Substitutions et concurrences," *Relations internationales* 6 (1976): 175.

2 Great Britain, the leading international investor since the beginning of the nineteenth century, did not pass similar legislation. On 10 January 1928, the ten-year-old French law was rescinded.

3 Liberalism was not completely unhindered. Governments could encourage or veto foreign issues for political or diplomatic reasons. They could also raise fiscal barriers to short-term capital movements.

4 International Monetary Fund (IMF), *Annual Report, 1967* (Washington, DC: IMF, 1967), 32. For additional information, tables, and sources referred to in this chapter, see Samir Saul, "Has Financial Internationalization Turned into Financial Globalization?" *Globalization and Autonomy Online Compendium,* http://www.globalautonomy.ca/global1/article.jsp?index=RA_Saul_FinancialIntl.xml.

5 Jeffrey A. Frieden, *Global Capitalism: Its Fall and Rise in the Twentieth Century* (New York: W.W. Norton and Company, 2006), 342-46.

6 International Monetary Fund, *Annual Report, 1984* (Washington, DC: IMF, 1984), 19, 421-22.

7 Peter Svedberg, "The Portfolio-Direct Composition of Private Foreign Investment in 1914 Revisited," *Economic Journal* 88, 352 (1978): 763, 768.

8 John H. Dunning, "Changes in the Level and Structure of International Production: The Last One Hundred Years," in *The Growth of International Business,* ed. Mark Casson (London: George Allen, 1983), 85.

9 Lance E. Davis and Robert A. Huttenback, *Mammon and the Pursuit of Empire: The Political Economy of British Imperialism, 1860-1912* (Cambridge: Cambridge University Press, 1986), 37. International exchange rates were stable until 1914. They fluctuated after the First World War with the onset of inflation, budget deficits, and other financial difficulties, but the dollar-pound parity did not change significantly until after the Second World War.

10 Michael Mussa et al., "Capital Account Liberalization: Theoretical and Practical Aspects," *IMF Occasional Paper* 172, 30 September 1998, 31.

11 P.L. Cottrell, *British Overseas Investment in the Nineteenth Century* (London: Macmillan, 1975), 27.

12 George Paish, "The Export of Capital and the Cost of Living," *The Statist*, 14 February 1914, Si-Sviii; Albert Henry Imlah, *Economic Elements in the Pax Britannica* (Cambridge, MA: Harvard University Press, 1958), 28.

13 Angus Maddison, *The World Economy: A Millennial Perspective* (Paris: Development Centre of the Organisation for Economic Co-operation and Development, 2001), 105.

14 Michael Edelstein, *Overseas Investment in the Age of High Imperialism* (New York: Columbia University Press, 1982), 25; Herbert Feis, *Europe the World's Banker, 1870-1914: An Account of European Foreign Investment and the Connection of World Finance with Diplomacy before the War* (New York: A.M. Kelley, 1964), xix.

15 Matthew Simon, "The Pattern of New British Portfolio Foreign Investment, 1865-1914," in *The Export of Capital from Britain 1870-1914*, ed. Alan R. Hall (London: Methuen, 1968), 24-25.

16 Davis and Huttenback, *Mammon*, 72.

17 Feis, *Europe the World's Banker*, 27; Simon, *Pattern of New British Portfolio Investment*, 23.

18 Pédro Arbulu and Jacques-Marie Vaslin, "La place de Paris dans la finance internationale du 19ième siècle," *Revue d'Économie Financière* 57 (2000): 31; Feis, *Europe the World's Banker*, xx, 47.

19 Feis, *Europe the World's Banker*, 51.

20 Ibid., 61, 71, 74.

21 Cleona Lewis, *America's Stake in International Investments* (Washington, DC: The Brookings Institute, 1938), 119.

22 Ibid., 445.

23 United Nations, *Les mouvements internationaux de capitaux entre les deux guerres* (New York: United Nations, 1949); Alan S. Milward, "Les placements français à l'étranger et les deux guerres mondiales," in *La position internationale de la France: Aspects économiques et financiers, XIXᵉ-XXᵉ siècles*, ed. Maurice Lévy-Leboyer, 301-2 (Paris: Éditions de l'École des hautes études en sciences sociales [EHESS], 1977).

24 United Nations, *Les mouvements*, 6; John H. Dunning, *Studies in International Investment* (London: George Allen and Unwin, 1970), 19.

25 Marc Flandreau and Chantale Rivière, "La grande 'retransformation'? Contrôles de capitaux et intégration financière internationale, 1880-1996," *Économie Internationale* 78 (1999): 11-58.

26 Ibid., 35-37.

27 Albert Fishlow, "Lessons from the Past: Capital Markets During the 19th Century and the Interwar Period," *International Organization* 39, 3 (1985): 418-19.

28 Peter B. Kenen, *Capital Mobility and Financial Integration: A Survey* (Princeton, NJ: International Finance Section, Princeton University, 1976).

29 Ibid., 62.

30 United Nations, *Le courant international des capitaux à long terme et les donations publiques, 1951-1959* (New York: United Nations, 1961), 2.

31 Stijn Claessens, "The Emergence of Equity Investment in Developing Countries: An Overview," *The World Bank Economic Review* 9, 1 (1995): 1.

32 Philip A. Lane and Gian Maria Milesi-Ferretti, "International Financial Integration," *IMF Working Paper* no. 03/86, April 2003, 7, 25, 26.

33 International Monetary Fund, *Report on the Measurement of International Capital Flows* (Washington, DC: IMF, 1992), 8.

34 William Poole, "A Perspective on US International Capital Flows," *Federal Reserve Bank of St. Louis Review* 87, 1 (2004): 3.

35 Organisation for Economic Co-operation and Development, *Endettement extérieur des pays en développement* (Paris: OECD, 1983) and *Financement et dette extérieure des pays en développement* (Paris: OECD, 1986-88); Rachel McCulloch and Peter A. Petri, "Equity Financing of East Asian Development," in *Capital Flows and Financial Crises,* ed. Miles Kahler (New York: Cornell University Press, 1998), 162.

36 *Bulletin Financier BBL* [Bulletin for international fiscal documentation], January – February 1993; William Easterly, "How Did Heavily Indebted Poor Countries Become Heavily Indebted? Reviewing Two Decades of Debt Relief," *World Development* 30, 10 (2002): 1677-96.

37 David Woodward, *The Next Crisis? Direct and Equity Investment in Developing Countries* (London: Zed, 2001), 29.

38 World Bank, *Private Capital Flows to Developing Countries: The Road to Financial Integration* (New York: Oxford University Press, 1997), 104.

39 Robert Lensink and Howard White, "Does the Revival of International Private Capital Flows Mean the End of Aid? An Analysis of Developing Countries' Access to Private Capital," *World Development* 26, 7 (1998): 1223.

40 Ibid.

41 Sergio L. Schmukler, "Financial Globalization: Gain and Pain for Developing Countries," *Federal Reserve Bank of Atlanta Economic Review* 89, 2 (2004): 41; Claessens, "Emergence of Equity Investment," 3.

42 Eduardo Fernandez-Arias and Peter J. Montiel, "The Surge in Capital Inflows to Developing Countries: An Analytical Overview," *World Bank Economic Review* 101, 1 (1996): 54.

43 Ignacio Trigueros, "Les entrées de capitaux et l'investissement: Le Mexique," in *Mouvements des capitaux et performances des investissements: Les leçons de l'Amérique latine,* ed. Ricardo Ffrench-Davis and Helmut Reisen (Paris: Organisation for Economic Co-operation and Development, 1998), 214.

44 Marcelle Chauvet and Fang Dong, "Leading Indicators of Country Risk and Currency Crises: The Asian Experience," *Federal Reserve Bank of Atlanta Economic Review* 89, 1 (2004): 27, 29.

45 UNCTAD (United Nations Conference on Trade and Development), *World Investment Report 2000: Cross-Border Mergers and Acquisitions and Development* (New York and Geneva: United Nations, 2000), 3-4; UNCTAD, *World Investment Report 2002: Transnational Corporations and Export Competitiveness* (New York and Geneva: United Nations, 2002), 14.

46 UNCTAD, *World Investment Report 1997: Transnational Corporations, Market Structure and Competition Policy* (New York and Geneva: United Nations, 1997), xv; UNCTAD, *World Investment Report 2000,* xv; UNCTAD, *World Investment Report 2001: Promoting Linkages* (New York and Geneva: United Nations, 2001), 9.

47 UNCTAD, *World Investment Report,* xvi, and *World Investment Report 2002,* 14-15.

48 See Appendix 1 in Saul, "Has Financial Internationalization Turned into Financial Globalization?"

49 Ibid., Appendix 2.

50 Ibid., Appendix 3.

51 Ibid., Appendix 4.

52 Ibid., Appendix 5.

53 UNCTAD, *World Investment Report 2001,* 53, and *World Investment Report 2003, FDI Policies for Development: National and International Perspectives* (New York and Geneva: United Nations 2002), 16.

54 Andras Uthoff and Daniel Titelman, "La relation entre l'épargne étrangère et l'épargne nationale dans le cadre de la libéralisation financière," in *Mouvements des capitaux et performances des investissements: Les leçons de l'Amérique latine,* ed. Ricardo Ffrench-Davis and Helmut Reisen (Paris: Organisation for Economic Co-operation and Development, 1998), 27-47.

55 See Appendix 6 in Saul, "Has Financial Internationalization Turned into Financial Globalization?"

56 UNCTAD, *World Investment Report 2001,* 121.

57 UNCTAD, *L'investissement étranger direct en Afrique* (New York and Geneva: United Nations, 1995), 14, 19, 46.

58 See Appendix 8 in Saul, "Has Financial Internationalization Turned into Financial Globalization?"

59 UNCTAD, *World Investment Report 1996: Investment, Trade and International Policy Agreements* (New York and Geneva: United Nations, 1996), 7.

60 See Appendix 9 in Saul, "Has Financial Internationalization Turned into Financial Globalization?"

61 UNCTAD, *World Investment Report 1996,* 30-32, 34-35, and *World Investment Report 2003,* 187-90.

62 Judd Polk, "The New World Economy," *Columbia Journal of World Business* 3, 1 (1968): 7-16, and "The New International Production," *World Development* 1, 5 (1973): 15-20.

63 John H. Dunning, "The Role of Foreign Direct Investment in a Globalizing Economy," *Banca Nazionale del Lavoro Quarterly Review* 48, 193 (1995): 137.

64 Charles-Albert Michalet, "Transnational Corporations and the Changing International Economic System," *Transnational Corporations* 3, 1 (1994): 17-18.

65 Paul Bairoch, "The Constituent Economic Principles of Globalization in Historical Perspective: Myths and Realities," *International Sociology* 15, 2 (2000): 205, 209.

66 UNCTAD, *World Investment Report 2001,* 85.

67 Maurice Obstfeld and Alan M. Taylor, *Global Capital Markets: Integration, Crisis, and Growth* (Cambridge: Cambridge University Press, 2004), 173-76.

Chapter 7: Global Industrial Enclaves

1 L.S. Stavrianos, *Global Rift: The Third World Comes of Age* (New York: William Morrow and Company, 1981), 33-34; Giovanni Arrighi, Beverley J. Silver, and Benjamin D. Brewer, "Industrial Convergence, Globalization, and the Persistence of the North-South Divide," *Studies in Comparative International Development* 38, 1 (2003): 21-22, 26-27.

2 Naomi Klein, *No Logo: Taking Aim at the Brand Bullies* (Toronto: Vintage, 2000), 205; Ronen Palan, *The Offshore World: Sovereign Markets, Virtual Places, and Nomad Millionaires* (Ithaca, NY: Cornell University Press, 2003), 51-22; Aihwa Ong, *Neoliberalism as Exception: Mutations in Citizenship and Sovereignty* (Durham, NC: Duke University Press, 2006), 106-7, 116, and 135-38.

3 Arjun Appadurai, "Grassroots Globalization and the Research Imagination," *Public Culture* 12, 1 (2000): 6.

4 Brink Lindsey, *Against the Dead Hand: The Uncertain Struggle for Global Capitalism* (New York: John Wiley and Sons, 2002), ix-x, 8; William Brittain-Caitlin, *Offshore: The Dark Side of the Global Economy* (New York: Farrar, Straus and Giroux, 2005), 24, 97; Steven McKay, *Satanic Mills or Silicon Islands? The Politics of High-Tech Production in the Phillipines*

(Ithaca, NY: Cornell University Press, 2006), 4, 13, 15-16; Ong, *Neoliberalism as Exception,* 3, 19, 103.

5 Arjun Appadurai, "Deep Democracy: Urban Governmentality and the Horizon of Politics," *Public Culture* 14, 1 (2002): 22.

6 Saskia Sassen employs the term *frontier zones* in "Spatialities and Temporalities of the Global: Elements for a Theorization," *Public Culture* 12, 1 (2000): 216.

7 Aturo Escobar, *Encountering Development: The Making and Unmaking of the Third World* (Princeton, NJ: Princeton University Press, 1995), 19, 218.

8 Manuel Castells, *The City and the Grassroots: A Cross-Cultural Theory of Urban Social Movements* (Berkeley: University of California Press, 1983), xix-xx.

9 Arif Dirlik, "Place-Based Imagination: Globalism and the Politics of Place," in *Places and Politics in an Age of Globalization,* ed. Roxann Prazniak and Arif Dirlik (Lanham, MD: Rowman and Littlefield, 2001), 17-19.

10 Sassen, "Spatialities and Temporalities of the Global," 216.

11 Jan Aart Scholte, *Globalization: A Critical Introduction* (New York: St. Martin's Press, 2000), xiv.

12 Dirlik, "Place-Based Imagination," 30-31.

13 Ibid., 42. See also Arturo Escobar, "Culture Sits in Places: Reflections on Globalism and Subaltern Strategies of Localization," *Political Geography* 20, 2 (2001): 139-74.

14 Reider Almas and Geoffrey Lawrence, "Introduction: The Global/Local Problematic," in *Globalization, Localization, and Sustainable Livelihoods,* ed. Reider Almas and Geoffrey Lawrence (Burlington, VT: Ashgate, 2003), 18, 22; Nancy A. Naples, "The Challenges and Possibilities of Transnational Feminist Praxis," in *Women's Activism and Globalization: Linking Local Struggles and Transnational Politics,* ed. Nancy Naples and Marisha Desai (New York: Routledge, 2002), 269.

15 Dirlik, "Place-Based Imagination," 36.

16 Ibid., 22.

17 Castells, *The City and the Grassroots,* 212; Dirlik, "Place-Based Imagination," 23.

18 Rex A. Lucas, *Minetown, Milltown, Railtown: Life in Canadian Communities of Single Industry* (Toronto: University of Toronto Press, 1974), xi.

19 Gerald Burke, *Towns in the Making* (New York: St. Martin's Press, 1971), 126-35; Leonardo Benevolo, *The Origins of Modern Town Planning* (London: Routledge, 1967), 110, 114, 118.

20 Sally Marks, *The Ebbing of European Ascendancy: An International History of the World* (London: Hodder Arnold, 2002), 13-15, 60.

21 Harold Kalman, *A History of Canadian Architecture* (Toronto: Oxford University Press, 1994), 657; Gerald Hodge, "The Roots of Canadian Planning," *American Planning Association Journal* 51, 1 (1985): 8-11; Michael Simpson, *Thomas Adams and the Modern Planning Movement* (London: Alexandrine Press, 1985), 75, 94; Marc A. Weiss, "Developing and Financing the 'Garden Metropolis': Urban Planning and Housing Policy in Twentieth-Century America," *Planning Perspectives* 5 (1990): 307; Robert Freestone, "An Imperial Aspect: The Australasian Town Planning Tour of 1914-1915," *Australian Journal of Politics and History* 44 (1998): 159-76. For more on the rise of corporate and town planning in the early twentieth century, see Alfred D. Chandler, *The Visible Hand: The Managerial Revolution in American Business* (Cambridge, MA: Harvard University Press, 1978); John S. Garner, ed., *The Company Town: Architecture and Society in the Early Industrial Age* (New York: Oxford University Press, 1992); John D. Fairfield, "Scientific Management of Urban Space: Professional City Planning and the Legacy of Progressive Reform," *Journal of Urban History*

20 (1994): 179-204; Margaret Crawford, *Building the Workingman's Paradise: The Design of American Company Towns* (New York: Verso, 1995).

22 Simpson, *Thomas Adams,* 112; Oiva Saarinen, "Single-Sector Communities in Northern Ontario: The Creation and Planning of Dependent Towns," in *Power and Place,* ed. Gilbert Stelter and Alan Artibise (Vancouver: UBC Press, 1986), 237; Neil White, "Creating Community: Industrial Paternalism and Town Planning in Corner Brook, Newfoundland, 1923-1955," *Urban History Review* 32, 2 (2004): 50-51.

23 Lucas, *Minetown, Milltown, Railtown,* xi.

24 Duane Swank, *Global Capital, Political Institutions, and Policy Change in Developed Welfare States* (Cambridge: Cambridge University Press, 2002), 3-6, 285-89.

25 Palan, *The Offshore World,* 119-23.

26 Ibid., 122-23.

27 Appadurai, "Deep Democracy," 21.

28 Lindsey, *Against the Dead Hand,* x, 3, 10.

29 Palan, *The Offshore World,* 51-52.

30 Gary Gereffi and Miguel Korzeniewicz. "Introduction: Global Commodity Chains," in *Commodity Chains and Global Capitalism,* ed. Gary Gerrefi and Miguel Korzeniewicz (Westport, CT: Praeger, 1994), 2-3; Joshua Cohen and Joel Rogers eds., *Can We Put an End to Sweatshops?* (Boston: Beacon Press, 2001), 7; Laura T. Reynolds, "Institutionalizing Flexibility: A Comparative Analysis of Fordist and Post-Fordist Models of Third World Agro-Export Production," in *Commodity Chains and Global Capitalism,* ed. Gary Ferrefi and Miguel Korzeniewicz (Westport, CT: Praeger, 1994), 157-58.

31 Rosalinda Pineda Ofreneo, "The Philippine Garment Industry," in *Global Production: The Apparel Industry in the Pacific Rim,* ed. Nora Hamilton, Lucie Cheng, and Edna Bonacich (Philadelphia, PA: Temple University Press, 1994), 162-79; Gereffi and Korzeniewicz, "Introduction," 4, 12.

32 Castells, *The City and the Grassroots,* 178; Dennis Shoesmith, *Export Processing Zones in Five Countries* (Hong Kong: Asia Partnership for Human Development, 1986); Diane Lauren Wolf, *Factory Daughters: Gender, Household Dynamics, and Rural Industrialization in Java* (Berkeley: University of California Press, 1992), 255-56; Paul Cooney, "The Mexican Crisis and the *Maquiladora* Boom: A Paradox of Development or the Logic of Neoliberalism?" *Latin American Perspectives* 28, 3 (2001): 62, 68; Manuel Belo Moreira, "Local Consequences and Responses to Global Integration: The Role of the State in the Less Favoured Zones," in *Globalization, Localization, and Sustainable Livelihoods,* ed. Reider Almas and Geoffrey Lawrence (Burlington, VT: Ashgate, 2003), 195; Lindsey, *Against the Dead Hand,* x, 8, 265.

33 Palan, *The Offshore World,* 190.

34 Appadurai, "Deep Democracy," 22; Sassen, "Spatialities and Temporalities," 217; McKay, *Satanic Mills or Silicon Islands?,* 4-5, 13-16; Ong, *Neoliberalism as Exception,* 7, 19, 108, 116.

35 Nancy Melissa Lutz, "Images of Docility: Asian Women and the World-Economy," in *Racism, Sexism, and the World System,* ed. Joan Smith (New York: Greenwood Press, 1988), 70; Klein, *No Logo,* 214.

36 Bruce E. Kaufman, "The Case for the Company Union," *Labor History* 41, 3 (2000): 321, 337, 348.

37 Jeremy Brecher and Tim Costello, *Global Village or Global Pillage: Economic Reconstruction from the Bottom Up* (Boston: South End Press, 1994), 87; Seung Hoon Lee and Ho Keun Song, "The Korean Garment Industry: From Authoritarian Patriarchism to Industrial Paternalism," in *Global Production: The Apparel Industry in the Pacific Rim,* ed. Nora Hamilton,

Lucie Cheng, and Edna Bonacich (Philadelphia, PA: Temple University Press, 1994), 148-49, 157.

38 Gary Gereffi and Mei-Lin Pan, "The Globalization of Taiwan's Garment Industry," in *Global Production: The Apparel Industry in the Pacific Rim*, ed. Nora Hamilton, Lucie Cheng, and Edna Bonacich (Philadelphia, PA: Temple University Press, 1994), 126; Gunseli Berik, "Mature Export-Led Growth and Gender Wage Inequality in Taiwan," *Feminist Economics* 6, 3 (2000): 19.

39 Berik, "Mature Export-Led Growth," 6.

40 Aihwa Ong, *Spirits of Resistance and Capitalist Discipline: Factory Women in Malaysia* (Albany: State University of New York Press, 1987), 148; Donella Caspersz, "Globalization and Labour: A Case Study of EPZ Workers in Malaysia," *Economic and Industrial Democracy* 19, 2 (1998): 270-71.

41 Caspersz, "Globalization and Labour," 265.

42 Wolf, *Factory Daughters*, 121-22.

43 Sassen, "Spatialities and Temporalities," 220.

44 Cirila Quintero-Ramirez, "Unions, Collaboration, and Labour Conditions in Mexican Maquiladoras," *International Studies Association*, 2001, http://www.isanet.org/archive/ramirez.html (accessed 11 January 2005).

45 Anita Chan and Zhu Xiaoyang, "Disciplinary Labor Regimes in Chinese Factories," *Critical Asian Studies* 35, 4 (2003): 561, 566, 573.

46 Kevin J. Middlebrook, "The Politics of Industrial Restructuring: Transnational Firms' Search for Flexible Production in the Mexican Automobile Industry," *Comparative Politics* 23, 3 (1991): 293; Huberto Juarez Nunez, "*Maquila* Workers in Mexico: The Prospects for Organization and International Solidarity," *Labor History* 43, 4 (2002): 443.

47 Harley Shaiken, *Mexico in the Global Economy: High Technology and Work Organization in Export Industries* (San Diego, CA: Center for US-Mexican Studies, 1990), 49.

48 Dale Hathaway, "Mexico's Frente Autentico del Trabajo and the Problem of Unionizing Maquiladoras," *Labor History* 43, 4 (2002): 433-34.

49 Appadurai, "Deep Democracy," 22.

50 Hathaway, "Mexico's Frente Autentico del Trabajo," 436; Quintero-Ramirez, "Unions, Collaboration, and Labour Conditions."

51 Barry Carr, "Globalization from Below: Labour Internationalism under NAFTA," *International Social Science Journal* 51, 159 (1999): 50, 52-53.

52 White, "Creating Community," 32; Noreen Kirkman, *Mount Isa: Oasis of the Outback* (Townsville, QLD: James Cook University, 1998).

53 White, "Creating Community," 52.

54 Bipasha Baruah, "Earning Their Keep and Keeping What They Earn: A Critique of Organizing Strategies for South Asian Women in the Informal Sector," *Gender, Work, and Organization* 11, 6 (2004): 610, 614.

55 Ibid., 622.

56 Appadurai, "Deep Democracy," 28-30, 35-39, 41.

57 Kathryn Kopinak, "Living the Gospel through Service to the Poor: The Convergence of Political and Religious Motivations in Organizing *Maquiladora* Workers in Juarez, Mexico," in *Race, Class, Gender: Bonds and Barriers*, ed. Jesse Vorst et al. (Winnipeg: Between the Lines, 1989), 217-44; Maria Fernandez-Kelly, *For We Are Sold, I and My People: Women and Industry in Mexico's Frontier* (Albany: State University of New York Press, 1983).

58 Kopinak, "Living the Gospel," 226-27; Patricia Marin and Cecilia Rodriguez, "Working on Racism: Centro Obrero, El Paso," in *Of Common Cloth: Women in the Global Textile*

Industry, ed. Wendy Chapkis and Cynthia Enloe (Amsterdam: Transnational Institute, 1983), 84–85.

59 Jorge Alberto Fernandez, "Redesigning the Strategy of the Frente Autentico del Trabajo in the *Maquiladoras*," *Labor History* 43, 4 (2002): 461.

60 Ibid., 463; Hathaway, "Mexico's Frente Autentico del Trabajo," 430-31, 433.

61 See Wendy Chapkis and Cynthia Enloe, *Of Common Cloth: Women in the Global Textile Industry* (Amsterdam: Transnational Institute, 1983); Leo Panitch and Ralph Miliband, "The New World Order and the Socialist Agenda," in *Socialist Register 1992*, ed. Ralph Miliband and Leo Panitch (London: The Merlin Press, 1992), 1-25.

62 Panitch and Miliband, "The New World Order," 22.

63 Nora Hamilton, Lucie Cheng, and Edna Bonacich, eds., *Global Production: The Apparel Industry in the Pacific Rim* (Philadelphia, PA: Temple University Press, 1994); Chapkis and Enloe, *Of Common Cloth*, 82.

64 Caspersz, "Globalization and Labour," 159, 261; Ong, *Spirits of Resistance*, 196-203; Wolf, *Factory Daughters*, 258-59.

65 Mary Beth Mills, *Thai Women in the Global Labor Force: Consuming Desires, Contested Selves* (New Brunswick, NJ: Rutgers University Press, 1999), 11, 167-69.

66 Ong, *Spirits of Resistance*, xv; Wolf, *Factory Daughters*, 131-33.

67 Caspersz, "Globalization and Labour," 255, 259.

68 Castells, *The City and the Grassroots*, 299.

69 Ronaldo Munck, "Globalization, Labor and the 'Polanyi Problem,'" *Labor History* 45, 3 (2004): 257.

70 Jeremy Brecher, Tim Costello, and Brendan Smith, *Globalization from Below: The Power of Solidarity* (Cambridge, MA: South End Press, 2000), x-xi; Manuel Castells and Martin Ince, *Conversations with Manuel Castells* (London: Blackwell Publishing, 2003), 58, 60; Munck, "Globalization, Labor and the 'Polanyi Problem,'" 255-56.

71 Jackie Smith, "Democratizing Globalization? Impacts and Limitations of Transnational Social Movements," Working Paper Series, Institute on Globalization and the Human Condition, McMaster University, Hamilton, Ontario, 2004, 9.

72 Ibid., 4, 7-8.

73 Klein, *No Logo*, 446.

74 Christian Levesque and Gregor Murray, "Local versus Global: Activating Local Union Power in the Global Economy," *Labor Studies Journal* 27, 3 (2002): 40; Jeff Faux, "A Global Strategy for Labour," *World Social Forum*, 2002, http://www.globalpolicynetwork.org (accessed 26 January 2005).

75 Panitch and Miliband, "New World Order," 21; Robert W. Cox, "Global Perestroika," in *Socialist Register 1992*, ed. Ralph Miliband and Leo Panitch (London: The Merlin Press, 1992), 40.

76 Gay Seidman, *Manufacturing Militance: Workers' Movements in Brazil and South Africa, 1970-1985* (Berkeley: University of California Press, 1994), 226, 262.

77 Robert Lambert, "Labour Movement Renewal in the Era of Globalization: Union Responses in the South," in *Global Unions? Theory and Strategies of Organized Labour in the Global Political Economy*, ed. Jeffrey Harrod and Robert O'Brien (London: Routledge, 2002), 203.

78 Peter Evans, "Fighting Marginalization with Transnational Networks: Counter-Hegemonic Globalization," *Contemporary Sociology* 29, 1 (2000): 233.

79 Brecher and Costello, *Global Village or Global Pillage*, 9; Brecher, Costello, and Smith, *Globalization from Below*, 42.

80 Brecher and Costello, *Global Village or Global Pillage*, 87.

81 Jackie Smith and Hank Johnston, "Introduction," in *Globalization and Resistance: Transnational Dimensions of Social Movements*, ed. Jackie Smith and Hank Johnston (New York: Rowman and Littlefield, 2002), 1-10.

82 Nancy A. Naples, "Challenges and Possibilities," 274-75.

83 Randy Stoecker, "Cyberspace vs. Face-to-Face: Community Organizing in the New Millennium," *Perspectives on Global Development and Technology* 1, 2 (2002): 156.

84 Geraldine Pratt and Brenda Yeoh, "Transnational (Counter) Topographies," *Gender, Place and Culture* 10, 2 (2003): 160.

85 Kopinak, "Living the Gospel," 218.

86 Munck, "Globalization, Labor, and the 'Polanyi Problem,'" 257; Dirlik, "Place-Based Imagination," 41.

87 Escobar, *Encountering Development*, 19; Robert O'Brien, "Labour and IPE: Rediscovering Human Agency," in *Global Political Economy: Contemporary Theories*, ed. Ronen Palan (London: Routledge, 2000), 98; Dirlik, "Place-Based Imagination"; Scholte, *Globalization*.

88 John D. French, "Towards Effective Transnational Labor Solidarity Between NAFTA North and NAFTA South," *Labor History* 43, 4 (2002): 457.

89 Baruah, "Earning Their Keep and Keeping What They Earn," 615.

90 Appadurai, "Grassroots Globalization," 17.

91 Leslie Salzinger, *Genders in Production: Making Workers in Mexico's Global Factories* (Berkeley: University of California Press, 2003), 25, 33.

92 Sidney Tarrow, "From Lumping to Splitting: Specifying Globalization and Resistance," in *Globalization and Resistance: Transnational Dimensions of Social Movements*, ed. Jackie Smith and Hank Johnson (New York: Rowman and Littlefield, 2002), 234.

93 Melissa W. Wright, "Crossing the Factory Frontier: Gender, Place, and Power in the Mexican Maquiladora," *Antipode* 29, 3 (1997): 298-99.

94 Appadurai, "Grassroots Globalization," 8; Escobar, *Encountering Development*, 218.

Chapter 8: Freedom of the Ether or the Electromagnetic Commons?

1 Minutes of the Opening Session, 4 October 1927, International Radiotelegraph Conference, Washington, p. 22, National Archives and Records Administration, College Park, Maryland (Archives II) (hereafter NARA), R(ecord)G(roup) 43, entry 136, box 19, file 574.106.

2 "Some Advantages of Participation by the US in the Proposed IRC, 9/13/1927," p. 1, 3, NARA, RG 43, entry 136, box 6, file 574.1.

3 The standard unit of time used to measure frequency, established at the 1927 Washington Radiotelegraph Convention, is the second. See "Discussion of Article 3, General Radiotelegraph Regulations, Proposals 269-288," NARA, entry 136, box 11, file 574 1a4-2.

4 Garrett Hardin, "The Tragedy of the Commons," *Science* 162 (1968): 1243-48; Marvin Soroos, "The International Commons: A Historical Perspective," *Environmental Review* 12, 1 (1998): 17-20.

5 See Stephen Krasner, "Global Communications and National Power," *World Politics* 43, 3 (1991): 337.

6 See Jeffrey Williamson, "Globalization, Convergence, and History," *Journal of Economic History* 56, 2 (1996): 1-30.

7 See Brigit Meyer and Peter Geschiere, eds., *Globalization and Identity: Dialectics of Flow and Closure* (Oxford: Oxford University Press, 1999).

8 Rowland F. Pocock, "'No Other Possible Market': The Royal Navy as Sponsor of Radio Telegraphy," in *From Semaphore to Short Waves*, ed. Frank A.J.L. James (London: Royal Society of Arts, 1998), 136-45.

9 Final Protocol of the Preliminary Conference on Wireless Telegraphy, Berlin, 13 August 1903, 97 British and Foreign State Papers 467, 83-85.

10 The ITU united the two existing European telegraph unions, the Austro-German Telegraph Union and the Western European Union. It oversaw developments in telegraph technology, harmonized rates, and established Morse code as the international standard.

11 David M. Leive, *International Telecommunications and International Law: The Regulation of the Radio Spectrum* (Dobbs Ferry, NY: Oceana Publications, 1970), 40-42.

12 *International Radiotelegraphic Convention, 1912*, article 8.

13 "Charles H. Hughes — President," undated (c. 1925), NARA, RG 43, entry 136, box 2, file 574.D 7.

14 Minutes of Sub-Committee 2, 11 October 1920, p. 2, NARA, RG 43, entry 69, box 1, file dossier B-2.

15 Alan B. Albarran and Gregory G. Pitts, *The Radio Broadcasting Industry* (Boston: Allyn and Bacon, 1996), 24; *Oxford English Dictionary* (Oxford: Oxford University Press, 1996), 183.

16 Chief Operator of the Government Radio Station, Santo Domingo, to American Legation, Dominican Republic, 24 February 1916, NARA, RG 43, entry 76, box 2, file 810.74/56.

17 Commanding Officer, 3rd Company (Signal), to Expeditionary Commander, 29 December 1915, NARA, RG 43, entry 76, box 2, file 874 810.74/17.

18 Minutes, Sub-Committee No. 5, on Improvement of Communication Facilities between the Five Great Powers, International Conference on Electrical Communication, 12 October 1920, NARA, RG 43, entry 69, box 1, file "Digests of Meetings of Sub-Committees" (2 of 2), p. 2. See also US legation, Berne, to Secretary of State, 22 November 1920, NARA, RG 43, entry 76, box 3, file 854.74/3.

19 Vice Consul H.T. Goodier, Japan, to Secretary of State, 2 March 1920, NARA, RG 43, entry 76, box 3, file 800.72/31; Minutes, Sub-Committee 5, International Conference on Electrical Communication, 14 October 1920, NARA, RG 43, entry 69, box 1, file "Digests of Meetings of Sub-Committees" (2 of 2).

20 *Radio Act of 1912*, Public Law 264, 62nd Cong. (August 13, 1912); George P. Oslin, *The Story of Telecommunications* (Macon, GA: Mercer University Press, 1992), 278, 282; David Kennedy, *Freedom from Fear: The American People in Depression and War, 1929-1945* (New York: Oxford University Press, 1999), 228.

21 Preston McGoodwin, RCA, Caracas, to Secretary of State, 8 April 1920, NARA, RG 43, entry 76, box 3, file 831.74/44; [Mr.] Gonzales, American Legation in Cuba, to Secretary of State, 18 September 1919, NARA, RG 43, entry 76, box 3, file 837.74/56; American Vice Consul, Ecuador, to Department of State, 22 April 1920, NARA, RG 43, entry 76, box 3, file 822.74/14.

22 Minutes of Sub-Committee 2, International Conference on Electrical Communication (hereafter ICEC), 11 October 1920, p. 5, NARA, RG 43, entry 69, box 1, file dossier B-2.

23 Minutes, First Plenary Session of the ICEC, 8 October 1920, p. 1, 2, NARA, RG 43, entry 69, box 1, file dossier B.

24 Minutes of Committee No. 1, ICEC, 12 October 1920, p. 4, NARA, RG 43, entry 69, box 1, file dossier B.

25 Ibid., 15 October 1920, NARA, RG 43, entry 69, box 1, file dossier B-1.

26 Ibid., 11 December 1920 and 12 December 1920.

27 Charles Bright, *Imperial Telegraphic Communication* (London: King, 1911), 124.

28 Ibid., 64.

29 Lesley Bennet Tribolet, *The International Aspects of Electrical Communications in the Pacific Area* (Baltimore, MD: Johns Hopkins Press, 1929), 1-3; Bright, *Imperial Telegraphic Communication*, 63.

30 Minutes, Conference between the American Delegates and Various Representatives of American Telegraph, Cable and Radio Companies, 26 May 1921, p. 4., NARA, RG 43, entry 72, box 1, file dossier no. A.

31 Walter Dillenz, "Broadcasting and Copyright" (paper presented at the "Regional Forum on the Impact of Emerging Technologies on the Law of Intellectual Property for Asia and the Pacific," Seoul, Korea, 30 August–1 September 1989), WIPO Publication 681 (E), 1990, p. 159, WIPO Archives, Geneva, E 2319F630 WIPO.R.

32 Minutes, Conference between the American Delegates and Various Representatives of American Telegraph, Cable and Radio Companies, 26 May 1921, p. 254, 256.

33 Ibid., 115.

34 Ibid., 106, 126, 174.

35 Ibid., 57.

36 Minutes of Sub-Committee 2, ICEC, 11 October 1920, p. 7.

37 Oslin, *Story of Telecommunications,* 275-81.

38 Albarran and Pitts, *Radio Broadcast Industry,* 25-26.

39 Ibid., 21, 28.

40 The most important suit was *US v. Zenith Radio Corp. et al.* (1926).

41 See Donald Read, *The Power of News: The History of Reuters* (Oxford: Oxford University Press, 1999).

42 IRC Press Release no. 17, 5 October 1927, NARA, RG 43, entry 136, box 20, file 574.108; State Department Press Releases, Enclosure 8, NARA, RG 43, entry 136, box 20, file 574.107a; "General Report of the Commission of Jurists at the Hague, 1922: Part 1, Rules for the Control of Radio in Time of War," in *American Journal of International Law* 17, supplement (1923): S242-S60.

43 Press Release, State Department, Re International Telegraph Conference, 28 September 1927, p. 3, 5, 8, NARA, RG 43, entry 136, box 2, file 574.107a. The proposals were published as *Proposals for the IRC of Washington,* known colloquially as the "Berne Book."

44 Appendix 43 to *American Final Report: Summary of Important Features of the International Radiotelegraph Convention signed at Washington, 25 Nov. 1927,* p. 1, NARA, RG 43, entry 136, box 7, file 574.1.

45 List of delegates to IRC, NARA, RG 43, entry 136, box 3, file 574.00201; "List of Companies, Organizations and Individuals to whom Circular Invitation of March 11, 1927, and of Subsequent Date has been Sent," NARA, RG 43, box 2, file 574a.

46 "Delegate Questionnaire," NARA, RG 43, entry 136, box 3, file 574.002; IRC Press Release no. 7, Sept 25, NARA, RG 43, entry 136, box 20, file 574.108.

47 "Final Report of the Executive Officer and the Secretary of the American Delegation," p. 4, 6, 7, NARA, RG 43, entry 136, box 5, file 574.1.

48 IRC Press Release no. 4, 15 September 1927, NARA, RG 43, entry 136, box 20, file 574.108.

49 IRC Press Release no. 23, 10 October 1927, NARA, RG 43, entry 136, box 20, file 574.108.

50 Ibid.

51 See IRC Press Release no. 9, 27 September 1927, NARA, RG 43, entry 136, box 20, file 574.108.

52 IRC Press Release no. 2, 10 September 1927, NARA, RG 43, entry 136, box 20, file 574.108.

53 Minutes, Committee no. 1, 10th session, 12 September 1927, NARA, RG 43, entry 136, box 8, file 574.1a101.

54 IRC Press Release no. 3, 14 September 1927, NARA, RG 43, entry 136, box 20, file 574.108.

55 Minutes of the American Delegation, Memorandum, 26 September 1927, NARA, RG 43, entry 136, box 4, file 574.1. By the opening of the conference, Germany had scaled back this request to include only frequencies over 2,850 metres.

56 Martin McLoone, "Music Hall Dope and British Propaganda? Cultural Identity and Early Radio Broadcasting in Ireland," *Historical Journal of Film, Radio and Television* 20, 3 (2000): 307.

57 Ibid., 311.

58 International Meteorological Committee, Sub-Committee no. 1 of Technical Committee, *Proposals for the IRC of Washington*, p. 137, NARA, RG 43, entry 136, box 6, file 574.1.

59 Ibid., 124, 125.

60 "International Radio Conference of Washington, Proposals of the USA, July 1927," Enclosure D to Appendix 1 of *Final Report of US Delegation*, p. 57, NARA, RG 43, entry 136, box 5, file 574.1.

61 "Proposal of the Polish Delegation, 27 October 1927," *Proposals for the IRC of Washington*, Appendix 6, p. 2, NARA, RG 43, entry 136, box 6, file 574.1.

62 *Radiotelegraph Convention and General Regulations,* article 19.6 and article 17.1.3.

63 Minutes, Technical Committee, Session 11, 11 November 1927, p. 2, 6, 9, NARA, RG 43, entry 136, box 18, file 574.1c701.

64 Minutes, 6th session, Technical Committee, 27 October 1927, NARA, RG 43, entry 136, box 18, file 574.1c701; Minutes, 4th Plenary Session, 10 November 1927, NARA, RG 43, entry 136, box 20, file 574.106.

65 "Proposals submitted by Italy," *Proposals for the IRC of Washington*, Appendix 6, p. 10 and 14, NARA, RG 43, entry 136, box 6, file 574.1.

66 "Appendix 39 — English Translation of Articles 1 to 9 as Approved by the Drafting Committee," 24 October 1927, NARA, RG 43, entry 136, box 7, file 574.1.

67 Minutes of Sub-Committee No. 1 of Technical Committee, 24 October 1927, NARA, RG 43, entry 136, box 18, file 574.1c7a01.

68 "Proposals for the IRC of Washington," pp. 125-27.

69 R. del Valle Sárraga, VP of Radui Club of Puerto Rico, to Secretary of Commerce, 22 September 1927, NARA, RG 43, entry 136, box 11, file 574.1a4-2.

70 Alfred Goldsmith to C.H. Taylor, RCA, 14 November 1927, NARA, RG 43, entry 136, box 11, file 574.1a4.

71 "Proposal Submitted by the Netherlands Delegation and Concurred in by the Curacao Delegation," NARA, RG 43, entry 136, box 7, file 574.1.

72 "Discussion of Technical Subjects Relating to Interference and Frequency Allocation," IRC, 1 October 1927, p. 1 (emphasis in original), 4, NARA, RG 43, entry 136, box 11, file 574.1a4-1.

73 "Statement by Judge Stephen Davis before the Committee on the Convention, 7 Oct. 1927," Appendix 39 of *English Translation of Articles 1 to 9 as Approved by the Drafting Committee 24 October, 1927*, NARA, RG 43, entry 136, box 5, file 574.1.

74 *Proposals for the IRC of Washington*, p. 108 and p. 501, NARA, RG 43, entry 136, box 6, file 574.1; *International Radio Conference*, article 14.1; "Proposals of the USA, July 1927," p. 69; *Report to the Minister of Marine and Fisheries by the Canadian Delegation to the International Radiotelegraph Conference, Washington, October and November, 1927* (Ottawa: Department of Marine and Fisheries, 1928), 17.

75 Philo C. Wasburn, "International Radio Broadcasting: Some Considerations for Political Sociology," *Journal of Political and Military Sociology* 13, 2 (1985): 37–41.

76 James G. Savage, *The Politics of International Telecommunications Regulation* (London: Westview Press, 1985), 92, 138–39.

77 *International Telecommunication Convention, Madrid, 1932 — Final Copy of Convention*, articles 1 and 17, NARA, RG 43, entry 186, box 1, file "Reports" (3 of 3).

78 Krasner, *Global Communications*, 347–49.

79 Dillenz, "Broadcasting and Copyright," 164–65.

80 Viktor Mayer-Schönberger and Deborah Hurley, "Globalization of Communication," in *Governance and a Globalizing World*, ed. Joseph Nye and John Donahue (Washington, DC: Brookings Institution Press, 2000), 131–51.

81 Leslie Pal, "Governing the Electronic Commons: Globalization, Autonomy, Legitimacy and the Internet," in *Unsettled Legitimacy: Political Community, Power, and Authority in a Global Era*, ed. Steven Bernstein and William D. Coleman (Vancouver: UBC Press, forthcoming).

82 Clive Kessler, "Globalization: Another False Universalism?" *Third World Quarterly* 21, 6 (2000): 939.

83 Klaus W. Grewlich, "Toward an International Competition Policy in Global Telecommunications," in *Globalism and Localism in Telecommunications*, ed. E.M. Noam and A.J. Wolfson (Amsterdam: Elsevier, 1997), 357.

84 John Tomlinson, *Globalization and Culture* (Cambridge: Cambridge University Press, 1999), chap. 4, passim; Jean-Pierre Chamoux, "After Privatization: Neocolonialism?" in *Globalism and Localism in Telecommunications*, ed. E.M. Noam and A.J. Wolfson (Amsterdam: Elsevier, 1997), 343.

Chapter 9: A Globalization Moment

1 Elliott Roosevelt, *As He Saw It* (New York: Duell, 1946), 109–12.

2 Robert D. Murphy, *Diplomat Among Warriors* (Garden City, NY: Doubleday, 1964), 172–73; William Roger Louis, *Imperialism at Bay: The United States and the Decolonization of the British Empire, 1941-1945* (New York: Oxford University Press, 1978), 438–39.

3 An interesting recent discussion of counter-pointed impulses can be found in Walter Russell Mead, *Special Providence: American Foreign Policy and How It Changed the World* (New York: Knopf, 2001).

4 A useful survey of US foreign policy during the presidencies of Theodore Roosevelt and William Howard Taft can be found in Walter LaFeber, *The American Age* (New York: Norton, 1989), 218–52. An indispensable source on Woodrow Wilson is N. Gordon Levin Jr., *Woodrow Wilson and World Politics: America's Response to War and Revolution* (New York: Oxford University Press, 1968).

5 Frank Freidel, *Franklin D. Roosevelt: A Rendezvous with Destiny* (Boston: Little Brown, 1990).

6 See, for example, Patrick J. Hearden, *Architects of Globalism: Building a New World Order during World War II* (Fayetteville: University of Arkansas Press, 2002); Warren F. Kimball, *The Juggler: Franklin Roosevelt as Wartime Statesman* (Princeton, NJ: Princeton University Press, 1991).

7 Quoted in James MacGregor Burns, *Roosevelt: The Soldier of Freedom* (New York: Harcourt Brace Jovanovich, 1970), 130.

8 Quoted in Robert Dallek, *Franklin D. Roosevelt and American Foreign Policy, 1932-1945* (New York: Oxford University Press, 1979), 324.

9 Transcript of Roosevelt-Molotov conversation, quoted in Louis, *Imperialism at Bay*, 156-57.

10 One overview of the Casablanca Conference can be found in Dallek, *Franklin D. Roosevelt and American Foreign Policy*, 369-79.

11 See US Department of State, *Foreign Relations of the United States: The Conferences at Washington, 1941-1942, and Casablanca, 1943* (Washington, DC: US Government Printing Office, 1968), 487-853 (hereafter cited as *FRUS: Casablanca*).

12 Roosevelt, *As He Saw It*, 115-16, 121-22.

13 Murphy, *Diplomat Among Warriors*, 168.

14 US Department of State, *Foreign Relations of the United States, 1943*, vol. 5, *The American Republics* (Washington, DC: US Government Printing Office, 1965), 656.

15 Roosevelt, *As He Saw It*, 85-86.

16 US Department of State, *Foreign Relations of the United States, 1941*, vol. 1 (Washington, DC: US Government Printing Office, 1958), 368-69.

17 Ibid., 76-77.

18 Kenneth W. Pendar, *Adventure in Diplomacy: The Emergence of General de Gaulle in North Africa* (New York: Dodd, Mead, 1945), 147-48.

19 US Department of State, *Foreign Relations of the United States, 1943*, vol. 5, *The American Republics*, 5:656; US Department of State, *Foreign Relations of the United States, 1943*, vol. 4, *The Near East and Africa* (Washington, DC: US Government Printing Office, 1965), 656-63.

20 Roosevelt, *As He Saw It*, 113-14.

21 *FRUS: Casablanca*, 703.

22 Roosevelt, *As He Saw It*, 75.

23 Elliott Roosevelt, ed., *F.D.R.: His Personal Letters* (New York: Duell, Sloan, and Pearce, 1950), 1413.

24 Roosevelt, *As He Saw It*, 115.

25 Ibid., 85-86.

26 Roland Robertson, *Globalization: Social Theory and Global Culture* (London: Sage, 1992), 8.

27 Quoted in Robert E. Sherwood, *Roosevelt and Hopkins: An Intimate History* (New York: Harper, 1950), 667 (emphasis added).

28 Martin Albrow, *The Global Age: State and Society beyond Modernity* (Cambridge: Polity Press, 1996), 88.

29 Thomas L. Friedman, *The Lexus and the Olive Tree* (New York: Anchor Books, 2000), 7-8.

30 Jan Aart Scholte, *Globalization: A Critical Introduction* (New York: St. Martin's Press, 2000), 16, and Anthony Giddens, *The Consequences of Modernity* (Stanford, CA: Stanford University Press, 1990), 64.

31 See, for example, Lloyd C. Gardner, *Economic Aspects of New Deal Diplomacy* (Boston: Beacon Press, 1971).

32 See Ibid., x, and Kimball, *The Juggler,* 127-28. A relevant and interesting moment also occurred during Roosevelt's journey home from Casablanca. On a brief stopover in Monrovia, the president met with some of the members of the US Army engineering unit based there. Most of the soldiers were African Americans, and the US ambassador remembered that some of them joked about having gotten to shake Roosevelt's hand, even if they had had to come to Liberia to do it. The ambassador also recalled the positive impression that the behaviour and achievements of the black Americans had made on Liberian society. See George Arthur Padmore, *The Memoirs of a Liberian Ambassador* (Lewiston, NY: E. Mellen Press, 1996), 152-53. My thanks to Mairi MacDonald for leading me to the Padmore memoir.

33 See, for example, Lloyd Gardner, *Economic Aspects of New Deal Diplomacy;* Hearden, *Architects of Globalism;* Michael J. Hogan, *The Marshall Plan: America, Britain, and the Reconstruction of Western Europe, 1947-1952* (Cambridge: Cambridge University Press, 1987); Kimball, *Juggler.*

34 See, for example, Jeffrey Sachs, "International Economics: Unlocking the Mysteries of Globalization," *Foreign Policy* 110 (Spring 1998): 97-109. The quotation from Adam Smith is on 99-100. See also Gene M. Grossman and Elhanan Helpman, *Innovation and Growth in the Global Economy* (Cambridge, MA: MIT Press, 1991) and Elhanan Helpman, *The Mystery of Economic Growth* (Cambridge, MA: Belknap Press of Harvard University Press, 2004).

35 Gilbert Rist, *The History of Development: From Western Origins to Global Faith* (Atlantic Highlands, NJ: Zed Books, 1997); Nils Gilman, *Mandarins of the Future: Modernization Theory in Cold War America* (Baltimore, MD: Johns Hopkins University Press, 2003); Michael E. Latham, *Modernization as Ideology: American Social Science and "Nation-Building" in the Kennedy Era* (Chapel Hill: University of North Carolina Press, 2000).

36 See, for example, Sherwood, *Roosevelt and Hopkins,* 719.

37 A valuable discussion of Roosevelt's ongoing concerns can be found in Hearden, *Architects of Globalism.*

38 Pendar, *Adventure in Diplomacy,* 146.

39 Macmillan, quoted in Alistair Horne, *Macmillan: 1894-1956* (London: Macmillan, 1988), 165.

40 Sherwood, *Roosevelt and Hopkins,* 685.

41 See, for example, a recent study and a far-sighted earlier one: Michael Mandelbaum, *The Case for Goliath: How America Acts as the World's Government in the Twenty-First Century* (New York: Public Affairs, 2005); Stanley Hoffmann, *Primacy or World Order: American Foreign Policy since the Cold War* (New York: McGraw-Hill, 1978).

42 See Rist, *The History of Development;* Gilman, *Mandarins of the Future;* Latham, *Modernization as Ideology;* and, in this volume, see Stephen M. Streeter, "Globalization, Autonomy, and the Third World: The Struggle for Hearts and Minds in Guatemala and Vietnam in the 1960s."

43 *FRUS: Casablanca,* 695-96.

44 See, for example, Eric Blanchard, "Gender, International Relations, and the Development of Feminist Security Theory," *Signs* 28, 4 (2003): 1289-1312; and Jill Steans, *Gender and International Relations: An Introduction* (Cambridge: Polity Press, 1998).

45 Rist, *History of Development,* 75.

46 See, for example, Walter LaFeber, "Roosevelt, Churchill and Indochina, 1942-1945," *American Historical Review* 80, 5 (975): 1277-95.

47 See, for example, John Lewis Gaddis, *Strategies of Containment*, rev. ed. (New York: Oxford University Press, 2005), 3-23; Kimball, *Juggler*, 7-20, 159-84.

48 Pendar, *Adventure in Diplomacy*, 151-52.

Chapter 10: Paradigm Shift and the Nuremberg Trials

1 Kriangsak Kittichaisaree, *International Criminal Law* (New York: Oxford University Press, 2001), 19.

2 Andrew Clapham, "Issues of Complexity, Complicity and Complementarity: From the Nuremberg Trials to the Dawn of the New International Criminal Court," in *From Nuremberg to The Hague: The Future of International Criminal Justice*, ed. Philippe Sands (Cambridge: Cambridge University Press, 2003), 33; Jackson Nyamuya Maogoto, *War Crimes and Realpolitik: International Justice from World War I to the 21st Century* (Boulder, CO: Lynne Rienner Publishers, 2004), 6.

3 Derek Heater, *World Citizenship: Cosmopolitan Thinking and Its Opponents* (London: Continuum, 2002), 28.

4 Derek Heater, *What Is Citizenship?* (Cambridge: Polity Press, 1999), 135.

5 Ibid., 97.

6 Steven R. Ratner and Jason S. Abrams, *Accountability for Human Rights Atrocities in International Law: Beyond the Nuremberg Legacy*, 2nd ed. (New York: Oxford University Press, 2001), 13.

7 Bruce Broomhall, *International Justice and the International Criminal Court: Between Sovereignty and the Rule of Law* (New York: Oxford University Press, 2003), 23.

8 David Held, *Democracy and the Global Order: From the Modern State to Cosmopolitan Governance* (Stanford, CA: Stanford University Press, 1995), 206.

9 Michael Ignatieff, *The Warrior's Honour: Ethnic War and the Modern Conscience* (Toronto: Penquin Books, 1999), 117.

10 Maogoto, *War Crimes and Realpolitik*, 129.

11 Kriangsak, *International Criminal Law*, 16.

12 "International Military Tribunal (Nuremberg), Judgment and Sentences, October 1, 1946," reprinted in *American Journal of International Law* 41, 1 (1947): 220 (hereafter IMT Judgment).

13 The Versailles Treaty, 28 June 1919: Part VII, art. 227, http://www.yale.edu/lawweb/avalon/imt/partvii.htm.

14 Dominic McGoldrick, "Criminal Trials Before International Tribunals: Legality and Legitimacy," in *The Permanent International Criminal Court: Legal and Policy Issues*, ed. Dominic McGoldrick, P.J. Rowe, and Eric Donnelly (Oxford: Hart, 2004), 12.

15 Gerry Simpson, "Politics, Sovereignty, and Remembrance," in *The Permanent International Criminal Court: Legal and Policy Issues*, ed. Dominic McGoldrick, P.J. Rowe, and Eric Donnelly (Oxford: Hart, 2004), 49.

16 Antonio Cassese, *International Criminal Law* (New York: Oxford University Press, 2003), 329.

17 Maogoto, *War Crimes and Realpolitik*, 57-62; Samantha Power, *"A Problem From Hell": America and the Age of Genocide* (New York: Perennial, 2002), 16.

18 Ibid., 62.

19 Moscow Conference, "Joint Four-Nation Declaration: Statement on Atrocities," October 1943, http://www.yale.edu/lawweb/avalon/wwii/moscow.htm.

20 London Agreement and Charter of the International Military Tribunal: Annex, August 8, 1945, http://www.yale.edu/lawweb/avalon/imt/proc/imtchart.htm.

21 Cassese, *International Criminal Law,* 332.

22 McGoldrick, "Criminal Trials," 15.

23 Ibid., 16.

24 Richard Overy, "The Nuremberg Trials: International Law in the Making," in *From Nuremberg to The Hague: The Future of International Criminal Justice,* ed. Philippe Sands (Cambridge: Cambridge University Press, 2003), 21.

25 Ibid.

26 IMT Judgment, 243.

27 Ibid., 249.

28 McGoldrick, "Criminal Trials," 45.

29 Ibid., 38.

30 Power, *"A Problem From Hell."*

31 IMT Judgment, 219.

32 Ibid., 221.

33 Overy, "Nuremberg Trials," 26.

34 IMT Judgment, 223.

35 Ibid., 272-333.

36 UN General Assembly, Resolution 95(1), Affirmation of the Principles of Law Recognized by the Charter of the Nuremberg Tribunal, 11 December 1946; International Law Commission, Principles of International Law Recognized in the Charter of the Nuremberg Tribunal and in the Judgment of the Tribunal. English text published in *Report of the International Law Commission,* 5 June–29 July 1950, Doc. A/1316, 11-14.

37 Broomhall, *International Justice,* 19.

38 James Crawford, "The Drafting of the Rome Statute," in *From Nuremberg to The Hague: The Future of International Criminal Justice,* ed. Philippe Sands (Cambridge: Cambridge University Press, 2003), 117.

39 Overy, "Nuremberg Trials," 1-2.

40 IMT Judgment, 216-17.

41 McGoldrick, "Criminal Trials," 19-20.

42 Overy, "Nuremberg Trials," 3-4.

43 Crawford, "Drafting of the Rome Statute," 112.

44 Leila Nadya Sadat, "The Evolution of the ICC: From The Hague to Rome and Back Again," in *The United States and the International Criminal Court: National Security and International Law,* ed. Sarah B. Sewall and Carl Kaysen (Oxford: Rowman and Littlefield, 2000), 38.

45 A.G. Hopkins, "Globalization — An Agenda for Historians," in *Globalization in World History,* ed. A.G. Hopkins (New York: Norton, 2002), 3.

46 Akira Iriye, *Global Community: The Role of International Organizations in the Making of the Contemporary World* (Berkeley: University of California Press, 2002), 41.

47 Ibid., 8

48 Charter of the United Nations, 1945.

49 Michael Ignatieff, *Rights Revolution* (Toronto: Anansi Press, 2000), 28.

50 UN General Assembly, Resolution 55/2, Millennium Declaration, 18 September 2000, UN Doc. A/55/L.2: para. 4-5.

51 Robert Jackson, "Sovereignty in World Politics," in *Sovereignty at the Millennium,* ed. Robert Jackson (Oxford: Blackwell, 1999), 10.

52 Broomhall, *International Justice*, 188.
53 Gregory Fox, "The Right to Political Participation in International Law," in *Law and Moral Action in World Politics*, ed. Cecilia Lynch and Michael Maurice Loriaux (Minneapolis: University of Minnesota Press, 2000), 77.
54 Thomas Risse and Kathryn Sikkink, "The Socialization of International Human Rights Norms into Domestic Practices: Introduction," in *The Power of Human Rights: International Norms and Domestic Change*, ed. Thomas Risse, Steve C. Ropp, and Kathryn Sikkink (Cambridge: Cambridge University Press, 1999), 17-24.
55 Ibid., 5.
56 Ibid., 16.
57 Cecilia Lynch, "Political Activism and International Law," in *Law and Moral Action in World Politics*, ed. Cecilia Lynch and Michael Maurice Loriaux (Minneapolis: University of Minnesota Press, 2000), 142.
58 Broomhall, *International Justice*, 59.
59 Kofi Annan, "Two Concepts of Sovereignty," *The Economist*, 18-24 September 1999, 49-50.
60 Heater, *What Is Citizenship?* 115.
61 Anthony Giddens, *Runaway World: How Globalization Is Reshaping Our Lives*, 2nd ed. (New York: Routledge, 2003), 50; Held, *Democracy and the Global Order*, 124.
62 Ignatieff, *Rights Revolution*, 36.
63 Olivier Russbach, "The Citizen's Right to International Law," in *Law and Moral Action in World Politics*, ed. Cecilia Lynch and Michael Maurice Loriaux (Minneapolis: University of Minnesota Press, 2000), 254.
64 Cassese, *International Criminal Law*, 335.
65 Anthony Giddens, *The Consequences of Modernity* (Stanford, CA: Stanford University Press, 1990), 4.
66 Tim Dunne and Nicholas J. Wheeler, "Introduction: Human Rights and the Fifty Years' Crisis," in *Human Rights in Global Politics*, ed. Tim Dunne and Nicholas J. Wheeler (Cambridge: Cambridge University Press, 1999), 1-28.
67 Cassese, *International Criminal Law*, 5.
68 Kriangsak, *International Criminal Law*, 4.
69 Maogoto, *War Crimes and Realpolitik*, 126.
70 Kriangsak, *International Criminal Law*, 326.
71 Clapham, "Issues of Complexity, Complicity and Complementarity," 43.
72 Cherie Booth, "Prospects and Issues from the International Criminal Court: Lessons from Yugoslavia and Rwanda," in *From Nuremberg to The Hague: The Future of International Criminal Justice*, ed. Philippe Sands (Cambridge: Cambridge University Press, 2003), 166.
73 Ibid., 159.
74 Overy, "Nuremberg Trials," 28-29.
75 United Nations, Rome Statute of the International Criminal Court, 17 July 1998, UN Doc. A/CONF.183./9 (hereafter Rome Statute).
76 Rome Statue, overview.
77 McGoldrick, "Criminal Trials," 10-11.
78 Simpson, "Politics, Sovereignty, and Remembrance," 60.
79 Rome Statute, art. 17.
80 Crawford, "Drafting of the Rome Statute," 113.
81 Rome Statute, arts. 85-102.
82 Ibid., art. 5.

83 Ibid., art. 5(2).

84 International Criminal Court, Assembly of States Parties, "The States Parties to the Rome Statute," http://www.icc-cpi.int/statesparties.html.

85 Nigel Dower, *An Introduction to Global Citizenship* (Edinburgh: Edinburgh University Press, 2003), 66.

86 Rome Statute, art. 25.

87 Cassese, *International Criminal Law*, 22.

88 Simpson, "Politics, Sovereignty, and Remembrance," 51.

89 Broomhall, *International Justice*, 59.

90 For example, see United Nations, *A More Secure World: Our Shared Responsibility*, Report of the Secretary-General's High Level Panel on Threats, Challenges and Change, 2004, http://www.un.org/secureworld/report3.pdf.

91 International Commission on Intervention and State Sovereignty, *The Responsibility to Protect* (Ottawa: International Development Research Centre, 2001), http://www.iciss.ca/menu-en.asp.

92 David Wippman, "The International Criminal Court," in *The Politics of International Law*, ed. Christian Reus-Smit (Cambridge: Cambridge University Press, 2004), 187.

93 David Held, "From Executive to Cosmopolitan Democracy," in *Taming Globalization: Frontiers of Governance*, ed. David Held and Mathias Koenig-Archibugi (Cambridge: Polity, 2003), 185.

Chapter 11: The US-Led Globalization Project in the Third World

1 Ian Taylor, "Globalisation Studies and the Developing World: Making International Political Economy Truly Global," *Third World Quarterly* 26, 7 (2005): 1025-42. For the lack of attention to the Third World in historical studies of the Cold War, see Odd Arne Westad, *The Global Cold War: Third World Interventions and the Making of Our Times* (New York: Cambridge University Press, 2005). On the need to begin scrutinizing US-Third World relations through the lens of globalization, see Dennis Merrill, "Conceptualizing the Third World: Language, Theory, and Method," *Diplomatic History* 26, 2 (2002): 323.

2 For an explanation of the "US-led globalization project" and its origins, see Mark T. Berger, *The Battle for Asia: From Decolonization to Globalization* (New York: Routledge Curzon, 2004), 25n3, 37-60.

3 John F. Kennedy, "Special Message to the Congress on Foreign Aid," 22 March 1961, *Public Papers of the President: John F. Kennedy,* http://www.presidency.ucsb.edu/ws/index.php?pid=8545&st=&st1=.

4 Mark H. Haefele, "Walt Rostow's Stages of Economic Growth: Ideas and Action," in *Staging Growth: Modernization, Development, and the Global Cold War*, ed. David C. Engerman (Amherst: University of Massachusetts Press, 2003), 81.

5 Jan Aart Scholte, *Globalization: A Critical Introduction*, 2nd ed. (Basingstoke: Palgrave Macmillan, 2005), 101-20.

6 David Ryan, "By Way of Introduction: The United States, Decolonization and the World System," in *The United States and Decolonization: Power and Freedom*, ed. David Ryan and Victor Pungong (New York: St. Martin's Press, 2000), 15; Ian Clark, *Globalization and Fragmentation: International Relations in the Twentieth Century* (New York: Oxford University Press, 1997), 142-45; Robbie Robertson, *The Three Waves of Globalization: A History of a Developing Global Consciousness* (London: Zed, 2002), 11.

7 Robert McNamara, "United States Policy in Vietnam," *Department of State Bulletin* 50 (13 April 1964): 565; Townsend Hoopes, *The Limits of Intervention: An Inside Account of How the Johnson Policy of Escalation in Vietnam Was Reversed* (New York: David McKay Co., 1969), 14-16.

8 Emily S. Rosenberg, *Spreading the American Dream: American Economic and Cultural Expansion, 1890-1945* (New York: Hill and Wang, 1982), 7.

9 Paul Bairoch, *Economics and World History: Myths and Paradoxes* (New York: Harvester Wheatsheaf, 1993), 32.

10 Mark Berger, "Decolonisation, Modernisation and Nation-Building: Political Development and the Appeal of Communism in Southeast Asia, 1945-1975," *Journal of Southeast Asian Studies* 34, 3 (2003): 422. For other historical antecedents of liberal developmentalism, see the essay by Ron Pruessen in this volume.

11 Walt W. Rostow, *The Stages of Economic Growth: A Non-Communist Manifesto* (Cambridge: Cambridge University Press, 1960).

12 Walt W. Rostow, "Guerrilla Warfare in the Underdeveloped Areas," *Department of State Bulletin* 45 (7 August 1961): 234.

13 Haefele, "Walt Rostow's Stages of Economic Growth," 86-88. On the connection between modernization theory and neoliberal globalization, see Nils Gilman, *Mandarins of the Future: Modernization Theory in Cold War America* (Baltimore, MD: Johns Hopkins University Press, 2003), 241-76.

14 Robert S. McNamara, *The Essence of Security* (New York: Harper and Row, 1968), 149.

15 Arturo Escobar, *Encountering Development: The Making and Unmaking of the Third World* (Princeton, NJ: Princeton University Press, 1995); Michael E. Latham, *Modernization as Ideology: American Social Science and "Nation-Building" in the Kennedy Era* (Chapel Hill: University of North Carolina Press, 2000).

16 Marc Frey, "Tools of Empire: Persuasion and the United States' Modernizing Mission in Southeast Asia," *Diplomatic History* 27, 4 (2003): 558.

17 Robert D. Dean, "Masculinity as Ideology: John F. Kennedy and the Domestic Politics of Foreign Policy," *Diplomatic History* 22, 1 (1998): 52. On Kennedy's fascination with guerrilla warfare as part of the "macho hubris of the era," see David Halberstam, *The Best and the Brightest* (New York: Random House, 1972), 122-23.

18 For a careful exploration of the links between war and globalization, see Paul James and Jonathan Friedman, "Globalizing War: A Critical Introduction," in *Globalization and Violence*, vol. 3, *Globalizing War and Intervention*, ed. Paul James and Tom Nairn (London: Sage, 2006), ix-xxxii. On the need for war to promote free trade and neoliberal globalization, see Tarak Barkawi, *Globalization and War* (Lanham: Rowman and Littlefield, 2006); Sohan Sharma and Surinder Kumar, "The Military Backbone of Globalisation," *Race and Class* 44, 3 (2003): 23-39.

19 For a useful definition of peasant autonomy, see Timothy Wickham-Crowley, *Exploring Revolution: Essays on Latin American Insurgency and Revolutionary Theory* (Armonk, NY: M.E. Sharpe, 1991), 176-77.

20 John Gerassi, ed., *Venceremos: The Speeches and Writings of Che Guevara* (New York: Macmillan, 1968), 289; Che Guevara, "Vietnam Must Not Stand Alone," *New Left Review* 43 (May-June 1967): 87; Manuel Piñeiro Losada, ed., *Che Guevara and the Latin American Revolutionary Movements* (Melbourne: Ocean Press, 2006).

21 For examples of contemporary studies, see Thomas Melville and Marjorie Melville, *Guatemala — Another Vietnam?* (Harmondsworth: Penguin, 1971) and Victor Perera, "Guatemala: Always La Violencia," *New York Times Magazine*, 13 June 1971. For examples of

scholarly comparisons, see Jeffrey Paige, "Social Theory and Peasant Revolution in Vietnam and Guatemala," *Theory and Society* 12, 6 (1983): 639-737, and Eric R. Wolf, *Peasant Wars of the Twentieth Century* (New York: Harper and Row, 1999).

22 Gerassi, ed., *Venceremos*, 286.

23 The Vietminh was a revolutionary organization formed by Ho Chi Minh in 1941 to liberate Vietnam from the Japanese occupation and French colonialism.

24 On the Guatemalan guerrillas contacts with Cuba, see Julio César Macías, *La guerrilla fue mi camino: Epitafio para César Montes* (Guatemala: Editorial Piedra Santa Arandi, 1999), 67-68, 78-81, 93-97, 112-15, 124, 176-80. On Soviet and Chinese assistance to North Vietnam, see Ilya V. Gaiduk, *Confronting Vietnam: Soviet Policy toward the Indochina Conflict, 1954-1963* (Washington, DC: Woodrow Wilson Center Press, 2003); Mari Olsen, *Soviet-Vietnam Relations and the Role of China, 1949-64: Changing Alliances* (New York: Routledge, 2006).

25 Gabriel Kolko, *Anatomy of a War: Vietnam, the United States, and the Modern Historical Experience* (New York: Pantheon, 1985), 18-21.

26 Paul J. Dosal, *Power in Transition: The Rise of Guatemala's Industrial Oligarchy, 1871-1994* (New York: Praeger, 1995).

27 US Department of the Army, *Area Handbook for Vietnam* (Washington, DC, 1962), 53. This is not to say, of course, that indigenous peoples living in Vietnam were not gravely affected by the war. See Mark W. McLeon, "Indigenous Peoples and the Vietnamese Revolution, 1930-1975," *Journal of World History* 10, 2 (1999): 353-89. For a Guatemalan guerrilla view of the differences between Guatemala and Vietnam regarding indigenous peoples, see Rolando Morán, *Entrevistas al comandante en jefe del Ejército Guerrillero de los Pobres, Rolando Morán* (Guatemala: El Ejército, 1982), 7-8, 23-24.

28 I use the less pejorative term *National Liberation Front* to represent the revolutionary organization in South Vietnam that the Americans referred to as the "Viet Cong."

29 According to various journalists, up to one thousand Green Berets operated in Guatemala during the 1960s. Official US sources admit only that a handful of Green Berets participated in special military-training teams in Guatemala.

30 Stephen M. Streeter, *Managing the Counterrevolution: The United States and Guatemala, 1954-1961* (Athens: Ohio University Press, 2000), 3. On casualties inflicted by the Vietnam War, see Charles Hirschman, Samuel Preston, and Vu Manh Loi, "Vietnamese Casualties During the American War: A New Estimate," *Population and Development Review* 21 (December 1995): 783-812.

31 Michael Adas, "A Colonial War in a Postcolonial Era: The United States' Occupation of Vietnam," in *America, the Vietnam War, and the World: Comparative and International Perspectives,* ed. Andreas W. Daum, Lloyd C. Gardner, and Wilfried Mausbach (New York: Cambridge University Press, 2003), 32-35; James L. Gibson, *The Perfect War: The War We Couldn't Lose and How We Did* (New York: Vintage Books, 1988).

32 Quoted in Stephen G. Rabe, *The Most Dangerous Area in the World: John F. Kennedy Confronts Communist Revolution in Latin America* (Chapel Hill: University of North Carolina Press, 1999), 2.

33 US Department of State, "United States Economic Assistance to South Viet Nam, 1954-1975: An Overview," 14 October 1975, Texas Tech Virtual Vietnam Archive, item 2390111001, http://star.vietnam.ttu.edu/virtualarchive/ (hereafter TTVVA followed by item number).

34 Quoted in Chester L. Cooper, *The Lost Crusade: America in Vietnam* (New York: Dodd, Mead, 1970), 168.

35 John Mecklin, *Mission in Torment: An Intimate Account of the US Role in Vietnam* (Garden City, NY: Doubleday, 1965), 20; Streeter, *Managing the Counterrevolution,* 137-63.

36 Nolting, telegram to Department of State, 5 April 1963, in US Department of State, *Foreign Relations of the United States, 1961-1963,* vol. 3 (Washington, DC: US Government Printing Office, 1991), doc. 81.

37 David W.P. Elliott, "Hanoi's Strategy in the Second Indochina War," in *The Vietnam War: Vietnamese and American Perspectives,* ed. Jayne Susan Werner and Luu Doan Huynh (Armonk, NY: M.E. Sharpe, 1993), 75.

38 Memorandum of conversation (Daspit, Post, Corrigan, Bell, Unda Murillo), 12 July 1963, US National Archives, RG 286, entry 167, box 10, folder "Guatemala FY 64." Author interviews with US AID officers William Bradford, Donald Fiester, and Peter Tobia, 1991.

39 John O'Donnell and Harvey C. Neese, eds., *Prelude to Tragedy: Vietnam, 1960-1965* (Annapolis, MD: Naval Institute Press, 2001), 33-37.

40 Susanne Jonas and David Tobis, *Guatemala* (New York: North American Congress on Latin America, 1974), 201.

41 Roy L. Prosterman and Jeffrey M. Riedinger, *Land Reform and Democratic Development* (Baltimore, MD: Johns Hopkins University Press, 1987), 7-33; Paige, "Social Theory"; Kolko, *Anatomy of a War,* 126.

42 Quoted in Gary L. Olson, *US Foreign Policy and the Third World Peasant: Land Reform in Asia and Latin America* (New York: Praeger, 1974), 104.

43 Streeter, *Managing the Counterrevolution,* 150-55.

44 Richard Hough et al., *Land and Labor in Guatemala: An Assessment* (Washington, DC: US Agency for International Development, 1982), 34.

45 For official US assessments of the strategic hamlet program, see US Department of State, *Foreign Relations of the United States, 1961-1963.* For the Vietnamese side, see Philip E. Catton, *Diem's Final Failure: Prelude to America's War in Vietnam* (Lawrence: University Press of Kansas, 2003).

46 Stephen Streeter, "Nation-Building in the Land of Eternal Counterinsurgency: Guatemala and the Contradictions of the Alliance for Progress," *Third World Quarterly* 27, 1 (2006): 57-68.

47 Deputy Secretary of Defense, memorandum to JFK, 3 May 1961, in US Department of State, *Foreign Relations of the United States, 1961-1963,* vol. 1, doc. 42. More than one observer noticed the similarity between the pacification programs in Guatemala and Vietnam. For an example, see N. Diamond, "Why They Shoot Americans," *Nation* 206 (5 February 1968): 166-67.

48 Eric M. Bergerud, *The Dynamics of Defeat: The Vietnam War in Hau Nghia Province* (Boulder, CO: Westview Press, 1991), 15-16, 268-72; Richard A. Hunt, *Pacification: The American Struggle for Vietnam's Hearts and Minds* (Boulder, CO: Westview Press, 1995), 36-38; David W.P. Elliott, *The Vietnamese War: Revolution and Social Change in the Mekong Delta* (Armonk, NY: M.E. Sharpe, 2003), 189.

49 Larry E. Cable, *Conflict of Myths: The Development of American Counterinsurgency Doctrine and the Vietnam War* (New York: New York University Press, 1988); Michael E. Latham, "Redirecting the Revolution? The USA and the Failure of Nation-Building in South Vietnam," *Third World Quarterly* 27, 1 (2006): 27-41.

50 Doris Kearns Goodwin, *Lyndon Johnson and the American Dream* (New York: Harper and Row, 1976), 267. For more on the faulty assumptions made by US officials in Vietnam, see William Rosenau, *US Internal Security Assistance to South Vietnam: Insurgency, Subversion, and Public Order* (New York: Routledge, 2005).

51 "Study in Anticipation of a Crisis in Guatemala," 21 April 1969, National Security Archive, George Washington University, Washington, DC.

52 Hilsman, memorandum to Secretary of State, 14 March 1964, in US Department of State, *Foreign Relations of the United States, 1964-1968*, vol. 1 (Washington, DC: US Government Printing Office, 1992), doc. 90.

53 Mecklin, *Mission in Torment*, 76-78.

54 Homer Bigart, "A 'Very Real War' in Vietnam," *New York Times*, 25 February 1962.

55 Robert Michael Pearce, *The Insurgent Environment* (Santa Monica, CA: RAND, 1969), 103.

56 David Stoll, *Between Two Armies in the Ixil Towns of Guatemala* (New York: Columbia University Press, 1993).

57 David Hunt, "Images of the Viet Cong," in *The United States and Viet Nam from War to Peace: Papers from an Interdisciplinary Conference on Reconciliation*, ed. Robert M. Slabey (Jefferson, NC: McFarland and Co., 1996), 59.

58 Quoted in Gilbert N. Dorland, *Legacy of Discord: Voices of the Vietnam War Era* (Washington, DC: Brassey's, 2001), 85.

59 For a possible explanation of why the RAND interviewers became more sympathetic to the Vietnamese revolutionaries after 1968, see David Hunt, "Revolution in the Delta," *Critical Asian Studies* 35, 4 (2003): 601.

60 RAND Corporation, "Viet Cong Motivation and Morale in 1964: A Preliminary Report," 1964, TTVVA, item 2311701004; John C. Donnell, *Viet Cong Recruitment: Why and How Men Join* (Santa Monica, CA: RAND, 1967); Robert K. Brigham, *ARVN: Life and Death in the South Vietnamese Army* (Lawrence: University Press of Kansas, 2006), 17-18.

61 Kolko, *Anatomy*, 194.

62 Maxwell Taylor, "The Current Situation in South Viet-Nam — November 1964," undated, in US Department of State, *Foreign Relations of the United States, 1964-1968*, doc. 426. For examples of studies that emphasize NLF coercive tactics, see Douglas Pike, *Viet Cong: The Organization and Techniques of the National Liberation Front of South Vietnam* (Cambridge, MA: MIT Press, 1966); Nathan Leites, *The Viet Cong Style of Politics* (Santa Monica, CA: RAND, 1969; Anthony James Joes, *The War for South Viet Nam, 1954-1975*, 2nd ed. (Westport, CT: Praeger, 2001).

63 Ron Robin, *The Making of the Cold War Enemy: Culture and Politics in the Military-Intellectual Complex* (Princeton, NJ: Princeton University Press, 2001), 185-99.

64 Quoted in Andrew F. Krepinevich Jr., *The Army and Vietnam* (Baltimore, MD: Johns Hopkins University Press, 1986), 222.

65 Konrad Kellen, *Conversations with Enemy Soldiers in Late 1968/Early 1969: A Study of Motivation and Morale* (Santa Monica, CA: RAND, 1970), 56.

66 Gregory R. Clark, ed., *Quotations on the Vietnam War* (Jefferson, NC: McFarland, 2001), entry 507.

67 David Hunt, "The My Tho Grapevine and the Sino-Soviet Split," in *A Companion to the Vietnam War*, ed. Marilyn Blatt Young and Robert Buzzanco (Malden, MA: Blackwell, 2002), 79-82.

68 Robert K. Brigham, *Guerrilla Diplomacy: The NLF's Foreign Relations and the Viet Nam War* (Ithaca, NY: Cornell University Press, 1999), 17.

69 On the shift from nationalism to international Socialism among Latin American revolutionaries, see Richard Gott, *Rural Guerrillas in Latin America*, 2nd ed. (Harmondsworth, UK: Penguin, 1973), 49.

70 Adolfo Gilly, "The Guerrilla Movement in Guatemala (Part 2)," *Monthly Review* 17 (June 1965): 32.

71 César Macías, *La guerrilla fue mi camino*, 189-203.

72 Carta abierta del comandante Luis Augusto Turcios Lima a la dirección nacional del movimiento revolucionario 13 de noviembre, 6 March 1965, Thomas J. Dodd Research Center, Storrs, Connecticut, North American Congress on Latin America Archive, box 153, folder "(4) [Politics, file no. 21]."

73 Gilly, "Guerrilla Movement," 19-20.

74 Ejército Guerrillero de los Pobres, *Articles from Compañero, the International Magazine of Guatemala's Guerrilla Army of the Poor, EGP* (San Francisco, CA: Solidarity, 1982).

75 "Monthly Guerrilla Report, January 1-31," 16 February 1966, A-358, National Security Archive, George Washington University, Washington, DC.

76 John Isbister, *Promises Not Kept: Poverty and the Betrayal of Third World Development*, 6th ed. (Bloomfield, CT: Kumarian Press, 2003), 145.

77 The maquilas in Guatemala fall into the category of export-processing zones discussed by Neil White in this volume.

78 For a critical evaluation of the Vietnamese Communist Party's leadership since 1975, see Gabriel Kolko, *Vietnam: Anatomy of a Peace* (New York: Routledge, 1997). On the loss of village autonomy, see Gerald Cannon Hickey, *Window on a War: An Anthropologist in the Vietnam Conflict* (Lubbock: Texas Tech University Press, 2002), 362-63. The failure of revolutionary movements in Latin America to transcend the discourse of liberal developmentalism is described in María Josefina Saldaña-Portillo, *The Revolutionary Imagination in the Americas and the Age of Development* (Durham, NC: Duke University Press, 2003). Other thoughtful evaluations of the decolonization movements in the Third World include Gerard Chaliand, *Revolution in the Third World*, rev. ed. (New York: Penguin, 1989), 197-224; Phillip Darby, "Colonial and Postcolonial Globalizations: A Critical Introduction," in *Globalization and Violence*, vol. 2., *Colonial and Postcolonial Globalizations*, ed. Paul James and Tom Nairn (London: Sage, 2006), ix-xxxi.

79 William J. Clinton, "Remarks at Vietnam National University in Hanoi, 17 November 2000," *Public Papers of the President: William J. Clinton*, http://www.presidency.ucsb.edu/ws/index.php?pid=1038&st=&st1=.

80 Francis Fukuyama, "The End of History?" *National Interest* 16 (Summer 1989): 3-18.

81 Kay B. Warren, *Indigenous Movements and Their Critics: Pan-Maya Activism in Guatemala* (Princeton, NJ: Princeton University Press, 1999); Victor Montejo, *Maya Intellectual Renaissance: Identity, Representation, and Leadership* (Austin: University of Texas Press, 2005); June C. Nash, *Mayan Visions: The Quest for Autonomy in an Age of Globalization* (New York: Routledge, 2001).

82 Binh Tran-Nam and Chi Do Pham, *The Vietnamese Economy: Awakening the Dormant Dragon* (New York: Routledge, 2002); Hans Stockton, ed., *The Future of Development in Vietnam and the Challenges of Globalization: Interdisciplinary Essays* (Lewiston, NY: Edwin Mellen Press, 2006).

83 For a review of the literature on how peasants are challenging neoliberal globalization, see David Barkin, "Who Are the Peasants?" *Latin American Research Review* 39, 3 (2004): 270-81.

Chapter 12: A Globalizing Moment

I would like to thank Professors Abdejjabar Bsaies, Lotfi Bouzaiane, William Coleman, and Mongi Bahloul for comments on an earlier draft of this paper.

1 According to Ronald W. Pruessen's essay in this volume, the origins of this strategy date back to 1943, when President Franklin D. Roosevelt began to ponder development reforms at the Casablanca Conference.

2 Philippe Norel, *L'invention du marché: Une histoire économique de la mondialisation* (Paris: Les Editions du Seuil, 2004), translation by Yassine Essid.

3 Gérard Chaliand, *Mythes révolutionnaires du tiers-monde* (Paris: Les Editions du Seuil, 1976), 26.

4 Samir Amin, *La nation arabe* (Paris: Editions de Minuit, 1976), 31.

5 Samia El Machat, *Les États-Unis et la Tunisie: De l'ambiguïté à l'entente* (Paris: L'Harmattan, 1996), 35, 95.

6 Ronald W. Pruessen (this volume).

7 Paul Bairoch, *Révolution industrielle et sous-développement* (Paris-La Haye: Les Editions Mouton, 1974), 98-71.

8 Yves Benot, *Le sous-développement* (Paris: Les Editions Maspero, 1976), 14.

9 Through the ratios of exports and imports to GDP, one may assess the inclusion of a country in the world economy by examining, as a criterion, the degree of openness of its economy. According to data from World Development Indicators 2006, the ratio of exports to GDP for the three Maghreb countries and for the period 1965-1970 was between 20 and 23 percent, whereas in 2001 and 2004 it was between 38 and 45 percent. With regard to the import to GDP ratio, Tunisia and Morocco had a ratio of between 15 and 20 percent between 1965 and 1970, a figure that had risen to 37 percent and 49 percent, respectively, by the period 2001-4. The case of Algeria is treated separately. The second criterion is the debt burden relative to GDP, which was around 37 percent for both countries between 1971 and 1980, but rose to 45 percent in Morocco and 65 percent in Tunisia in 2001-4. By comparing these data from one period to another, it is clear that the integration of the Maghreb into the world economy occurred well after the 1960s. World Bank, *World Development Indicators 2006*, World Bank Group, http://devdata.worldbank.org/wdi2006/contents/Section2.htm, and Agnès Chevalier and Véronique Kessler, "Croissance et insertion internationale du Maghreb: Questions sur l'avenir des relations avec l'Europe," in *Maghreb: Les anées de transition*, ed. Bassma Kodmani-Darwich and May Chartouni-Dubarry (Paris: Masson, 1990), 257-67.

10 Even Socialism is based on materialism and the nineteenth-century ideology of progress. This ideology seeks to challenge the universal claims of capitalism. Yet, as a matter of obedience to Western thinking, Socialism is wedded to capitalism, and it could not fully satisfy those countries seeking a viable alternative that would not only ensure their economic development but also satisfy their thirst for an autonomous identity. Indeed, the term *economics* was born with the writings of Leon Walras, who claimed to make the study of the economy an exact science. If we consider the writings of Lionel Robbins, for whom there is no rationality other than the capitalist one, it can be argued that this trend was strengthened by the neoclassical school.

11 Sixty thousand French *Coopérants*, or technical assistants, have served in Algeria since 1962. This cooperation was of great help in addressing temporarily the lack of domestic skills.

12 The ideological currents from the Machrek have always been greeted with a degree of suspicion that has been fuelled by interference by countries in the Middle East — mainly by Nasser of Egypt, who felt that the struggles of the Maghreb should be integrated with struggles for autonomy within the wider Arab world. The reference to the Arabism *(al-qawmiyya al-arabiyya)* at Machrek is powerful and deeply rooted in a collective consciousness based on the experience of Nasserism's concrete policies. In the Maghreb, this period corresponds to the peoples' search for an understanding and reconstruction of specific national experiences.

13 Paul Balta, "Vie politique au Maghreb," in *L'État du Maghreb,* ed. Camille and Yves Lacoste (Paris: Editions la Découverte, 1991), 356–60.

14 Eric Berr and François Combarnous, "L'impact du consensus de Washington sur les pays en développement: Une évaluation empirique," Documents de travail 100, Centre d'Economie du Développement de l'Université Montesquieu Bordeaux IV.

15 A. Bedoui, "Etat et développement: Essai d'analyse de la spécificité et des limites du rôle de l'Etat en Tunisie" (Thèse de Doctorat d'Etat, Université el-Manar, 2005), 403.

16 It is true that most developing countries have chosen the path of import-substitution, which involves the importation of capital goods, but few countries, particularly Algeria, that are anxious to achieve economic independence opted for the local production of capital goods, as was the case in the Soviet Union under the first three five-year plans.

17 Michel Chauvin, *Tiers-monde: La fin des idées reçues* (Paris: Syros-Alternatives, 1991).

18 Arghiri Emmanuel, *L'échange inégal: Essai sur les antagonismes dans les rapports internationaux* (Paris: Maspero, 1975) and *Les Profits et les Crises* (Paris: Maspero, 1974); Pierre Philippe Rey, *Colonialisme, néo-colonialisme et transition vers le capitalisme* (Paris: Maspero, 1971); Samir Amin, *Le Développement inégal: Essai sur les formations sociales du capitalisme périphérique* (Paris: Editions de Minuit, 2001); Samir Amin, *Critique du capitalisme* (Paris: PUF, 2002); Charles Bettelheim, *Planification et croissance accélérée* (Paris: Maspero, 1965) and *La Transition vers l'économie socialiste* (Paris: Maspero, 1968) and *Problèmes théoriques et pratiques de la planification* (Paris, Maspero, 1970).

19 Paul Bairoch, *Le tiers-monde dans l'impasse* (Paris: Gallimard, 1971), 249.

20 Yves Fuchs, *La coopération, aide ou néo-colonialisme?* (Paris: Editions sociales, 1973); Pierre Jalée, *Le pillage du tiers monde* (Paris: Maspero, 1966).

21 As Esambert points out: "We are at a time when the Shah of Iran lays in the bed of Cyrus and Darius, while the Iraqi President is taken down for the continuation of Nebuchadnezzar, where Egyptian hieroglyphics reflect the announcement of their destiny. The French will want more than Gallic Celts, the Israelis find the rules for their behaviour in the prophecies and in the history of the Hebrew language." Bernard Esambert, *La guerre économique mondiale* (Paris: Editions Orban, 1991), 279.

22 The concept of modernity encompasses two different realities in the Maghreb and Machrek. In the Machrek countries, modernity is linked to the Arab nationality, Arabism, pan-Arab behaviour, and speaking Arabic. In the Maghreb, modernity is usually associated with Europe and the European languages, whereas a sense of the archaic is often linked to those things Arab. Bassma Kodmani-Darwish, "Mahgreb/Machrek histoire d'une relation complexe," in *Maghreb, les années de transition,* ed. Bassma Kodmani-Darwich and May Chartouni-Dubarry (Paris: Masson, 1990), 269–90.

23 Marshall Sahlins, *Âge de pierre, âge d'abondance: L'économie des sociétés primitives,* préface de P. Clastres (1972; repr., Paris: Gallimard, 1976) and *Stone Age Economics* (Paris: Aldine de Gruyter, 1972).

24 Olivier Carré, "Evolution de la pensée arabe au Proche-Orient depuis 1967," *Revue Française des sciences politiques* 23, 5 (1973): 1046-79. One must not lose sight that, for a period, Nasser's Egypt was seen as the heart and mind of Arab culture and remained a source of symbols and representations for all Arab peoples. Nasserism is first and foremost a loyalty to the man who mobilized part of the Arab elite, including those from the Maghreb, around the idea of Arab nationalism and Arab unity (a United Arab Republic was established on 1 February 1958 by the addition of Syria and Yemen). Nasser's charisma was tarnished by the breakup of the union and by the 1967 defeat of Egypt by Israel. That defeat marked the failure of Nasserism as a doctrine of pan-Arabism. In any case, his vision never found a real echo in the political and economic models of the Maghreb countries, although on the cultural level Egypt has long maintained its leadership. With the exception of Nasser's fervent disciple, Khaddafi, whose attempts at forming Arab unions have all failed, Nasser's political vision has no legacy.

25 Obviously nobody could deny the contribution of the Arabs, themselves largely dependent on inputs from other people. I am referring here to such areas as economics or sociology. Ibn Khaldun, for example, is an emblematic figure for Arab Third Worldism. He was claimed as the "father" of economics, sociology, and economic development theory. I can also mention writings about science and the Qur'an in which eminent scientists have tried to see each verse as an anticipation of modern discoveries. Some Muslims argue that the Qur'an contains scientific truths that were unknown to the men of the time (the sixth and seventh centuries AD). Those who support this view see it as an argument about the nature of the Qur'anic revealed text: if this book contains knowledge that no man of the time possessed, it is evidence that it is of divine origin. I refer here to Maurice Bucaille's *The Bible, the Quran and Science,* published by Seghers in 1976 and translated and read widely throughout the Arab and Muslim world, which has served to consolidate the confidence of Muslim people in the Qur'an as a kind of second proof, although it was more ecumenical than propaganda. Georges Antonio Saliba and Rushidi Rashid themselves express this trend, but their contribution lies in a field that is related to exact science and less subject to criticism. The magazine *Arabic Science and Philosophy,* a historical journal first published in 1991 by Cambridge University Press, is a very serious publication, but it was confined to a small circle because few people in the Arab world know the works of Rashid and Saliba.

26 Jean François Revel, *La tentation totalitaire* (Paris: Laffont, 1976) and *Ni Marx ni Jésus: De la seconde révolution américaine à la seconde révolution mondiale* (Paris: Laffont, 1970); Edward F. Denison and Jean Pierre Poullier, *Why Growth Rates Differ? Postwar Experience in Nine Western Countries* (Washington, DC: Brookings Institution, 1967); Pascal Bruckner, *Les Sanglots de l'homme blanc: Tiers-monde, culpabilité, haine de soi* (Paris: Seuil, 1983); Chaliand, *Mythes révolutionnaires du tiers-monde.* Although written in the 1990s, Alain Peyrefitte's *La société de confiance* (Paris: Editions Odile Jacob, 1995) sums up the challenge to the Third World theoretical vulgate.

27 Jalée, *Le pillage du tiers monde.*

28 Alain Touraine, *Un nouveau paradigme* (Paris: Fayard, 2005), 39.

29 The Boumedienne years (1965-78) in Algeria were marked by a massive accumulation: privilege was granted to hydrocarbons and basic industries, and a dominant role was given to the state and public sector. This policy met its limits, resulting in extreme dependence on hydrocarbons and the mediocre performance of the productive sectors: increased costs of industrialization in the areas of investment and operations resulted in a sharp dependence on technology. As a result, starting in 1980, Algeria slowed the pace of investment, it made

an effort to improve existing industrial capabilities, it initiated a restructuring of public enterprises to encourage private investment, and it introduced a policy to limit external debt. Morocco had shown internal and external economic imbalances and the decline of its economy reached a negative growth rate of -1.3 percent in 1981. Its debt grew to US$18 billion in 1988. For Tunisia, the growth rate was negative in 1987.

30 François Partant, *La fin du développement: Naissance d'une alternative* (Paris: Les Editions Maspero, Cahier libres no. 373, 1982).

31 In the Maghreb, Muslim sensitivity seems to coincide with a reformism that differs from countries such as Egypt, where the first movement of radical Islam dates from the 1940s. With the failure of economic development based on Western ideological models, whether Socialist or capitalist, Islamic trends in the Maghreb strengthened by turning to their benefit the historical illegitimacy of the parties in power (like the FLN in Algeria and the PSD [Socialist Destourian Party] in Tunisia) and by introducing claims for religious legitimacy that were fed by the everyday difficulties of North African populations in Algeria and Morocco and, to a lesser extent, Tunisia. For that reason, the name "Muslim Brotherhood" is inadequate in North Africa. The movement of the Muslim Brotherhood is dated in time and localized in space. Maghreb currents of radical Islam have differed tactically and doctrinally from this Egyptian movement. See Camille and Yves Lacoste, eds., *Maghreb, peuples et civilisations* (1995; repr., Paris: La Découverte, 2004), 131-40; François Burgat, *L'islamisme en face* (Paris: La Découverte, 1995).

32 In the Maghreb, Arabization had a dual role: it was a factor in social integration and the consolidation of national unity and identity, and it ensured that the North African states would stand out from France, placing them on an equal footing with Middle Eastern countries. Arabization was conducted at an accelerated pace in Algeria, probably because this country had the greatest need to cement its unity, mainly at the expense of the Tamazight language.

33 F. Nahavandi, "Développement et globalisation," in *Globalisation et néolibéralisme dans le tiers-monde*, ed. F. Nahavandi (Paris: L'Harmattan, 2000), 9-27.

34 John Williamson, "What Should the World Bank Think about the Washington Consensus?" *The World Bank Research Observer* 15, 2 (2000): 254.

35 *Al-Hayat*, 13 February 2004.

36 Bruce Bueno de Mesquita and George W. Downs, "Richer but Not Freer," *Foreign Affairs* 84, 5 (2005): 77.

Chapter 13: Snakes That Are Rainbows

1 The passages in italics are from Deborah Bird Rose's account of the Yarralin community's mythology of the Rainbow Snake as harbinger and creator in *Dingo Makes Us Human: Life and Land in an Aboriginal Australian Culture* (Cambridge: Cambridge University Press, 1992), 98.

2 John R. Searle, *The Construction of Social Reality* (New York: Free Press, 1995), 13-23.

3 Searle, *Construction of Social Reality*.

4 Ibid., 27-29.

5 James Fearon and Alexander Wendt, "Rationalism v. Constructivism: A Skeptical View," in *Handbook of International Relations*, ed. Walter Carlsnaes, Thomas Risse-Kappen, and Beth A. Simmons (London: Sage, 2002), 52-72; John Gerard Ruggie, "International Responses to Technology: Concepts and Trends," *International Organization* 29, 3 (1975): 557-

83, and *Constructing the World Polity: Essays on International Institutionalization* (London: Routledge, 1998); Vivienne Kondos and Gillian Cowlishaw, "Introduction: Conditions of Possibility," *TAJA (The Australian Journal of Anthropology)* 8, 1 (1995): 1-14.

6 Peter L. Berger and Thomas Luckmann, *The Social Construction of Reality: A Treatise in the Sociology of Knowledge* (Garden City, NY: Doubleday, 1966), 20.

7 L.R. Hiatt, *Arguments about Aborigines: Australia and the Evolution of Social Anthropology* (Cambridge: Cambridge University Press, 1996), 115-19.

8 Ronald M. Berndt and Catherine H. Berndt, *The World of the First Australians* (Adelaide: Rigby Press, 1985), 230.

9 Ibid., 336.

10 Ian Keen, *Aboriginal Economy and Society: Australia at the Threshold of Colonisation* (South Melbourne, Victoria: Oxford University Press, 2004), 210.

11 Ibid., 229-31.

12 Ibid., 261.

13 Michael Jackson, *At Home in the World* (Durham, NC: Duke University Press, 1995).

14 Fred R. Myers, *Pintupi Country, Pintupi Self: Sentiment, Place, and Politics among Western Desert Aborigines*, Smithsonian Series in Ethnographic Inquiry (Washington/Canberra: Smithsonian Institution Press/Australian Institute of Aboriginal Studies, 1986), 47.

15 Ibid., 49-50.

16 Ibid., 55-56.

17 Cited in Hiatt, *Arguments about Aborigines*, 94-97.

18 Myers, *Pintupi Country*, 69.

19 Ibid., 70.

20 The arguments about different accounts of human origins have, to a considerable extent, "obscured the *modus vivendi* to which religious people and scientists generally subscribed": C.A. Bayly, *The Birth of the Modern World, 1780-1914: Global Connections and Comparisons*, The Blackwell History of the World (Malden, MA: Blackwell, 2004), 363. See also Sara Sohmer, "The Melanesian Mission and Victorian Anthropology," in *Darwin's Laboratory: Evolutionary Theory and Natural History in the Pacific*, ed. Roy M. MacLeod and Philip F. Rehbock (Honolulu: University of Hawaii Press, 1994), 317-18, and Niels Gunson, "British Missionaries and Their Contribution to Science in the Pacific Islands," also in *Darwin's Laboratory*, 287-88.

21 C.A. Bayly, "The British and Indigenous Peoples, 1760-1860: Power, Perception and Identity," in *Empire and Others: British Encounters with Indigenous Peoples, 1600-1850*, ed. M.J. Daunton and Rick Halpern (Philadelphia: University of Pennsylvania Press, 1999), 33-34.

22 Bayly, *Birth of the Modern World*, 330.

23 Catherine Hall, "William Knibb and the Constitution of the New Black Subject," in *Empire and Others: British Encounters with Indigenous Peoples, 1600-1850*, ed. M.J. Daunton and Rick Halpern (Philadelphia: University of Pennsylvania Press, 1999), 305.

24 Henry Richard Fox Bourne, *The Aborigines Protection Society: Chapters in Its History* (London: P.S. King and Son, 1899), 3.

25 Bain Attwood, *The Making of the Aborigines* (Sydney: Allen and Unwin, 1989) and *Rights for Aborigines* (Sydney: Allen and Unwin, 2003); Heather Goodall, *Invasion to Embassy: Land in Aboriginal Politics in New South Wales, 1770-1972* (St. Leonards, NSW: Allen and Unwin, in association with Black Books, 1996).

26 Attwood, *Rights for Aborigines*, 8.

27 Andrew Markus, *Governing Savages* (Sydney: Allen and Unwin, 1990), 72.

28 Attwood, *Rights for Aborigines*, 8.

29 Irene Watson, *Looking at You Looking at Me: An Aboriginal History of the South-East of South Australia* (Nairne, SA: I. Watson, 2002), 89-93; Attwood, *Making of the Aborigines*, xi, 7-25. For the most detailed account of the imposition of global moral prescriptions for missionary architecture and design and for indigenous clothing and mobility, see the Comaroffs' study of South African missions in the second half of the nineteenth century: Jean Comaroff and John L. Comaroff, *Of Revelation and Revolution*, vol. 2, *The Dialectics of Modernity on a South African Frontier* (Chicago: University of Chicago Press, 1997), 275-322.

30 Attwood, *Rights for Aborigines*, 28.

31 From a letter dated 23 August 1936 to *The Ladder*, cited in Andrew Markus, "After the Outward Appearance: Scientists, Administrators and Politicians," in *All That Dirt, Aborigines 1938: An Australia 1938 Monograph*, ed. Bill Gammage and Andrew Markus (Canberra: History Project Incorporated, Australian National University, 1982), 83. See also the World Council of Churches, *Justice for Aboriginal Australians: Report of the World Council of Churches Team Visit to the Aborigines, June 15 to July 3, 1981* (Sydney: Australian Council of Churches, 1981) and the account of indigenous theologian Djiniyihi Gondarra in Henry Reynolds, *Dispossession: Black Australians and White Invaders* (Sydney: Allen and Unwin, 1989), 180-81.

32 Markus, *Governing Savages*, 180.

33 Attwood, *Rights for Aborigines*, 6-7; M.F. Christie, *Aborigines in Colonial Victoria, 1835-86* (Sydney: Sydney University Press, 1979), 168; Goodall, *Invasion to Embassy*.

34 Ravi de Costa, "Identity, Authority and the Moral Worlds of Indigenous Petitions," *Comparative Studies in Society and History* 46, 3 (2006): 669-98.

35 Bain Attwood and Andrew Markus, eds., *The Struggle for Aboriginal Rights: A Documentary History* (St. Leonards, NSW: Allen and Unwin, 1999), 38-39.

36 Attwood, *Rights for Aborigines*, 28-30.

37 Attwood, *Rights for Aborigines*; Bain Attwood and Andrew Markus, *Thinking Black: William Cooper and the Australian Aborigines' League* (Canberra, ACT: Aboriginal Studies Press, 2004); de Costa, "Identity, Authority, and Moral Worlds of Indigenous Petitions"; Andrew Markus, "William Cooper and the 1937 Petition to the King," *Aboriginal History* 7, 1 (1983): 46-60; Andrew Markus and Monash University, Department of History, *Blood from a Stone: William Cooper and the Australian Aborigines' League* (Clayton, Victoria: Dept. of History, Monash University, 1986).

38 Attwood, *Making of the Aborigines*, 102. Another indicator was the franchise. Although the size of the indigenous voting population was never significant in the nineteenth century, recently historians have argued that "such slender opportunities as were offered to Aborigines to participate in settler political processes went to mission-trained men," Julie Evans et al., *Equal Subjects, Unequal Rights: Indigenous Peoples in British Settler Colonies, 1830-1910* (Manchester: Manchester University Press, 2003), 83.

39 Goodall, *Invasion to Embassy*, 76-79.

40 Andrew Bank, "Losing Faith in the Civilizing Mission: The Premature Decline of Humanitarian Liberalism at the Cape, 1840-60," in *Empire and Others: British Encounters with Indigenous Peoples, 1600-1850*, ed. M.J. Daunton and Rick Halpern (Philadelphia: University of Pennsylvania Press, 1999), 364-83.

41 J.R. Miller, *Skyscrapers Hide the Heavens: A History of Indian-White Relations in Canada*, 3rd ed. (Toronto: University of Toronto Press, 2000); John Chesterman, *Civil Rights: How Indigenous Australians Won Formal Equality* (St. Lucia, QLD: University of Queensland Press, 2005).

42 On the distinction between settler states and resource states, see Juergen Osterhammel, *Colonialism: A Theoretical Overview* (Princeton, NJ: Markus Wiener Publishers, 1997).

43 Attwood, *Rights for Aborigines*, 340.

44 Transcript of *First in Line* program, 22 August 1989, cited in Coral Dow, "Aboriginal Tent Embassy: Icon or Eyesore?" 4 April 2000, Parliament of Australia, Parliamentary Library, http://www.aph.gov.au/library/pubs/chron/1999-2000/2000chro3.htm.

45 Roberta B. Sykes, *Black Majority* (Hawthorn, Victoria: Hudson Publishing, 1989), 163.

46 Scott Robinson, "The Aboriginal Embassy: An Account of the Protests of 1972," *Aboriginal History* 18, 1 (1994): 49-63.

47 *The Age*, 14 April 1995.

48 Scott Robinson, "The Aboriginal Embassy, 1972" (master's thesis, Australian National University, 1993), 54.

49 Gary Foley, "The Aboriginal Embassy, January-July 1972," The Koori History Website, http://www.kooriweb.org/foley/images/history/1970s/emb72/embassydx.html.

50 The Tent Embassy remained for many months, despite repeated police interference. At the end of 1972, the newly elected Labor government enacted a suite of reforms in indigenous affairs, including the creation of a land rights regime in which non-alienable title would be vested in traditional indigenous communities and managed by new indigenous-run land councils. See Edward Gough Whitlam, *The Whitlam Government, 1972-1975* (Ringwood, Victoria: Viking, 1985).

51 Greg Cowan, "Nomadic Resistance: Tent Embassies and Collapsible Architecture, Illegal Architecture and Protest," Koori History Website, http://www.kooriweb.org/foley/images/history/1970s/emb72/embarchit.htm.

52 Marilyn Lake, *Faith: Faith Bandler, Gentle Activist* (Crows Nest, NSW: Allen and Unwin, 2002), 140.

53 Robinson, *Aboriginal History*, 53. Note that the correct name of the organization is the Indian Claims Commission, not the Canadian Claims Commission.

54 Bruce McGuinness, "Going International — Handle with Care!" *Identity* 3, 11 (1979): n.p.

55 Thomas Friedman, "It's a Flat World, After All," *New York Times Magazine*, 3 April 2005, 35.

56 Jan Aart Scholte, *Globalization: A Critical Introduction*, 2nd ed. (New York: Palgrave Macmillan, 2005).

Chapter 14: Globalization and US Empire

1 Henry Kissinger, *Diplomacy* (New York: Simon and Schuster, 1994), 790. In addition to Kissinger's book, information for this narrative is drawn primarily from Michael Mandelbaum and Strobe Talbott, *Reagan and Gorbachev* (New York: Vintage Books, 1987); Jason Manning, "Reykjavik," *The Eighties Club: The Politics and Pop Culture of the 1980s*, 2000, http://eightiesclub.tripod.com/id322.htm; and George P. Schultz, *Turmoil and Triumph: My Years as Secretary of State* (New York: Charles Scribner's Sons, 1993).

2 Manning, "Reykjavik."

3 Kissinger, *Diplomacy*, 790.

4 Ibid., 791.

5 Manning, "Reykjavik."

6 Ibid.

7 Manning, "Reykjavik."

8 Kissinger, *Diplomacy*, 787; Strobe Talbott, *Deadly Gambits: The Reagan Administration and the Stalemate in Nuclear Arms Control* (New York: Vintage Books, 1985).

9 Fred Halliday, *The Making of the Second Cold War* (London: Verso, 1983).

10 George Kennan, "The Sources of Soviet Conduct," *Foreign Affairs* 25 (July 1947): 566-82; Thomas Bodenheimer and Robert Gould, *Rollback! Right-Wing Power in US Foreign Policy* (Cambridge, MA: South End Press, 1989). At the time, there was a heated strategic debate between advocates of containment and proponents of rollback — the former being the "moderates" and the latter the "radical conservatives." In light of historical developments, however, it seems more sensible to regard the two policies as consecutive phases in the struggle to overcome the barriers that the Soviet regime posed to the expansion of US hegemony.

11 Kissinger, *Diplomacy*, 790.

12 Ibid.

13 "Reagan Proposes US Seek New Way to Block Missiles," *New York Times*, 24 March 1983: A20.

14 Kissinger, *Diplomacy*, 778.

15 CNN Interactive, The Reagan-Gorbachev transcripts, Reykjavik, Iceland, 11-16 October 1986, *Cold War*, episode 22, "Star Wars," 2004, http://www.cnn.com/specials/cold.war/ episodes/22/documents/reykjavik.

16 Ibid., 4.

17 See also Frances Fitzgerald, *Way Out There in The Blue: Reagan, Star Wars and the End of the Cold War* (New York: Simon and Schuster, 2000); Richard Pipes, "How to Cope with the Soviet Threat: A Long-Term Strategy for the West," *Commentary* 78, 2 (1984): 13-14. From the Soviet perspective, the credibility of the SDI threat was no doubt enhanced by the recent precedent of the zero option conflict and the unsettling realization that the Americans/NATO actually meant business. On the other hand, the fact that SDI, unlike Pershing and Cruise missiles, was not an operational system but in its early stages of development should not lead to the erroneous conclusion that it was all an American bluff that could have been called by a more astute political negotiator than Gorbachev. It is the other way around. The effectiveness of the partly fictitious Star Wars weapon in the US negotiating arsenal highlights the precariousness of the Soviet situation in military and economic terms. The Soviet leadership, therefore, needed only this final push over the brink to realize that the factual systemic incommensurability, the "imbalance of power," and hence the vulnerability of the Soviet position was too glaring to be ignored, SDI notwithstanding.

18 CNN Interactive, The Reagan-Gorbachev transcripts, Reykjavik.

19 Kissinger, *Diplomacy*, 778.

20 Manning, "Reykjavik," 3.

21 History Central, "World History 1986-87," 2000. http://www.multied.com/dates/1986. html.

22 Kissinger, *Diplomacy*, 794.

23 Of course, there were other historical and domestic factors that affected the disintegration of the Soviet Union. See, for instance, Alexander Dallin and Gail W. Lapidus, eds., *The Soviet System: From Crisis to Collapse*, rev. ed. (Boulder, CO: Westview, 1991), and Geoffrey Hosking and Robert Service, eds., *Reinterpreting Russia* (New York: Oxford University Press, 1999). The nuclear arms race between the United States and Russia continues however, and subsequent agreements and treaties (such as the 2002 Moscow Treaty on Strategic Offensive Reductions) have followed a predictable trajectory of ever-expanding

US predominance (US withdrawal from the Comprehensive Test Ban Treaty in 1999 and continued testing of the missile defense system), while at the same time trying to force the terms of the Anti-Ballistic Missile Treaty on Russia. See Walter LaFeber, *America, Russia and the Cold War, 1945-1996* (New York: McGraw-Hill, 2001); James Putzel, "The 'New' Imperialism and Possibilities for Coexistence" (Discussion Paper 2, Crisis States Programme, LSE, Development Studies Institute, London, 2004); Angela A. Stent, "Russia: Farewell to Empire?" *World Policy Journal* 19 (Fall 2002): 83-89.

24 A virtual discussion organized by the Globalization and Autonomy project, spring 2003. The first paragraphs of this section follow my analysis in "The Forces Driving Globalization: Modalities, Actors and Processes," in *Jorden runt igen – Nya bidrag till en gammal globalhistoria* [Around the world again — New contributions to an old global history], ed. Arne Jarrick and Alf Johansson (Stockholm: Almqvist and Wiksell, 2004), 134-35.

25 Jan Aart Scholte, "What is Globalization? The Definition Issue – Again" (Working Paper Series, Institute on Globalization and the Human Condition, McMaster University, Hamilton, Ontario, 2003).

26 Ulf Hedetoft, *The Global Turn: National Encounters with the World* (Aalborg: Aalborg University Press, 2003) and "The Forces Driving Globalization"; Michael Mann, "Has Globalization Ended the Rise and Rise of the Nation-State?" *Review of International Political Economy* 4, 3 (1997): 472-96, and *Incoherent Empire* (London: Verso, 2003); Øyvind Østerud, *Globaliseringen og nasjonalstaten* [Globalization and the nation state] (Oslo: Universitetsforlaget, 1999).

27 Michael Hardt and Antonio Negri, *Empire* (Cambridge, MA: Harvard University Press, 2000); David Harvey, *The New Imperialism* (Oxford: Oxford University Press, 2003); Michael Ignatieff, *Blood and Belonging* (London: Chatto and Windus, 1993); Robert Kagan, *Paradise and Power: America and Europe in the New World Order* (London: Atlantic Books, 2003); Joseph S. Nye, *The Paradox of American Power: Why the World's Only Superpower Can't Go It Alone* (Oxford: Oxford University Press, 2002); Emmanuel Todd, *After the Empire: The Breakdown of the American Order*, trans. C. Jon Delogu (New York: Columbia University Press, 2003).

28 In this context, *autonomy* refers to political units that possess the freedom and space to govern, manage, act, and possibly participate in or be consulted about rule making, but only in conditions ultimately determined by an extraneous and dominant agency (or agencies). The implication is that the autonomy of states can be extended as their sovereignty is limited or neutralized.

29 "Interests" in this chapter are not taken to be static, let alone essentialist features of contemporary statehood; they are not determined once and for all, but are in a constant process of interpretation and adaptation by political actors and institutions within limits set by economic, political, diplomatic, and historical considerations, by the "bounded rationality" of international competition and cooperation, and by path dependencies determined by ideas, institutions, and perceptions of identity. They are constructed, but not arbitrary; they are changeable, but within limits. In this (discursive and reflexive) sense, they are extremely real and, once defined and pursued as political preferences, have tangible outcomes and consequences, which tend, in turn, to define goals, instruments, and limits of the doable. In other words, the fact that interests are in theory changeable does not mean that they do change significantly in historical practice. The argumentative tenor of this contribution is that American interests in the domain under scrutiny have been relatively permanent in the postwar period, but they have been subject to changing instruments of deployment and have entered into varying configurations of realism and idealism

(discussed further below). See also Seyom Brown, *Faces of Power: Constancy and Change in United States Foreign Policy from Truman to Clinton* (New York: Columbia University Press, 1994); Peter Trubowitz, *Defining the National Interest: Conflict and Change in American Foreign Policy* (Chicago: University of Chicago Press, 1998). For a neoconservative reading of American interests informed by idealist principles of a just international order, see William Kristol and Robert Kagan, "National Interest and Global Responsibility," in *The Neocon Reader,* ed. Irwin Stelzer (New York: Grove Press, 2004), 57-74.

30 James Mittelman, *The Globalization Syndrome* (Princeton, NJ: Princeton University Press, 2000); A.G. Hopkins, ed., *Globalization in World History* (London: Pimlico, 2002).

31 Susan Strange, *The Retreat of the State: The Diffusion of Power in the World Economy* (Cambridge: Cambridge University Press, 1996); Tom Nairn, "America vs. Globalization," openDemocracy, 2003, http://www.opendemocracy.net; Charles A. Kupchan, *The End of the American Era* (New York: Alfred A. Knopf, 2003).

32 Andrew J. Bacevich, *American Empire: The Realities and Consequences of US Diplomacy* (Cambridge, MA: Harvard University Press, 2002); Stephen Howe, "American Empire: The History and Future of an Idea," openDemocracy, 2003, http://www.opendemocracy. net; Robert Hunter Wade, "The Invisible Hand of the American Empire," openDemocracy, 2003, http://www.opendemocracy.net; see also the chapters by Pruessen and Streeter in this volume.

33 Johan Galtung, *On the Coming Decline and Fall of the US Empire* (Lund: The Transnational Foundation for Peace and Future Research, 2004).

34 Bruce E. Moon, "The United States and Globalization," in *Political Economy and the Changing Global Order,* ed. Richard Stubbs and Geoffrey R.D. Underhill (Oxford: Oxford University Press, 2000), 349.

35 Terms like *unipolarity* and *multipolarity* are better thought of as metaphorical terms used to denote a unique and hierarchical pattern of global power distribution than as scientific concepts. One can certainly conceptualize a global order in which the United States enjoys dominance, even hegemony, in some domains, while still recognizing that other, though less powerful, "poles" exist.

36 Cited in John Pilger, *The New Rulers of the World* (London: Verso, 2002), 98. The implication is not that postwar US foreign policy did not entail an "idealist" component, only that it was different from today, in terms of formulation, target, and instruments. It was defined by US desires to shape a global order (in terms of institutions, loyalties, and structures of dependence) in the fields of military, political, and economic activity, and it was geared to the major task of combating the Communist menace. Permutations of US idealism in foreign policy domains serve both as the normative justification for interests in the context of *realpolitik* and as useful instruments in the pursuit of long-term goals. See also Judith Goldstein, *Ideas, Interests and the American Trade Policy* (Ithaca, NY: Cornell University Press, 1994); Louis J. Halle, *The Cold War as History* (New York: Harper and Row, 1967); Michael Hunt, *Ideology and US Foreign Policy* (New Haven, CT: Yale University Press, 1988); Michael Mandelbaum, *The Ideas that Conquered the World* (New York: Public Affairs, 2002); Robert E. Osgood, *Ideals and Self-Interest in America's Foreign Relations: The Great Transformation of the Twentieth Century* (Chicago: University of Chicago Press, 1953); William Appleman Williams, *The Tragedy of American Diplomacy* (New York: W.W. Norton, 1988).

37 Wade, *Invisible Hand,* 1.

38 Moon, "United States and Globalization," 342.

39 Ibid., 344.

40 The scope of this chapter does not permit a detailed exploration of this consistency — imperialism by design, as it may appropriately be termed — in US global policies: see Bacevich, *American Empire* and also Geir Lundestad, *"Empire" by Integration: The United States and European Integration, 1945-1997* (Oxford: Oxford University Press, 1998). But it should be noted that the concept should be envisaged primarily as a continuity in policy goals; secondarily, as discursive and action-oriented attempts to utilize, orchestrate, or engineer propitious conditions; and only then as factual initiatives to overcome significant obstacles to US power. The first implication is that "consistency" does not apply to the instruments deployed at various times; the second implication is that this perspective does not mean that everything has been (and can be) successfully pre-planned by US policy makers, who have often had to resort to "seizing the day" while taking advantage of windows of opportunity not of their own making; and the third implication is that, for the same reason, consistency does not preclude bumps along the road, occasional setbacks, contradictory relations between politics and economics, strains in external relations (for instance, in trans-Atlantic affairs), tensions between foreign and domestic policies, or generally unintended consequences of policy preferences and their outcomes. Many of these tensions, problems, paradoxes, and results have been caused by the globalist policy line – or, alternatively, their (attempted) resolution has been defined by it.

41 Putzel, "'New' Imperialism," 5.

42 Which is not to say that other countries or corporate interests of other national origins (British, Chinese, German – even Danish or Dutch) are excluded from the benefits of globalization – only that the influence and modalities of US power imply that the global order is overwhelmingly and disproportionately skewed in its favour.

43 Wade, *Invisible Hand,* 1; Joseph S. Nye, *Bound to Lead: The Changing Nature of American Power* (New York: Basic Books, 1990), *The Paradox of American Power,* and *Soft Power: The Means to Success in World Politics* (New York: Public Affairs, 2004).

44 G.W.F. Hegel, *Science of Logic,* vol. 1 (1812-16; repr., New York: Prometheus Books, 1989).

45 See, for example, Paul Hirst and Grahame Thompson, *Globalization in Question: The International Economy and the Possibilities of Governance* (Cambridge: Polity Press, 1996); Niall Ferguson, "Sinking Globalization," *Foreign Affairs* 84, 2 (2005): 64-77.

46 See Thomas W. Zeiler, *Free Trade, Free World: America and the Advent of GATT* (Chapel Hill: University of North Carolina Press, 1999).

47 Even though the UN is the institutional embodiment of internationalism, it too was shaped under the tutelage of the United States, and in its institutional structure (e.g., the composition of the Security Council and the right of veto) it still carries vestiges of this history: Stephen C. Schlesinger, *Act of Creation: The Founding of the United Nations* (Boulder, CO: Westview Press, 2003).

48 Wade, "The Invisible Hand"; US Department of Defense, *Joint Vision 2020* (Washington, DC: US Government Printing Office, 2000); *USA Patriot Act,* Public Law 107-56, *U.S. Statutes at Large* 115 Stat. 272 (2001); White House, *National Security Strategy of the United States of America,* 25 September 2002, http://www.whitehouse.gov/nsc/nss.html.

49 Charles Wolf and Brian Rosen, "Public Democracy: How to Think about and Improve It" (RAND occasional paper, Santa Monica, California, 6 October 2004).

50 Edgar Grande and Louis W. Pauly, eds., *Complex Sovereignty: Reconstituting Political Authority in the 21st Century* (Toronto: University of Toronto Press, 2005); Ulf Hedetoft, "Sovereignty Revisited: European Reconfigurations, Global Challenges, and Implications for Small States," in *Global Ordering: Institutions and Autonomy in a Changing World,* ed. Louis W. Pauly and William D. Coleman (Vancouver: UBC Press, 2008), 214-33.

51 The concepts of empire and hegemony are often used interchangeably. In this chapter, however, *empire* refers to the total capacity for "external" power projection on the part of a given state (here the US) and the structural and substantive results that impact relations between "core" and "periphery." Empire entails domination (or predominance). *Hegemony* refers to the extent to which these (neo-imperial) relations are matched by the successful absorption and acceptance of such relations of domination by the dominated peoples. *Hegemony*, in other words, refers solely to culture and ideology, whereas *empire* is a more comprehensive concept, which may or may not entail hegemonic relations. In this particular case, the transition from levels one and two (economic-financial and political-military domination) to level three (cultural hegemony) marks the most precarious moment in attempts to conflate globalization and US empire.

52 Ron Suskind, "Without a Doubt," *New York Times Magazine,* 17 October 2004. See also Ron Suskind, *The Price of Loyalty: George W. Bush, the White House, and the Education of Paul O'Neill* (New York: Simon and Schuster, 2004).

53 Niall Ferguson, *Colossus: The Price of America's Empire* (Harmondsworth: Penguin, 2004); see also William E. Odom and Robert Dujarric, *America's Inadvertent Empire* (New Haven, CT: Yale University Press, 2004).

54 Alberto Giovannini, "Bretton Woods and its Precursors: Rules versus Discretion in the History of International Monetary Regimes" (Working Paper Series, no. 4001, National Bureau of Economic Research, Washington, DC, February 1992); Scott Nearing and Joseph Freeman, *Dollar Diplomacy: A Study in American Imperialism* (New York: B.W. Huebsch and Viking Press, 1925); Georg Schild, *Bretton Woods and Dumbarton Oaks: American Economic and Political Postwar Planning in the Summer of 1944* (New York: St. Martin's Press, 1995).

55 Benjamin Cohen, "Bretton Woods System" (text prepared for the *Routledge Encyclopedia of International Political Economy,* 2004), http://www.polsci.ucsb.edu/faculty/cohen/in-press/bretton.html; Barry J. Eichengreen, *Globalizing Capital: A History of the International Monetary System* (Princeton, NJ: Princeton University Press, 1996); Richard N. Gardner, *Sterling-Dollar Diplomacy* (Oxford: Oxford University Press, 1969); Harold James, *International Monetary Cooperation since Bretton Woods* (Oxford: Oxford University Press, 1996).

56 Benjamin Cohen, *International Monetary Relations in the New Global Economy* (Cheltenham: Edward Elgar, 2004).

57 Ibid.

58 That currency pegging still goes on and is used as an instrument for gaining national trading advantages was evident in the period between 1994 and 2005, when China pegged the Yuan to the US dollar. The example further demonstrates that such behaviour is not taken lightly by the global superpower.

59 There is more than mere psychology to this protection of gold reserves. Unlike dollar notes, there is a direct relationship between gold — as one, albeit unique, example of the world of marketable commodities — and its value. Thus the dollar as a measure of universal value symbolizes what the equivalent value in gold concretely embodies materially. The dollar, in other words, *must* have an underlying, concrete measure of reference. The fact that this measure is gold is, in a sense, contingent; that a specific measure needs to exist is not.

60 Robert O. Keohane and Joseph S. Nye, *Power and Interdependence* (Boston: Little and Brown, 1977).

61 See Masood Ahmed, Timothy Lane, and Marianne Schulze-Ghattas, "Refocusing IMF Conditionality," *Finance and Development* 38, 4 (2001), http://www.imf.org/external/pubs/

ft/fandd/2001/12/ahmed.htm; William D. Coleman, "Agricultural Trade and the World Trade Organization," in *Global Ordering: Institutions and Autonomy in a Changing World*, ed. Louis W. Pauly and William D. Coleman (Vancouver: UBC Press, 2008), 64-84; Rosemary Foot, S. Neil Macfarlane, and Michael Mastanduno, eds., *US Hegemony and International Organizations* (Cambridge: Cambridge University Press, 2003); Peter Sutherland, "The Man Who Built the WTO: An Interview with Peter Sutherland," openDemocracy, 2004, http://www.opendemocracy.net; Robert Hunter Wade, "The Rising Inequality of World Income Distribution," *Finance and Development* 38, 4 (2001), http://www.imf.org/external/pubs/ft/fandd/2001/12/wade.htm; Robert Hunter Wade, "What Strategies Are Viable for Developing Countries Today? The World Trade Organization and the Shrinking of 'Development Space'" (Working Paper no. 31, Crisis States Programme, LSE, Development Studies Institute, London, 2003). For a somewhat different take on the history and role of the WTO, one that views it as the lesser of many evils, see Kent Jones, *Who's Afraid of the WTO?* (Oxford: Oxford University Press, 2004).

62 See Robert O. Keohane, "The Theory of Hegemonic Stability and Changes in International Economic Regimes, 1967-1977," in *Change in the International System*, ed. Ole R. Holsti, Randolph M. Siverson, and Alexander L. George (Boulder, CO: Westview, 1980), 131-62, and *After Hegemony* (Princeton, NJ: Princeton University Press, 1984), 32ff.

63 John Williamson, "What Washington Means by Policy Reform," in *Latin American Adjustment: How Much Has Happened?* ed. John Williamson (Washington, DC: Institute for International Economics, 1990).

64 As a case in point, see one scholar's assessment of the throes of Russian foreign policy making in the early years of the current decade: Angela Stent, "Russia: Farewell to Empire?" *World Policy Journal* 19 (Fall 2002): 83-84.

65 As is evidenced by the protracted conflict between subsidies to Airbus (EU) and Boeing (US), which has simmered for years in the WTO. The American justification for subsidizing Boeing and refusing parallelism between the two cases is that Boeing is an important provider of technology to the Armed Services and, therefore, has a security-related status. The case also suggests that, although in some areas it may be true, as realists contend, there is a relative disconnect between foreign and domestic politics in the United States, and the links are often conspicuous and the impact of synergies wide-ranging. See also William Hartung and Michelle Ciarrocca, "The Military–Industrial–Think Tank Complex: Corporate Think Tanks and the Doctrine of Aggressive Militarism," *International Monitor* 24, 1 and 2 (2003), http://multinationalmonitor.org, and Robert O. Keohane and Helen Milner, eds., *Internationalization and Domestic Politics* (Cambridge: Cambridge University Press, 1996).

66 David H. Levey and Stuart S. Brown, "US Hegemony Has a Strong Foundation," *International Herald Tribune*, 19-20 February 2005; Wade, *Invisible Hand*.

67 Hedetoft, *Global Turn*, chap. 8; Nye, *Paradox of American Power*.

68 Ivo Daalder and James M. Lindsay, *America Unbound: The Bush Revolution in American Foreign Policy* (Washington, DC: The Brookings Institution, 2003); Philip H. Gordon and Jeremy Shapiro, *Allies at War: America, Europe and the Crisis over Iraq* (New York: McGraw-Hill, 2004); Stefan Halper and Jonathan Clarke, *America Alone: The Neo-Conservatives and the Global Order* (Cambridge: Cambridge University Press, 2004); Samuel Huntington, *The Clash of Civilizations and the Remaking of World Order* (New York: Simon and Schuster, 1996); Irwin Stelzer, ed., *The Neocon Reader* (New York: Grove Press, 2004).

69 White House, *National Security*.

70 For an interesting example of such discursive synergy, see the article on the front page of *International Herald Tribune*, 26 January 2005.

71 John Milbank, "Sovereignty, Empire, Capital and Terror," *South Atlantic Quarterly* 101, 2 (2002): 305-23.

72 Anne-Marie Slaughter, *A New World Order* (Princeton, NJ: Princeton University Press, 2004).

73 David Halberstam, *War in a Time of Peace: Bush, Clinton, and the Generals* (New York: Scribner, 2001); White House, *National Security*.

74 Nye, *Bound to Lead*.

75 Especially after 9/11, as the moment of exception *par excellence,* see Giorgio Agamben, *State of Exception* (Chicago: University of Chicago Press, 2005); Fred Hålliday, *Two Days That Shook the World* (London: Saqi Books, 2001); Carl Schmitt, *The Concept of the Political* (1932; repr., Chicago: University of Chicago Press, 1996); George W. Bush, "Agenda for America," 2004, http://www.georgewbush.com (accessed 28 October 2004); Kupchan, *End of the American;* Michael Ignatieff, *Empire Lite: Nation-Building in Bosnia, Kosovo and Afghanistan* (London: Vintage, 2003); Mandelbaum, *Ideas that Conquered.*

76 Ken Booth and Tim Dunne, eds., *Worlds in Collision: Terror and the Future of Global Order* (Basingstoke: Palgrave, 2002).

77 Tariq Ali, *The Clash of Fundamentalisms* (London: Verso, 2002).

78 See various contributions to Stelzer, ed., *The Neocon Reader.*

79 Kenneth Waltz, "The Nuclear Future" (public lecture, delivered to the Danish Institute for International Studies, Copenhagen, 17 May 2005).

80 Francis Fukuyama, *The End of History and the Last Man* (New York: Free Press, 1992); Immanuel Kant, *Zum Ewigen Frieden* [Perpetual peace] (1795; repr., Stuttgart: Reclam, 1984).

81 Halper and Clarke, *America Alone.*

82 William Clark, "The Real Reasons for the Upcoming War with Iraq," revised in 2004, with additional commentary in 2005, Independent Media Center, 2003, http://www.ratical.org/ratville/CAH/RRriraqWar.html; William F. Engdahl, "A New American Century? Iraq and the Hidden Euro-Dollar Wars," *Current Concerns* 4 (2003), http://www.currentconcerns.ch/archive/2003/04/20030409.php.

83 As was the case during the Cold War — namely, the role of Radio Free Europe in the erosion of the USSR's ideological predominance in the East, which was yet another topic addressed to no avail by Gorbachev at Reykjavik: CNN Interactive, The Reagan-Gorbachev transcripts.

84 The reverse side of this narrative is that American interests cannot but lead to very selective reactions to dictatorships. See Stanley Hoffmann, "America Alone in the World," *The American Prospect,* 22 September 2002, http://www.prospect.org/cs/articles?article=america_alone_in_the_world. A case in point is the killing in May 2005 of hundreds, maybe thousands, of protesters and insurgents against the dictatorial policies of the regime in Uzbekistan while the US military forces in the country sat idly by and political pronouncements from Washington about the need for an Uzbek democracy were conspicuously absent.

85 Galtung, *Coming Decline*; Paul Kennedy, *The Rise and Fall of the Great Powers* (New York: Random House/Vintage Books, 1989); Nairn, *America versus Globalization;* Todd, *After the Empire;* Immanuel Wallerstein, *The Decline of American Power: The US in a Chaotic World* (New York: W.W. Norton, 2003).

86 Ulf Hedetoft, "Contemporary Cinema: Between Cultural Globalization and National Interpretation," in *Cinema and Nation,* ed. Mette Hjort and Scott MacKenzie (London: Routledge, 2000), 278–97; George Ritzer, *The McDonaldization of Society* (Thousand Oaks, CA: Pine Forge Press, 1993); Alexander Stephan, ed., *The Americanization of Europe: Culture, Diplomacy, and Anti-Americanism after 1945* (Oxford: Berghahn, 2005).

Works Cited

Abend, Lisa. "Specters of the Secular: Spiritism in Nineteenth-Century Spain." *European History Quarterly* 34, 4 (2004): 507-34.

Abu Manneh, Butrus. *Studies on Islam and the Ottoman Empire in the 19th Century, 1826-1876.* Istanbul: Isis Press, 2001.

Adas, Michael. "A Colonial War in a Postcolonial Era: The United States' Occupation of Vietnam." In *America, the Vietnam War, and the World: Comparative and International Perspectives,* ed. Andreas W. Daum, Lloyd C. Gardner, and Wilfried Mausbach, 27-42. New York: Cambridge University Press, 2003.

Agamben, Giorgio. *State of Exception.* Chicago: University of Chicago Press, 2005.

Ahmad, Feroz. *Turkey: The Quest for Identity.* Oxford: Oneworld, 2003.

Ahmed, Masood, Timothy Lane, and Marianne Schulze-Ghattas. "Refocusing IMF Conditionality." *Finance and Development* 38, 4 (2001), http://www.imf.org/external/pubs/ft/fandd/2001/12/ahmed.htm.

Aksan, Virginia. "Breaking the Spell of Baron de Tott: Reframing the Question of Military Reform in the Ottoman Empire, 1760-1830." *International History Review* 24, 2 (2002): 253-77.

—. *Ottoman Wars, 1700-1870: An Empire Besieged.* Harlow: Pearson Education, 2007.

Albarran, Alan B., and Gregory G. Pitts. *The Radio Broadcasting Industry.* Boston: Allyn and Bacon, 1996.

Albrow, Martin. *The Global Age: State and Society beyond Modernity.* Cambridge: Polity Press, 1996.

Ali, Tariq. *The Clash of Fundamentalisms.* London: Verso, 2002.

Almas, Reider, and Geoffrey Lawrence. "Introduction: The Global/Local Problematic." In *Globalization, Localization, and Sustainable Livelihoods,* ed. Reider Almas and Geoffrey Lawrence, 3-24. Burlington, VT: Ashgate, 2003.

Amin, Samir. *La nation Arabe.* Paris: Editions de Minuit, 1976.

328

—. *Le Développement inégal: Essai sur les formations sociales du capitalisme périphérique*. Paris: Editions de Minuit, 2001.

—. *Critique du capitalisme*. Paris: PUF, 2002.

Anderson, Benedict. *Imagined Communities: Reflections on the Origin and Spread of Nationalism*. 2nd ed. London: Verso Books, 1991.

Anderson, David M., and David Killingray, eds. *Policing the Empire: Government, Authority, and Control, 1830-1940*. Manchester, UK: Manchester University Press, 1991.

Annan, Kofi. "Two Concepts of Sovereignty." *The Economist*, 18-24 September 1999.

Antunes, Cátia. *Globalisation in the Early Modern Period: The Economic Relationship between Amsterdam and Lisbon, 1640-1705*. Amsterdam: Aksant, 2004.

Appadurai, Arjun. *Modernity at Large: Cultural Dimensions of Globalization*. Minneapolis: University of Minnesota Press, 1996.

—. "Grassroots Globalization and the Research Imagination" *Public Culture* 12, 1 (2000): 1-19.

—. "Deep Democracy: Urban Governmentality and the Horizon of Politics." *Public Culture* 14, 1 (2002): 21-47.

Arbulu, Pédro, and Jacques-Marie Vaslin. "La place de Paris dans la finance internationale du 19ième siècle." *Revue d'Économie Financière* 57 (2000): 29-36.

Armitage, David. "Three Concepts of Atlantic History." In *The British Atlantic World, 1500-1800*, ed. David Armitage and Michael J. Braddick, 11-27. London: Palgrave, 2002.

Arrighi, Giovanni, Beverley J. Silver, and Benjamin D. Brewer. "Industrial Convergence, Globalization, and the Persistence of the North-South Divide." *Studies in Comparative International Development* 38, 1 (2003): 3-31.

Asendorf, Christoph. *Batteries of Life: On the History of Things and Their Perception in Modernity*. Berkeley: University of California Press, 1993.

Attwood, Bain. *The Making of the Aborigines*. Sydney: Allen and Unwin, 1989.

—. *Rights for Aborigines*. Sydney: Allen and Unwin, 2003.

Attwood, Bain, and Andrew Markus. *Thinking Black: William Cooper and the Australian Aborigines' League*. Canberra, ACT: Aboriginal Studies Press, 2004.

—, eds. *The Struggle for Aboriginal Rights, a Documentary History*. St. Leonards, NSW: Allen and Unwin, 1999.

Aubrée, Marion, and François Laplatine. *La table, le livre, et les esprits: Naissance, évolution et actualité du mouvement social spirite entre France et Brésil*. Paris: Lattès, 1990.

Aydınlı, Ersel. "The Turkish Pendulum between Globalization and Security: From the Late Ottoman Era to the 1930s." *Middle East Studies* 40, 33 (2004): 102-33.

Bacevich, Andrew J. *American Empire: The Realities and Consequences of US Diplomacy*. Cambridge, MA: Harvard University Press, 2002.

Bairoch, Paul. *Le tiers-monde dans l'impasse*. Paris: Gallimard, 1971.

—. *Révolution industrielle et sous-développement*. Paris-La Haye: Les Editions Mouton, 1974.

—. *Economics and World History: Myths and Paradoxes*. New York: Harvester Wheatsheaf, 1993.

—. "The Constituent Economic Principles of Globalization in Historical Perspective: Myths and Realities." *International Sociology* 15, 2 (2000): 197-214.

Ballantyne, Tony. "Empire, Knowledge and Culture: From Proto-Globalization to Modern Globalization. In *Globalization in World History*, ed. A.G. Hopkins, 115-40. London: Pimlico, 2002.

Balta, Paul. "Vie politique au Maghreb." In *L'État du Maghreb*, ed. Camille and Yves Lacoste. Paris: Editions la Découverte, 1991.

Bank, Andrew. "Losing Faith in the Civilizing Mission: The Premature Decline of Humanitarian Liberalism at the Cape, 1840-60." In *Empire and Others: British Encounters with*

Indigenous Peoples, 1600-1850, ed. M.J. Daunton and Rick Halpern, 364-83. Philadelphia: University of Pennsylvania Press, 1999.

Barfield, Thomas. *The Perilous Frontier: Nomadic Empires and China, 221 BC to AD 1757.* Cambridge: Blackwell, 1989.

Barkawi, Tarak. *Globalization and War.* Lanham: Rowman and Littlefield, 2006.

Barkin, David. "Who Are the Peasants?" *Latin American Research Review* 39, 3 (2004): 270-81.

Baruah, Bipasha. "Earning Their Keep and Keeping What They Earn: A Critique of Organizing Strategies for South Asian Women in the Informal Sector." *Gender, Work, and Organization* 11, 6 (2004): 605-26.

Basham, Diana. *The Trial of Woman: Feminism and the Occult Sciences in Victorian Literature and Society.* London: Macmillan, 1992.

Bastide, Roger. *Les religions africaines au Brésil: Vers une sociologie des interpénétrations de civilisations.* Paris: Presses Universitaires de France, 1960.

Bayart, Jean-François. *Le gouvernement du monde: Une critique politique de la globalisation.* Paris: Fayard, 2004.

Bayly, C.A. "The British and Indigenous Peoples, 1760-1860: Power, Perception and Identity." In *Empire and Others: British Encounters with Indigenous Peoples, 1600-1850,* ed. M.J. Daunton and Rick Halpern, 19-41. Philadelphia: University of Pennsylvania Press, 1999.

—. *The Birth of the Modern World, 1780-1914: Global Connections and Comparisons.* The Blackwell History of the World. Malden, MA: Blackwell, 2004.

Bayly, C.A., Steven Beckert, Matthew Connelly, Isabel Hofmeyr, Wendy Kozol, and Patricia Seed. "On Transnational History." *American Historical Review* 111, 5 (2006): 1441-64.

Beauchamp, Ken. *History of Telegraphy.* London: Institution of Electrical Engineers, 2001.

Beck, Ulrich. *Power in the Global Age: A New Global Political Economy.* Malden, MA: Polity, 2005.

Beckwith, Christopher. *The Tibetan Empire in Central Asia: A History of the Struggle for Great Power among Tibetans, Turks, Arabs, and Chinese during the Early Middle Ages.* Princeton, NJ: Princeton University Press, 1987.

Bedoui, A. "État et développement: Essai d'analyse de la spécificité et des limites du rôle de l'État en Tunisie." Thèse de Doctorat d'État, Université el-Manar, 2005.

Bektas, Yakup. "Displaying the American Genius: The Electromagnetic Telegraph in the Wider World." *British Journal for the History of Science,* 34, 2 (2001): 199-232.

Benevolo, Leonardo. *The Origins of Modern Town Planning.* London: Routledge, 1967.

Bennison, Amira. "Muslim Universalism and Western Globalization." In *Globalization in World History,* ed. A.G. Hopkins, 74-97. London: Pimlico, 2002.

Benot, Yves. *Le sous-développement.* Paris: Les Editions Maspero, 1976.

Bentley, Jerry H. "Cross-Cultural Interaction and Periodization in World History." *American Historical Review* 101, 3 (1996): 749-70.

Benton, Lauren A. *Law and Colonial Cultures: Legal Regimes in World History, 1400-1900.* Cambridge: Cambridge University Press, 2002.

Berger, Mark. "Decolonisation, Modernisation and Nation-Building: Political Development and the Appeal of Communism in Southeast Asia, 1945-1975." *Journal of Southeast Asian Studies* 34, 3 (2003): 421-48.

—. *The Battle for Asia: From Decolonization to Globalization.* New York: Routledge Curzon, 2004.

Berger, Peter L., and Thomas Luckmann. *The Social Construction of Reality: A Treatise in the Sociology of Knowledge.* Garden City, NY: Doubleday, 1966.

Bergerud, Eric M. *The Dynamics of Defeat: The Vietnam War in Hau Nghia Province.* Boulder, CO: Westview Press, 1991.

Berik, Gunseli. "Mature Export-Led Growth and Gender Wage Inequality in Taiwan." *Feminist Economics* 6, 3 (2000): 1-26.

Bermudez, Armando Andres. "Notas para la historia del espiritismo en Cuba." *Etnología y Folklore* 4, 1 (1967): 5-22.

Berndt, Ronald M., and Catherine H. Berndt. *The World of the First Australians.* Adelaide: Rigby Press, 1985.

Berr, Eric, and François Combarnous, "L'impact du consensus de Washington sur les pays en développement: Une évaluation empirique." Documents de travail 100, Centre d'Economie du Développement de l'Université Montesquieu Bordeaux IV.

Bettelheim, Charles. *Planification et croissance accélérée.* Paris: Maspero, 1965.

—. *La Transition vers l'économie socialiste.* Paris: Maspero, 1968.

—. *Problèmes théoriques et pratiques de la planification.* Paris: Maspero, 1970.

Bigart, Homer. "A 'Very Real War' in Vietnam." *New York Times,* 25 February 1962.

Birchal, Sérgio de Oliveira. "The Transfer of Technology to Latecomer Economies in the Nineteenth Century: The Case of Minas Gerais, Brazil." *Business History* 43, 4 (2001): 48-67.

Blanchard, Eric. "Gender, International Relations, and the Development of Feminist Security Theory." *Signs* 28, 4 (2003): 1289-1312.

Blondheim, Menahem. *News over the Wires: The Telegraph and the Flow of Public Information in America, 1844-1897.* Cambridge, MA: Harvard University Press, 1994.

Bodenheimer, Thomas, and Robert Gould. *Rollback! Right-Wing Power in US Foreign Policy.* Cambridge, MA: South End Press, 1989.

Booth, Cherie. "Prospects and Issues from the International Criminal Court: Lessons from Yugoslavia and Rwanda." In *From Nuremberg to The Hague: The Future of International Criminal Justice,* ed. Philippe Sands, 166-92. Cambridge: Cambridge University Press, 2003.

Booth, Ken, and Tim Dunne, eds. *Worlds in Collision: Terror and the Future of Global Order.* Basingstoke: Palgrave, 2002.

Bourne, Henry Richard Fox. *The Aborigines Protection Society: Chapters in Its History.* London: P.S. King and Son, 1899.

Boxer, C.R. *Portuguese India in the Mid-Seventeenth Century.* Delhi: Oxford University Press, 1980.

Brandon, George. *Santería from Africa to the New World: The Dead Sell Memories.* Bloomington: Indiana University Press, 1993.

Braude, Ann. *Radical Spirits: Spiritualism and Women's Rights in Nineteenth Century America.* Boston: Beacon Press, 1989.

Brecher, Jeremy, and Tim Costello. *Global Village or Global Pillage: Economic Reconstruction from the Bottom Up.* Boston: South End Press, 1994.

Brecher, Jeremy, Tim Costello, and Brendan Smith. *Globalization from Below: The Power of Solidarity.* Cambridge, MA: South End Press, 2000.

Brigham, Robert K. *Guerrilla Diplomacy: The NLF's Foreign Relations and the Viet Nam War.* Ithaca, NY: Cornell University Press, 1999.

—. *ARVN: Life and Death in the South Vietnamese Army.* Lawrence: University Press of Kansas, 2006.

Bright, Charles. *Imperial Telegraphic Communication.* London: King, 1911.

Brittain-Caitlin, William. *Offshore: The Dark Side of the Global Economy.* New York: Farrar, Straus and Giroux, 2005.

Brook, Timothy. "Time and Global History." Paper presented at the fourth meeting of the Globalization and Autonomy Research Project, Munk Centre, University of Toronto, September 2005.

Broomhall, Bruce. *International Justice and the International Criminal Court: Between Sovereignty and the Rule of Law.* New York: Oxford University Press, 2003.

Brown, Seyom. *Faces of Power: Constancy and Change in United States Foreign Policy from Truman to Clinton.* New York: Columbia University Press, 1994.

Bruckner, Pascal. *Les Sanglots de l'homme blanc: Tiers-monde, culpabilité, haine de soi.* Paris: Seuil, 1983.

Bucaille, Maurice. *La Bible, le Coran et la Science.* Paris: Seghers, 1976

Bueno de Mesquita, Bruce, and George W. Downs. "Richer but Not Freer." *Foreign Affairs* 84, 5 (2005): 77-86.

Bulletin Financier BBL [Bulletin for international fiscal documentation], January - February 1993.

Burgat, François. *L'islamisme en face.* Paris: La Découverte, 1995.

Burke, Gerald. *Towns in the Making.* New York: St. Martin's Press, 1971.

Burns, James MacGregor. *Roosevelt: The Soldier of Freedom.* New York: Harcourt Brace Jovanovich, 1970.

Bush, George W. "Agenda for America," 2004, http://www.georgewbush.com (accessed 28 October 2004).

Cable, Larry E. *Conflict of Myths: The Development of American Counterinsurgency Doctrine and the Vietnam War.* New York: New York University Press, 1988.

Cañizares-Esguerra, Jorge. *How to Write the History of the New World: Histories, Epistemologies, and Identities in the Eighteenth-Century Atlantic World.* Stanford, CA: Stanford University Press, 2001.

Carey, James W. *Communication as Culture: Essays on Media and Society.* New York: Routledge, 1989.

Carlson, Linda. *Company Towns of the Pacific Northwest.* Seattle: University of Washington Press, 2003.

Carr, Barry. "Globalization from Below: Labour Internationalism under NAFTA." *International Social Science Journal* 51, 159 (1999): 49-60.

Carré, Olivier. "Evolution de la pensée arabe au Proche-Orient depuis 1967." *Revue Française des sciences politiques* 23, 5 (1973): 1046-79.

Caspersz, Donella. "Globalization and Labour: A Case Study of EPZ Workers in Malaysia." *Economic and Industrial Democracy* 19, 2 (1998): 253-86.

Cassese, Antonio. *International Criminal Law.* New York: Oxford University Press, 2003.

Castells, Manuel. *The City and the Grassroots: A Cross-Cultural Theory of Urban Social Movements.* Berkeley: University of California Press, 1983.

—. *The Rise of the Network Society.* Cambridge, MA: Blackwell, 1996.

Castells, Manuel, and Martin Ince. *Conversations with Manuel Castells.* London: Blackwell Publishing, 2003.

Castoriadis, Cornelius. *Philosophy, Politics, Autonomy.* New York: Oxford University Press, 1991.

Catton, Philip E. *Diem's Final Failure: Prelude to America's War in Vietnam.* Lawrence: University Press of Kansas, 2003.

César Macías, Julio. *La guerrilla fue mi camino: Epitafio para César Montes.* Guatemala: Editorial Piedra Santa Arandi, 1999.

Cevdet, Ahmed. *Tarih.* 12 vols. Istanbul, 1858-83.

Chaliand, Gérard. *Mythes révolutionnaires du tiers-monde*. Paris: Les Editions du Seuil, 1976.

——. *Revolution in the Third World*. Rev. ed. New York: Penguin, 1989.

Chamoux, Jean-Pierre. "After Privatization: Neocolonialism?" In *Globalism and Localism in Telecommunications*, ed. E.M. Noam and A.J. Wolfson, 343–50. Amsterdam: Elsevier, 1997.

Chan, Anita, and Zhu Xiaoyang. "Disciplinary Labor Regimes in Chinese Factories." *Critical Asian Studies* 35, 4 (2003): 559–84.

Chandler, Alfred D. *The Visible Hand: The Managerial Revolution in American Business*. Cambridge, MA: Harvard University Press, 1978.

Chapkis, Wendy, and Cynthia Enloe, eds. *Of Common Cloth: Women in the Global Textile Industry*. Amsterdam: Transnational Institute, 1983.

Chauvet, Marcelle, and Fang Dong. "Leading Indicators of Country Risk and Currency Crises: The Asian Experience." *Federal Reserve Bank of Atlanta Economic Review* 89, 1 (2004): 25–37.

Chauvin, Michel. *Tiers-monde: La fin des idées reçues*. Paris: Syros-Alternatives, 1991.

Chesterman, John. *Civil Rights: How Indigenous Australians Won Formal Equality*. St. Lucia, QLD: University of Queensland Press, 2005.

Chevalier, Agnès, and Véronique Kessler. "Croissance et insertion internationale du Maghreb: Questions sur l'avenir des relations avec l'Europe." In *Maghreb: Les anées de transition*, ed. Bassma Kodmani-Darwich and May Chartouni-Dubarry, 257–67. Paris: Masson, 1990.

Christie, M.F. *Aborigines in Colonial Victoria, 1835-86*. Sydney: Sydney University Press, 1979.

Claessens, Stijn. "The Emergence of Equity Investment in Developing Countries: An Overview." *The World Bank Economic Review* 9, 1 (1995): 1–17.

Clapham, Andrew. "Issues of Complexity, Complicity and Complementarity: From the Nuremberg Trials to the Dawn of the New International Criminal Court." In *From Nuremberg to The Hague: The Future of International Criminal Justice*, ed. Philippe Sands, 30–67. Cambridge: Cambridge University Press, 2003.

Clark, Gregory R., ed. *Quotations on the Vietnam War*. Jefferson, NC: McFarland, 2001.

Clark, Ian. *Globalization and Fragmentation: International Relations in the Twentieth Century*. New York: Oxford University Press, 1997.

Clark, William. "The Real Reasons for the Upcoming War with Iraq," revised in 2004, with additional commentary in 2005. Independent Media Center, 2003. http://www.ratical. org/ratville/CAH/RRriraqWar.html.

Clinton, William J. "Remarks at Vietnam National University in Hanoi, 17 November 2000." *Public Papers of the President: William J. Clinton*. http://www.presidency.ucsb.edu/ ws/index.php?pid=1038&st=&st1=.

Cloete, Henricus, *Theses Philologico-Juricae*. Lugduni: Batavorum, 1811.

CNN Interactive. The Reagan-Gorbachev transcripts, Reykjavik, Iceland, 11-16 October 1986, *Cold War*, episode 22, "Star Wars," 2004. http://www.cnn.com/specials/cold.war/ episodes/22/documents/reykjavik.

Cohen, Benjamin. "Bretton Woods System." Text prepared for the *Routledge Encyclopedia of International Political Economy*, 2004. http://www.polsci.ucsb.edu/faculty/cohen/inpress/ bretton.html.

——. *International Monetary Relations in the New Global Economy*. Cheltenham: Edward Elgar, 2004.

Cohen, Joshua, and Joel Rogers, eds. *Can We Put an End to Sweatshops?* Boston: Beacon Press, 2001.

Coleman, William D. "Agricultural Trade and the World Trade Organization." In *Global Ordering: Institutions and Autonomy in a Changing World,* ed. Louis W. Pauly and William D. Coleman, 64-84. Vancouver: UBC Press, 2008.

Coleman, William D., and John W. Weaver, eds. *Property Rights: Struggles over Autonomy in a Global Age.* Vancouver: UBC Press, under review.

Comaroff, Jean, and John L. Comaroff. *Of Revelation and Revolution.* Vol. 2, *The Dialectics of Modernity on a South African Frontier.* Chicago: University of Chicago Press, 1997.

Cooney, Paul. "The Mexican Crisis and the *Maquiladora* Boom: A Paradox of Development or the Logic of Neoliberalism?" *Latin American Perspectives* 28, 3 (2001): 55-82.

Cooper, Chester L. *The Lost Crusade: America in Vietnam.* New York: Dodd, Mead, 1970.

Cooper, Frederick. *Colonialism in Question: Theory, Knowledge, History.* Berkeley: University of California Press, 2005.

Cottrell, P.L. *British Overseas Investment in the Nineteenth Century.* London: Macmillan, 1975.

Cowan, Greg. "Nomadic Resistance: Tent Embassies and Collapsible Architecture, Illegal Architecture and Protest." Koori History Website. http://www.kooriweb.org/foley images/history/1970s/emb72/embarchit.htm.

Cox, Robert W. "Global Perestroika." In *Socialist Register 1992,* ed. Ralph Miliband and Leo Panitch, 26-43. London: The Merlin Press, 1992.

Crabtree, Adam. *From Mesmer to Freud: Magnetic Sleep and the Roots of Psychological Healing.* New Haven, CT: Yale University Press, 1993.

Crawford, James. "The Drafting of the Rome Statute." In *From Nuremberg to The Hague: The Future of International Criminal Justice,* ed. Philippe Sands, 109-56. Cambridge: Cambridge University Press, 2003.

Crawford, Margaret. *Building the Workingman's Paradise: The Design of American Company Towns.* New York: Verso, 1995.

Crosby, Alfred W. *Ecological Imperialism: The Biological Expansion of Europe, 900-1900.* Canto ed. Cambridge: Cambridge University Press, 2003.

Curtin, Philip D. *The World and the West: The European Challenge and the Overseas Response in the Age of Empire.* Cambridge: Cambridge University Press, 2000.

Daalder, Ivo, and James M. Lindsay. *America Unbound: The Bush Revolution in American Foreign Policy.* Washington, DC: The Brookings Institution, 2003.

Dalai Lama XIV. *The Spirit of Tibet: Universal Heritage.* Ed. A.A. Shiromany. New Delhi: Allied Publishers, 1995.

Dallek, Robert. *Franklin D. Roosevelt and American Foreign Policy, 1932-1945.* New York: Oxford University Press, 1979.

Dallin, Alexander, and Gail W. Lapidus, eds. *The Soviet System: From Crisis to Collapse.* Rev. ed. Boulder, CO: Westview, 1991.

Damazio, Sylvia. *Da elite ao povo: O espiritismo no Rio de Janeiro.* Rio de Janeiro: Bertrand, 1994.

Darby, Phillip. "Colonial and Postcolonial Globalizations: A Critical Introduction." In *Globalization and Violence.* Vol. 2, *Colonial and Postcolonial Globalizations,* ed. Paul James and Tom Nairn, ix-xxxi. London: Sage, 2006.

Darwin, John. *After Tamerlane: The Global History of Empire.* London: Penguin Books, 2007.

Davis, Lance E., and Robert A. Huttenback. *Mammon and the Pursuit of Empire: The Political Economy of British Imperialism, 1860-1912.* Cambridge: Cambridge University Press, 1986.

Davison, Roderic. "Foreign and Environmental Contributions to the Political Modernization of Turkey." In *Essays in Ottoman and Turkish History,* ed. Roderic Davison, 73-95. Austin: University of Texas Press, 1990.

—. "Britain, the International Spectrum, and the Eastern Question 1827-1841." *New Perspectives on Turkey* 7 (1992): 15-35.

Dean, Robert D. "Masculinity as Ideology: John F. Kennedy and the Domestic Politics of Foreign Policy." *Diplomatic History* 22, 1 (1998): 29-62.

Debeir, Jean-Claude. "Le problème des exportations de capitaux français de 1919 à 1930: Substitutions et concurrences." *Relations internationales* 6 (1976): 171-82.

de Costa, Ravi. "Identity, Authority and the Moral Worlds of Indigenous Petitions." *Comparative Studies in Society and History* 46, 3 (2006): 669-98.

Denison, Edward F., and Jean Pierre Poullier. *Why Growth Rates Differ? Postwar Experience in Nine Western Countries.* Washington, DC: Brookings Institution, 1967.

Deringil, Selim. *The Well-Protected Domains: Ideology and the Legitimation of Power in the Ottoman Empire, 1876-1909.* London: I.B. Tauris, 1998.

Desideri, Ippolito. *An Account of Tibet: The Travels of Ippolito Desideri.* London: Routledge, 1932.

De Villiers, C.C. *Geslagsregister van die Kaapse Families: Geheel Omgewerkte Uitgawe Hersien en Angevul de C. Pama.* 3 vols. Kaapstad: A.A. Balkema, 1966.

de Vries, Jan, and A. Van der Woude, *The First Modern Economy: Success, Failure and the Perseverance of the Dutch Economy.* Cambridge: Cambridge University Press, 1997.

Diacon, Todd. *Stringing Together a Nation: Cândido Mariano da Silva Rondon and the Construction of a Modern Brazil, 1906-1930.* Durham, NC: Duke University Press, 2004.

Diamond, N. "Why They Shoot Americans." *Nation* 206 (5 February 1968): 166-67.

Didier, Hugues, trans. "Récit de João Cabral (1628)." In *Les Portugais au Tibet: Les premières relations Jésuites (1624-1635).* Paris: Chandeigne, 2002.

Dillenz, Walter. "Broadcasting and Copyright." Paper presented at the "Regional Forum on the Impact of Emerging Technologies on the Law of Intellectual Property for Asia and the Pacific," Seoul, Korea, 30 August–1 September 1989. WIPO Publication 681 (E), 1990, WIPO Archives, Geneva, E 2319F630 WIPO.R.

Dirlik, Arif. "Place-Based Imagination: Globalism and the Politics of Place." In *Places and Politics in an Age of Globalization,* ed. Roxann Prazniak and Arif Dirlik, 15-52. Lanham, MD: Rowman and Littlefield, 2001.

—. *Global Modernity: Modernity in the Age of Global Capitalism.* Boulder, CO: Paradigm, 2007.

Donnell, John C. *Viet Cong Recruitment: Why and How Men Join.* Santa Monica, CA: RAND, 1967.

Dorland, Gilbert N. *Legacy of Discord: Voices of the Vietnam War Era.* Washington, DC: Brassey's, 2001.

Dosal, Paul J. *Power in Transition: The Rise of Guatemala's Industrial Oligarchy, 1871-1994.* New York: Praeger, 1995.

Dow, Coral. "Aboriginal Tent Embassy: Icon or Eyesore?" 4 April 2000, Parliament of Australia, Parliamentary Library. http://www.aph.gov.au/library/pubs/chron/1999-2000/2000chr03.htm.

Dower, Nigel. *An Introduction to Global Citizenship.* Edinburgh: Edinburgh University Press, 2003.

Downey, Gregory J. *Telegraph Messenger Boys: Labor, Technology, and Geography, 1850-1950.* New York: Routledge, 2002.

Doyal, Len, and Ian Gough. *A Theory of Human Need.* New York: Guilford Press, 1991.

Drayton, Richard. "The Collaboration of Labor: Slaves, Empires, and Globalizations in the Atlantic World, ca. 1600-1850." In *Globalization in World History,* ed. A.G. Hopkins, 99-115. New York: Norton, 2002.

Drescher, Seymour. "The Long Goodbye: Dutch Capitalism and Antislavery in Comparative Perspective." *American Historical Review* 99, 1 (1994): 44-69.

Dunne, Tim, and Nicholas J. Wheeler. "Introduction: Human Rights and the Fifty Years' Crisis." In *Human Rights in Global Politics*, ed. Tim Dunne and Nicholas J. Wheeler, 1-28. Cambridge: Cambridge University Press, 1999.

Dunning, John H. *Studies in International Investment.* London: George Allen and Unwin, 1970.

—. "Changes in the Level and Structure of International Production: The Last One Hundred Years." In *The Growth of International Business*, ed. Mark Casson, 84-139. London: George Allen, 1983.

—. "The Role of Foreign Direct Investment in a Globalizing Economy." *Banca Nazionale del Lavoro Quarterly Review* 48, 193 (1995): 125-44.

During, Simon. *Modern Enchantments: The Cultural Power of Secular Magic.* Cambridge, MA: Harvard University Press, 2002.

Easterly, William. "How Did Heavily Indebted Poor Countries Become Heavily Indebted? Reviewing Two Decades of Debt Relief." *World Development* 30, 10 (2002): 1677-96.

Edelman, Nicole. *Voyantes, guérisseuses et vissionnaires en France, 1785-1914.* Paris: Albin Michel, 1995.

Edelstein, Michael. *Overseas Investment in the Age of High Imperialism.* New York: Columbia University Press, 1982.

Efendi, Esad. *Üss-ü Zafer.* Istanbul: n.p., 1927.

Eichengreen, Barry J. *Globalizing Capital: A History of the International Monetary System.* Princeton, NJ: Princeton University Press, 1996.

Ejército Guerrillero de los Pobres. *Articles from Compañero, the International Magazine of Guatemala's Guerrilla Army of the Poor, EGP.* San Francisco, CA: Solidarity, 1982.

Elkins, Caroline. *Imperial Reckoning: The Untold Story of Britain's Gulag in Kenya.* New York: Henry Holt, 2005.

Elliott, David W.P. "Hanoi's Strategy in the Second Indochina War." In *The Vietnam War: Vietnamese and American Perspectives*, ed. Jayne Susan Werner and Luu Doan Huynh, 66-94. Armonk, NY: M.E. Sharpe, 1993.

—. *The Vietnamese War: Revolution and Social Change in the Mekong Delta.* Armonk, NY: M.E. Sharpe, 2003.

El Machat, Samia. *Les États-Unis et la Tunisie: De l'ambiguïté à l'entente.* Paris: L'Harmattan, 1996.

Elphick, Richard. *Khoikhoi and the Founding of White South Africa.* Johannesburg: Ravan Press, 1985.

Emmanuel, Arghiri. *Les Profits et les Crises.* Paris: Maspéro, 1974.

—. *L'échange inégal: Essai sur les antagonismes dans les rapports internationaux.* Paris: Maspero, 1975.

Engdahl, F. William. "A New American Century? Iraq and the Hidden Euro-Dollar Wars." *Current Concerns* 4 (2003), http://www.currentconcerns.ch/archive/2003/04/20030409.php.

Erdem, Hakan, "Recruitment of 'Victorious Soldiers of Muhammad' in the Arab Provinces, 1826-1828." In *Histories of the Modern Middle East: New Directions*, ed. Israel Gershoni, Hakan Erdem, and Ursula Woköck, 189-204. Boulder, CO: Lynne Rienner, 2002.

Esambert, Bernard. *La guerre économique mondiale.* Paris: Editions Orban, 1991.

Escobar, Arturo. *Encountering Development: The Making and Unmaking of the Third World.* Princeton, NJ: Princeton University Press, 1995.

—. "Culture Sits in Places: Reflections on Globalism and Subaltern Strategies of Localization." *Political Geography* 20, 2 (2001): 139-74.

Evans, Julie, Patricia Grimshaw, David Philips, and Shurlee Swain. *Equal Subjects, Unequal Rights: Indigenous Peoples in British Settler Colonies, 1830-1910.* Manchester: Manchester University Press, 2003.

Evans, Peter. "Fighting Marginalization with Transnational Networks: Counter-Hegemonic Globalization." *Contemporary Sociology* 29, 1 (2000): 230-41.

Fahmy, Khaled. *All the Pasha's Men: Mehmed Ali, His Army and the Making of Modern Egypt,* Cambridge: Cambridge University Press, 1997.

Fairfield, John D. "Scientific Management of Urban Space: Professional City Planning and the Legacy of Progressive Reform." *Journal of Urban History* 20 (1994): 179-204.

Faux, Jeff. "A Global Strategy for Labour." *World Social Forum,* 2002. http://www.globalpoli -cynetwork.org (accessed 26 January 2005).

Fearon, James, and Alexander Wendt. "Rationalism v. Constructivism: A Skeptical View." In *Handbook of International Relations,* ed. Walter Carlsnaes, Thomas Risse-Kappen, and Beth A. Simmons, 52-72. London: Sage, 2002.

Feis, Herbert. *Europe the World's Banker, 1870-1914: An Account of European Foreign Investment and the Connection of World Finance with Diplomacy before the War.* New York: A.M. Kelley, 1964.

Ferguson, Niall. *Colossus: The Price of America's Empire.* Harmondsworth: Penguin, 2004.

—. "Sinking Globalization." *Foreign Affairs* 84, 2 (2005): 64-77.

Fernandez, Jorge Alberto. "Redesigning the Strategy of the Frente Autentico del Trabajo in the Maquiladoras." *Labor History* 43, 4 (2002): 461-63.

Fernandez-Arias, Eduardo, and Peter J. Montiel. "The Surge in Capital Inflows to Developing Countries: An Analytical Overview." *World Bank Economic Review* 101, 1 (1996): 51-77.

Fernandez-Kelly, Maria. *For We Are Sold, I and My People: Women and Industry in Mexico's Frontier.* Albany: State University of New York Press, 1983.

Ffrench-Davis, Ricardo, and Helmut Reisen, eds. *Mouvements des capitaux et performances des investissements: Les leçons de l'Amérique latine.* Paris: Organisation for Economic Co-operation and Development, 1998.

Findley, Carter. "The Advent of Ideology in the Islamic Middle East (Part I)." *Studia Islamica* 55 (1982): 143-69.

Fishlow, Albert. "Lessons from the Past: Capital Markets during the 19th Century and the Interwar Period." *International Organization* 39, 3 (1985): 383-439.

Fitzgerald, Frances. *Way Out There in The Blue: Reagan, Star Wars and the End of the Cold War.* New York: Simon and Schuster, 2000.

Flandreau, Marc, and Chantale Rivière. "La grande 'retransformation'? Contrôles de capitaux et intégration financière internationale, 1880-1996." *Économie Internationale* 78 (1999): 11-58.

Foley, Gary. "The Aboriginal Embassy, January-July 1972." The Koori History Website. http://www.kooriweb.org/foley/images/history/1970s/emb72/embassydx.html.

Foot, Rosemary, S. Neil MacFarlane, and Michael Mastanduno, eds. *US Hegemony and International Organizations.* Cambridge: Cambridge University Press, 2003.

Fortna, Benjamin. *Imperial Classroom: Islam, the State and Education in the Late Ottoman Empire.* Oxford: Oxford University Press, 2002.

Fox, Gregory. "The Right to Political Participation in International Law." In *Law and Moral Action in World Politics,* ed. Cecilia Lynch and Michael Loriaux, 77-107. Minneapolis: University of Minnesota Press, 2000.

Freestone, Robert. "An Imperial Aspect: The Australasian Town Planning Tour of 1914-1915." *Australian Journal of Politics and History* 44 (1998): 159-76.

Freidel, Frank. *Franklin D. Roosevelt: A Rendezvous with Destiny.* Boston: Little Brown, 1990.

French, John D. "Towards Effective Transnational Labor Solidarity between NAFTA North and NAFTA South." *Labor History* 43, 4 (2002): 451-59.

Frey, Marc. "Tools of Empire: Persuasion and the United States' Modernizing Mission in Southeast Asia." *Diplomatic History* 27, 4 (2003): 543-68.

Frieden, Jeffrey A. *Global Capitalism: Its Fall and Rise in the Twentieth Century.* New York: W.W. Norton and Company, 2006.

Friedman, Thomas L. *The Lexus and the Olive Tree.* New York: Anchor Books, 2000.

—. "It's a Flat World, after All." *New York Times Magazine,* 3 April 2005.

Fuchs, Yves. *La coopération, aide ou néo-colonialisme?* Paris: Editions sociales, 1973.

Fukuyama, Francis. "The End of History?" *National Interest* 16 (Summer 1989): 3-18.

—. *The End of History and the Last Man.* New York: Free Press, 1992.

Gabaccia, Donna. "A Long Atlantic in a Wider World." *Atlantic Studies* 1, 1 (2004): 1-27.

Gaddis, John Lewis. *Strategies of Containment.* Rev. ed. New York: Oxford University Press, 2005.

Gaiduk, Ilya V. *Confronting Vietnam: Soviet Policy toward the Indochina Conflict, 1954-1963.* Washington, DC: Woodrow Wilson Center Press, 2003.

Galbi [Ge'erbi], "Pingding Xizang beiwen" [An epigraphic record of the pacification of Tibet]. In *Qing zhengfu yu lamajiao* [The Qing government and lamaism], ed. Zhang Yuxin. Xuchang: Xizang renmin chubanshe, 1988.

Galtung, Johan. *On the Coming Decline and Fall of the US Empire.* Lund: The Transnational Foundation for Peace and Future Research, 2004.

Garner, John S., ed. *The Company Town: Architecture and Society in the Early Industrial Age.* New York: Oxford University Press, 1992.

Gardner, Lloyd C. *Economic Aspects of New Deal Diplomacy.* Boston: Beacon Press, 1971.

Gardner, Richard N. *Sterling-Dollar Diplomacy.* Oxford: Oxford University Press, 1969.

"General Report of the Commission of Jurists at the Hague, 1922: Part 1, Rules for the Control of Radio in Time of War," in *American Journal of International Law* 17 (1923): S242-S60.

Gerassi, John, ed. *Venceremos: The Speeches and Writings of Che Guevara.* New York: Macmillan, 1968.

Gereffi, Gary, and Mei-Lin Pan. "The Globalization of Taiwan's Garment Industry." In *Global Production: The Apparel Industry in the Pacific Rim,* ed. Nora Hamilton, Lucie Cheng, and Edna Bonacich, 126-46. Philadelphia, PA: Temple University Press, 1994.

Gereffi, Gary, and Miguel Korzeniewicz. "Introduction: Global Commodity Chains." In *Commodity Chains and Global Capitalism,* ed. Gary Gerrefi and Miguel Korzeniewicz, 1-14. Westport, CT: Praeger, 1994.

Gibson, James L. *The Perfect War: The War We Couldn't Lose and How We Did.* New York: Vintage Books, 1988.

Giddens, Anthony. *The Consequences of Modernity.* Stanford, CA: Stanford University Press, 1990.

—. *Runaway World: How Globalization Is Reshaping Our Lives.* 2nd ed. New York: Routledge, 2003.

Gilly, Adolfo. "The Guerrilla Movement in Guatemala (Part 2)." *Monthly Review* 17 (June 1965): 7-41.

Gilman, Nils. *Mandarins of the Future: Modernization Theory in Cold War America.* Baltimore, MD: Johns Hopkins University Press, 2003.

Gilpin, Robert. *Global Political Economy: Understanding the International Economic Order.* Princeton, NJ: Princeton University Press, 2001.

Gilroy, Paul. *The Black Atlantic: Modernity and Double Consciousness.* Cambridge, MA: Harvard University Press, 1993.

Giovannini, Alberto. "Bretton Woods and Its Precursors: Rules versus Discretion in the History of International Monetary Regimes." Working Paper Series, no. 4001, National Bureau of Economic Research, Washington, DC, February 1992.

Giumbelli, Emerson. *O cuidados dos mortos: Acusação e legitimação do espiritismo.* Rio de Janeiro: Arquivo Nacional, 1997.

Göçek, Fatma Müge. *Social Constructions of Nationalism in the Middle East.* Albany: SUNY Press, 2002.

Goldstein, Judith. *Ideas, Interests and American Trade Policy.* Ithaca, NY: Cornell University Press, 1994.

Goodall, Heather. *Invasion to Embassy: Land in Aboriginal Politics in New South Wales, 1770-1972.* St. Leonards, NSW: Allen and Unwin, in association with Black Books, 1996.

Goodwin, Doris Kearns. *Lyndon Johnson and the American Dream.* New York: Harper and Row, 1976.

Gordon, John Steele. *A Thread Across the Ocean: The Heroic Story of the Transatlantic Cable.* New York: Walker and Company, 2002.

Gordon, Philip H., and Jeremy Shapiro. *Allies at War: America, Europe and the Crisis over Iraq.* New York: McGraw-Hill, 2004.

Gott, Richard. *Rural Guerrillas in Latin America.* 2nd ed. Harmondsworth, UK: Penguin, 1973.

Gough, Ian. "Lists and Thresholds: Comparing the Doyal-Gough Theory of Human Need with Nussbaum's Capabilities Approach. WeD Working Paper 01, ESRC Research Group on Wellbeing in Developing Countries, Bath, United Kingdom, 2003. http//www.bath.ac.uk/econ-dev/wellbeing/research/workingpaperpdf/wedo1.pdf

Grande, Edgar, and Louis W. Pauly, eds. *Complex Sovereignty: Reconstituting Political Authority in the 21st Century.* Toronto: University of Toronto Press, 2005.

Grewlich, Klaus W. "Toward an International Competition Policy in Global Telecommunications." In *Globalism and Localism in Telecommunications,* ed. E.M. Noam and A.J. Wolfson, 351-59. Amsterdam: Elsevier, 1997.

Grossman, Gene M., and Elhanan Helpman. *Innovation and Growth in the Global Economy.* Cambridge, MA: MIT Press, 1991.

Guevara, Che. "Vietnam Must Not Stand Alone." *New Left Review* 43 (May-June 1967): 79-91.

Gunning, Tom. "Phantom Images and Modern Manifestations: Spirit Photography, Magic Theater, Trick Films, and Photography's Uncanny." In *Fugitive Images: From Photography to Video,* ed. Patrice Petro, 42-71. Bloomington: Indiana University Press, 1995.

Gunson, Niels. "British Missionaries and Their Contribution to Science in the Pacific Islands." In *Darwin's Laboratory: Evolutionary Theory and Natural History in the Pacific,* ed. Roy M. MacLeod and Philip F. Rehbock, 283-316. Honolulu: University of Hawaii Press, 1994.

Haas, Peter M. "Introduction: Epistemic Communities and International Policy Coordination." *International Organization* 46, 1 (1992): 1-35.

Hacking, Ian. "Telepathy: Origins of Randomization in Experimental Design." *Isis* 79, 3 (1988): 427-51.

Haefele, Mark H. "Walt Rostow's Stages of Economic Growth: Ideas and Action." In *Staging Growth: Modernization, Development, and the Global Cold War,* ed. David C. Engerman, 81-103. Amherst: University of Massachusetts Press, 2003.

Halberstam, David. *The Best and the Brightest.* New York: Random House, 1972.

—. *War in a Time of Peace: Bush, Clinton, and the Generals.* New York: Scribner, 2001.

Hall, Catherine. "William Knibb and the Constitution of the New Black Subject." In *Empire and Others: British Encounters with Indigenous Peoples, 1600-1850,* ed. M.J. Daunton and Rick Halpern, 303-24. Philadelphia: University of Pennsylvania Press, 1999.

Halle, Louis J. *The Cold War as History.* New York: Harper and Row, 1967.

Halliday, Fred. *The Making of the Second Cold War.* London: Verso, 1983.

—. *Two Days That Shook the World.* London: Saqi Books, 2001.

Halper, Stefan, and Jonathan Clarke. *America Alone: The Neo-Conservatives and the Global Order.* Cambridge: Cambridge University Press, 2004.

Hamilton, Nora, Lucie Cheng, and Edna Bonacich, eds. *Global Production: The Apparel Industry in the Pacific Rim.* Philadelphia, PA: Temple University Press, 1994.

Harcourt, Wendy. "Rethinking Difference and Equality: Women and the Politics of Place." In *Places and Politics in an Age of Globalization,* ed. Roxann Prazniak and Arif Dirlik, 299-322. New York: Rowman and Littlefield, 2001.

Hardin, Garret. "The Tragedy of the Commons." *Science* 162 (1968): 1243-48.

Harding, Walter, ed. *The Cape of Good Hope Government Proclamations from 1806 to 1825, as Now in Force and Unrepealed and Ordinances Passed in Council from 1825 to 1838.* Cape Town: A.S. Robertson, 1838.

Hardt, Michael, and Antonio Negri. *Empire.* Cambridge, MA: Harvard University Press, 2000.

Hartung, William, and Michelle Ciarrocca. "The Military–Industrial–Think Tank Complex: Corporate Think Tanks and the Doctrine of Aggressive Militarism." *International Monitor* 24, 1 and 2 (2003), http://multinationalmonitor.org.

Harvey, David. *The New Imperialism.* Oxford: Oxford University Press, 2003.

Hathaway, Dale. "Mexico's Frente Autentico del Trabajo and the Problem of Unionizing Maquiladoras." *Labor History* 43, 4 (2002): 427-38.

Hay, Douglas, and Paul Craven, eds. *Masters, Servants, and Magistrates in the British Empire, 1562-1955.* Chapel Hill: University of North Carolina Press, 2004.

Headrick, Daniel R. *The Tentacles of Progress: Technology Transfer in the Age of Imperialism, 1850-1940.* Oxford: Oxford University Press, 1988.

—. *The Invisible Weapon: Telecommunications and International Politics, 1851-1945.* Oxford: Oxford University Press, 1991.

Hearden, Patrick J. *Architects of Globalism: Building a New World Order during World War II.* Fayetteville: University of Arkansas Press, 2002.

Heater, Derek. *What is Citizenship?* Cambridge: Polity Press, 1999.

—. *World Citizenship: Cosmopolitan Thinking and Its Opponents.* London: Continuum, 2002.

Hedetoft, Ulf. "Contemporary Cinema: Between Cultural Globalization and National Interpretation." In *Cinema and Nation,* ed. Mette Hjort and Scott MacKenzie, 278-97. London: Routledge, 2000.

—. *The Global Turn: National Encounters with the World.* Aalborg: Aalborg University Press, 2003.

—. "The Forces Driving Globalization: Modalities, Actors and Processes." In *Jorden runt igen – Nya bidrag till en gammal globalhistoria* [Around the world again – New contributions to an old global history], ed. Arne Jarrick and Alf Johansson, 124-46. Stockholm: Almqvist and Wiksell, 2004.

——. "Sovereignty Revisited: European Reconfigurations, Global Challenges, and Implications for Small States." In *Global Ordering: Institutions and Autonomy in a Changing World*, ed. Louis W. Pauly and William D. Coleman, 214-33. Vancouver: UBC Press, 2008.

Hedin, Sven. *Southern Tibet, 1906-1908.* 9 vols. Stockholm: Lithographic Institute of the General Staff of the Swedish Army, 1917.

Hegel, G.W.F. *Science of Logic.* 1812-16. Vol. 1. Trans. A.V. Miller. New York: Prometheus Books, 1989.

Held, David. *Democracy and the Global Order: From the Modern State to Cosmopolitan Governance.* Stanford, CA: Stanford University Press, 1995.

——. "From Executive to Cosmopolitan Democracy." In *Taming Globalization: Frontiers of Governance*, ed. David Held and Mathias Koenig-Archibugi, 160-86. Cambridge, UK: Polity, 2003.

Held, David, Anthony McGrew, David Goldblatt, and Jonathan Perraton. *Global Transformations: Politics, Economics and Culture.* Stanford, CA: Stanford University Press, 1999.

Helpman, Elhanan. *The Mystery of Economic Growth.* Cambridge, MA: Belknap Press of Harvard University Press, 2004.

Hess, David. *Spirits and Scientists: Ideology, Spiritism, and Brazilian Culture.* Philadelphia: University of Pennsylvania Press, 1991.

Hiatt, L.R. *Arguments about Aborigines: Australia and the Evolution of Social Anthropology.* Cambridge: Cambridge University Press, 1996.

Hickey, Gerald Cannon. *Window on a War: An Anthropologist in the Vietnam Conflict.* Lubbock: Texas Tech University Press, 2002.

Hirschman, Samuel, Samuel Preston, and Vu Manh Loi. "Vietnamese Casualties During the American War: A New Estimate." *Population and Development Review* 21 (December 1995): 783-812.

Hirst, Paul Q., and Grahame Thompson. *Globalization in Question: The International Economy and the Possibilities of Governance.* Cambridge: Polity Press, 1996.

History Central. "World History 1986-87," 2000. http://www.multied.com/dates/1986.html.

Hitchcock, Robert K. "Human Rights and Indigenous Peoples in Africa and Asia." In *Human Rights and Diversity: Area Studies Revisited*, ed. David P. Forsythe and Patrice C. McMahon, 205-23. Lincoln: University of Nebraska Press, 2003.

Hobsbawm, Eric. *On History.* New York: The New Press, 1997.

Hodge, Gerald. "The Roots of Canadian Planning." *American Planning Association Journal* 51, 1 (1985): 8-22.

Hoffmann, Stanley. *Primacy or World Order: American Foreign Policy since the Cold War.* New York: McGraw-Hill, 1978.

——. "America Alone in the World." *The American Prospect,* 22 September 2002, http://www.prospect.org/cs/articles?article=america_alone_in_the_world.

Hogan, Michael J. *The Marshall Plan: America, Britain, and the Reconstruction of Western Europe, 1947-1952.* Cambridge: Cambridge University Press, 1987.

Holton, Sandra Stanley. "'To Educate Women into Rebellion': Elizabeth Cady Stanton and the Creation of a Transatlantic Network of Radical Suffragists." *American Historical Review* 99, 4 (1994): 1112-36.

Hoon Lee, Seung, and Ho Keun Song. "The Korean Garment Industry: From Authoritarian Patriarchism to Industrial Paternalism." In *Global Production: The Apparel Industry in the*

Pacific Rim, ed. Nora Hamilton, Lucie Cheng, and Edna Bonacich, 147-61. Philadelphia, PA: Temple University Press, 1994.

Hoopes, Townsend. *The Limits of Intervention: An Inside Account of How the Johnson Policy of Escalation in Vietnam Was Reversed.* New York: David McKay Co., 1969.

Hopkins, A.G. "Globalization — An Agenda for Historians." In *Globalization in World History,* ed. A.G. Hopkins, 1-10. New York: Norton, 2002.

—, ed. *Globalization in World History.* London: Pimlico, 2002.

—. "The History of Globalization — and the Globalization of History?" In *Globalization in World History,* ed. A.G. Hopkins, 11-36. London: Pimlico, 2002.

Horne, Alistair. *Macmillan: 1894-1956.* London: Macmillan, 1988.

Hosking, Geoffrey, and Robert Service, eds. *Reinterpreting Russia.* New York: Oxford University Press, 1999.

Hough, Richard, John Kelley, Stephen Miller, Fred L. Mann, Russell DeRossier, and Mitchell A. Seligson. *Land and Labor in Guatemala: An Assessment.* Washington, DC: US Agency for International Development, 1982.

Howard, Rhoda. *Human Rights and the Search for Community.* Boulder, CO: Westview Press, 1995.

Howe, Stephen. "American Empire: The History and Future of an Idea." openDemocracy, 2003. http://www.opendemocracy.net.

Hunt, David. "Images of the Viet Cong." In *The United States and Viet Nam from War to Peace: Papers from an Interdisciplinary Conference on Reconciliation,* ed. Robert M. Slabey, 51-63. Jefferson, NC: McFarland and Co., 1996.

—. "The My Tho Grapevine and the Sino-Soviet Split." In *A Companion to the Vietnam War,* ed. Marilyn Blatt Young and Robert Buzzanco, 79-92. Malden, MA: Blackwell, 2002.

—. "Revolution in the Delta." *Critical Asian Studies* 35, 4 (2003): 599-620.

Hunt, Michael. *Ideology and US Foreign Policy.* New Haven, CT: Yale University Press, 1988.

Hunt, Richard A. *Pacification: The American Struggle for Vietnam's Hearts and Minds.* Boulder, CO: Westview Press, 1995.

Huntington, Samuel. *The Clash of Civilizations and the Remaking of World Order.* New York: Simon and Schuster, 1996.

Ignatieff, Michael. *Blood and Belonging.* London: Chatto and Windus, 1993.

—. *The Warrior's Honour: Ethnic War and the Modern Conscience.* Toronto: Penguin Books, 1999.

—. *The Rights Revolution.* Toronto: Anansi Press, 2000.

—. *Empire Lite: Nation-Building in Bosnia, Kosovo and Afghanistan.* London: Vintage, 2003.

Imlah, Albert Henry. *Economic Elements in the Pax Britannica.* Cambridge, MA: Harvard University Press, 1958.

International Commission on Intervention and State Sovereignty. *The Responsibility to Protect.* Ottawa: International Development Research Centre, 2001. http://www.iciss.ca/menu-en.asp.

International Criminal Court. Assembly of States Parties. "The States Parties to the Rome Statute," http://www.icc-cpi.int/statesparties.html.

International Law Commission. Principles of International Law Recognized in the Charter of the Nuremberg Tribunal and in the Judgment of the Tribunal. English text published in *Report of the International Law Commission,* 5 June–29 July 1950, Document A/1316, 11-14.

"International Military Tribunal (Nuremberg), Judgment and Sentences, 1946, October 1." Reprinted in *American Journal of International Law* 41, 1 (1947): 172-333.

International Monetary Fund (IMF). *Annual Report, 1967.* Washington, DC: IMF, 1967.

—. *Annual Report, 1984.* Washington, DC: IMF, 1984.

—. *Report on the Measurement of International Capital Flows.* Washington, DC: IMF, 1992.

Iriye, Akira. *Global Community: The Role of International Organizations in the Making of the Contemporary World.* Berkeley: University of California Press, 2002.

Isbister, John. *Promises Not Kept: Poverty and the Betrayal of Third World Development.* 6th ed. Bloomfield, CT: Kumarian Press, 2003.

Israel, Jonathan. *Empires and Entrepots: The Dutch, the Spanish Monarchy, and the Jews, 1585-1713.* London: The Hambledon Press, 1990.

—. *The Dutch Republic: Its Rise, Greatness, and Fall, 1477-1806.* Oxford: Clarendon Press, 1998.

Jackson, Michael. *At Home in the World.* Durham, NC: Duke University Press, 1995.

Jackson, Robert. "Sovereignty in World Politics: A Glance at the Conceptual Landscape." In *Sovereignty at the Millennium,* ed. Robert Jackson, 9-34. Oxford: Blackwell, 1999.

Jalée, Pierre. *Le pillage du tiers monde.* Paris: Maspero, 1966.

James, Harold. *International Monetary Cooperation since Bretton Woods.* Oxford: Oxford University Press, 1996.

James, Paul, and Jonathan Friedman. "Globalizing War: A Critical Introduction." In *Globalization and Violence.* Vol. 3, *Globalizing War and Intervention,* ed. Paul James and Tom Nairn, ix-xxxii. London: Sage, 2006.

Joes, Anthony James. *The War for South Viet Nam, 1954-1975.* 2nd ed. Westport, CT: Praeger, 2001.

Jonas, Susanne, and David Tobis. *Guatemala.* New York: North American Congress on Latin America, 1974.

Jones, Kent. *Who's Afraid of the WTO?* Oxford: Oxford University Press, 2004.

Kaapse Argiefstukke, Kaapse Plakkaatboek, Deel III (1754-1786). Kaapstad: Cape Times, 1949.

Kagan, Robert. *Paradise and Power: America and Europe in the New World Order.* London: Atlantic Books, 2003.

Kalman, Harold. *A History of Canadian Architecture.* Toronto: Oxford University Press, 1994.

Kangxi manwen zhupi zouzhe quanyi [Complete translation of Kangxi's vermilion rescripts in Manchu]. Beijing: Zhongguo shehui kexue chubanshe, 1996.

Kant, Immanuel. *Zum Ewigen Frieden* [Perpetual peace]. 1795; Reprint, Stuttgart: Reclam, 1984.

Kanunnâme-yi asâkir-i mansure-yi Muhammadiye. Istanbul: n.p., 1829.

Kardec, Allan. *The Book on Mediums, or, Guide for Mediums and Invocators.* Trans. Emma A. Wood. 1861; Reprint, York Beach, ME: Samuel Weiser, 1970.

Karpat, Kemal. "The *Hijra* from Russia and the Balkans: The Process of Self-Definition in the Late Ottoman State." In *Muslim Travellers: Pilgrimage, Migration and the Religious Imagination,* ed. Dale F. Eickelman and James Piscatori, 131-52. Berkeley: University of California Press, 1990.

Kaufman, Bruce E. "The Case for the Company Union." *Labor History* 41, 3 (2000): 321-50.

Keen, Ian. *Aboriginal Economy and Society: Australia at the Threshold of Colonisation.* South Melbourne, Victoria: Oxford University Press, 2004.

Kellen, Konrad. *Conversations with Enemy Soldiers in Late 1968/Early 1969: A Study of Motivation and Morale.* Santa Monica, CA: RAND, 1970.

Kenen, Peter B. *Capital Mobility and Financial Integration: A Survey.* Princeton, NJ: International Finance Section, Princeton University, 1976.

Kennan, George. "The Sources of Soviet Conduct." *Foreign Affairs* 25 (July 1947): 566-82.

Kennedy, David. *Freedom from Fear: The American People in Depression and War, 1929-1945.* New York: Oxford University Press, 1999.

Kennedy, John F. "Special Message to the Congress on Foreign Aid," 22 March 1961. *Public Papers of the President: John F. Kennedy,* http://www.presidency.ucsb.edu/ws/index.php?pid=8545&st=&st1=.

Kennedy, Paul, 1989. *The Rise and Fall of the Great Powers.* New York: Random House/Vintage Books, 1989.

Keohane, Robert O. "The Theory of Hegemonic Stability and Changes in International Economic Regimes, 1967-1977." In *Change in the International System,* ed. Ole R. Holsti, Randolph M. Siverson, and Alexander L. George, 131-62. Boulder, CO: Westview, 1980.

—. *After Hegemony.* Princeton, NJ: Princeton University Press, 1984.

Keohane, Robert O., and Helen Milner, eds. *Internationalization and Domestic Politics.* Cambridge: Cambridge University Press, 1996.

Keohane, Robert O., and Joseph S. Nye. *Power and Interdependence.* Boston: Little and Brown, 1977.

Kessler, Clive S. "Globalization: Another False Universalism?" *Third World Quarterly* 21, 6 (2000): 931-42.

Kimball, Warren F. *The Juggler: Franklin Roosevelt as Wartime Statesman.* Princeton, NJ: Princeton University Press, 1991.

Kirkman, Noreen. *Mount Isa: Oasis of the Outback.* Townsville, QLD: James Cook University, 1998.

Kırlı, Cengiz. "The Struggle Over Space: The Coffeehouses of Istanbul, 1700-1845." PhD diss., SUNY Binghamton, 2000.

Kissinger, Henry. *Diplomacy.* New York: Simon and Schuster, 1994.

Kittichaisaree, Kriangsak. *International Criminal Law.* New York: Oxford University Press, 2001.

Klein, Naomi. *No Logo: Taking Aim at the Brand Bullies.* Toronto: Vintage, 2000.

Kodmani-Darwish, Bassma, "Mahgreb/Machrek Histoire d'une relation complexe." In *Maghreb, les années de transition,* ed. Bassma Kodmani-Darwich and May Chartouni-Dubarry, 269-90. Paris: Masson, 1990.

Kolko, Gabriel. *Anatomy of a War: Vietnam, the United States, and the Modern Historical Experience.* New York: Pantheon Books, 1985.

—. *Vietnam: Anatomy of a Peace.* New York: Routledge, 1997.

Kondos, Vivienne, and Gillian Cowlishaw. "Introduction: Conditions of Possibility." *TAJA (The Australian Journal of Anthropology)* 6, 1 (1995): 1-14.

Kopinak, Kathryn. "Living the Gospel through Service to the Poor: The Convergence of Political and Religious Motivations in Organizing *Maquiladora* Workers in Juarez, Mexico." In *Race, Class, Gender: Bonds and Barriers,* ed. Jesse Vorst et al., 217-44. Winnipeg: Between the Lines, 1989.

Krasner, Stephen. "Global Communications and National Power." *World Politics* 43, 3 (1991): 336-66.

Krepinevich, Andrew F., Jr. *The Army and Vietnam.* Baltimore, MD: Johns Hopkins University Press, 1986.

Kristol, William, and Robert Kagan. "National Interest and Global Responsibility." In *The Neocon Reader,* ed. Irwin Stelzer, 57-74. New York: Grove Press, 2004.

Kselman, Thomas. *Death and the Afterlife in Nineteenth-Century France.* Princeton, NJ: Princeton University Press, 1993.

Kupchan, Charles A. *The End of the American Era.* New York: Alfred A. Knopf, 2003.

Lacoste, Camille and Yves, eds. *Maghreb, peuples et civilisations.* 1995; Reprint, Paris: La Découverte, 2004.

LaFeber, Walter. "Roosevelt, Churchill and Indochina, 1942-1945." *American Historical Review* 80, 5 (1975): 1277-95.

—. *The American Age*. New York: Norton, 1989.

—. *America, Russia and the Cold War, 1945-1996*. 9th ed. New York: McGraw-Hill, 2001.

Lake, Marilyn. *Faith: Faith Bandler, Gentle Activist*. Crows Nest, NSW: Allen and Unwin, 2002.

Lambert, Robert. "Labour Movement Renewal in the Era of Globalization: Union Responses in the South." In *Global Unions? Theory and Strategies of Organized Labour in the Global Political Economy*, ed. Jeffrey Harrod and Robert O'Brien, 185-203. London: Routledge, 2002.

Lane, Philip A., and Gian Maria Milesi-Ferretti. "International Financial Integration," *IMF Working Paper* no. 03/86, April 2003.

Latham, Michael E. *Modernization as Ideology: American Social Science and "Nation-Building" in the Kennedy Era*. Chapel Hill: University of North Carolina Press, 2000.

—. "Redirecting the Revolution? The USA and the Failure of Nation-Building in South Vietnam." *Third World Quarterly* 27, 1 (2006): 27-41.

Latham, Robert, and Saskia Sassen, "Digital Formations: Constructing an Object of Study." In *Digital Formations: IT and New Architectures in the Global Realm*, ed. Latham and Sassen, 1-33. Princeton, NJ: Princeton University Press, 2005

Leites, Nathan. *The Viet Cong Style of Politics*. Santa Monica, CA: RAND, 1969.

Leive, David M. *International Telecommunications and International Law: The Regulation of the Radio Spectrum*. Dobbs Ferry, NY: Oceana Publications, 1970.

Lensink, Robert, and Howard White. "Does the Revival of International Private Capital Flows Mean the End of Aid? An Analysis of Developing Countries' Access to Private Capital." *World Development* 26, 7 (1998): 1221-34.

Levesque, Christian, and Gregor Murray. "Local versus Global: Activating Local Union Power in the Global Economy." *Labor Studies Journal* 27, 3 (2002): 39-65.

Levey, David H., and Stuart S. Brown. "U.S. Hegemony has a Strong Foundation." *International Herald Tribune*, 19-20 February 2005.

Levin, N. Gordon, Jr. *Woodrow Wilson and World Politics: America's Response to War and Revolution*. New York: Oxford University Press, 1968.

Levy, Avigdor. "The Military Policy of Sultan Mahmud II, 1808-1839." PhD diss., Harvard University, 1968.

Lewis, Bernard. *The Emergence of Modern Turkey*. Oxford: Oxford University Press, 1968.

Lewis, Cleona. *America's Stake in International Investments*. Washington, DC: The Brookings Institute, 1938.

Lindsey, Brink. *Against the Dead Hand: The Uncertain Struggle for Global Capitalism*. New York: John Wiley and Sons, 2002.

London Agreement and Charter of the International Military Tribunal: Annex, 8 August 1945. http://www.yale.edu/lawweb/avalon/imt/proc/imtchart.htm.

Louis, William Roger. *Imperialism at Bay: The United States and the Decolonization of the British Empire, 1941-1945*. New York: Oxford University Press, 1978.

Lubrano, Annteresa. *The Telegraph: How Technological Innovation Caused Social Change*. New York: Garland Publishing, 1997.

Lucas, Rex A. *Minetown, Milltown, Railtown: Life in Canadian Communities of Single Industry*. Toronto: University of Toronto Press, 1974.

Lundestad, Geir. *"Empire" by Integration: The United States and European Integration, 1945-1997*. Oxford: Oxford University Press, 1998.

Lutz, Nancy Melissa. "Images of Docility: Asian Women and the World-Economy." In *Racism, Sexism, and the World System*, ed. Joan Smith, 57-74. New York: Greenwood Press, 1988.

Lynch, Cecilia. "Political Activism and International Law." In *Law and Moral Action in World Politics*, ed. Cecilia Lynch and Michael Loriaux, 140-74. Minneapolis: University of Minnesota Press, 2000.

Macías, Julio César. *La guerrilla fue mi camino: Epitafio para César Montes*. Guatemala: Editorial Piedra Santa Arandi, 1999.

Maciel, Laura Antunes. "Cultura e tecnologia: A constituição do serviço telegráfico no Brasil." *Revista Brasileira de História* 21, 41 (2001): 127-44.

Maddison, Angus. *The World Economy: A Millennial Perspective*. Paris: Development Centre of the Organisation for Economic Co-operation and Development, 2001.

Makdisi, Ussama. *The Culture of Sectarianism: Community, History, and Violence in Nineteenth-Century Ottoman Lebanon*. Berkeley: University of California Press, 2000.

Mandelbaum, Michael. *The Ideas that Conquered the World*. New York: Public Affairs, 2002.

—. *The Case for Goliath: How America Acts as the World's Government in the Twenty-First Century*. New York: Public Affairs, 2005.

Mandelbaum, Michael, and Strobe Talbott. *Reagan and Gorbachev*. New York: Vintage Books, 1987.

Mann, Michael. "Has Globalization Ended the Rise and Rise of the Nation-State?" *Review of International Political Economy* 4, 3 (1997): 472-96.

—. *Incoherent Empire*. London: Verso, 2003.

Manning, Jason. "Reykjavik." *The Eighties Club: The Politics and Pop Culture of the 1980s*, 2000. http://eightiesclub.tripod.com/id322.htm.

Maogoto, Jackson Nyamuya. *War Crimes and Realpolitik: International Justice from World War I to the 21st Century*. Boulder, CO: Lynne Rienner Publishers, 2004.

Margold, Jane. "Reformulating the Compliant Image: Filipina Activists in the Global Factory." *Urban Anthropology* 28, 1 (1999): 1-28.

Marin, Patricia, and Cecilia Rodriguez. "Working on Racism: Centro Obrero, El Paso." In *Of Common Cloth: Women in the Global Textile Industry*, ed. Wendy Chapkis and Cynthia Enloe, 81-85. Amsterdam: Transnational Institute, 1983.

Marks, Sally. *The Ebbing of European Ascendancy: An International History of the World*. London: Hodder Arnold, 2002.

Markus, Andrew. "After the Outward Appearance: Scientists, Administrators and Politicians." In *All That Dirt, Aborigines 1938: An Australia 1938 Monograph*, ed. Bill Gammage and Andrew Markus, 83-106. Canberra: History Project Incorporated Australian National University, 1982.

—. "William Cooper and the 1937 Petition to the King." *Aboriginal History* 7, 1 (1983): 46-60.

—. *Governing Savages*. Sydney: Allen and Unwin, 1990.

Markus, Andrew, and Monash University, Department of History. *Blood from a Stone: William Cooper and the Australian Aborigines' League*. Monash Publications in History 2. Clayton, Victoria: Dept. of History, Monash University, 1986.

Marx, Karl, and Friedrich Engels. "Manifesto of the Communist Party." In *The Marx-Engels Reader*, 2nd ed., ed. Robert Tucker, 469-500. New York: W.W. Norton, 1978.

Mathews, Freya. *The Ecological Self*. London: Routledge, 1991.

Matlock, Jann. "Ghostly Politics." *Diacritics* 30, 3 (2000): 53-71.

Matory, J. Lorand. *Black Atlantic Religion: Tradition, Transnationalism, and Matriarchy in the Afro-Brazilian Candomble*. Princeton, NJ: Princeton University Press, 2005.

Mayer-Schönberger, Viktor, and Deborah Hurley. "Globalization of Communication." In *Governance and a Globalizing World,* ed. Joseph Nye and John Donahue, 135-51. Washington, DC: Brookings Institution Press, 2000.

McCarthy, Justin. *Death and Exile: The Ethnic Cleansing of Ottoman Muslims, 1821-1922.* Princeton, NJ: Darwin, 1995.

McCulloch, Rachel, and Peter A. Petri. "Equity Financing of East Asian Development." In *Capital Flows and Financial Crises,* ed. Miles Kahler, 158-85. New York: Cornell University Press, 1998.

McFadden, Margaret H. *Golden Cables of Sympathy: The Transatlantic Sources of Nineteenth-Century Feminism.* Lexington: University of Kentucky Press, 1999.

McGarry, Molly. *Ghosts of Futures Past: Spiritualism and the Cultural Politics of Nineteenth-Century America.* Berkeley: University of California Press, 2008.

McGoldrick, Dominic. "Criminal Trials Before International Tribunals: Legality and Legitimacy." In *The Permanent International Criminal Court: Legal and Policy Issues,* eds. Dominic McGoldrick, P.J. Rowe, and Eric Donnelly, 9-46. Oxford: Hart Publishing, 2004.

McGuinness, Bruce. "Going International — Handle with Care!" *Identity* 3, 11 (1979): n.p.

McKay, Steven. *Satanic Mills or Silicon Islands? The Politics of High-Tech Production in the Philippines.* Ithaca, NY: Cornell University Press, 2006.

McLeon, Mark W. "Indigenous Peoples and the Vietnamese Revolution, 1930-1975." *Journal of World History* 10, 2 (1999): 353-89.

McLoone, Martin. "Music Hall Dope and British Propaganda? Cultural Identity and Early Radio Broadcasting in Ireland." *Historical Journal of Film, Radio and Television* 20, 3 (2000): 301-15.

McMahon, Robert J. "The Republic as Empire: American Foreign Policy in the Twentieth Century." In *Perspectives on Modern America: Making Sense of the Twentieth Century,* ed. Harvard Sitkoff, 80-100. New York: Oxford University Press, 2001.

McMullin, Stan. *Anatomy of a Seance: A History of Spirit Communication in Central Canada.* Montreal and Kingston: McGill-Queen's University Press, 2004.

McNamara, Robert. "United States Policy in Vietnam." *Department of State Bulletin* 50 (13 April 1964): 562-70.

—. *The Essence of Security.* New York: Harper and Row, 1968.

McNeill, J.R. "The End of the Old Atlantic World: America, Africa, Europe, 1770-1888." In *Atlantic American Societies from Columbus through Abolition, 1492-1888,* ed. Alan L. Karras and J.R. McNeill, 245-68. London: Routedge, 1992.

Mead, Walter Russell. *Special Providence: American Foreign Policy and How It Changed the World.* New York: Knopf, 2001.

Mecklin, John. *Mission in Torment: An Intimate Account of the US Role in Vietnam.* Garden City, NY: Doubleday, 1965.

Melville, Thomas, and Marjorie Melville. *Guatemala — Another Vietnam?* Harmondsworth: Penguin, 1971.

Merrill, Dennis. "Conceptualizing the Third World: Language, Theory, and Method." *Diplomatic History* 26, 2 (2002): 317-24.

Meyer, Brigit, and Peter Geschiere, eds. *Globalization and Identity: Dialectics of Flow and Closure.* Oxford: Oxford University Press, 1999.

Michalet, Charles-Albert. "Transnational Corporations and the Changing International Economic System." *Transnational Corporations* 3, 1 (1994): 9-21.

Middlebrook, Kevin J. "The Politics of Industrial Restructuring: Transnational Firms' Search for Flexible Production in the Mexican Automobile Industry." *Comparative Politics* 23, 3 (1991): 275-97.

Milbank, John. "Sovereignty, Empire, Capital and Terror." *South Atlantic Quarterly* 101, 2 (2002): 305-23.

Miller, J.R. *Skyscrapers Hide the Heavens: A History of Indian-White Relations in Canada.* 3rd ed. Toronto: University of Toronto Press, 2000.

Mills, Mary Beth. *Thai Women in the Global Labor Force: Consuming Desires, Contested Selves.* New Brunswick, NJ: Rutgers University Press, 1999.

Milward, Alan S. "Les placements français à l'étranger et les deux guerres mondiales." In *La position internationale de la France: Aspects économiques et financiers, XIXᵉ-XXᵉ Siècles*, ed. Maurice Lévy-Leboyer, 299-311. Paris: Éditions de l'école des hautes études en sciences sociales (EHESS), 1977.

Mittelman, James. *The Globalization Syndrome.* Princeton, NJ: Princeton University Press, 2000.

Mody, Ashoka, and Antu Panini Murshid. "Growing Up with Capital Flows" *IMF Working Paper* no. 02/75, April 2002.

Monroe, John Warne. Laboratories of Faith: Mesmerism, Spiritism, and Occultism in Modern France. Ithaca, NY: Cornell University Press, 2007.

Montejo, Victor. *Maya Intellectual Renaissance: Identity, Representation, and Leadership.* Austin: University of Texas Press, 2005.

Moon, Bruce E. "The United States and Globalization." In *Political Economy and the Changing Global Order,* ed. Richard Stubbs and Geoffrey R.D. Underhill, 342-51. Oxford: Oxford University Press, 2000.

Morán, Rolando. *Entrevistas al comandante en jefe del Ejército Guerrillero de los Pobres, Rolando Morán.* Guatemala: El Ejército, 1982.

Moreira, Manuel Belo. "Local Consequences and Responses to Global Integration: The Role of the State in the Less Favoured Zones." In *Globalization, Localization, and Sustainable Livelihoods,* ed. Reider Almas and Geoffrey Lawrence, 189-203. Burlington, VT: Ashgate, 2003.

Morus, Iwan Rhys. "Currents from the Underworld: Electricity and the Technology of Display in Early Victorian England." *Isis* 84, 1 (1993): 50-89.

—. "The Electric Ariel: Telegraphy and Commercial Culture in Early Victorian England." *Victorian Studies* 39, 3 (1996): 339-78.

Moscow Conference. "Joint Four-Nation Declaration: Statement on Atrocities," October 1943. http://www.yale.edu/lawweb/avalon/wwii/moscow.htm (accessed 20 December 2006).

Motyl, Alexander J. "Why Empires Reemerge: Imperial Collapse and Imperial Revival in Comparative Perspective." *Comparative Politics* 31, 2 (1999): 127-45.

Munck, Ronaldo. "Globalization, Labor and the 'Polanyi Problem.'" *Labor History* 45, 3 (2004): 251-69.

Murphy, Robert D. *Diplomat Among Warriors.* Garden City, NY: Doubleday, 1964.

Mussa, Michael, Barry J. Eichengreen, Enrica Detragiache, and Giovanni Dell'Ariccia. "Capital Account Liberalization: Theoretical and Practical Aspects." *IMF Occasional Paper* 172, 30 September 1998.

Muthu, Sankar. *Enlightenment against Empire.* Princeton, NJ: Princeton University Press, 2003.

Myers, Fred R. *Pintupi Country, Pintupi Self: Sentiment, Place, and Politics among Western Desert Aborigines*. Smithsonian Series in Ethnographic Inquiry. Washington/Canberra: Smithsonian Institution Press/Australian Institute of Aboriginal Studies, 1986.

Nahavandi, F. "Développement et globalisation." In *Globalisation et néolibéralisme dans le tiers-monde*, ed. F. Nahavandi, 9-27. Paris: L'Harmattan, 2000.

Nairn, Tom. "America vs. Globalization." openDemocracy, 2003. http://www.opendemocracy.net.

Naples, Nancy A. "The Challenges and Possibilities of Transnational Feminist Praxis." In *Women's Activism and Globalization: Linking Local Struggles and Transnational Politics*, ed. Nancy Naples and Marisha Desai, 267-81. New York: Routledge, 2002.

Nash, June C. *Mayan Visions: The Quest for Autonomy in an Age of Globalization*. New York: Routledge, 2001.

Nearing, Scott, and Joseph Freeman. *Dollar Diplomacy: A Study in American Imperialism*. New York: B.W. Huebsch and Viking Press, 1925.

New, Chester W. *The Life of Henry Brougham to 1830*. Oxford: Clarendon Press, 1961.

Nickles, David Paull. *Under the Wire: How the Telegraph Changed Diplomacy*. Cambridge, MA: Harvard University Press, 2003.

Noakes, Richard J. "Telegraphy is an Occult Art: Cromwell Fleetwood Varley and the Diffusion of Electricity to the Other World." *British Journal for the History of Science* 32, 4 (1999): 421-59.

—. "'Instruments to Lay Hold of Spirits': Technologizing the Bodies of Victorian Spiritualism." In *Bodies/Machines*, ed. Iwan Rhys Morus, 125-63. Oxford: Berg, 2002.

Norel, Philippe. *L'invention du marché: Une histoire économique de la mondialisation*. Paris: Les Editions du Seuil, 2004.

Novais, Fernando, ed. *História da Vida Privada No Brasil*. Vol. 3. São Paulo: Companhia das Letras, 1998.

Nunez, Huberto Juarez. "*Maquila* Workers in Mexico: The Prospects for Organization and International Solidarity." *Labor History* 43, 4 (2002): 439-50.

Nussbaum, Martha. "Human Functioning and Social Justice: In Defense of Aristotelian Essentialism." *Political Theory* 20 (May 1992): 202-42.

Nye, Joseph S. *Bound to Lead: The Changing Nature of American Power*. New York: Basic Books, 1990.

—. *The Paradox of American Power: Why the World's Only Superpower Can't Go It Alone*. Oxford: Oxford University Press, 2002.

—. *Soft Power: The Means to Success in World Politics*. New York: Public Affairs, 2004.

O'Brien, Robert. "Labour and IPE: Rediscovering Human Agency." In *Global Political Economy: Contemporary Theories*, ed. Ronen Palan, 89-99. London: Routledge, 2000.

Obstfeld, Maurice, and Alan M. Taylor. *Global Capital Markets: Integration, Crisis, and Growth*. Cambridge: Cambridge University Press, 2004.

Odom, William E., and Robert Dujarric. *America's Inadvertent Empire*. New Haven, CT: Yale University Press, 2004.

O'Donnell, John, and Harvey C. Neese, eds. *Prelude to Tragedy: Vietnam, 1960-1965*. Annapolis, MD: Naval Institute Press, 2001.

Ofreneo, Rosalinda Pineda. "The Philippine Garment Industry." In *Global Production: The Apparel Industry in the Pacific Rim*, ed. Nora Hamilton, Lucie Cheng, and Edna Bonacich, 162-79. Philadelphia, PA: Temple University Press, 1994.

Olsen, Mari. *Soviet-Vietnam Relations and the Role of China, 1949-64: Changing Alliances*. New York: Routledge, 2006.

Olson, Gary L. *US Foreign Policy and the Third World Peasant: Land Reform in Asia and Latin America*. New York: Praeger, 1974.

Ong, Aihwa. *Spirits of Resistance and Capitalist Discipline: Factory Women in Malaysia*. Albany: State University of New York Press, 1987.

—. *Neoliberalism as Exception: Mutations in Citizenship and Sovereignty*. Durham, NC: Duke University Press, 2006.

Oppenheim, Janet. *The Other World: Spiritualism and Psychical Research in England, 1850-1914*. Cambridge: Cambridge University Press, 1985.

Organisation for Economic Co-operation and Development. *Endettement extérieur des pays en développement*. Paris: OECD, 1983.

—. *Financement et dette extérieure des pays en développement*. Paris: OECD, 1986-88.

Osgood, Robert E. *Ideals and Self-Interest in America's Foreign Relations: The Great Transformation of the Twentieth Century*. Chicago: University of Chicago Press, 1953.

Oslin, George P. *The Story of Telecommunications*. Macon, GA: Mercer University Press, 1992.

Osterhammel, Jürgen. *Colonialism: A Theoretical Overview*. Princeton, NJ: Markus Wiener, 1997.

Østerud, Øyvind. *Globaliseringen og nasjonalstaten* [Globalization and the nation state]. Oslo: Universitetsforlaget, 1999.

Otis, Laura. *Networking: Communicating with Bodies and Machines in the Nineteenth Century*. Ann Arbor: University of Michigan Press, 2001.

Overy, Richard. "The Nuremberg Trials: International Law in the Making." In *From Nuremberg to The Hague: The Future of International Criminal Justice,* ed. Philippe Sands, 1-29. Cambridge: Cambridge University Press, 2003.

Owen, Alex. *The Darkened Room: Women, Power and Spiritualism in Late Victorian England*. Philadelphia: University of Pennsylvania Press, 1989.

Padmore, George Arthur. *The Memoirs of a Liberian Ambassador*. Lewiston, NY: E. Mellen Press, 1996.

Paige, Jeffrey. "Social Theory and Peasant Revolution in Vietnam and Guatemala." *Theory and Society* 12, 6 (1983): 699-737.

Paish, George. "The Export of Capital and the Cost of Living." *The Statist,* 14 February 1914, Si-Sviii.

Pal, Leslie. "Governing the Electronic Commons: Globalization, Autonomy, Legitimacy and the Internet." In *Unsettled Legitimacy: Political Community, Power, and Authority in a Global Era,* ed. Steven Bernstein and William D. Coleman. Vancouver: UBC Press, forthcoming.

Palan, Ronen. *The Offshore World: Sovereign Markets, Virtual Places, and Nomad Millionaires*. Ithaca, NY: Cornell University Press, 2003.

Palmié, Stephan. *Wizards and Scientists: Explorations in Afro-Cuban Modernity and Tradition*. Durham, NC: Duke University Press, 2002.

Panaite, Viorel. "The *Re'ayas* of the Tributary-Protected Principalities: The Sixteenth through the Eighteenth Centuries." *International Journal of Turkish Studies* 9, 1-2 (2003): 79-104.

Panitch, Leo, and Ralph Miliband. "The New World Order and the Socialist Agenda." In *Socialist Register 1992,* ed. Ralph Miliband and Leo Panitch, 1-25. London: The Merlin Press, 1992.

Papers Relating to the Manumission of Steyntje and Her Children with an Appendix. Cape Town: George Greig, 1827.

Partant, François. *La fin du développement: Naissance d'une alternative*. Paris: Les Editions F. Maspero, Cahiers libres no. 373, 1982.

Pearce, Robert Michael. *The Insurgent Environment*. Santa Monica, CA: RAND, 1969.

Pels, Peter. "Spirits and Modernity: Alfred Wallace, Edward Tylor and the Visual Politics of Facts." In *Magic and Modernity: Interfaces of Revelation and Concealment*, ed. Birgit Meyer and Peter Pels, 241-71. Stanford, CA: Stanford University Press, 2003.

Pendar, Kenneth W. *Adventure in Diplomacy: The Emergence of General de Gaulle in North Africa*. New York: Dodd, Mead, 1945.

Perdue, Peter. *China Marches West: The Qing Conquest of Central Eurasia*. Cambridge, MA: Harvard University Press, 2005.

Perera, Victor. "Guatemala: Always La Violencia." *New York Times Magazine*, 13 June 1971.

Petech, Luciano. *China and Tibet in the Early 18th Century*. Leiden: Brill, 1950.

—. *Selected Papers on Asian History*. Rome: Istituto Italiano per il Medio ed Estremo Oriente, 1988.

Peters, John Durham. *Speaking into the Air: A History of the Idea of Communication*. Chicago: University of Chicago Press, 1999.

Peyrefitte, Alain. *La société de confiance*. Paris: Editions Odile Jacob, 1995.

Pierce, Richard A. *Russian Central Asia, 1867-1917: A Study in Colonial Rule*. Berkeley: University of California Press, 1960.

Pike, Douglas. *Viet Cong: The Organization and Techniques of the National Liberation Front of South Vietnam*. Cambridge, MA: MIT Press, 1966.

Pilger, John. *The New Rulers of the World*. London: Verso, 2002.

Piñeiro Losada, Manuel, ed. *Che Guevara and the Latin American Revolutionary Movements*. 2nd ed. Melbourne: Ocean Press, 2006.

Pipes, Richard. "How to Cope with the Soviet Threat: A Long-Term Strategy for the West." *Commentary* 78, 2 (1984): 13-14.

Pocock, Rowland F. "'No Other Possible Market': The Royal Navy as Sponsor of Radio Telegraphy." In *From Semaphore to Short Waves*, ed. Frank A.J.L. James, 136-45. London: Royal Society of Arts, 1998.

Polk, Judd. "The New World Economy." *Columbia Journal of World Business* 3, 1 (1968): 7-16.

—. "The New International Production." *World Development* 1, 5 (1973): 15-20.

Poole, William. "A Perspective on US International Capital Flows." *Federal Reserve Bank of St. Louis Review* 87, 1 (2004): 1-8.

Porter, Jennifer. "The Spirit(s) of Science: Paradoxical Positivism as Religious Discourse among Spiritualists." *Science as Culture* 14, 1 (2005): 1-21.

Power, Samantha. *"A Problem From Hell": America and the Age of Genocide*. New York: Perennial, 2002.

Pratt, Geraldine, and Brenda Yeoh. "Transnational (Counter) Topographies." *Gender, Place and Culture* 10, 2 (2003): 159-66.

Prosterman, Roy L., and Jeffrey M. Riedinger. *Land Reform and Democratic Development*. Baltimore, MD: Johns Hopkins University Press, 1987.

Putzel, James. "The 'New' Imperialism and Possibilities for Coexistence." Discussion Paper 2, Crisis States Programme, LSE, Development Studies Institute, London, 2004.

Quintero-Ramirez, Cirila. "Unions, Collaboration, and Labour Conditions in Mexican Maquiladoras." *International Studies Association*, 2001, http://www.isanet.org/archive/ramirez. html (accessed 11 January 2005).

Rabe, Stephen G. *The Most Dangerous Area in the World: John F. Kennedy Confronts Communist Revolution in Latin America*. Chapel Hill: University of North Carolina Press, 1999.

RAND Corporation, "Viet Cong Motivation and Morale in 1964: A Preliminary Report," 1964. Texas Tech Virtual Vietnam Archive, item 2311701004. http://star.vietnam.ttu.edu/virtualarchive/.

Ratner, Steven R., and Jason S. Abrams. *Accountability for Human Rights Atrocities in International Law: Beyond the Nuremberg Legacy.* 2nd ed. New York: Oxford University Press, 2001.

Read, Donald. *The Power of News: The History of Reuters.* Oxford: Oxford University Press, 1999.

"Reagan Proposes US Seek New Way to Block Missiles." *New York Times,* 24 March 1983: A20.

Reed, Howard. "The Destruction of the Janissaries by Mahmud II in June, 1826." PhD diss., Princeton University, 1951.

Report to the Minister of Marine and Fisheries by the Canadian Delegation to the International Radiotelegraph Conference, Washington, October and November, 1927. Ottawa: Department of Marine and Fisheries, 1928.

Revel, Jean François. *Ni Marx ni Jésus: De la seconde révolution américaine à la seconde révolution mondiale.* Paris: Laffont, 1970.

—. *La tentation totalitaire.* Paris: Laffont, 1976.

Rey, Pierre Philippe. *Colonialisme, néo-colonialisme et transition vers le capitalisme.* Paris: Maspero, 1971.

Reynolds, Henry. *Dispossession: Black Australians and White Invaders.* Sydney: Allen and Unwin, 1989.

Reynolds, Laura T. "Institutionalizing Flexibility: A Comparative Analysis of Fordist and Post-Fordist Models of Third World Agro-Export Production." In *Commodity Chains and Global Capitalism,* ed. Gary Gereffi and Miguel Korzeniewicz, 143-61. Westport, CT: Praeger, 1994.

Risse, Thomas, and Kathryn Sikkink. "The Socialization of International Human Rights Norms into Domestic Practices: Introduction." In *The Power of Human Rights: International Norms and Domestic Change,* ed. Thomas Risse, Steven C. Ropp, and Kathryn Sikkink, 1-38. Cambridge: Cambridge University Press, 1999.

Rist, Gilbert. *The History of Development: From Western Origins to Global Faith.* Atlantic Highlands, NJ: Zed Books, 1997.

Ritzer, George. *The McDonaldization of Society.* Thousand Oaks, CA: Pine Forge Press, 1993.

Roach, Joseph. *Cities of the Dead: Circum-Atlantic Performance.* New York: Columbia University Press, 1996.

Robertson, Robbie. *The Three Waves of Globalization: A History of a Developing Global Consciousness.* London: Zed, 2002.

Robertson, Roland. *Globalization: Social Theory and Global Culture.* London: Sage, 1992.

Robin, Ron. *The Making of the Cold War Enemy: Culture and Politics in the Military-Intellectual Complex.* Princeton, NJ: Princeton University Press, 2001.

Robinson, Scott. "The Aboriginal Embassy, 1972." Master's thesis, Australian National University, 1993.

—. "The Aboriginal Embassy: An Account of the Protests of 1972." *Aboriginal History* 18, 1 (1994): 49-63.

Rodgers, Daniel T. *Atlantic Crossings: Social Politics in a Progressive Age.* Cambridge, MA: Belknap Press of Harvard University Press, 1998.

Rogan, Eugene. *Frontiers of the State in the Late Ottoman Empire: Transjordan, 1850-1921.* Cambridge: Cambridge University Press, 1999.

Roosevelt, Elliott. *As He Saw It.* New York: Duell, 1946.

—, ed. *F.D.R.: His Personal Letters*. New York: Duell, Sloan, and Pearce, 1950.

Rose, Deborah Bird. *Dingo Makes Us Human: Life and Land in an Aboriginal Australian Culture*. Cambridge: Cambridge University Press, 1992.

Rosenau, James N. *Distant Proximities: Dynamics beyond Globalization*. Princeton, NJ: Princeton University Press, 2003.

Rosenau, William. *US Internal Security Assistance to South Vietnam: Insurgency, Subversion, and Public Order*. New York: Routledge, 2005.

Rosenberg, Emily S. *Spreading the American Dream: American Economic and Cultural Expansion, 1890-1945*. New York: Hill and Wang, 1982.

Rostow, Walt W. *The Stages of Economic Growth: A Non-Communist Manifesto*. Cambridge: Cambridge University Press, 1960.

—. "Guerrilla Warfare in the Underdeveloped Areas." *Department of State Bulletin* 45 (7 August 1961): 233-38.

Rozwadowski, Helen M. "Technology and Ocean-Scape: Defining the Deep Sea in the Mid-Nineteenth Century." *History and Technology* 17, 33 (2001): 217-47.

Ruggie, John Gerard. "International Responses to Technology: Concepts and Trends." *International Organization* 29, 3 (1975): 557-83.

—. *Constructing the World Polity: Essays on International Institutionalization*. London: Routledge, 1998.

Russbach, Olivier. "The Citizen's Right to International Law." In *Law and Moral Action in World Politics*, ed. Cecilia Lynch and Michael Loriaux, 253-69. Minneapolis: University of Minnesota Press, 2000.

Ryan, David. "By Way of Introduction: The United States, Decolonization and the World System." In *The United States and Decolonization: Power and Freedom*, ed. David Ryan and Victor Pungong, 1-23. New York: St. Martin's Press, 2000.

Saarinen, Oiva. "Single-Sector Communities in Northern Ontario: The Creation and Planning of Dependent Towns." In *Power and Place*, ed. Gilbert Stelter and Alan Artibise, 219-64. Vancouver: UBC Press, 1986.

Sachs, Jeffrey. "International Economics: Unlocking the Mysteries of Globalization." *Foreign Policy* 110 (Spring 1998): 97-109.

Sadat, Leila Nadya. "The Evolution of the ICC: From The Hague to Rome and Back Again." In *The United States and the International Criminal Court: National Security and International Law*, ed. Sarah B. Sewall and Carl Kaysen. Oxford: Rowman and Littlefield, 2000.

Safrastjan, Ruben. "Ottomanism in Turkey in the Epoch of Reforms in XIXC: Ideology and Policy I." *Etudes Balkaniques* 24 (1988): 72-86.

Sahlins, Marshall. *Stone Age Economics*. Paris: Aldine de Gruyter, 1972.

—. *Âge de pierre, âge d'abondance: L'économie des sociétés primitives*. Preface by P. Clastres. 1972; Reprint, Paris: Gallimard, 1976.

Saldaña-Portillo, María Josefina. *The Revolutionary Imagination in the Americas and the Age of Development*. Durham, NC: Duke University Press, 2003.

Salzinger, Leslie. *Genders in Production: Making Workers in Mexico's Global Factories*. Berkeley: University of California Press, 2003.

Sassen, Saskia. "Spatialities and Temporalities of the Global: Elements for a Theorization." *Public Culture* 12, 1 (2000): 215-32.

—. *Territory, Authority, Rights: From Medieval to Global Assemblages*. Princeton, NJ: Princeton University Press, 2006.

Saul, Samir. "Has Financial Internationalization Turned into Financial Globalization?" *Globalization and Autonomy Compendium,* http://www.globalautonomy.ca/global1/article. jsp?index=RA_Saul_FinancialIntl.xml.

Savage, James G. *The Politics of International Telecommunications Regulation.* London: Westview Press, 1989.

Schaebler, Birgit. "Civilizing Others: Global Modernity and the Local Boundaries (French/ German, Ottoman and Arab) of Savagery." In *Globalization and the Muslim World: Culture, Religion and Modernity,* ed. Birgit Schaebler and Leif Stenberg, 3-9. Syracuse: Syracuse University Press, 2004.

Schild, Georg. *Bretton Woods and Dumbarton Oaks: American Economic and Political Postwar Planning in the Summer of 1944.* New York: St. Martin's Press, 1995.

Schlesinger, Stephen C. *Act of Creation: The Founding of the United Nations.* Boulder, CO: Westview Press, 2003.

Schmitt, Carl. *The Concept of the Political.* Trans. George Schwab. 1932; Reprint, Chicago: University of Chicago Press, 1996.

Schmukler, Sergio L. "Financial Globalization: Gain and Pain for Developing Countries." *Federal Reserve Bank of Atlanta Economic Review* 89, 2 (2004): 39-66.

Scholte, Jan Aart. *Globalization: A Critical Introduction.* New York: St. Martin's Press, 2000.

—. "What Is Globalization? The Definitional Issue – Again." In *Working Paper Series,* Centre for the Study of Globalisation and Regionalisation, 109/02, University of Warwick, 2002.

—. "What is Globalization? The Definition Issue – Again." Working Paper Series, Institute on Globalization and the Human Condition, McMaster University, Hamilton, Ontario, 2003.

—. *Globalization: A Critical Introduction.* 2nd ed. New York: Palgrave Macmillan, 2005.

Schultz, George P. *Turmoil and Triumph: My Years as Secretary of State.* New York: Charles Scribner's Sons, 1993.

Sconce, Jeffrey. *Haunted Media: Electronic Presence from Telegraphy to Television.* Durham, NC: Duke University Press, 2000.

Searle, John R. *The Construction of Social Reality.* New York: Free Press, 1995.

Seidman, Gay. *Manufacturing Militance: Workers' Movements in Brazil and South Africa, 1970-1985.* Berkeley: University of California Press, 1994.

Sevcenko, Nicolau. "A capital irradiante: Técnica, ritmos, e ritos do Rio." In *História da Vida Privada No Brasil.* Vol. 3, ed. Fernando Novais, 513-619. São Paulo: Companhia das Letras, 1998.

Shaiken, Harley. *Mexico in the Global Economy: High Technology and Work Organization in Export Industries.* San Diego, CA: Center for US-Mexican Studies, 1990.

Sharma, Sohan, and Surinder Kumar. "The Military Backbone of Globalisation." *Race and Class* 44, 3 (2003): 23-39.

Sharp, Lynn L. *Secular Spirituality: Reincarnation and Spiritism in Nineteenth-Century France.* Lanham, MD: Lexington Books, 2006.

Shell, Robert Carl-Heinz. *Children of Bondage: A Social History of the Slave Society at the Cape of Good Hope, 1652-1838.* Hanover/Lebanon: Wesleyan University Press/University Press of New England, 1994.

Sherwood, Robert E. *Roosevelt and Hopkins: An Intimate History.* New York: Harper, 1950.

Shoesmith, Dennis. *Export Processing Zones in Five Countries.* Hong Kong: Asia Partnership for Human Development, 1986.

Simon, Matthew. "The Pattern of New British Portfolio Foreign Investment, 1865-1914." In *The Export of Capital from Britain, 1870-1914,* ed. Alan R. Hall, 15-44. London: Methuen, 1968.

Simpson, Gerry. "Politics, Sovereignty, and Remembrance." In *The Permanent International Criminal Court: Legal and Policy Issues,* ed. Dominic McGoldrick, P.J. Rowe, and Eric Donnelly, 47-61. Oxford: Hart Publishing, 2004.

Simpson, Michael. *Thomas Adams and the Modern Planning Movement.* London: Alexandrine Press, 1985.

Slaughter, Anne-Marie. *A New World Order.* Princeton, NJ: Princeton University Press, 2004.

Smith, Jackie. "Democratizing Globalization? Impacts and Limitations of Transnational Social Movements." Working Paper Series, Institute on Globalization and the Human Condition, McMaster University, Hamilton, Ontario, 2004.

Smith, Jackie, and Hank Johnston. "Introduction." In *Globalization and Resistance: Transnational Dimensions of Social Movements,* ed. Jackie Smith and Hank Johnston, 1-10. New York: Rowman and Littlefield, 2002.

Smith, Warren W., Jr. *Tibetan Nation: A History of Tibetan Nationalism and Sino-Tibetan Relations.* Boulder, CO: Westview Press, 1996.

Smuts, Michael Andrianus. *Specimen Iuridicum Inaugurale Specimen.* Lugduni Batavorum, 1807.

Sohmer, Sara. "The Melanesian Mission and Victorian Anthropology." In *Darwin's Laboratory: Evolutionary Theory and Natural History in the Pacific,* ed. Roy M. MacLeod and Philip F. Rehbock, 317-38. Honolulu: University of Hawaii Press, 1994.

Sollors, Werner. "Dr. Benjamin Franklin's Celestial Telegraph, or Indian Blessings to Gas-Lit American Drawing Rooms." *Social Science Information* 22, 6 (1983): 983-1004.

Soroos, Marvin S. "The International Commons: A Historical Perspective." *Environmental Review* 12, 1 (1988): 1-22.

Standage, Tom. *The Victorian Internet: The Remarkable Story of the Telegraph and the Nineteenth Century's On-line Pioneers.* New York: Berkley Books, 1998.

Stavrianos, L.S. *Global Rift: The Third World Comes of Age.* New York: William Morrow and Company, 1981.

Steans, Jill. *Gender and International Relations: An Introduction.* Cambridge: Polity Press, 1998.

Stelzer, Irwin, ed. *The Neocon Reader.* New York: Grove Press, 2004.

Stent, Angela A. "Russia: Farewell to Empire?" *World Policy Journal* 19 (Fall 2002): 83-89.

Stephan, Alexander, ed. *The Americanization of Europe: Culture, Diplomacy, and Anti-Americanism after 1945.* Oxford: Berghahn, 2005.

Stinchcombe, Arthur. *Sugar Island Slavery in the Age of Enlightenment: The Political Economy of the Caribbean World.* Princeton, NJ: Princeton University Press, 1995.

Stocking, George. "Animism in Theory and Practice: E.B. Tylor's Unpublished 'Notes on Spiritualism.'" *Man* 6, 1 (1971): 88-104.

Stockton, Hans, ed. *The Future of Development in Vietnam and the Challenges of Globalization: Interdisciplinary Essays.* Lewiston, NY: Edwin Mellen Press, 2006.

Stoecker, Randy. "Cyberspace vs. Face-to-Face: Community Organizing in the New Millennium." *Perspectives on Global Development and Technology* 1, 2 (2002): 143-64.

Stoll, David. *Between Two Armies in the Ixil Towns of Guatemala.* New York: Columbia University Press, 1993.

Stolow, Jeremy. "Salvation by Electricity." In *Religion: Beyond a Concept,* ed. Hent de Vries, 669-86. New York: Fordham University Press, 2007.

Strange, Susan. *The Retreat of the State: The Diffusion of Power in the World Economy.* Cambridge: Cambridge University Press, 1996.

Streeter, Stephen M. *Managing the Counterrevolution: The United States and Guatemala, 1954-1961.* Athens: Ohio University Press, 2000.

—. "Nation-Building in the Land of Eternal Counterinsurgency: Guatemala and the Contradictions of the Alliance for Progress." *Third World Quarterly* 27, 1 (2006): 57-68.

Suskind, Ron. *The Price of Loyalty: George W. Bush, the White House, and the Education of Paul O'Neill.* New York: Simon and Schuster, 2004.

—. "Without a Doubt." *New York Times Magazine*, 17 October 2004.

Süssekind, Flora. *Cinematograph of Words: Literature, Technique and Modernization in Brazil.* Stanford, CA: Stanford University Press, 1997.

Sutherland, Peter. "The Man Who Built the WTO: An Interview with Peter Sutherland." openDemocracy, 2004. http://www.opendemocracy.net.

Svedberg, Peter. "The Portfolio-Direct Composition of Private Foreign Investment in 1914 Revisited." *Economic Journal* 88, 352 (1978): 763-77.

Swank, Duane. *Global Capital, Political Institutions, and Policy Change in Developed Welfare States.* Cambridge: Cambridge University Press, 2002.

Sykes, Roberta B. *Black Majority.* Hawthorn, Victoria: Hudson Publishing, 1989.

Talbott, Strobe. *Deadly Gambits: The Reagan Administration and the Stalemate in Nuclear Arms Control.* New York: Vintage Books, 1985.

Tarrow, Sidney. "From Lumping to Splitting: Specifying Globalization and Resistance." In *Globalization and Resistance: Transnational Dimensions of Social Movements,* ed. Jackie Smith and Hank Johnston, 229-49. New York: Rowman and Littlefield, 2002.

Taves, Ann. *Fits, Trances and Visions: Experiencing Religion and Explaining Experience from Wesley to James.* Princeton, NJ: Princeton University Press, 1999.

Taylor, Charles. *Modern Social Imaginaries.* Durham, NC: Duke University Press, 2004.

Taylor, Ian. "Globalisation Studies and the Developing World: Making International Political Economy Truly Global." *Third World Quarterly* 26, 7 (2005): 1025-42.

Theal, George McCall, ed. *Records of the Cape Colony from October 1812 to April 1814.* London: William Clowes and Sons, 1901.

Thompson, Leonard. *A History of South Africa.* New Haven, CT: Yale University Press, 1995.

Thompson, Neville. *Earl Bathurst and the British Empire, 1762-1834.* Barnsley: Leo Cooper, 1999.

Thurschwell, Pamela. *Literature, Technology and Magical Thinking, 1880-1920.* Cambridge: Cambridge University Press, 2001.

Todd, Emmanuel. *After the Empire: The Breakdown of the American Order.* Trans. C. Jon Delogu. New York: Columbia University Press, 2003.

Tomlinson, John. *Globalization and Culture.* Cambridge: Cambridge University Press, 1999.

Touraine, Alain. *Un nouveau paradigme.* Paris: Fayard, 2005.

Tran-Nam, Binh, and Chi Do Pham. *The Vietnamese Economy: Awakening the Dormant Dragon.* New York: Routledge, 2002.

Tribolet, Lesley Bennett. *The International Aspects of Electrical Communications in the Pacific Area.* Baltimore, MD: Johns Hopkins Press, 1929.

Trigueros, Ignacio. "Les entrées de capitaux et l'investissement: Le Mexique." In *Mouvements des capitaux et performances des investissements: Les leçons de l'Amérique latine,* ed. Ricardo Ffrench-Davis and Helmut Reisen, 211-34. Paris: Organisation for Economic Co-operation and Development, 1998.

Trubowitz, Peter. *Defining the National Interest: Conflict and Change in American Foreign Policy.* Chicago: University of Chicago Press, 1998.

Tsing, Anna Lowenhaupt. *Friction: An Ethnography of Global Connection.* Princeton, NJ: Princeton University Press, 2005.

Turner, Philip. "Capital Flows in the 1980s: A Survey of Major Trends." Bank of International Settlements, Economic Papers, no. 30, April 1991, http://www.bis.org/publ/econ30.htm.

UNCTAD (United Nations Conference on Trade and Development). *L'investissement étranger direct en Afrique.* New York and Geneva: United Nations, 1995.

—. *World Investment Report 1996: Investment, Trade and International Policy Agreements.* New York and Geneva: United Nations, 1996.

—. *World Investment Report 1997: Transnational Corporations, Market Structure and Competition Policy.* New York and Geneva: United Nations, 1997.

—. *World Investment Report 2000: Cross-Border Mergers and Acquisitions and Development.* New York and Geneva: United Nations, 2000.

—. *World Investment Report 2001: Promoting Linkages.* New York and Geneva: United Nations, 2001.

—. *World Investment Report 2002: Transnational Corporations and Export Competitiveness.* New York and Geneva: United Nations, 2002.

—. *World Investment Report 2003: FDI Policies for Development: National and International Perspectives.* New York and Geneva: United Nations, 2003.

United Nations. *Le courant international des capitaux à long terme et les donations publiques, 1951-1959.* New York: United Nations, 1961.

—. *Le courant international des capitaux à long terme et les donations publiques, 1959-1961.* New York: United Nations, 1963.

—. Rome Statute of the International Criminal Court, 17 July 1998. UN Doc. A/ CONF.183./9.

—. *A More Secure World: Our Shared Responsibility.* Report of the Secretary-General's High Level Panel on Threats, Challenges and Change, 2004. http://www.un.org/secureworld/report3.pdf.

—. *Les mouvements internationaux de capitaux entre les deux guerres.* New York: United Nations, 1949.

UN General Assembly. Resolution 95(I), Affirmation of the Principles of Law Recognized by the Charter of the Nuremberg Tribunal, 11 December 1946. In *Report of the International Law Commission,* 5 June–29 July 1950, Doc. A/1316, 11-14.

—. Resolution 55/2, Millennium Declaration, 18 September 2000. UN Doc. A/55/L.2.

US Department of the Army. *Area Handbook for Vietnam.* Washington, DC: Government Printing Office, 1962.

US Department of Defense. *Joint Vision 2020.* Washington, DC: US Government Printing Office, 2000.

US Department of State. *Foreign Relations of the United States, 1941.* Vol. 1. Washington, DC: US Government Printing Office, 1958.

—. *Foreign Relations of the United States, 1943.* Vol. 5, *The American Republics.* Washington, DC: US Government Printing Office, 1965.

—. *Foreign Relations of the United States, 1943.* Vol. 4, *The Near East and Africa.* Washington, DC: US Government Printing Office, 1965.

—. *Foreign Relations of the United States: The Conferences at Washington, 1941-1942, and Casablanca, 1943.* Washington, DC: US Government Printing Office, 1968.

—. *Foreign Relations of the United States, 1961-1963.* 3 vols. Washington, DC: US Government Printing Office, 1988-91.

—. *Foreign Relations of the United States, 1964-1968.* Vol. 1. Washington, DC: US Government Printing Office, 1992.

—. "United States Economic Assistance to South Vietnam, 1954-1975: An Overview," 14 October 1975. Texas Tech Virtual Vietnam Archive, item 2390111001. http://star.vietnam. ttu.edu/virtualarchive/.

Uthoff, Andras, and Daniel Titelman. "La relation entre l'épargne étrangère et l'épargne nationale dans le cadre de la libéralisation financière." In *Mouvements des capitaux et performances des investissements: Les leçons de l'Amérique latine,* ed. Ricardo Ffrench-Davis and Helmut Reisen, 27-47. Paris: Organisation for Economic Co-operation and Development, 1998.

Uzunçarşılı, İ. *Osmanlı Devleti Teşkilatından Kapukulu Ocakları.* Ankara: Türk Tarih Kurumu, 1943.

van der Veer, Peter. *Imperial Encounters: Religion and Modernity in India and Britain.* Princeton, NJ: Princeton University Press, 2001.

Vasconcelos, João. "Espíritos clandestinos: Espiritismo, pesquisa psíquica e antropologia da religião entre 1850 e 1920." *Religião e Sociedade* 23, 2 (2003): 92-126.

Versailles Treaty. 28 June 1919. http://www.yale.edu/lawweb/avalon/imt/menu.htm.

Viswanathan, Gauri. "The Ordinary Business of Occultism." *Critical Inquiry* 27, 1 (2000): 1-20.

von Moltke, Baron Heinrich. *The Russians in Bulgaria and Rumelia in 1828-1829, During the Campaigns of the Danube, the Sieges of Brailow, Varna, Silistria, Shumla, and the Passage of the Balkans.* Trans. Marshal Diebitch. London: John Murray, 1854.

—. *Lettres d'Maréchal de Moltke sur l'Orient.* Trans. Alfred Marchand. Paris: Librairie Fischbacher, 1872.

Waddams, S.M. *Law, Politics and the Church of England: The Career of Stephen Lushington, 1782-1873.* Cambridge: Cambridge University Press, 1992.

Wade, Robert Hunter. "The Rising Inequality of World Income Distribution." *Finance and Development* 38, 4 (2001), http://www.imf.org/external/pubs/ft/fandd/2001/12/wade.htm.

—. "The Invisible Hand of the American Empire," openDemocracy, 2003. http://www. opendemocracy.net.

—. "What Strategies Are Viable for Developing Countries Today? The World Trade Organization and the Shrinking of 'Development Space.'" Working Paper no. 31, Crisis States Programme, LSE, Development Studies Institute, London, 2003.

Wadge, Elisabeth. "The Scientific Spirit and the Spiritualist Scientist: Moving in the Right Circles." *Victorian Review* 26, 1 (2000): 24-42.

Wallerstein, Immanuel. *The Decline of American Power: The US in a Chaotic World.* New York: W.W. Norton, 2003.

—. *World-Systems Analysis: An Introduction.* Durham, NC: Duke University Press, 2004.

Waltz, Kenneth. "The Nuclear Future." Public lecture, delivered to the Danish Institute for International Studies, Copenhagen, 17 May 2005.

Warren, Kay B. *Indigenous Movements and Their Critics: Pan-Maya Activism in Guatemala.* Princeton, NJ: Princeton University Press, 1999.

Wasburn, Philo C. "International Radio Broadcasting: Some Considerations for Political Sociology." *Journal of Political and Military Sociology* 13, 2 (1985): 37-41.

Watson, Irene. *Looking at You Looking at Me: An Aboriginal History of the South-East of South Australia.* Nairne, SA: I. Watson, 2002.

Watson, R.L. *The Slave Question: Liberty and Property in South Africa.* 1990; Reprint, Johannesburg: Witwatersrand University Press, 1991.

—. *The Great Land Rush and the Making of the Modern World, 1650-1900*. Montreal and Kingston: McGill-Queen's University Press, 2003.

Weiss, Marc A. "Developing and Financing the 'Garden Metropolis': Urban Planning and Housing Policy in Twentieth-Century America." *Planning Perspectives* 5 (1990): 307-19.

Westad, Odd Arne. *The Global Cold War: Third World Interventions and the Making of Our Times*. New York: Cambridge University Press, 2005.

White, Neil. "Creating Community: Industrial Paternalism and Town Planning in Corner Brook, Newfoundland, 1923-1955." *Urban History Review* 32, 2 (2004): 45-58.

White House. *National Security Strategy of the United States of America*, 25 September 2002. http://www.whitehouse.gov/nsc/nss.html (accessed 3 November 2003).

Whitlam, Edward Gough. *The Whitlam Government, 1972-1975*. Ringwood, Victoria: Viking, 1985.

Wickham-Crowley, Timothy. *Exploring Revolution: Essays on Latin American Insurgency and Revolutionary Theory*. Armonk, NY: M.E. Sharpe, 1991.

Williams, William Appleman. *The Tragedy of American Diplomacy*. New York: W.W. Norton, 1988.

Williamson, Jeffrey. "Globalization, Convergence, and History." *Journal of Economic History* 56, 2 (1996): 1-30.

Williamson, John. "What Washington Means by Policy Reform." In *Latin American Adjustment: How Much Has Happened?* ed. John Williamson, 54-84. Washington, DC: Institute for International Economics, 1990.

—. "What Should the World Bank Think about the Washington Consensus?" *The World Bank Research Observer* 15, 2 (2000): 251-64.

Winichakul, Thongchai. *Siam Mapped: A History of the Geo-Body of a Nation*. Honolulu: University of Hawaii Press, 1994.

Wippman, David. "The International Criminal Court." In *The Politics of International Law*, ed. Christian Reus-Smit, 151-88. Cambridge: Cambridge University Press, 2004.

Wolf, Charles, and Brian Rosen. "Public Diplomacy: How to Think about and Improve It." RAND occasional paper, Santa Monica, California, 6 October 2004.

Wolf, Diane Lauren. *Factory Daughters: Gender, Household Dynamics, and Rural Industrialization in Java*. Berkeley: University of California Press, 1992.

Wolf, Eric R. *Peasant Wars of the Twentieth Century*. 2nd ed. New York: Harper and Row, 1999.

Wong, Yu Ching, and Charles Adams. "Trends in Global and Regional Foreign Direct Investment Flows." Paper presented at "Conference on Foreign Direct Investment: Opportunities and Challenges for Cambodia, Laos, and Vietnam," organized by the IMF and the State Bank of Vietnam, Hanoi, 16-17 August 2002.

Wood, Marcus. *Slavery, Empathy, and Pornography*. Oxford: Oxford University Press, 2002.

Woods, Ngaire. *The Globalizers: The IMF, the World Bank, and their Borrowers*. Ithaca, NY: Cornell University Press, 2006.

Woodward, David. *The Next Crisis? Direct and Equity Investment in Developing Countries*. London: Zed Books, 2001.

Worden, Nigel. *Slavery in Dutch South Africa*. Cambridge: Cambridge University Press, 1985.

World Bank. *Private Capital Flows to Developing Countries: The Road to Financial Integration*. New York: Oxford University Press, 1997.

—. *06 World Development Indicators*. World Bank Group. http://devdata.worldbank.org/wdi2006/contents/cover.htm.

World Council of Churches. *Justice for Aboriginal Australians: Report of the World Council of Churches Team Visit to the Aborigines, 15 June to 3 July.* Sydney: Australian Council of Churches, 1981.

Wright, Melissa W. "Crossing the Factory Frontier: Gender, Place, and Power in the Mexican Maquiladora." *Antipode* 29, 3 (1997): 278-302.

Wu, Shu-hui. "How the Qing Army Entered Tibet in 1728 after the Tibetan Civil War." *Zentrale-Asiatische Studien* 26 (1996): 122-38.

Zboiński, H. *Armée ottomane: Son organisation actuelle telle qu'elle résulte de l'exécution de la loi de 1869.* Paris: Librairie militaire de J. Dumaine, 1877.

Ze'evi, Dror. "*Kul* and Getting Cooler: The Dissolution of Elite Collective Identity and the Formation of Official Nationalism in the Ottoman Empire." *Mediterranean Historical Review* 11, 2 (1996): 177-95.

Zeiler, Thomas W. *Free Trade, Free World: America and the Advent of GATT.* Chapel Hill: University of North Carolina Press, 1999.

Zhang, Yuxin, ed. *Qing zhengfu yu lamajiao* [The Qing government and lamaism]. Xuchang: Xizang renmin chubanshe, 1988.

Zucheng, Gu, ed. *Ming-Qing zhi Zang shiyao* [Historical outline of Ming and Qing policies to control Tibet]. Lhasa: Xizang renmin chubanshe, 1999.

Zürcher, Erik J. "The Ottoman Conscription System in Theory and Practice." In *Arming the State: Military Conscription in the Middle East and Central Asia, 1775-1925,* ed. Erik J. Zürcher, 79-94. London: I.B. Tauris, 1999.

Contributors

Virginia H. Aksan is a professor in the Department of History at Mc-Master University and author of *Ottoman Wars 1700-1870*. Her current research interests include transimperial intellectual encounters, the circulation of knowledge, and cultures of the premodern Mediterranean.

Timothy Brook is concurrently principal of St. John's College, University of British Columbia, and Shaw Professor of Chinese at Oxford University. He is the author most recently of *Vermeer's Hat: The Seventeenth Century and the Dawn of the Global World* and co-author of *Death by a Thousand Cuts*.

William D. Coleman is Canada Research Chair on Globalization Studies and Public Policy. He is also founder and director of the Institute on Globalization and the Human Condition and professor of political science at McMaster University. His research interests include theories of globalization, global dimensions of public policy, and the politics of agriculture and food.

Ravi de Costa is an assistant professor in the Faculty of Environmental Studies at York University, Toronto. His research interests include globalization and indigenous peoples and comparative research on Aboriginal-settler relations in Australia and Canada.

Yassine Essid is professor of medieval history at the University of Tunis, Tunisia, and president of the Groupe d'Etudes et de Recherches Interdisciplinaires sur la Méditerranée (GERIM). His research interests include the history of Islamic economic thought, global Islam, and the food anthropology of the Mediterranean.

Daniel Gorman is assistant professor of history and political science at the University of Waterloo. He also teaches in the Balsillie School of International Affairs. His research interests include the history of the British Empire, the historical antecedents of global governance, and intellectual property.

Ulf Hedetoft is professor of nationality and migration studies and director of the SAXO Institute at the University of Copenhagen. He is also director of the Academy for Migration Studies in Denmark (AMID).

Adrian L. Jones is a PhD student of international relations in the Department of Political Science at McMaster University. His research and teaching interests include international law and global governance, particularly in the areas of international human rights and international criminal justice.

Ronald W. Pruessen is the former chair of the University of Toronto's Department of History. His research and teaching focus on US foreign policy and globalization issues, and his current projects include work on the way post-1945 decolonization and "development" efforts helped to produce the conditions for what was eventually labelled "globalization."

Samir Saul is professor of history at the Université de Montréal. His research themes include modern international economic history and imperialism, with a special emphasis on modern France and its former empire, as well as the Arab world.

Jeremy Stolow teaches media history in the Department of Communication Studies at Concordia University, Montreal. His areas of research are religion, media, technology, and cultural history.

Stephen M. Streeter is an associate professor in the Department of History at McMaster University. He is also a member of the Institute on Globalization and the Human Condition. His research interests include the history of US foreign relations, Latin America, and the Vietnam War.

John C. Weaver is a Distinguished University Professor at McMaster University. His last book, *The Great Land Rush and the Making of the Modern World, 1650-1900,* was the recipient of the Wallace Ferguson Prize of the Canadian Historical Association and the Book Award of the North American Conference on British Studies. He recently finished a book on suicide and the human condition.

Neil White recently received his PhD in history from McMaster University. His dissertation contrasted the creation and development of company towns in Australia and Canada. He is engaged currently, at Columbia University's Center for the History and Ethics of Public Health, in postdoctoral research into the politics and regulation of pollution at American and Canadian lead smelters.

Index

PRINTED AND BOUND IN CANADA BY FRIESENS
SET IN BEMBO BY GEORGE KIRKPATRICK

Text design: GEORGE KIRKPATRICK
Copy editor: LESLEY ERICKSON
Indexer: ANNETTE LOREK